Encyclopedia of Family Life

Encyclopedia of Family Life

Volume 5
Single-parent families – Zero Population Growth movement
Index

Editor

Carl L. Bankston III
University of Southwestern Louisiana

Project Editor

R. Kent Rasmussen

SALEM PRESS, INC.
Pasadena, California   Hackensack, New Jersey

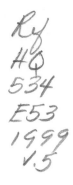

Managing Editor: Christina J. Moose
Project Editor: R. Kent Rasmussen
Manuscript Editor: Robert Michaels
Development Editor: Wendy Sacket
Research Supervisor: Jeffry Jensen
Acquisitions Editor: Mark Rehn
Photograph Editor: Karrie Hyatt
Production Editor: Joyce I. Buchea
Design and Layout: James Hutson
Indexer: Robert Michaels

Frontispiece: Hazel Hankin

Copyright © 1999, by SALEM PRESS, INC.

Library of Congress Cataloging-in-Publication Data

Encyclopedia of Family Life / editor, Carl L. Bankston III; project editor, R. Kent Rasmussen.
p.   ; cm.
Includes bibliographical references (p.   ) and index.
ISBN 0-89356-940-2 (set)
ISBN 0-89356-993-3 (vol. 5)
1. Family—North America—Encyclopedias. 2. Domestic relations—North America—Encyclopedias. 3. Family services—North America—Encyclopedias. I. Bankston, Carl L. (Carl Leon), 1952-   . II. Rasmussen, R. Kent.
HQ534.E53   1999
306.85'097'03—dc21   98-42491
                                                                                   CIP

First Printing

PRINTED IN THE UNITED STATES OF AMERICA

Contents

Encyclopedia of Family Life

Single-parent families

RELEVANT ISSUES: Economics and work; Parenting and family relationships

SIGNIFICANCE: The single-parent, mother-child family, the fastest growing family type in the world, is and will continue to represent a common experience in the lives of women and children

There are two types of single-parent families recognized by the U.S. Bureau of the Census: single-parent, mother-child families and single-parent, father-child families. In both cases there is an "own" child or children under eighteen, residing in the household with a single parent or householder who is eighteen years of age or older. "Own" children in a family are sons and daughters of the householder, including stepchildren and adopted children. The U.S. Census excludes householders under eighteen years of age.

Growth of Single-Parent Families. During the second half of the twentieth century, single-parent families increased in the United States and around the world. Between 1950 and 1994 in the United States the proportion of single-parent families almost quadrupled. In 1950 approximately 1.5 million (1,495,000) single-parent families comprised 7.4 percent of all families with children. By 1994 nearly 9 million (8,961,000) single-parent families accounted for 26.3 percent of all families with children. The increase was steady, with the most rapid growth occurring between 1970 and 1980.

As a concomitant pattern, the proportion of children living in single-parent households increased during this time. In 1994, 24.5 percent of all children in the United States lived in single-parent families. In other words, 1 of every 4 children lived in a single-parent family, accounting for 15.3 million children. The 1994 figure of 1 in every 4 children living in single-parent families compares to approximately 3 million (3,002,000) children living in single-parent families in 1950, or 10 percent of all children in the United States at that time. These point-in-time or prevalence figures are high, but not as high as the figures for children who will spend some period of their childhood in single-parent families. Modern estimates are that three in every five children born in the United States in the 1990's will have spent an average of six years living in a single-parent family. The duration of single-parent families is another aspect of their growth.

Prevalence of Single-Parent Families. There are important variations by sex and race for single-parent families in the United States. In 1994, 59.5 percent of African American children under eighteen years of age lived in single-parent families. Among Hispanics 29.1 percent of children lived in single-parent families. Among whites 18.7 percent of children lived in single-parent families. Across all races, the sex of the single parent is disproportionately female. Among whites, 82.4 percent of single-parent families are headed by females. Among Hispanics, 77.6 percent of single-parent families are headed by females. Among African Americans, 91.9 percent of single-parent families are headed by females. The single-parent, father-child family receives a lot of popular attention, but single-father families represent only about 10 percent of single-parent families in the United States and worldwide. The greatest number and percentage of single-parent families are headed by females. Worldwide, female-headed families are approximately 25 percent of all families. Although not synonymous with mother-child families, most female-headed households contain children.

Marriage, Divorce, and Single-Parent Families. As there is variation in the prevalence of single-parent families through time and among countries, there is variation in causes. Historically, young women of the servant classes were at greatest risk of single, out-of-wedlock parenthood, often because they were impregnated by masters or relatives. Frequently, these pregnancies were cause for dismissal of unfortunate mothers-to-be, who were cast into poverty. However, single-parent, mother-child families were sometimes associated with the economic well-being of women. In the nineteenth century Scottish Lowlands, unmarried girls could keep their jobs if they became pregnant rather than having to return in shame as an economic burden to their families. Parents and clergy took a relaxed view of pregnancy at that time, believing that while unfortunate, "It's nae sae bad as stealing." Similarly, in the Austrian provinces, with a high demand for farm labor, out-of-wedlock births were socially accepted and reached 30 to 50 percent. In the past, high rates of out-of-wedlock births occurred when the status of women was very

Single-mother families have become the fastest-growing type of family unit in the world. (Don Franklin)

depressed, but it also occurred when it was relatively good.

In modern Western society, the single greatest cause of single-parent households is marriage. Most children living in single-parent families are born into married-couple families. These families are then transformed by death, desertion, or divorce into single-parent families. In the United States the divorce rate rose sharply in the 1960's and continued to rise until the beginning of the 1980's. After 1965 remarriages also began to decline. In consequence, the number of one-parent households resulting from divorce increased by 450 percent between 1960 and 1983. The increase

in mother-only families is due in large part to the increase in formerly married mothers. However, while the divorce rate stabilized during the 1980's, mother-headed families continued to increase. Thus, marriage is not the only cause of the prevalence of mother-child families.

Out-of-Wedlock Births. The never-married comprise a smaller but rapidly growing component of single parents. Before 1940 the out-of-wedlock birth rate was very low in the United States compared to other countries; it began to climb in the 1960's. Of the never-married with their own children, approximately 80 percent are eighteen to thirty-four years of age. In 1960 in the United

States there were 73,000 never-married women age eighteen to thirty-four with children. This rose to 324,000 in 1970. In 1980 there were 1.4 million never-married persons with their own children. These never-married parents are predominantly in their twenties. More than one-third are twenty to twenty-four years old. Another 25 percent are ages twenty-five to twenty-nine. Approximately 4 percent (56,000) are under age eighteen. For some never-married parents, marriage is not a viable option. This includes gay and lesbian parents who would be listed as single parents, although they are in stable unions. Also included among never-married single parents are heterosexual couples who cohabit but are not legally married.

Women can bear children out of wedlock in a variety of contexts, including as a result of planned as well as unplanned pregnancies. Two categories of never-married or previously married women are notable for making the choice to bear and rear children out of wedlock. The first and largest category comprises those who have children within a common law or consensual heterosexual relationship. The composition of this group varies from country to country and comprises a variety of household arrangements, including those who do not live together, which in some countries can bring its practitioners social security and taxation benefits. Research indicates that women in these de facto arrangements are as likely to have chosen them as men, although more women have expectations of eventual marriage. The second and smaller category comprises women who want to limit the involvement of men. Such mother-only families are formed by the birth of a mother's own baby, usually through artificial insemination, or by adoption (which is also a possibility for father-only families).

The phenomenon of single women using artificial insemination appeared in the mid-1970's. Groups that formed in the United Kingdom and in the United States to support women choosing this option stressed two themes: human rights and reproductive freedom. In 1991 the Birmingham

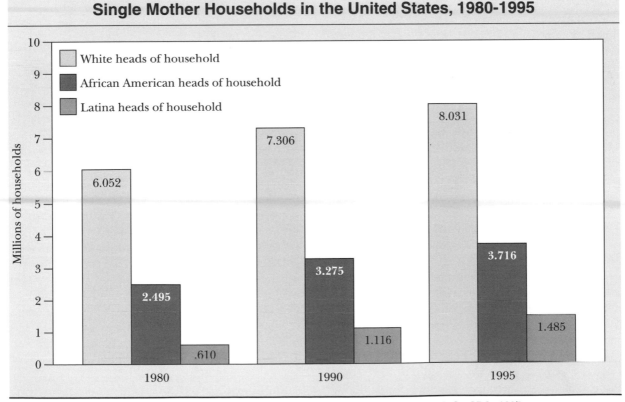

Single Mother Households in the United States, 1980-1995

Source: U.S. Bureau of the Census, *Statistical Abstract of the United States: 1997.* Washington, D.C.: GPO, 1997.

branch of the British Pregnancy Advisory Service made headlines by announcing that it would assist women who did not want to engage in sexual intercourse in having "virgin births" via artificial insemination. Lesbian women use artificial insemination to conceive children. Other single women using artificial insemination give personal reasons such as lack of a suitable partner. The typical heterosexual woman who has conceived using artificial insemination is thirty to thirty-nine years of age, has not married or has experienced a marital breakup, and believes that time is running out because of her age. There is evidence that children of these families develop as well as other children. Lesbian mothers tend to have high levels of education and professional training and often report more support and practical help from their partners than wives receive from husbands. Mother-child relationships among lesbian mothers are reported to be close, and children's cognition and social competence is normal or above average. Mother-only parenthood appears to work out for mothers and children when mothers have good social, economic, and personal resources.

Economic Circumstances of Single-Parent Families. The major source of income for U.S. families is the earnings of primary breadwinners. The ability of single parents with children to earn income is a critical determinant of their economic status. Because of differences in labor force participation and wages, female breadwinners earn less than half as much as male breadwinners. Even women who are employed full-time and year-round earn significantly less than men. On average, fully employed women earn about 60 percent as much as men. For single parents this is a critical difference. Moreover, for many single parents, full-time, year-round employment is not possible either because of their parenting responsibilities or because employers are more likely to discriminate against women with children—a situation sometimes referred to as "the mommy track."

For single parents employed at minimum wage, full-time, year-round work does not provide an income above the poverty level. Although government subsidies for single parents, such as Aid to Families with Dependent Children (AFDC), are low (AFDC payments typically have been below $200 per month), medical benefits tied to AFDC

programs have tended, historically, to be better than at minimum wage jobs. Women have most commonly been maids, cashiers, nursing aids, child-care workers, and waitresses. These jobs usually provide no health care coverage, and often the income derived from them is not sufficient to cover job-related expenses—in particular, child care.

Frequently, the wages of single mothers are low in part because they are mothers and have invested their time and energy in child care. Compared with men, mothers are less likely to have continuous work histories and are less likely to have received on-the-job training. Some employers discriminate against women because they have children. The ratio of dependents to earners is higher in single-parent than in dual-parent families. Not only do the major breadwinners in mother-child families earn lower incomes than men, but contributions from fathers are also usually low or nonexistent. About 40 percent of absent white fathers and 20 percent of absent African American fathers pay child support. Of those who pay, support payments account for about 10 percent of the income of single white mothers and three percent of the income of single African American mothers.

In addition to low wages and little alimony and child support from absent fathers, a third cause of poverty in mother-only families is the relatively low benefits they receive from the government. Among single mothers, widows who receive survivor insurance benefits are less likely to be poor than single women receiving AFDC (a program that assists mother-only families as well as some father-only families). Widows are a group of single mothers who receive a larger portion of their income through public benefits. The average survivor's benefit is double the benefit from AFDC. Increasing the benefits for divorced, separated, and never-married mothers to the level of benefits received by other survivors would be consistent with a policy to allow poor women to stay home and raise their children. Otherwise, the low levels of support from government, absent fathers, and minimum-wage jobs contribute to inadequate and often disastrous economic circumstances for mother-child families.

More than half (57.7 percent) of children living in single-parent, female-headed families in 1994 lived below the poverty level. This included 82 percent of children living in African American mother-child families (approximately 4 million children) and 46 percent of children living in white and Hispanic mother-child families (approximately 6 million children). If single mothers lived in economic circumstances similar to those of men, they would take 10 million children with them out of poverty. Helping low-income, single mothers means helping children.

Problems and Advantages of Single-Parent Families. The greatest problem facing single-parent, mother-only families is poverty. The extent to which poverty is a problem of mothers and their dependent children has resulted in the term "feminization of poverty."

In addition to money problems, single-parent families have problems with time. The single parent must do everything alone that two parents do together. There is subtle discrimination against single parents by such institutions as the schools, which frequently assume that for every student there are two parents, one of whom stays at home full time. This is true even though the majority of elementary school teachers are women working outside the home. Low incomes go hand in hand with inflexible work schedules. Low-income jobs are highly visible and offer little personal autonomy, compared to jobs paying high incomes. Many schools do not offer after-school programs. Accordingly, working single parents are frequently faced with a choice of leaving children alone after school (latchkey children) or risking unemployment.

In spite of the economic and temporal hardships faced by many single-parent families, such families also have advantages. Single parents tend to be more focused on the needs of their children than dual parents, and there is less violence in single-parent households than in dual-parent households. In fact, violence is sometimes the reason for divorce. There is also evidence that children in single-parent households tend to express greater freedom from gender stereotypes and are generally more independent and self-reliant than children in dual-parent households. There is, of course, tremendous variation among single-parent families. Given similar economic circumstances, there is no systematic evidence suggesting single-parent families are inherently less functional for children than other family forms. There also is no evidence that the single-parent, mother-child family is declining in prevalence or duration.

—*Elizabeth Maret*

BIBLIOGRAPHY

Burns, Ailsa, and Cath Scott. *Mother-Headed Families and Why They Have Increased.* Mahwah, N.J.: Lawrence Erlbaum, 1994. Written in Australia, this book explores the causes and implications of why mother-headed families now comprise a large underprivileged class across the Western world.

Garfinkel, Irwin, and Sara S. McLanahan. *Single Mothers and Their Children.* Washington, D.C.: The Urban Institute, 1986. Discusses the rapid increase in families headed by women and assesses the impact of changes in domestic policy occurring in the Reagan Administration.

Kurz, Demie. *For Richer, For Poorer: Mothers Confront Divorce.* New York: Routledge, 1994. Illuminates through interviews with 129 divorced mothers why women are leaving their marriages and what their lives are like as divorced mothers, while illustrating not only the hardships but also the freedom from domination, violence, and destructive emotional influences.

Marsiglio, William, ed. *Fatherhood: Contemporary Theory, Research, and Social Policy.* Thousand Oaks, Calif.: Sage Publications, 1995. Written by sociologists and professionals in family social work, this volume is part of a series on men and masculinity that focuses on legal, economic, and policy questions as well as father-child interactions in child-care experiences.

Spatter-Roth, Roberta, Beverly Barr, Heidi Harman, and Lois Shaw. *Welfare That Works: The Working Lives of AFDC Recipients.* Washington, D.C.: The Institute for Women's Policy Research, 1995. Presents findings from an ongoing investigation into the survival strategies of single mothers on AFDC while challenging the notion that welfare creates dependency and raising questions about the feasibility of time-limited welfare as a strategy for raising single mothers out of poverty.

Sweet, James, and Larry Bumpass. *American Families and Households.* New York: Russell Sage Foundation, 1990. Descriptive study planned, commissioned, and monitored by the National

Committee for Research on the 1980 census that investigates U.S. families and households and is a good research tool for those who want basic quantitative information.

See also Aid to Families with Dependent Children (AFDC); Big Brothers and Big Sisters of America (BBBSA); Child rearing; Child support; Children born out of wedlock; Divorce; Family demographics; Family economics; Family-friendly programs; Feminization of poverty; Latchkey children; Parenting; Poverty; Social capital; Unwed fathers; Welfare; Widowhood.

B. F. Skinner, who applied principles learned in studies of animal behavior to studying human beings. (Alfred A. Knopf, Inc.)

Skinner, B. F.

BORN: March 20, 1904, Susquehanna, Pa.
DIED: August 18, 1990, Cambridge, Mass.
AREA OF ACHIEVEMENT: Behavioral psychology
SIGNIFICANCE: Skinner proposed that the only "scientific" study of animal behavior involved the operation of positive and negative reinforcement of behavior itself, a principle he extended to human behavior

Influenced by behavioral psychologist John B. Watson, B. F. Skinner began to focus on the observable behavior of rats and later pigeons during his graduate studies at Harvard University. Skinner rejected untestable concepts such as "mind" or "thinking" and concentrated on the objective facts of animals' responses to their environment. To remove confusing influences from the environment, Skinner reduced rats' research task to a single operation, such as pressing a lever to obtain a pellet of food. By allowing animals to master further tasks one by one with suitable rewards ("positive reinforcement"), he was able to produce quite complex behavior. This method was called "operant conditioning," and the simplified environment came to be called a "Skinner box."

The results obtained with the Skinner box included training a rat to obtain a marble that could be traded for food and teaching pigeons to play a kind of ping-pong by rewarding each correct move with a grain of corn. Operant conditioning methods were applied to human learning. In the 1940's and 1950's Skinner produced a teaching machine and "programmed instruction" that led students through easy steps of learning, with positive reinforcement being the achievement of the correct answer. This method was particularly effective with slow learners, who profited when learning was divided into a series of small tasks that could be mastered one at a time. Skinner's method continues to be used in computerized instruction.

Skinner gained notoriety with his controlled-environment device for rearing babies, called variously the "aircrib" and the "Heir-Conditioner." The device was a closed, glass-fronted crib with a warmed, filtered air supply that eliminated the need for blankets or heavy baby clothes. Many hanging toys enriched the environment, and babies were allowed frequent contact with parents and other adults. Skinner estimated that his two daughters spent no more time in this crib environment than most other children did in playpens. Such assertions did not prevent a public outcry from individuals who confused the crib with the barren Skinner box and assumed that Skinner was conducting nefarious experiments on his own children. The crib was distributed commercially on a limited basis, and those who used it liked it. Nevertheless, it did not survive.

Skinner married Yvonne Blue in 1936 and moved from Harvard to the University of Minnesota that same year. In 1945 he became chairman of the psychology department at Indiana University in Bloomington. He returned to Harvard in 1948 and continued to work there after his formal retirement in 1974. In his later years Skinner became interested in the human and philosophical implications of behaviorism, producing his two best-known works—the utopian novel *Walden Two* (1948) and *Beyond Freedom and Dignity* (1971)—which argued for an organized human society in which people behaved toward one another in such a way that traditional notions of "freedom" and "dignity" would become unnecessary. Both books aroused much controversy. Skinner's output included some two dozen other works ranging from textbooks to popular books on behavior.

—*Robert M. Hawthorne, Jr.*

See also Bruner, Jerome; Child care; Child rearing; Educating children; Watson, John B.

Slavery

RELEVANT ISSUES: Kinship and genealogy; Marriage and dating; Parenting and family relationships

SIGNIFICANCE: Despite immense obstacles, African American slaves forged strong family bonds and created communities that valued marriage, nurtured children, cared for the aged, and preserved commitment to nuclear family groups

The laws governing slavery made it impossible for slaves to enjoy secure family lives. Not only could slaveholders sell any of their slaves, regardless of family ties, but slaves could not legally marry. Moreover, any child born to a slave woman was legally a slave, even if the father was a free African American or a white man. None of these deterrents to stable family life, however, kept slaves from valuing and trying to maintain family groups and kinship ties, and slaves were able, even in the face of immense obstacles, to shape a family-oriented culture that provided them emotional support, self-esteem, and a measure of autonomy from the white culture that controlled so much of their lives.

Marriage. Although slave marriage vows were not legally binding, slaves themselves—and most masters—recognized the commitments of those who claimed to be married. Most owners encouraged marriages: Marriage was regarded as the foundation of moral society. Moreover, family ties and responsibilities increased owners' hold on their slaves, since masters could determine whether to allow relationships to continue and could dictate the conditions under which they survived. Being able to separate spouses or family members was a powerful threat that slave owners held over their workers.

Some slaveholders arranged marriages, but most allowed their slaves to choose their own mates. Although most owners preferred that their slaves select spouses from their own holdings, they usually allowed marriages with slaves owned by others. Despite their positions of authority, owners probably worried about the ill effects of having workers discontented by thwarted love. Hence, the majority of slave marriages were marriages of love, not arrangement.

Most slaves marked their commitment by a ceremony of some sort, ranging from elaborate weddings that imitated those of whites (and were sometimes even arranged and attended by white families) to simply moving in together. Often weddings were accompanied by the folk custom of "jumping the broomstick" to see who would have the most authority in the relationship.

In wedding ceremonies, couples usually refrained from pledging to be together "till death do us part," as there was little assurance that they would have the final say in the matter. "What God has brought together, let no man put asunder" was not a realistic pronouncement at slave weddings, since owners could legally sunder couples at any time. Instead, some slaves vowed to stay married "till death or distance do us part." If slave couples were separated by the sale of one spouse, more often than not the sale was considered, realistically, tantamount to the spouse's death. Remarriage was the norm after such breakups, and children from former unions were assimilated into the new households. Nevertheless, a majority of slave marriages lasted for many years.

Most married slaves lived in single-family cabins. If husbands or wives were lucky (and, usually, light-skinned), they were perhaps assigned to work in the "big house" of the master or engage in a special craft, such as blacksmithing or carpentry. However, most slaves, male and female, were field hands. Field workers usually spent from dawn to dusk, six days a week, plowing, planting, weeding, or harvesting. Some owners gave their hands Saturday afternoons off to take care of their own chores—washing clothes, hunting, making and mending clothes, making candles, repairing their cabins, or tending their own gardens. Even then, slave couples had little time to spend together. Slaves who had married "abroad"—that is, to someone not owned by the same master—might or might not have been allowed to spend weekday evenings with their spouses.

Children and Childhood. On average, slave women had around seven children. Pregnant women were often not given adequate prenatal care. Infant mortality among African Americans was greater than among whites, probably because of the lack of care and poor diets during pregnancy and early childhood. Pregnant women were typically expected to perform their normal duties to within a month of giving birth and to be back on the job a few weeks following birth. Generally, nursing mothers could leave their work long enough to feed their infants only three or four times a day, and they were expected to wean their babies at what for the time was an early age. Slave

women too elderly to do field work often tended infants and young children, while older children were frequently left unsupervised.

Most slave children were allowed to have real childhoods of carefree play. They did not, however, get to spend a great deal of time with their parents, who would be away from them from dawn to dusk. Youngsters were not usually expected to work until they were eight to twelve years old, and then they were gradually assimilated into the workforce. They would, over several years, begin to be assigned duties. At first they performed light chores and spent fewer hours working than adults, but in the course of adolescence they came to take on the full workload of adults. Many children did not realize their condition of bondage until they were close to working age. Their realization sometimes came when their white playmates would go off to school without them or when the masters' children began to assume authority over them.

Parents and Parenting. Slaves, like nineteenth century Americans in general, considered fathers to be the head of the household. Even though parents could be subjected to various humiliations at the hand of their owners and had to be deferential in public, African American families tried to preserve the dignity of parents, especially fathers, within the household. Since white owners provided slave families with food staples, clothing, and housing, many of the roles traditionally assigned to fathers were preempted by slaveholders. Moreover, white masters and mistresses could discipline any slave; parents were often helpless in protecting themselves and their families from verbal and physical abuse. Some female slaves had to submit to being raped by their white masters or were even forced to live the lives of concubines. Husbands, parents, and siblings were helpless to defend their loved ones from this fate. Children were often shielded from knowledge of the worst abuses of slavery, such as rapes or whippings, but they ultimately learned of the full implications of bondage. Many slave narratives describe how youngsters were traumatized when they first witnessed a lashing or other event that made them fully cognizant of their own condition.

Although slave parents tried to shield their children from the effects of slavery, they also had to teach their children survival skills. Harsh punishments were meted out to children who violated racial codes of conduct. Children had to learn early on to be deferential in the presence of whites and to submit to the authority of even young white children. They also had to learn to protect the community in the slave quarters. Discretion and not repeating conversations they heard were of great importance. Parents whose children violated survival codes of conduct usually responded with

One of the first priorities of African Americans after they were freed from bondage was reuniting their families. (Archive Photos)

Harriet Beecher Stowe's novel Uncle Tom's Cabin *(1852) brought the plight of southern slave families to the attention of whites in the nonslave northern states.* (Library of Congress)

severe punishments, including slaps, shakings, and hard spankings, for children who did not learn these survival behaviors endangered themselves, their families, and communities.

Despite the many ways slavery undermined traditional parental roles, African American parents remained providers for their families. There was enough food on most plantations, but it was not plentiful and lacked variety. Diets often lacked protein unless they were supplemented by game. Male slaves were sometimes allowed to supplement their families' food allotments by hunting, fishing, and trapping. Parents of both sexes sometimes tended personal gardens. Mothers cooked, cleaned, and sewed. Although most masters provided male slaves with blankets and clothes, women were usually given cloth and expected to make their own dresses and children's clothes. Generally, boys as well as girls wore baggy, dresslike garments until they reached the age of ten or twelve. When young boys reached this age, they were given their own chores to do and also graduated into wearing pants. With these changes, they came of age.

Parents' role in family life revolved around the satisfaction of families' daily needs. Slave narratives reveal strong bonds of love between parents and children, especially between children and mothers. Loving home lives offered slaves a psychological buffer that offset the damages of slavery and provided a sanctuary where they could be themselves away from the scrutiny of whites. Moreover, the culture that flourished in the slave quarters fostered strong family and community values and practices that differed significantly from those of white Americans.

By the mid-nineteenth century, African Americans were usually several generations removed from their African heritage, yet some Africanisms remained central to their lives. Their music retained African rhythms; their games were often adaptations of African games. Many slaves preferred folk remedies to the medicines prescribed by white practitioners Although most slaves became Christians, their Christianity was generally of a more exuberant kind than that of whites, and it often existed side by side with beliefs in conjuring and voodoo. Moreover, the values of the slave community did not always mirror those of the white culture that shaped so much of their lives.

For example, in an era when white America demanded chastity of unmarried women, African American communities often followed the practice of many African tribes, accepting as normal some premarital sexual experimentation while expecting fidelity after marriage. Marriage to blood cousins was also usually taboo in African American communities, although it was fairly common in white society. Extended kinship networks were maintained, and the elderly were valued as they had been in Africa.

Attitudes and Assumptions. Common assumptions about the family life of African Americans have been rooted in misperceptions that arose both during the era of slavery and in modern times. In the nineteenth century, slavery apologists and antislavery proponents alike often maintained that blacks did not possess the same capacity for familial love as did whites, were by nature promiscuous, and were too childlike to take seriously the responsibilities of family life. These assumptions were held despite massive evidence to the contrary. Of course, such beliefs made it easier to condone slavery, especially the practice of selling individuals away from their families.

Slave owners, however, often acknowledged in practice their slaves' family feelings. As the law allowed owners to sell slaves without regard to family and kinship ties, many did so, but others took pains to keep families together—at least until economic factors outweighed their good intentions. Most owners sold slaves, even removing them from their families, if they got into serious financial trouble. In such cases, owners often arranged family breakups while parents or spouses were away to avoid emotional scenes as much as possible. Such precautions are evidence of their anticipation of heartfelt responses to their actions; records by persons who witnessed children being sold away from their parents, spouses being separated from each other, and brothers being taken away from their sisters bear testimony to the heartbreak such separations caused.

In the mid-twentieth century it was commonly believed that slavery led to a matriarchal structure in many modern African American families, with mothers providing economic stability and fathers either emasculated or absent. By the 1970's, however, studies refuted assumptions that modern manifestations of African American family life or modern dysfunctions in African American families could be accounted for by slavery. Studies of the family life of slaves showed that they valued nuclear families and kinship ties. Most slave families were dual-parent families, and in the years following emancipation thousands of African Americans tried desperately to reunite families forcibly separated during slavery, creating new communities with strong kinship and friendship ties that provided support networks. Such evidence suggests that the matriarchal family structures and dysfunctions found in some twentieth century African American families have more recent origins than slavery.

Genealogy. Family trees show that slaves often used naming patterns that emphasized kinship ties, especially in the nineteenth century. In the first two centuries of slavery in America, masters commonly assigned names to slaves they purchased and to children born as their property. Slaves, however, resisted this coopting of their identity. Many had private names used only in the slave quarters, and when allowed to name their children, slaves often followed African customs, naming offspring after events or seasons. Males were commonly named after their fathers, grandfathers, or other family members but almost never after a master, although sometimes female slaves might be given the name of a particularly favored mistress. Genealogy also reveals many slave families with racially mixed lineages. Children of slave women raped by white men were usually assimilated into their mothers' homes and raised without any acknowledgment of kinship from their white fathers.

African Americans who try to trace their family roots often have a difficult time finding records before 1870, the first year the United States census named most African Americans, since slaves were listed as numbers only. Plantation records sometimes list births, deaths, and sales; letters and diaries might shed light on family histories. Nonetheless, tracing family lines during slavery is quite difficult; tracing lineages back to African origins is usually impossible. In this respect, slavery has had an ongoing effect on African Americans' sense of family.
—*Grace McEntee*

BIBLIOGRAPHY

Blassingame, John W. *The Slave Community: Plantation Life in the Antebellum South*. Rev. ed. New York: Oxford University Press, 1979. Classic work by the first African American to write a major study of slavery and the first to base his study mostly on accounts of former slaves.

Finkelman, Paul, ed. *Women and the Family in a Slave Society*. New York: Garland, 1989. Essays mostly published in the 1970's and 1980's that cover an array of topics dealing with marriage, family, and sexuality in Southern slave cultures.

Genovese, Eugene D. *Roll, Jordan, Roll: The World the Slaves Made*. New York: Vintage, 1974. Seminal, thoroughly documented work covering all aspects of slave society and a classic that challenged and changed previous assumptions about slave culture.

Gutman, Herbert G. *The Black Family in Slavery and Freedom, 1750-1925*. New York: Vintage Books, 1976. Landmark book written to refute Daniel Patrick Moynihan's *The Negro Family in America*, which claimed that a "pathology" brought on by centuries of slavery explained "the deterioration of the Negro family" in the United States.

Kolchin, Peter. *American Slavery, 1619-1877*. New York: Hill & Wang, 1993. Traces the evolution of slavery in America and puts it in historic context with other forms of servitude.

Redford, Dorothy Spruill, with Michael D'Orso. *Somerset Homecoming: Recovering a Lost Heritage*. New York: Doubleday, 1988. First-person account of Redford's success in tracing her family's roots and what she discovered about slave families in the process.

See also African Americans; Antimiscegenation laws; Child rearing; Communities; Haley, Alex; Life expectancy; Literature and families; Men's roles; Parenting.

Social capital

RELEVANT ISSUES: Aging; Children and child development; Education; Parenting and family relationships

SIGNIFICANCE: Because family relationships are among the most important human relationships, the family can be a major source of social capital

The term "social capital" refers to relationships among people that can produce desirable outcomes. In economics, capital is wealth that is put

Helping a family member with homework contributes to the entire family's social capital. (Hazel Hankin)

into investment for future profit rather than for immediate consumption. Traditionally, capital refers to money put into business activities, but in the mid-twentieth century, it became common for economists and other social scientists to refer to knowledge, skills, and experience as "human capital," because these can be seen as forms of wealth that yield profits. There is some debate about when social scientists began using the phrase "social capital," but the term achieved great popularity during the 1980's and 1990's. Social capital theorists have argued that certain kinds of social relationships can be profitable, just as financial investments or a knowledge of engineering can be profitable. If people work together well or trust each other, their relationships can pay off.

Types of Social Capital. In families, both human capital and social capital can produce benefits for children. The education and skills of mothers, as forms of maternal human capital, have been identified as particularly crucial to child development. Early and continuing supportive interpersonal relationships, as forms of social capital, can help children develop attitudes and behaviors that will be advantageous throughout life. Parents who provide their children with guidance, attention, and discipline make investments in children that result in higher levels of education and better citizenship. Brothers and sisters who provide one another with information or help one another with homework contribute to one anothers' future opportunities.

Participation in civic networks is one of the clearest types of social capital outside the family sphere. Religious affiliation is a common source of associations among citizens. People may also participate in advantageous social relationships by becoming involved in labor unions, parent-teacher associations, sports clubs, fraternal groups, veterans groups, service clubs, professional societies, literary societies, hobby groups, and political groups. All of these kinds of participation have benefits for individuals and communities. Civically engaged communities have demonstrated more successful outcomes in social and economic projects than communities that are not civically engaged. Since individuals who grow up in stable, supportive families tend to become involved in community groups, social capital in families can contribute to social capital in communities.

A number of authors, including Robert Putnam and Francis Fukuyama, have identified trust as a particularly important form of social capital. People who trust each other can work together efficiently in business or in community projects. In this way, they invest their trust in enterprises. Because people often learn trust from the relationships in their families, the types of family relationships that prevail in a society can determine how much trust there is in society at large.

Erosion of Social Capital. There are a number of trends that may be leading to a loss of social capital in American society. Circumstances placing more families at risk of problems include increasing numbers of children living in poverty, lack of health insurance coverage, insufficient vaccinations, homelessness, domestic abuse, and neglect of children. Declining traditional neighborhoods and neighborhood recreational activities, such as bowling, limit opportunities for social interaction.

Two-parent and extended families are often able to invest more time and attention in children than single-parent families. In addition, these types of families are generally better able to exercise discipline over children and to guide them toward productive futures. Researchers have gen-erally found that children from single parent families are more likely than other children to engage in substance abuse, to display aggressive or violent behavior, and to suffer from a variety of psychological problems. Students from one-parent families often show a greater tendency to display behaviors and attitudes toward school that result in poor school performance. It is thus possible that changes in American family structure away from the two-parent family may result in the erosion of social capital.

Generating Social Capital in Families. Families can generate social capital by fostering closer and more cooperative relationships among family members and by becoming more involved in schools and community organizations. Activists, therapists, public officials, and others can inform families of the potential benefits of increased time spent in interactions within the household with family and friends. To encourage the growth of social capital, public officials can attempt to reduce the obstacles that may be created in families with single parents, no wage earners, large numbers of members, younger household leaders, poor health, or other disadvantages. Additional options for developing social capital include early education centers, community programs for children, social support resources, and worksite schools.

—*Gwenelle S. O'Neal*

BIBLIOGRAPHY

Fukuyama, Francis. *Trust: The Social Virtues and the Creation of Prosperity.* New York: Free Press, 1995.

Kozol, Jonathan. *Savage Inequalities: Children in America's Schools.* New York: Crown Publishers, 1991.

Putnam, Robert D. "Bowling Alone: America's Declining Social Capital." *Current* (June, 1995).

Rose, Mike. *Lives on the Boundary: A Moving Account of the Struggles and Achievements of America's Educational Underclass.* New York: Penguin, 1990.

Salazar-Stanton, Ricardo D. "A Social Capital Framework for Understanding the Socialization of Racial Minority Children and Youths." *Harvard Educational Review* 67 (Spring, 1997).

See also Bonding and attachment; Child abuse; Child rearing; Health of children; Health problems; Homeless families; Poverty; Single-parent families.

Social Security

RELEVANT ISSUES: Aging; Demographics; Economics and work; Law

SIGNIFICANCE: Social Security provides protection against income losses that can accompany the disability, death, or old age of working persons

The Old-Age, Survivors, and Disability Insurance (OASDI) programs, commonly known as Social Security, provide monthly benefits to retired and disabled workers, their dependents, and survivors. In December, 1995, average monthly benefits of $720 were paid to 43.4 million persons, or 16 percent of the U.S. population. Retired workers, widows, widowers, parents, and disabled workers were 84 percent of OASDI beneficiaries and together received 71 percent of benefits; children of deceased, disabled, or retired workers made up 8 percent of beneficiaries and received 21 percent of benefits; and wives and husbands of disabled or retired workers made up 8 percent of beneficiaries and received 8 percent of benefits. 65 percent of all beneficiaries were between the ages of sixty-five and eighty-four; 14 percent between the ages of fifty and sixty-four; and about 7 percent each were between the ages of eighteen and forty-nine, eighty-five and older, or under eighteen. About 60 percent of the 40.4 million adult beneficiaries were women.

Social Security provides at least half of total income for a majority of beneficiaries. In 1994 Social Security accounted for 50 percent or more of income for 66 percent of beneficiaries and 90 percent or more of income for 30 percent of beneficiaries. Social Security helps reduce poverty. In 1994 Social Security enabled 42 percent of all aged households—either married couples living together with husbands or wives aged 65 or older or persons 65 or older who did not live with spouses—to live above the poverty level. Social Security as a share of total income varies greatly by income level. In 1994 Social Security was 23 percent of total income for the highest income quintile of the aged, compared to 81 percent for the lowest quintile. In general, aged households with less income from assets, earnings, and private pensions increasingly rely on Social Security as a main source of economic well-being.

The OASDI Programs have been the subject of public concern in large part due to anticipated costs associated with the growing and increasing life expectancy of the elderly population. In 1995, 12.5 percent of the total U.S. population was 65 years of age and over. By the year 2040 the number of U.S. elderly is expected to double, with one in five individuals sixty-five years of age and over. This increase is primarily attributed to the aging of some seventy-six million baby boomers, those born between 1946 and 1964. Life expectancy is estimated to increase from 72.5 years for men and 79.3 years for women in 1996 to 78.4 and 84.1 respectively in 2070. Federal expenditures for the OASDI programs increased from $11 billion in 1960 to $117.1 billion in 1980 to $301.1 billion in 1993. As a percentage of total federal expenditures for public programs, however, the costs of the OASDI Programs have actually declined from 44.2 percent in 1960 to 38.6 percent in 1980 to 37.4 percent in 1993.

Costs of Medicare, the related health care program for the elderly, have increased from $7.1 billion in 1970 to $34.9 billion in 1980 to $148 billion in 1993. Unlike the OASDI program, Medicare as a percent of total federal expenditures for public programs has increased from 9 percent in 1970 to 11.5 percent in 1980 to 18.4 percent in 1993. As the population of the United States ages, related expenses are expected to rise in real dollar terms as well as a share of total Federal expenditures on public programs, driven more by the costs of Medicare than by the OASDI programs. Unless something is done to control modern spending levels, Social Security and Medicare are expected to run cash deficits, increasing from $232 billion and $114 billion respectively in 2020 to $1.3 trillion and $1.9 trillion respectively by 2040. Invariably, these projected increases in program costs, coupled with interest payments on the anticipated federal debt, are likely to create much pressure to curtail or crowd out means-tested, selective programs, such as Supplemental Security Income and Food Stamps, which benefit primarily low-income individuals and families.

Development of Social Security in the United States. Old-age benefits were provided for retired workers in the original Social Security Act of 1935, which covered only workers in commerce and industry, then about 40 percent of the workforce. The 1935 Act provided monthly benefits to retired

Social Security payments are the primary source of income for many elderly Americans. (James L. Shaffer)

workers sixty-five years of age and over and a lump-sum death benefit to the estate of these workers. In 1939 benefits were extended to dependents of retired workers (wives sixty-five years of age and older and children under sixteen) and to survivors of deceased workers (widows sixty-five years of age and older, mothers caring for an eligible child, children under the age of sixteen, and dependent parents). In 1956 benefits were further extended to disabled workers fifty to sixty-four years of age and to the disabled children over the age of eighteen of retired, disabled, or deceased workers, if they became disabled before they were eighteen (changed to disabled before the age of twenty-two in 1973). Benefits for disabled workers under fifty years of age were provided in 1960. The Medicare insurance program was created in 1965. As a result of the Social Security amendments of 1972, monthly cash OASDI benefits have been automatically adjusted since 1975 to keep pace with inflation.

Social Security was originally conceived as one leg of a three-legged income stool for retirees. Personal savings and private pensions were the two other legs, and both of these were expected to constitute the major portion of retirement income. That view was challenged by a 1975 Advisory Council, which saw Social Security as the nation's primary pension plan, providing more retirement income than private savings.

Benefits. Benefits can be paid to workers and their dependents or survivors if workers have worked long enough in covered employment to be "insured" for these benefits. Insured status is determined by a formula applied to workers' average monthly earnings indexed to the increase in average annual wages. For workers with many years of low earnings, Social Security provides a special minimum benefit based on the number of years of covered employment.

Workers must be at least sixty-two years old to be eligible for retirement benefits. There is no minimum age requirement for disability benefits. A benefit is payable to a spouse of a retired or disabled worker when a currently married spouse is at least sixty-two years old; is caring for one or more of the worker's entitled children who are disabled or have not reached the age of sixteen; or when a divorced spouse is at least sixty-two, is not married, and the marriage lasted at least ten years

before the divorce became final. A divorced spouse may be entitled independently of the worker's retirement if both the worker and divorced spouse are sixty-two years of age and if the divorce has been final for at least two years.

A monthly survivor benefit is payable to a widow, widower, or divorced spouse of a worker who was fully insured at the time of death. The widow, widower, or divorced spouse must be unmarried (unless the remarriage occurred after the widow or widower first became eligible for benefits as a widow or widower) and must be either sixty years of age or older or fifty to fifty-nine years of age and disabled throughout a waiting period of five consecutive calendar months that began no later than seven years after the month the worker died or after the end of his or her entitlement to benefits as a widowed mother or father.

A monthly benefit is payable to an unmarried child; eligible dependent grandchild; or a retired, disabled, or deceased worker who was fully or currently insured at death. The child or grandchild must either be younger than eighteen, a full-time elementary or secondary student younger than nineteen, or a disabled person eighteen years of age or older whose disability began before twenty-two years of age. A grandchild is eligible for benefits on a grandparent's earning record if the grandchild was adopted by the grandparent and may be entitled under certain circumstances even if no adoption took place. If adopted by the surviving spouse of that grandparent, the child would be eligible if he or she lived with or received one-half support from the grandparent prior to the grandparent's death.

A monthly survivor benefit is payable to a mother, father, surviving divorced father, or surviving divorced mother if the deceased worker on whose account the benefit is payable was fully or currently insured at the time of death and the mother, father, surviving divorced father, or surviving divorced mother is not married and cares for one or more entitled children of the worker. These payments continue as long as the youngest child being cared for is younger than sixteen or disabled. A monthly survivor benefit is payable to a parent sixty-two years of age or older of a deceased fully-insured worker. The worker must have been providing at least one-half of the parent's support.

Social Security benefits are often discussed in terms of how much of a person's preretirement earnings the benefits represent. Replacement rates (the percentage of a person's earnings in the year before retirement) vary by income level. For example, for individuals born in 1935 and expected to reach normal retirement age in 2000, replacement rates are 51.7 percent for low earners (those whose earnings are equal to 45 percent of the Social Security average-wage index), 42.4 percent for average earners (those whose earnings are equal to the Social Security average-wage index), and 25.6 percent for maximum earners (those whose earnings are equal to the maximum wage taxable for Social Security purposes).

Social Security benefits may be reduced, withheld, or increased for various reasons, thereby affecting the economic well-being of families. Individuals may be entitled to benefits both as workers, based on their own earnings, and also as dependents (spouse, widow, or widower) of other workers. In these cases, individuals do not collect both benefits. The amount of benefits that spouses, widows, or widowers receive is offset dollar for dollar by the amount of benefits to which they are entitled as workers. The benefit based on one's own work record is always received first, and the only part of the dependent benefit payable is that which it is greater than the worker benefit. In her essay in *Social Security in the Twenty-First Century* (1997), Karen Holden has shown that two-earner couples are at a distinct economic disadvantage when one spouse dies. In effect, the replacement-rate formula used to determine benefit levels of different couples with identical covered annual incomes is such that as couples share earnings more equally, protection against the death of one spouse declines. Such declines are more likely to plunge into poverty the far larger percentage of elderly widows who hover above the poverty line. Ironically, the increased sharing of earning roles between spouses, assumed to increase women's access to protective wage-based insurance, substantially lowers the economic protection provided to them as widows, compared with one-earner couples.

Social Security law also reduces benefits for non-disabled recipients who earn income from work above a certain amount. In 1997 recipients under sixty-five years of age could have earned up to $8,640 a year in wages or self-employment income without having their benefits reduced. Individuals between the ages of sixty-five and sixty-nine could have earned up to $13,500. For earnings above these amounts, recipients under age sixty-five lose $1 of benefits for each $2 of earnings, and those between sixty-five and sixty-nine lost $1 in benefits for every $3 of earnings. The earnings limit does not apply to recipients who are older than sixty-nine or to those who are disabled. The earnings limits rise each year indexed to the rise in average wages in the economy. At issue is the extent to which the incentive structure of Social Security encourages retirement (discourages work) for those under age seventy. Research has shown that labor force participation rates of older workers, particularly men, have decreased over the past several decades, but the influence of Social Security compared to other factors on this trend remains questionable.

Financing Mechanism of Social Security. There has been much debate about how financially sound Social Security is. The primary source of revenue of OASDI is the payroll tax paid by covered workers and matched by covered employers (7.56 percent of wages in 1996). In 1996 approximately 96 percent of the paid workforce in the United States was covered under Social Security. Excluded were state and local employees, federal civilian employees, and students. Taxes are based on earnings up to the annual maximum taxable wage base, which was $62,700 in 1996. Self-employed individuals pay contributions on their annual net earnings up to the same maximum as employees, but at a rate that is equal to the combined em-

Public Opinion on Social Security

Public opinion polls taken when federal government leaders were discussing Social Security reform in 1996 revealed a widespread consensus on giving people more control over their financial futures. For example, one poll found that nearly 70 percent of Americans favored a proposal that would allow them to control investment of part of the money that they are forced to pay in payroll taxes. This figure was 81 percent among persons under thirty years old.

ployee-employer tax rate. Revenue from the OAS and DI portion of the tax is credited to trust funds from which monthly benefits and administrative expenses are paid.

A declining trend in the ratio of workers to OASDI beneficiaries suggests that fewer workers contribute more of their incomes to support increasing numbers of beneficiaries. In 1960, 5.1 taxpaying workers supported each beneficiary, whereas in 1995 the number of taxpaying workers supporting each beneficiary had declined to 3.3. As the number of taxpayers per recipient declined, Social Security as a percentage of workers' payroll increased from 1.2 percent in 1955 to 11.5 percent in 1995. By 2040 no more than two, and perhaps as few as 1.6, taxpaying workers are expected to support Social Security beneficiaries, while Social Security is expected to range between 17.5 percent to 22.2 percent of workers' payroll. At issue is the extent to which all retirees come to rely on Social Security as a larger share of total income, thereby becoming increasingly dependent on workers whose proportionately shrinking take-home pay must also meet workers' own financial obligations. The debate over Social Security reform promises to be lively, as workers seek to maximize their take home pay and elders seek to protect their economic well-being.

—*Richard K. Caputo*

BIBLIOGRAPHY

Berkowitz, Edward D. *America's Welfare State from Roosevelt to Reagan.* Baltimore: The Johns Hopkins University Press, 1991. Historical overview of Social Security and other programs, tracing the ebb and flow of OASDI's popularity.

Committee on Ways and Means, U.S. House of Representatives. *1996 Green Book.* Washington, D.C.: U.S. Government Printing Office, 1996. Provides detailed background material and data on programs within the Committee's jurisdiction, including Social Security, Medicare, and the Railroad Retirement System.

Kingston, Eric R., and James H. Schultz, eds. *Social Security in the Twenty-First Century.* New York: Oxford University Press, 1997. Collection of essays that examines how Social Security affects families and the economy, including such issues as its impact on work, its fairness to women, and its financial stability.

Peterson, Peter G. *Will America Grow Up Before It Grows Old?* New York: Random House, 1996. Alarming view of how changing demographics may adversely affect families and the economy unless major changes are made in how the U.S. finances and limits Social Security benefits, such as switching from an income-based to a consumption-based tax and raising to seventy the age at which persons become eligible for Social Security.

Schultz, James H. *The Economics of Aging.* 6th ed. Westport, Conn.: Auburn House, 1995. Thorough examination of changes in retirement patterns, problems of older workers, and the complexity of retirement preparation and a discussion of pension plans and health costs.

Social Security Administration. *Annual Statistical Supplement, 1996 to the Social Security Bulletin.* Washington, D.C.: U.S. Government Printing Office, 1996. Presents more than 250 tables of detailed data on the U.S. network of income programs, as well as brief historical summaries of and discussions about recent legislative changes that affect these programs.

See also Aging and elderly care; Baby boomers; Disabilities; Intergenerational income transfer; Life expectancy; Nursing and convalescent homes; Poverty; Retirement; Senior citizen centers; Support Organizations.

Social workers

RELEVANT ISSUES: Children and child development; Parenting and family relationships; Sociology

SIGNIFICANCE: The profession of social work has had a significant impact on the lives of children and families in legislating policy, designing services, and effecting treatment methods

From the beginning of its existence, social work has been a profession that has been concerned with the social conditions of society and its effects on people. Working with individuals and families has been one of the central themes of social work and has remained so into the late twentieth century.

The basic tenets and programs of any social welfare system reflect the values and norms of society itself. Approaches to social welfare are tailored around the customs, traditions, and past experiences of a given society. The tradition of social welfare in the United States stems directly from the British system of social welfare and indirectly from the Judeo-Christian tenet of duty to others in need. The Elizabethan Poor Law of 1601 (passed in London, England), was the culmination of centuries of work in respect to the poor. This law brought together in one statute the principles of relief for the poor. It stressed local administration and financing of relief, included grants-in-aid to the unemployable, apprenticeships for the young, and work relief for able-bodied adults. It struggled with the concept that civil government must accept responsibility for the poor over the reinforcement of feudal social structure. Parents were legally liable for the support of their children and grandchildren and children were responsible for the care of their needy parents and grandparents. The Poor Law recognized that there would be times of involuntary unemployment (hence grants-in-aid to the unemployable) and firmly established the right to public assistance. This was the pattern for the poor laws that were subsequently enacted in the American colonies.

Early Social Welfare Organizations. Early social welfare organizations in colonial America were typically private religious or cultural societies—for example, the Quakers, the Scots Charitable Societies, the German Society of New York and the French Benevolent Society. These groups assisted the poor who were members of their church or ethnic group. Their assistance was given in partnership with whatever public aid was distributed by the colonies. It was not until after the Revolutionary War, when the numbers of poor increased dramatically, that demands were made by the American people to change the system of private, piecemeal aid to an organized system in which relief could be administered and supervised.

The earliest established, coordinated social welfare organizations in the United States were the Charity Organization Societies. The structure of these societies was adopted from England. Many private relief agencies had been established in America, especially in large cities. These agencies' programs were uncoordinated and sometimes overlapped with each other. In the Charity Organization Societies private agencies joined together to provide direct services to individuals and families and to plan and coordinate the efforts of private agencies to meet the pressing social problems in the urban centers. The Charity Organization Societies conducted detailed investigations of applicants to determine which services or financial help they required, maintained a central registration system of clients, and used volunteers as "friendly visitors," whose job it was to teach individuals and families how to become better people. Since poverty was seen as the result of personal failings, these volunteers attempted to "model" correct and proper behavior and the correct values one should have so as not to be poor.

Concurrent with the Charity Organization movement was the establishment of settlement houses. Modeled after Toynbee Hall in London, England, the settlement house movement was begun by the daughters of ministers, usually from the middle and upper classes. These women lived in impoverished neighborhoods and used the missionary approach of teaching residents how to live moral lives and improve their circumstances. However, they were also very involved in social reform movements to improve housing, health, and living conditions. The settlement houses taught immigrants English, hygiene, and occupational skills. The settlement house workers did not see poverty as totally the result of personal failings; they emphasized the role the environment and its conditions played in contributing to and prolonging poverty. The most noted leader in the settlement house movement was Jane Addams, who founded Hull House in Chicago, Illinois, in 1889.

Child Welfare. Of all social welfare activities, none has been more important than those dealing with children and their families. From the charity organization societies to settlement houses, all those who worked for social betterment saw in children the possibility of constructive altruism—the possibility of changing the nature of poverty by preventing it with children. If future generations were to possess the strength of mind, body, and character to become good, productive, responsible citizens, it was necessary to protect children.

From the colonial period to the early nineteenth century, childhood was not considered a special phase of human development. Children were considered to be miniature adults, who were aggressive and sinful and therefore in need of

Social workers often visit clients' homes to look after the welfare of children. (Ben Klaffke)

close supervision and stern treatment. By the mid-nineteenth century, however, the concept of childhood and child rearing was undergoing significant change. Children were coming to be seen as moldable by their parents and were thus seen as needing special treatment, especially a relaxed and healthy home life. The importance of the family in the lives of children was gaining in significance as a way to prevent poverty and help children develop into productive, healthy people. However, if families themselves were needy and not able to adequately care for children's upbringing, the children were removed from the home and placed in almshouses or orphanages if their parents had died. Children placed in almshouses numbered in the thousands, and by 1830 people began to demand that children's almshouses be abolished. Most of these institutions were large, with anywhere from five hundred to two thousand children under one roof. The managers were rigid and demanded obedience and precision. They often provided poor care.

The first children's organization in America to adopt family care, or placing-out, was the New York Children's Aid Society, founded by Charles Loring Brace in 1853. Alarmed at the increasing rates of juvenile delinquency and crime among New York youth, Brace attempted several approaches to help these children. The Children's Aid Society became noted for its placing-out program, in which boys and girls from New York were placed in farm homes in the central part of the country. Believing that the opportunity to work in a farm environment would improve the lives of these children, Brace and the Children's Aid Society eventually removed more than fifty thousand children from New York City in twenty-five years. This was the beginning of foster home care.

Protective Services for Children. Agencies providing protective services in America trace their origin to the case of Mary Ellen in 1875. Mary Ellen was severely beaten and neglected by a couple who had raised her since infancy. Unaware of legal approaches that could be taken to protect her, concerned community citizens appealed to the Society for the Prevention of Cruelty to Animals (SPCA). After the Society brought the child to the court's attention, she was removed from the home and placed with another family. The abusive couple were sentenced to prison. Following this

case, the Society for the Prevention of Cruelty to Children (SPCC) was established in New York. Before long, other states began forming protective service agencies and enacting legislation protecting children from abuse and neglect. From the beginning, protective services had two focuses: a law enforcement approach that emphasized punishment for abusive or neglectful parents and a rehabilitative approach that focused on the importance of helping parents and keeping families intact. In the 1900's the rehabilitative approach became the most widely used one. The emphasis in child protective services in the 1990's has been on "family preservation," whereby a broader range of services focuses on the whole family rather than on individual family members. Family preservation is not only used when placement is imminent but also offered to highly vulnerable families in which children are at risk but not yet in crisis.

Social Work as a Profession. Social work is the professional activity of helping individuals, groups, families, organizations, and communities to enhance or restore their capacity for social functioning and to create societal conditions that allow them to pursue their goals. Social work is distinct from other professions by virtue of its responsibility and mandate to provide social services.

A social worker requires training and expertise in a wide range of areas. Social work continues to emphasize a broad-based approach which requires a wide range of skills that enables social workers to intervene effectively in the common personal and emotional problems of clients and the common social problems faced by groups, organizations, and the larger community. In working with individuals, families, groups, or communities, social workers use a problem-solving approach and practice at three levels: the micro level, working one-to-one with individuals; the mezzo level, working with families and other small groups; and the macro level, working with organizations and communities, including seeking changes in statutes and social policies.

The specific activities of social workers include, but are not limited to, social casework, case management, group therapy, and community organizing. Social casework is aimed at helping individuals on a one-to-one basis to solve personal and social problems. Social casework services are provided by almost every social welfare agency that

Part of a social worker's job is to help clients cope with government rules and paperwork. (James L. Shaffer)

offers direct services. These services can include counseling, placement of children in foster or adoptive homes, drug and alcohol rehabilitation services, probation or parole services, and mental health work. Case management involves supervising and monitoring services to clients from a variety of agencies, including the coordination of services between and within agencies. Group therapy aims at facilitating the social, behavioral, and emotional adjustment of individuals through the group process. Many clients respond to treatment better in group settings than in one-on-one situations. Community organizing seeks to stimulate and assist local communities in evaluating, planning, and coordinating efforts to provide for communities' health, welfare, and recreational needs.

During the 1950's and 1960's child welfare was identified as a special form and a highly professional branch of social work practice. It has been recognized as one of the only practical fields in which social workers have long been in control of their own programs. Social workers involved in child welfare must possess knowledge of human behavior and development, systems theory, problem-solving methods, ethics, policy analysis, and dynamics of family behavior and treatment. Social workers involved with families use systems theory as their model for assessing the family and for structuring treatment. A holistic approach is used, whereby families are seen as units, and all efforts are directed toward understanding families in their social, economic, political, and geographical environment. Treatment is usually based on emphasizing the strengths and coping skills of families rather than their weaknesses and negative sides. Families' strengths are utilized to assist them in working through their problems. Social workers work with families in almost all settings, including hospitals, mental health facilities, correctional institutions, and school systems. Social workers, viewing the family as society's most valuable asset, will continue to work with families and children in the twenty-first century. —*Robin Sakina Mama*

BIBLIOGRAPHY

Ashby, L. *Saving the Waifs: Reformers and Dependent Children, 1890-1917.* Philadelphia: Temple University Press. Examines the many attempts to provide services to children and their families and presents a close examination of both agency services and policy changes.

Costin, Lela, Cynthia Bell, and Susan Downs. *Child Welfare: Policies and Practice.* White Plains, N.Y.: Longman, 1991. Comprehensive book that examines in detail all the modern issues affecting children and child welfare services.

Helton, Lonnie, and Maggie Jackson. *Social Work Practice with Families: A Diversity Model.* Boston: Allyn & Bacon, 1997. Concise book that looks at family and children's services and treatment approaches, with a specific focus on how social workers provide services to diverse groups of clients.

Kamerman, Sheila B., and Alfred Kahn. *Social Services for Children, Youth and Families in the United States.* New York: Columbia University School of Social Work, 1989. One of the best books on the history of social work involving families and children that is comprehensive in scope and detailed in its breadth of knowledge.

Langsam, Miriam. *Children West: A History of the Placing-Out of the New York Children's Aid Society.* Madison, Wis: State Historical Society, 1964. Detailed description of Charles Loring Brace's placing-out of children into farming communities and a good source on the beginnings of the child foster home movement.

Sidel, Ruth. *Women and Children Last: The Plight of Poor Women in Affluent America.* New York: Penguin Books, 1987. Excellent discussion of the situation of poor women and their children in America, covering social welfare policy and family policy involving young and older women.

Trattner, Walter I. *From Poor Law to Welfare State: A History of Social Welfare in America.* 4th ed. New York: Free Press, 1989. Thorough, comprehensive examination of how the social welfare system started in the United States and a detailed overview of the British system of social welfare as well as an overview of early forms of social welfare from the ancient Greeks on.

Zastrow, Charles. *Introduction to Social Work and Social Welfare.* 6th ed. Pacific Grove, Calif.: Brooks/Cole, 1996. Introductory book on social work as a profession and all the fields in which social workers practice.

See also Addams, Jane; Aid to Families with Dependent Children (AFDC); Child Abuse Prevention and Treatment Act (CAPTA); Child Welfare League of America (CWLA); Children's Defense Fund (CDF); Family: concept and history; Family counseling; Family therapy; Foster homes; Hull House; Poverty; Settlement houses; Welfare.

Son preference

RELEVANT ISSUES: Kinship and genealogy; Parenting and family relationships

SIGNIFICANCE: Throughout social history the preference for sons, particularly the preference for first-born males, has affected husband-wife and sibling relationships and at times has even affected families' community status

In Asia, particularly China, Japan, and Korea, there has traditionally been a preference for sons.

It has been believed that it is the eldest son's duty or, more accurately, the duty of the eldest son's wife to care for aged parents. In Asian families mothers-in-law have enjoyed a great deal of power because they have been in charge of their sons' wives within the extended families. Thus, sons, particularly the eldest, were greatly prized. Eldest sons had inheritance rights greater than those of other sons or daughters. Among traditional Asian families, those with sons were seen as particularly lucky. In Japan, families displayed their luck on Boy's Day by flying carp flags, a symbol of courage and endurance, for each boy in the family.

It was not until 1998 that the English monarchy accepted succession to the throne by a first-born female child. Queen Elizabeth II, who had been queen for forty-six years but who had succeeded to the throne only because she had no brothers, accepted the provision passed by Parliament that females be permitted to succeed to the throne. Early in the sixteenth century the English monarch Henry VIII married three times before he was able to get a male heir to the throne, Edward VI. The English novelist Jane Austen, writing in the late eighteenth and early nineteenth centuries, depicted how burdensome it was for families to have daughters whom they had to marry off and for whom they had to provide dowries.

Traditional attitudes influence immigrants to America. The European preference for sons and the laws that have preferred sons in matters of inheritance were carried to the New World by European immigrants. This preference was further strengthened because in the European tradition wives took their husbands' names. Thus, families wanted sons to carry on the family name. Likewise, Asian immigrants carried with them the preference for sons, the eldest of whom would marry and provide wives to take care of parents in their old age.

Social conditions have changed attitudes. Twentieth century American laws treat males and females equally. Thus, sons and daughters are equally eligible to inherit families' possessions. Many women do not take their husband's names when they marry. Thus, family names can continue through daughters as well as sons. Since males and females may enjoy equal educational and employment opportunities according to the law, families must no longer provide dowries so that daughters can bring material goods into marriage.

There is little reason for parents to be concerned whether their children will provide for them in old age. Most employers provide pension plans and most workers make Social Security contributions, which provide income for elderly and disabled persons and Medicare for the aged. Thus, son preference has waned in the United States and Canada. —*Annita Marie Ward*

See also Chinese Americans; Dowry; Family values; Japanese Americans; Korean Americans; Primogeniture; Religion; Vietnamese Americans.

Southeast Asian Americans

RELEVANT ISSUES: Parenting and family relationships; Race and ethnicity; Religious beliefs and practices

SIGNIFICANCE: There are substantial Southeast Asian populations throughout North America, each with distinctive family customs

Since 1975 large numbers of Southeast Asian immigrants from Laos, Cambodia, Thailand, and Vietnam have settled throughout the United States and southern Canada. Most of those from Laos, Cambodia, and Vietnam arrived in North America as refugees after socialist governments came to power in those countries at the end of the Vietnam War. The Hmong, a minority group from the mountains of Laos, were among these refugees. The Thais arrived in North America as immigrants, not refugees, with the largest numbers entering as students or as spouses of U.S. or Canadian citizens. However, much of the Thai settlement is also a consequence of American involvement in the war in Southeast Asia from 1965 to 1975, because Thailand borders Cambodia and Laos and the war established many links between America and Thailand.

California holds the largest concentrations of Southeast Asians in North America. Of the 149,014 Laotians in the 1990 U.S. Census, 58,058, or 39 percent, lived in California. Similarly, California was home to 32,064, or 35 percent, of the 91,275 U.S. Thais; 68,190, or 46 percent, of the 147,411 U.S. Cambodians; 46,892, or 52 percent, of the 90,082 U.S. Hmong; and 280,223, or 46 percent, of the 614,547 U.S. Vietnamese. Canada

Many Southeast Asian immigrants have begun their residence in the United States in public housing. (Ben Klaffke)

has a relatively small Thai population, found chiefly in Toronto, but by the late 1980's it was home to more than 100,000 Southeast Asians from the other groups. About three-quarters of Canadian Southeast Asians are Vietnamese, and they are primarily concentrated in Ontario Province, particularly in Toronto.

Size and Youth of Families. The Southeast Asians come from countries in which large families are customary and, as a consequence, their families tend to be much larger than those of other Americans. In the United States, for example, U.S. Census data show that the average American family had only 3.16 people per family. The average Canadian family was slightly larger. The average Cambodian family, by contrast, had 5.03 people, the average Laotian family 5.01, the average Vietnamese family 4.36, and the average Hmong family 6.58. Only the Thais, with an average family size of 3.48 people, were close to other

Americans. This is probably a reflection of the fact that so many Thais came to the United States as students or were married to non-Asian Americans.

Partly as a result of large family size, Southeast Asians tend to be younger than other Americans. In 1990 about one-fourth of all Americans were younger than eighteen. That same year nearly half of all Cambodian Americans and Laotian Americans were younger than eighteen. More than one-third of Vietnamese Americans and nearly two-thirds of Hmong Americans were younger than eighteen. Only the Thais were similar to other Americans. The extreme youth of the refugee groups means that passing on traditional family customs and relations is an especially large task for Laotian, Cambodian, Hmong, and Vietnamese parents.

Family Relations. Husbands are regarded as the heads of families among all Southeast Asian groups, but women often wield a great deal of power, especially over matters having to do with the household. Children in traditional Southeast Asian families are expected to show a great deal of respect for elders. Older brothers and sisters are expected to take responsibility for younger siblings, and younger children are expected to defer

Wherever sizeable communities of Southeast Asians—such as these Laotian residents of Stockton, California—live, they are apt to form community centers. (Ben Klaffke)

to their older siblings. The psychologist Nathan Caplan has argued that highly cooperative family relations may be one of the reasons why Southeast Asian children often do well in American schools, since brothers and sisters frequently help one another in doing schoolwork.

Since women are regarded as the core of the family and the central carriers of tradition in all Southeast Asian cultures, parents tend to place higher expectations and restrictions on daughters than on sons. This sometimes causes resentment on the part of American-born daughters and may lead to frictions within families. Both sons and daughters sometimes come into conflict with parents when the children attempt to live out American values of individual independence.

Marriage and Wedding Customs. The wedding customs of Thais, Laotians, and Cambodians are quite similar. In common traditional Thai and Laotian weddings, bridegrooms visit brides'

These Vietnamese American high school graduates typify the drive of Southeast Asian immigrants to better their condition through education. (James L. Shaffer)

houses on the evening before the wedding. Buddhist monks bless elaborate begging bowls filled with water. Then a long strand of cotton thread is tied around couples' and monks' wrists and looped around the blessed water. This ceremony is intended to unite the souls (known in both Lao and Thai as *kwan*) of the betrothed.

The next morning, monks, friends, and relatives sprinkle couples with the consecrated water. Later in the day, brides and bridegrooms sit together, dressed in traditional clothing, in front of a feast and wedding gifts in the presence of their families and guests. The monks recite prayers for couples' happiness and well-being.

In Cambodian weddings the ceremony usually begins in the morning at the brides' homes, where Buddhist monks chant blessings. Locks of hair are cut from the heads of the betrothed. Cotton threads soaked in holy water are tied around the wrists of brides and bridegrooms. A circle of married couples then passes around a candle in order to bless the marriages. Such weddings are followed by a large feast, which may be held in a private home or in a restaurant, depending on the convenience and means of the families.

Among the Hmong, marriages are traditionally arranged by go-betweens, who negotiate a price to be paid to the brides' families. Marriages are made public by a two-day feast. In Laos, if families could not agree on a bride-price or if prospective husbands were unacceptable to brides' families, suitors would often elope with the young women or kidnap them. Because the Hmong in America who have tried in some instances to follow this practice have been charged with kidnapping and rape, this custom has become very rare.

Wedding customs of Vietnamese Americans are quite different from those of other Southeast Asians, because the Vietnamese have been much more influenced by Chinese civilization than other Southeast Asians and many Vietnamese are Roman Catholics. Although Roman Catholic and Buddhist Vietnamese maintain many social ties with one another, marriages of people of different religious faiths are fairly rare. Roman Catholic and Buddhist Vietnamese in North America often live in separate communities. Although wedding customs differ among Vietnamese of different religions, wedding feasts following marriage ceremonies are a central tradition for all.

Family Holiday Celebrations. Holiday celebrations are important to Southeast Asian American families, because they provide opportunities for elders to pass on traditions and customs to younger people. Among all groups, New Year's celebrations are the most widely held and most important. The Laotian, Cambodian, and Thai New Year is usually held in mid-April. Thais and Laotians in America frequently dress in traditional clothes and hold cultural exhibitions during New Year's events, and they enjoy the custom of throwing water on each other. The Cambodians hold parties and dances and sometimes play a customary game in which young men and women throw a rolled-up scarf back and forth. At the Hmong New Year's Festival, held at the time of the new moon in December, young men and women play a similar courting game, tossing a ball back and forth. The Vietnamese New Year, held in January or February, is a lively three-day celebration with a variety of family and community rituals.

—*Carl L. Bankston III*

BIBLIOGRAPHY

Caplan, Nathan, John K. Whitmore, and Marcella H. Choy. *The Boat People and Achievement in America: A Study of Family Life, and Cultural Values.* Ann Arbor: University of Michigan Press, 1989.

Chan, Sucheng, ed. *Hmong Means Free: Life in Laos and America.* Philadelphia: Temple University Press, 1994.

Ng, Franklin, ed. *Asian American Encyclopedia.* 6 vols. New York: Marshall Cavendish, 1995.

Proudfoot, Robert. *Even the Birds Don't Sound the Same Here: The Laotian Refugees' Search for Heart in American Culture.* New York: Peter Lang Publishing, 1990.

Tenhula, John. *Voices from Southeast Asia: The Refugee Experience in the United States.* New York: Holmes & Meier, 1991.

Zhou, Min, and Carl L. Bankston III. *Growing Up American: The Adaptation of Vietnamese Children to American Society.* New York: Russell Sage Foundation, 1998.

See also Chinese Americans; East Indians and Pakistanis; Filipino Americans; Japanese Americans; Korean Americans; Pacific Islanders; Patriarchs; Vietnamese Americans.

Dr. Benjamin Spock's book on baby care has been used by more than 40 million families. (Archive Photos)

Spock, Benjamin

BORN: May 2, 1903, New Haven, Conn.
DIED: March 15, 1998, San Diego, Calif.
AREA OF ACHIEVEMENT: Children and child development
SIGNIFICANCE: In his publications and activities related to practical child care and developmental psychology, Spock sought to advise parents on matters and issues previously ignored or misunderstood by pediatricians

Benjamin Spock was the first person ever to train professionally in both pediatrics and psychoanalysis. His best-seller on child care, *The Common Sense Book of Baby and Child Care* (1946), was a dramatic contrast to earlier child-care books. Advocating previously controversial methods of child care, Spock emphasized the psychological aspects of child development and progressive childhood education at every level of development. His well-received book gave parents much more information than any previous publication on child care, selling three-quarters of a million copies in its first year of publication. By the mid-1950's the popularity of Spock's work was evidenced by references to it on popular prime-time television programs such as *I Love Lucy*. Eventually translated into thirty-nine languages and with more than forty million copies sold worldwide, Spock's book soon became the standard reference text for many parents. The fortieth-anniversary edition, *Dr. Spock's Baby and Child Care* (1985), included a completely updated medical-pediatric section written by the book's new coauthor, Dr. Michael B. Rothenberg.

A Yale graduate and winner of a 1924 Olympic gold medal in rowing, Spock began his medical career as a pediatrician in New York City during the Depression in the 1930's. He went on to serve in the U.S. Navy during World War II and later taught pediatric and psychiatric residents at the Rochester Child Health Project, the University of Pittsburgh, and Western Reserve University.

During the 1960's he became a vocal opponent of nuclear testing. He was particularly troubled by President John F. Kennedy's 1962 announcement that the United States had to resume nuclear testing to stay ahead of the Soviet Union. As a member of the National Committee for a Sane Nuclear Policy (SANE), Spock served as the organization's spokesman, warning of the possible risks to children, both physical and mental, of radiation exposure. Also opposed to the military draft and the escalation of U.S. involvement in Vietnam, he led peace demonstrations throughout the country. His involvement as a political activist led to an unsuccessful 1972 bid for the presidency as the nominee of the People's Party (socialist).

As a third party candidate, Spock attacked the Democrats and Republicans for their "imperialist" foreign policy and "unfair" domestic policy. Despite receiving a total of only seventy-nine thousand votes in the ten states in which he was on the ballot, the election loss did not discourage him from continuing to serve as an advocate for children, the poor, the elderly, and nuclear disarmament. In 1989 Spock and Mary Morgan, his second wife, published an autobiography entitled *Spock on Spock: A Memoir of Growing Up with the Century*. He has also written or collaborated on at least fourteen other books.

—*Donald C. Simmons, Jr.*

See also Brazelton, T. Berry; Child rearing; Childhood fears and anxieties; Freudian psychology; Motherhood; News media and families; Parenting.

Stepfamilies

RELEVANT ISSUES: Children and child development; Divorce; Kinship and genealogy; Law; Marriage and dating; Parenting and family relationships; Religious beliefs and practices
SIGNIFICANCE: Directly influenced by divorce rates, cohabitation, and widowhood, the stepfamily is becoming a common family form in which parents, children, and larger kinship systems attempt to remodel themselves along the lines of the nuclear family

The relationship between stepparents and stepchildren is sometimes described by the terms "stepparenting," "blended families," and "stepfamilies." However, no matter what name is applied, the family structure and the definition remain the same. Stepfamilies may be defined as families that contain a parent and children from a previous union and the parent's current partner. The children from the previous union are "stepchildren," and the current partner is the "stepparent." Both partners may have children from previous unions and may also have mutual children from the current union. The defining criterion is that they all reside in the same household.

A stepfamily may be defined as a family which is formed as the final phase of a process beginning with the disintegration of a previous marriage, either by death or divorce. The most common form of stepfamily includes a mother and her biological children living with a new spouse who is not the birth father of the children. In addition, the birth father is a noncustodial parent who does not live with the children. Cohabiting persons may also form stepfamilies, in which children are biologically related to only one parent and in which nonmarital childbearing occurs. In Canada and the United States, never-married women have increasingly chosen to parent their children rather than put them up adoption. Many such children have stepfathers who are not married to their mothers. Studies that limit the definition of stepfamilies to married couples misclassify a significant proportion of families and underestimate the prevalence and the duration of the stepfamily experience, which includes cohabiting partners and nonmarital childbearing. To define stepfamilies only in terms of marriage underestimates an important trend in stepfamilies: According to researchers, when cohabitation is taken into account, about two-fifths of all women and thirty percent of all children are likely to spend time in stepfamilies.

Stepparenthood. The stepfamily is becoming an increasingly common and complex family form. Stepfamilies are less likely to be formed within the first two years after divorce. In 1978, 10 percent of all children under the age of eighteen were reported living with a natural parent and a stepparent. Many other persons living in single-parent households have a stepparent married to a noncustodial parent. Some stepfamilies are based on widowhood and others on divorce; there are stepmother and stepfather families and one- and two-stepparent families. Each has unique structural and socioemotional characteristics. Stepparents may find that marriages with children are not easily extinguished. In fact, divorce may be defined as marriage carried on by other means, with a bond of hostility replacing the erotic bond. Partners and children involved in remarriage bring with them

an emotional and material inheritance that cannot be ignored. Many of the most powerful reminders of this inheritance stem from family contacts with public institutions that surround and shape family life.

The experience of remarriage brings many stepfamilies under much greater public scrutiny than they experienced during their first marriage. Family arrangements that would normally be designated as private and a matter of personal choice are shaped explicitly by legal policies and structures. The challenges commonly experienced by stepfamilies include a complex kin network with issues of divided loyalties, jealousy, guilt, and unclear boundaries. Role ambiguity of stepparents and stepkin and conflicts over finances and child rearing may become complicated. Stepparenting makes instant parenting necessary with little time for the development of the spousal relationship. New stepparents are generally unprepared for the stresses they are likely to experience or how to deal with them. The traditional nuclear family may not represent an adequate model for the stepfamily.

Challenges in Stepfamilies. Negative myths have been associated with stepparent-stepchildren families. Stories depict the doom and gloom of raising others' children, who are supposedly jealous, manipulative nuisances trying to ruin the lives of their stepparents, or of stepparents who mistreat their stepchildren whenever the opportunity arises. These negative myths about stepfamilies are so prominent that they can be found in books, plays, and movies depicting mean and murderous stepchildren and stepparents and in fairy tales such as Cinderella, with her "wicked" stepmother. Despite the many myths that prevail around the stepfamily relationship, children from stepfamily environments may exhibit fewer behavioral problems than children who live with their birth parents.

Although the success rate of children coming from stepfamily arrangements is high, the many challenges that arise in stepfamily households may not be ignored. The relationships between stepparents and stepchildren contribute to the understanding of the specific problems these families encounter. For several reasons, the first two years of stepfamilies' existence may be the most difficult. Both the adults and children entering step-

Negative myths about stepparents provided a focus for a series of horror films about murderous stepfathers that began with The Stepfather *in 1986.* (Museum of Modern Art, Film Stills Archive)

Trouble Signals in Stepfamilies

The American Academy of Child and Adolescent Psychiatry offers tips on problems in stepfamilies that may call for professional psychiatric help:

- A child is openly torn between two parents or households

- A child directs anger toward a particular family member or openly resents a parent or stepparent

- One parent suffers from too much stress to be of help to a troubled child

- A parent or stepparent openly favors one child over others

- A child is disciplined only by his or her parent without the involvement of the stepparent

- Family derives no evident pleasure from usually pleasurable activities

family relationships are usually anxious about being accepted by one another. It takes time for stepfamily members to adjust to one another and to their new roles. In some cases one adult may assume multiple roles, becoming a parent and a spouse for the first time. Adults who become instant parents have questions about the issue of discipline and how to balance discipline while seeking acceptance from their new spouses' children. Children may feel torn between their loyalty to a birth parent with whom they no longer live and the stepparent who has replaced the birth parent in the household.

Children may feel a loss when stepfamilies first form. The new arrangement certifies that the original family unit no longer exists. Some children not only live with a person they consider a stranger, but also live in a different house or perhaps even a different neighborhood or state. Once a biological parent marries a new spouse, a new extended family is formed. Thus, children acquire an additional set of grandparents, aunts, uncles, and cousins. Remarriage creates a different kind of family system, with children often living with one biological parent and a stepparent or dividing their family lives between maternal and paternal homes. Divorce, remarriage, and stepfamily relationships remain emotion laden, creating personal and legal dilemmas for members of immediate and extended families.

Need for Mutual Respect. Members of blended or remarriage families commonly have competing ideas or concepts. Such families do not re-create a nuclear family. In blended families, there are few guidelines or specifically prescribed roles. Families must deal with past history, conflicting loyalties and feelings, and possibly financial strains. Strong commitment to the marriage relationship with the gradual involvement of all family members in solving common problems will provide blended families with the opportunity to create acceptance, care, and mutual respect. Stepparents who are friends with their stepchildren may exert considerable influence on them, but they usually do so more through the special relationship they develop with the children than by filling a parental role. One of the most important factors in satisfactory family life is a strong bond between husbands and wives.

One common pattern involves remarriage after family members have belonged to a single-parent family for an extended time. Usually, the new partner is a single adult without children. The new partner imports a closed system and attempts to restore a closed system. Often he or she is eager to prove himself or herself as a parent but has little or no experience. For example, a man wants to "become a father to the kids" as well as a husband to their mother. The random-to-open behavior he sees from the children strikes him as disorderly and disrespectful. In some cases he may be aided by the mother in his attempts to impose order, but in others she may be more neutral. Conflict between the adults is the exception, because at this stage in the relationship the biological parent is usually reluctant to escalate conflicts of any kind. Thus, conflicts tend to be concentrated between stepfathers and their stepchildren. Adolescents in particular vigorously resist the loss of freedom and mutual respect they enjoyed with their mother. It takes time to learn how to deal with children in a stepparent relationship.

Frustration grows in many new stepfamilies when an idealistic new stepparent or a remarrying biological parent who feels overly guilty assumes the responsibility for everyone's happiness. When new coparents sacrifice their own personal needs and expect everyone to thank them for their self-lessness, disappointment, resentments, and stress may result. Typical stepparents try to guide, support, protect, and nurture their partners' and their own children. The environment in which they attempt to do this is often different from that of most biological parents. Unlike most biological parents, stepparents must often resolve the complex challenges surrounding stepchild visitation, education, holidays, loyalty conflicts, worship, health, and socializing with two or three other coparents who may be hostile or indifferent. Stepparents often feel powerless to shape or change stressful or unfair stepchild support, custody, or visitation rules imposed by former spouses' divorce decrees or prior court judgments. Erotic attraction between stepparents and stepchildren or between adolescent stepsiblings may be more likely than in a typical biological families. Thoughtful adult modeling, guidance, and enforcement of personal modesty and privacy rules is specially important in most stepfamily homes.

Adoptions are grouped into four categories: independent, intercountry, relinquishment or agency, and stepparent. Stepparent adoptions refer to the adoption of the children of one's spouse. In most states stepparent adoptions occur more frequency than other types of adoptions and are twice as common as nonstepparent adoptions. Adoption should be approached cautiously, and the stability of the new marriage should be established prior to considering adoption. Before consulting an attorney, one biological parent should consult with the other biological parent to establish whether the latter is opposed to having his or her child adopted by a stepparent. The former should also discuss it with the child, who may oppose being adopted, viewing adoption as an attempt to exclude the noncustodial parent.

Rights and Responsibilities of Stepparents. Blending families can raise legal questions about financial responsibilities, relationships with former spouses, and the authority of stepparents to discipline the children. Stepfamilies are aware or must become aware of the links between family members' adjustment and the legal circumstances facing them. For example, if the remarriage ends in divorce or death, additional questions arise about support obligations and custody or visitation rights. Generally, the natural parent remains obligated to support the children, but the stepparent will also be legally obligated to support the stepchildren regardless of whether the natural parent provides any support or not. In order to adopt stepchildren who are less than eighteen years old, written consent must be obtained from the natural parents. When the children are adopted, all legal rights and responsibilities of the noncustodial natural parent cease. The adopted children become the children of the adopting parent. Adopted stepchildren will inherit property as any parent or child.

Death of a Stepchild. The death of a stepchild sets into motion complex issues that may vary from family to family for many reasons. The length and quality of the marriage and the nature of the relationship between the biological parent and the deceased child plays a primary role in the grief that follows. Variations may depend on whether the stepparent has parented the child for many years and invested much time and love in the relationship or on whether personality conflicts made a warm relationship impossible. The circumstances of death may also influence how the death is handled. Open communication between biological parents and stepparents is extremely important as all members of the family try to assimilate the details of the child's death. A stepparent may feel almost invisible to the spouse, the other stepchildren, extended family members, friends, clergy, or medical personnel. Stepparents may find themselves excluded from important discussions about medical decisions or funeral arrangements. Old unresolved emotional issues between biological parents may become more pronounced after the child's death, especially if there were conflicts over the parenting process. The biological parents may need to cling to each other as they struggle with the loss, making the stepparent feel further isolated and threatened. Even the most intact families and stepfamilies may experience the most severe test after the death of a child. For stepparents, the experience of grief may be a precarious journey as they try to balance their feelings and other familial relationships.

Stepfamilies represent one of the numerous family structures that provide the setting for child development and family growth and support. Although it is thought that stepchildren are slightly more prone to problems in behavior, social relations, and school achievement than nonstepchildren, there are large individual differences among children from all family structures. The success rate of children coming from stepfamily arrangements is high. Blended families may become more common in the twenty-first century than traditional families if the modern trends of divorce, remarriage, cohabitation, and nonmarital childbearing continue. —*Lessie L. Bass*

BIBLIOGRAPHY

Fine, Mark A., and David R. Fine. "Recent Changes in Laws Affecting Stepfamilies: Suggestions for Legal Reform." *Family Relations* 41 (July, 1992). Examination of legal questions relating to stepparenting issues, with specific proposals for changes in the law.

Jones, Merry B., and Jo A. Schiller. *Stepmothers: Keeping It Together with Your Husband and His Kids.* New York: Carol Publishing Group, 1992. Practical guide aimed for new stepmothers.

Nowell, David Z. *Stepparent Is Not a Bad Word: Advice and Perspectives for Parenting Your Stepchildren.* Nashville, Tenn.: T. Nelson, 1994. Practical guidebook for stepparents.offering numerous observations from blended families with which the authors have worked.

Schectman, Jacqueline M. *The Stepmother in Fairy Tales.* Boston, Mass.: Sigo Press, 1991. Exploration of negative cultural stereotypes of "wicked" stepmothers.

Visher, Emily B., and John S. Visher. *Stepfamilies: A Guide to Working with Stepparents and Stepchildren.* New York: Brunner-Mazel Publishers, 1979. Manual for family counselors containing practical advice supported by documented case studies.

See also Adoption processes; Alternative family types; Blended families; Child custody; Child rearing; Cohabitation; Remarriage; Serial monogamy.

Sterilization

RELEVANT ISSUES: Health and medicine; Marriage and dating; Parenting and family relationships

SIGNIFICANCE: Sterilization is the most common method of contraception for married couples in both the United States and Canada

Both men and women may undergo sterilization. Although sterilization can sometimes be reversed, male and female sterilization should be considered permanent. Furthermore, the question of sterilization raises ethical issues that medical professionals and others must confront.

Male Sterilization. In males, sterilization is called "vasectomy." This procedure is both simple to perform and safe for almost all men. In addition, it is less expensive than female sterilization. The procedure is most often done in the medical office by a urologist or other surgeon and takes about thirty minutes. The man's pubic hair is clipped from the scrotum and penis and the area is numbed with an anesthetic similar to that used in a dentist's office. Following sterile surgical procedures, the surgeon makes a small incision on either side of the scrotum, locates the vas deferens (the ducts that carry sperm), and then ties and cuts them. The surgeon may also use a "no scalpel" technique. Cutting and tying the vas deferens prevents the sperm from reaching the penis during ejaculation. The man rests briefly, then goes home. He is advised to "take it easy" for about forty-eight hours and apply ice packs to the scrotum to reduce swelling. He is able to resume most normal activities, including sexual intercourse, in two to three days but should avoid strenuous activity for a week. Complications are rare.

Following vasectomy, men are not sterile until all the sperm in the vas have been ejaculated, so that a couple must use another form of contraception until there is no sperm remaining in the semen, usually after about fifteen ejaculations. Some men worry about changes in their sexual ability, but vasectomy does not interfere with either erection or ejaculation. No long-term health problems, including heart disease, have been demonstrated conclusively following vasectomy. However, some studies suggest a slight increase in the risk of prostate cancer.

Female Sterilization. Female sterilization requires that women enter the hospital, although for most women this can be done safely on an outpatient surgical basis, in which they enter and leave the hospital on the same day as surgery. Most women undergo general anesthesia, although one technique called "minilaparotomy" requires only local anesthesia and mild sedation. Female sterilization is considered safe for most women, but it is slightly riskier and considerably more expensive than vasectomy.

The woman is anesthetized and the surgeon makes one or two small incisions, usually in the abdomen (one near the umbilicus and possibly one just at the pubic hair line), instills carbon dioxide or other gas into the abdomen to better see the tubes, locates the tubes and then clips, binds, or cuts them. The surgeon may or may not cauterize the cut ends. Tubal ligation, as it is called, prevents the egg and the sperm from meeting. Following surgery, the woman is observed until she is medically stable and feels well enough to return home. She must rest for about twenty-four hours following the procedure and avoid heavy lifting for one week. She may resume sexual intercourse in about a week. The surgeon should evaluate the woman a week after surgery to be sure she is healing properly.

Complications following tubal ligation are fairly rare, but they may include anesthesia-related problems, infection, or bleeding. Women who have tubal ligations are slightly more at risk of an ectopic (tubal) pregnancy than women who have not had their tubes tied. Some women have changes in the amount of bleeding or the severity of menstrual cramps following tubal ligation. However, medical studies have not been conclusive about so-called post-tubal-ligation syndrome. Heavier bleeding and increased cramping may be prevalent in women who stop taking oral contraceptives after undergoing sterilization.

Occasionally, hysterectomy (removal of the uterus) is used to sterilize women. Hysterectomy involves a much higher risk of complications than tubal ligation and is considered inappropriate if used strictly for sterilization. Other medical conditions may make it appropriate, however.

Effects on the Family. Thanks to safe and effective surgical sterilization techniques, couples are now able to conclusively limit the number of children they have. This has a number of potential consequences for families. Couples may elect to have no children at all. For those who choose to have children, the amount of time a "stay-at-home" parent is out of the workforce is potentially

shorter. With fewer children and two potential wage earners, families' income may be higher. This could result in less financial strain in providing for families or in more disposable family income. Families with greater disposable income are able to provide more material goods and educational opportunities for themselves and their children. The family's emotional and psychological resources may be less strained by having only the number of children they want. Couples' sexual life is unhindered by contraceptive concerns and logistics.

On the other hand, sterilization may cause stress in a relationship. Because both male and female sterilization is usually not reversible, couples or individuals who change their minds about the number of children they want may regret their decision. Studies have shown that those most likely to regret sterilization are those who have lost children, divorced, remarried, felt coerced into undergoing sterilization, or underwent sterilization because of unhappiness with other contraceptive methods. Very young persons or those in unhappy or unstable marriages may later regret the decision to be sterilized. Women who have just been pregnant or had an abortion are also more likely to regret sterilization.

Hysterectomy

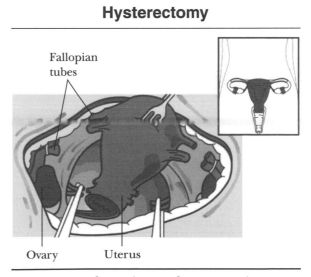

Fallopian tubes

Ovary   Uterus

The uterus, and sometimes such accompanying organs as the ovaries and Fallopian tubes, may be removed to treat disease conditions or as a contraceptive measure; the inset shows the location of the uterus.

Major surgery is required for both men and women who wish to reverse their sterilizations. Sometimes reversal cannot even be attempted because of the technique involved. Even if patients have had a potentially reversible sterilization, reversal surgery results in pregnancy only 16 to 70 percent of the time. Reversal surgery is extremely costly and not covered under most health insurance policies. Efforts are under way to devise silicon plugs or other techniques that would allow for reversible sterilization, but by the late 1990's this option was not available.

Ethical and Legal Issues. Sterilization raises legal and ethical issues of concern to families. One such issue is, who has the right to decide to be sterilized? While the American legal tradition suggests that the individuals concerned should have the right to make such a decision, some feel that society or other individuals also have a stake in the matter. For example, some churches oppose sterilization because they believe that marriages are for procreation. Some physicians refuse to perform sterilizations on individuals who have no children, while others require that both spouses consent to sterilization.

Another ethical concern relates to involuntary sterilization. Early in the twentieth century about thirty states passed laws allowing for the sterilization of persons judged mentally ill or criminally insane. Under these laws, more than thirty thousand people were sterilized by 1939. Some leaders in the eugenics movement openly advocated sterilization on racial grounds. Members of ethnic minorities in the United States still argue that sterilization is more strongly encouraged for minority peoples, especially those who are poor or rely on government assistance, than for white Americans. Some think, for example, that federal policies allowing the government to subsidize sterilizations but not abortions subtly coerce minority women into opting for sterilization.

Another important ethical issue is the question of who can best judge persons' fitness to be parents or their fitness to create families. Whether persons who have been convicted of child abuse should be required to undergo sterilization as a condition of parole or whether mentally or physically handicapped persons should be allowed to become parents are further ethical questions raised by the issue of sterilization. Furthermore, mentally re-tarded children have been shown to be at greater risk of sexual abuse and exploitation. This poses the question of whether parents of profoundly retarded children should be empowered to have their children sterilized for their own good and whether institutions caring for handicapped people should be allowed to forcibly sterilize their patients in order to prevent unintended pregnancy.

The U.S. Supreme Court has recognized the legal right of procreation under the Fourteenth Amendment, and most state laws concerning mandatory sterilization have either been struck down or are rarely implemented. Long-acting methods of birth control that are reversible (such as hormone injections or implants) have to some extent lessened the pressure to sterilize persons who would be considered risky parents. Nevertheless, the ethical questions remain. —*Rebecca Lovell Scott*

BIBLIOGRAPHY
Boston Women's Health Book Collective. *The New Our Bodies, Ourselves.* New York: Simon & Schuster, 1992.
Hatcher, R. A., et al. *Contraceptive Technology.* 16th ed. New York: Irvington Publishers, 1994.
Humber, J. M., and R. F. Almeder. *Biomedical Ethics Reviews 1992.* Totowa, N.J.: The Humana Press, 1993.
Sobsey, D., et al. *Disability, Sexuality, and Abuse: An Annotated Bibliography.* Baltimore, Md.: Paul H. Brooks, 1991.
Winikoff, B., et al. *The Contraceptive Handbook: A Guide to Safe and Effective Choices.* Yonkers, N.Y.: Consumer Reports Books, 1992.

See also Birth control; Childlessness; Eugenics; Family size; Fertility and infertility; Health problems; Reproductive technologies.

Stranger anxiety

RELEVANT ISSUES: Children and child development; Health and medicine; Parenting and family relationships
SIGNIFICANCE: Whereas almost all one-year-olds show some avoidance of intrusive adults and some two-year-olds still show strong fear and shyness, only a very small percentage of teenagers and adults have an anxiety disorder called "social phobia"

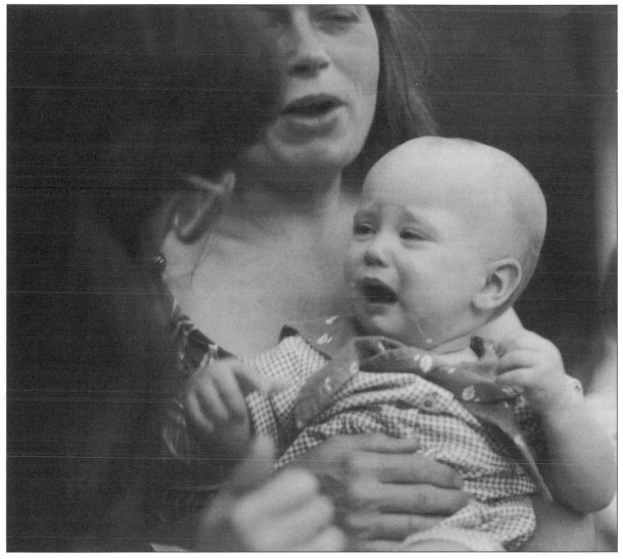

Like true strangers, well-meaning relatives or friends can frighten an infant if the child is not given time to get reacquainted with a person not seen for some time. (Long Hare Photographs)

The term "stranger anxiety" was used by psychoanalytic researcher Rene Spitz to describe how infants beginning at about eight months of age exhibit negative reactions toward strangers. Psychologists prefer the term "stranger reaction," because infants show both positive and negative reactions to strangers and because the term "anxiety" may imply that the behavior is abnormal. In fact, both Spitz and many subsequent researchers have found that reactions such as pulling back, looking away, and crying when touched are common in one-year-olds.

Another problem with the term "stranger anxiety" is that it seems to imply that babies are afraid only of true strangers. Many mothers, however, report wary or even fearful behavior when well-meaning friends or relatives who have not been seen recently try to pick up their babies without giving them a chance to get reacquainted. This quite typical reaction in one-year-olds can be embarrassing to some mothers. Other mothers view such behavior as a sign that their babies know them and prefer not to be separated. Negative reactions to strangers are more likely if babies are

Even a cuddly Disneyland creature may cause a child anxiety if it is a stranger to the child. (Cindy Beres)

not in physical contact with their mothers and if unfamiliar persons are intrusive—that is, if they approach rapidly and touch or try to pick up the babies. Most children warm up after a few minutes and are willing to interact with strangers. In the second year of life, negative reactions to strangers are clearly compounded by toddlers' concerns about being left alone, which is known as "separation anxiety."

Usually, stranger and separation anxiety subside in children when they reach about three years of age. Some infants and toddlers, however, are consistently upset by new persons, objects, and situations. Jerome Kagan and his colleagues studied such extremely shy and fearful toddlers, whom they called "inhibited," and found that most were still cautious and avoidant in unfamiliar situations when they were eight years old.

Psychiatrists have studied a type of anxiety disorder they call "social phobia." Phobias are extreme fears that are out of proportion to reality, leading to automatic avoidance of feared situations. Social phobia is an extreme fear of social situations, as in the case of persons who fear giving speeches in which they may be evaluated by others. Social phobias develop in later childhood or adolescence in a very small percentage of the population. It seems likely that there is a relationship between very strong and long lasting stranger anxiety in infants and social phobia in later life. However, infants' fear of strangers is almost universal and usually relatively short-lived. Social phobia is rare, long lasting, and extreme. Thus, there is little reason to be concerned about stranger anxiety in infancy.

—*George A. Morgan*

See also Attachment theory; Baby-sitters; Childhood fears and anxieties; Kagan, Jerome.

Straus, Murray

BORN: June 18, 1926, New York, N.Y.
AREA OF ACHIEVEMENT: Parenting and family relationships
SIGNIFICANCE: Straus is one of America's foremost authorities on family violence and an influential critic of the corporal punishment of children

A professor in the sociology and anthropology department at the University of New Hampshire since the 1960's, Murray Straus is one of America's best-known and most influential authorities on family violence. Early in his career, he helped to develop techniques for developing and measuring attitudes and behavior in families. His research in the early 1970's provided evidence that there was a link between family violence and male dominance of the family. He found that the more the father was the center of the family and the more authority the father held, the more likely it was that he would engage in violent acts.

In the academic year of 1989-1990, Straus served as president of the Society for the Study of Social Problems. At approximately the same time he also began some of his most controversial work, studying corporal punishment in families. Straus and his fellow researchers found that although physical punishment, such as spanking, did tend to improve the immediate behavior of children, it also increased the probability that they would engage in delinquency and violent behavior later in life. Straus embarked on a public campaign to urge parents to stop using physical punishment on their children. By the late 1990's Murray Straus had become one of America's most outspoken critics of corporal punishment.

—*Carl L. Bankston III*

See also Child abuse; Corporal punishment; Domestic violence; Parenting.

Substitute caregivers

RELEVANT ISSUES: Children and child development; Economics and work; Parenting and family relationships
SIGNIFICANCE: Substitute caregivers are persons other than parents who care for children on a regular basis

Substitute caregivers can be familial or nonfamilial. Familial caregivers are commonly grandparents and siblings—either children's or parents'. Nonfamilial substitute caregivers can be domestic workers, such as nannies and governesses, who are hired by parents to care for children in the parents' home. Nonfamilial substitute caregivers also include child-care workers, who provide care for other people's children in caregivers' homes and who may be paid either by parents or through outside funding sources, such as public assistance programs. Daily child care is

Grandmothers are among the most common substitute caregivers. (Dick Hemingway)

also provided by workers in institutions, such as nursery schools and day-care centers. Boarding schools, orphanages, group homes, and facilities operated by the juvenile justice system care for children on a full-time basis. Of all the types of substitute caregivers, the role of foster parents most closely resembles that of parents. Foster parents are sometimes related to the children they care for, but more frequently they are not.

In the past twenty-five years both the numbers and the percentages of working mothers with children of all ages has increased dramatically, giving rise to the need for substitute caregivers. In the 1970's, when the women's rights movement was in full swing, there was much controversy about mothers who worked and left their children to the care of others. The position of the organized women's movement was that women, including mothers, have as much right as men to the rewards of gainful employment. At the same time, many people, including those in the women's movement, were concerned about the impact that mothers' daily absence had on children, particularly young children. Many persons worried about so-called latchkey children, who were left unattended for approximately three hours each afternoon between the end of the school day and their mothers' return from work. Conservatives frequently combined these shared concerns with the opinion that it was essential to uphold the traditional family, in which women's place was in the home, where they were devoted to household tasks, child care, and the support of their husbands. This view was exemplified by President Richard M. Nixon when he vetoed the Comprehensive Child Development Act in 1970, arguing that he did not believe that the moral authority of the federal government should be used to support communal approaches to child rearing.

By the 1990's this controversy had become largely moot, because changes in family structure and the economy had made it essential for the majority of mothers to work outside the home. In contrast to Nixon, President George Bush approved an increase in child-care funding in 1990 through the Child Care and Development Block Grant. Like Nixon, Bush espoused the cause of the traditional family. Bush's most unqualified support was reserved for business, however, and by 1990 American businesses needed working mothers as much as mothers needed the employment opportunities provided by businesses. While federal and state governments have taken greater responsibility for making substitute child care available, quality remains problematic. The wages and salaries of substitute caregivers remain abysmally low, making it difficult to attract and retain trained and experienced workers.

—Jenifer Wolf

See also Au pairs; Baby-sitters; Child care; Child Care and Development Block Grant Act; Day care; Family caregiving; Foster homes; Latchkey children; Nannies.

Sudden infant death syndrome (SIDS)

RELEVANT ISSUES: Children and child development; Health and medicine

SIGNIFICANCE: A tragic occurrence, sudden infant death syndrome takes the lives of infants unexpectedly and for no apparent reason

Sudden infant death syndrome (SIDS) is a term used to describe the sudden, unexplained deaths of infants after all other medical causes of death have been ruled out by autopsy, investigation of infants' environment, and a complete review of infants' medical histories. It has been estimated that up to seven thousand cases of SIDS occur in the United States each year. SIDS typically occurs in infants between the ages of one month and one year of age; the majority of incidences take place by the end of the sixth month. Most cases of SIDS occur at night, when infants are asleep. SIDS is nondiscriminatory, affecting infants of all races, ethnicities, and socioeconomic backgrounds. It has been reported that 60 percent of SIDS cases involve males while 40 percent involve females and that more SIDS cases are reported in the fall and winter than in spring and summer.

There is no medical explanation for SIDS. Researchers have inconclusively hypothesized that SIDS may be caused by infection or other physiological stressors, by birth defects caused by poor maternal health as a result of mothers' smoking or taking drugs while pregnant, or by infants' failure to develop. It is believed possible that there is a time in infants' lives when they are simply more vulnerable to SIDS. Research has taken two distinct directions in trying to solve the SIDS mystery: One has been to determine the cause of SIDS and the other to identify ways to reduce the number of SIDS deaths.

SIDS cannot be prevented, but researchers have identified risk factors that may have a negative effect on infants. As a result, various recommendations have been made to hopefully decrease the incidence of SIDS. The American Academy of Pediatrics recommends that all healthy infants sleep on their backs to decrease the risk for SIDS. Most research has investigated the effects of sleep position on SIDS. Findings show that the incidence of SIDS has decreased since 1989, when parents were first advised to position their infants on their backs. The academy is quick to point out, however, that because of the complexity of SIDS the decreased number of cases since 1989 cannot be attributed solely to supine sleeping position. Other recommendations have been made by the U.S. Consumer Product Safety Committee, which has requested that parents use firm bedding materials, and by the National Institute of Child Health and Human Development, which has urged mothers to breast-feed their infants. SIDS is likely the

Medical research in the late 1990's found that placing infants on their backs while they sleep significantly reduces their chances of succumbing to SIDS. (Cindy Beres)

A Month in Which to Remember SIDS Victims

October is National Sudden Infant Death Syndrome Awareness Month. Sponsored by the SIDS Alliance, based in Baltimore, Maryland, the annual event works to increase public awareness of the fact that SIDS is the leading cause of death among infants more than a week old. It also works to stimulate contributions for medical research and family services.

result of a complex combination of many factors, including sleeping position, bedding material, infant nutrition and health, and maternal health and lifestyle.

Many support networks provide education and counseling about SIDS. Most hospitals and county health districts also offer support services to assist individuals who have lost children to SIDS. The American SIDS Institute and the National SIDS Network offer feedback to parents and siblings and provide the latest in research findings and recommendations about this complex and mysterious cause of infant death. —*Alan J. Coelho*

See also Birth defects; Child care; Child rearing; Child safety; Death; Health of children.

Suicide

RELEVANT ISSUES: Aging; Children and child development; Health and medicine; Parenting and family relationships

SIGNIFICANCE: Suicide is among the leading causes of death in the United States and Canada and a source of long-term distress for surviving family members

Every day men and women, young and old act on the belief that death is preferable to life. It is estimated that each self-inflicted death has a strong and enduring impact on at least six other people. Many suicides can be prevented through awareness of risk factors and skillful response to people who are experiencing depression, anxiety, and frustration.

Suicide as a Major Cause of Death. A suicidal death occurs about every two hours in Canada and about every seventeen minutes in the United States. Suicide has been determined to be among the leading causes of death in the United States, Canada, and many other nations ever since such data began to be collected. Suicide is the eighth leading cause of death in the United States, taking more than thirty thousand lives each year. It is the fifth leading cause of death in Canada, taking about 3,500 lives per year. Although there are many more suicides in the United States, with its larger population, than in Canada, Canada has a higher suicide rate: fourteen per 100,000 as compared with twelve per 100,000 in the United States. These rates are about average for industrialized nations which, as a group, have experienced a leveling off of suicide rates after their steady rise between the mid-1980's and the mid-1990's.

There are several notable similarities in suicides in North America, whether in Canada or the United States. Men are about four times more likely than women to commit suicide. The risk of death by suicide is higher for males at all age levels than for women and increases as men move through the life course. Men over the age of sixty-five have the highest suicide rates. Women are at the greatest risk of suicide in their early adult years. Young women are most likely to attempt suicide, but elderly men are most likely to end their own lives, most often by using firearms and other lethal methods. Youth suicide, defined as suicide committed by persons between the ages of fifteen and twenty-four, has more than tripled in the United States and Canada since the end of World War II. Teenagers and young adults are at particularly high risk of self-inflicted death, because they are at relatively low risk of dying from heart disease and cancer, the two leading causes of death. In both the United States and Canada, surveys have found that it is not uncommon for people to have had thoughts about suicide or even to have made attempts at some point in their lives, usually while they were in their teens or in their later adult years. It is clear that many people have moments when they think about suicide, although most do not act on their impulses.

In the United States, the suicide rate has consistently been higher among whites than among African Americans or Asian Americans. Some Native American groups, especially their youth, have had very high suicide rates. Suicide rates are also high

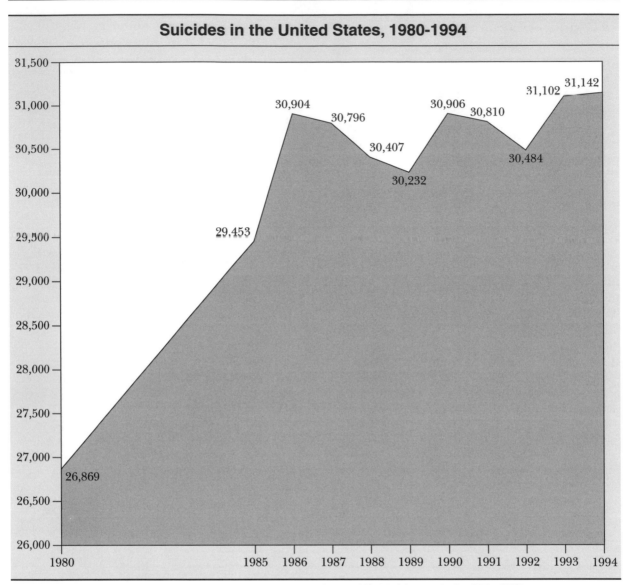

Suicides in the United States, 1980-1994

Source: U.S. Bureau of the Census, *Statistical Abstract of the United States: 1997*. Washington, D.C.: GPO, 1997.

among Native Canadians in the Yukon and Northwest Territories.

General Risk Factors for Suicide. The factors placing people at higher risk of committing suicide include living alone, having few connections to society (limited contacts with family, limited social life), experiencing the recent death of a loved one, experiencing the recent loss of an important relationship for reasons other than death, having a progressively disabling condition or terminal illness, using alcoholic beverages to excess (including binge drinking) or using other mind-altering drugs, being depressed, and being affected by either personal or society-wide periods of economic crisis. Most people undergoing these experiences do not commit suicide, and it would be a mistake to assume that they are suicidal. For example, some people enjoy living alone. Similarly, the stress of a progressively disabling condition or terminal illness is borne by many people who continue to find meaning in their lives and have no inclination to commit suicide. It is not difficult situations themselves, but how persons interpret and cope with them that is most important. Nevertheless, there is a general tendency for suicidal thoughts and actions to occur more frequently in people who are experiencing one or more of these situations.

As might be expected, the risk increases when several of these factors are present at the same time. For example, depressed persons might lose close personal relationships, become more depressed, withdraw, and use alcohol or drugs in an attempt to mask their emotional pain. There is also continual interaction between individuals, families, and societal events. For example, unemployment and business failures in a distressed economy place extra pressures on families, leading to increased risk of suicidal behavior. Young people may feel that their opportunities are being blocked; elderly people may fear that they are outliving their resources.

Youth at High Risk of Suicide. Although suicide is one of the major causes of death among teenagers and young adults, some young people are at higher risk than others. Young people are at greater risk of committing suicide if other members of their families have made suicide attempts or if they themselves have attempted suicide. If they have undergone recent behavioral changes, which may lead them to withdraw from previous interests and activities or engage in sudden bursts of pleasure seeking and risk taking, they may be at greater risk of committing suicide. Hopelessness, apathy, or dread may be factors leading to suicide, whereby young people may express directly or indirectly that they want to end their lives. This may be indicated when their thought processes become narrow and rigid, leading them to ignore shades of meaning and alternative possibilities and causing them to consider only extreme

courses of action. Additionally, they may also become touchy, unpredictable, and quick to anger, overreacting to small frustrations or provocations.

This high-risk profile is often associated with problems within the family. Studies have found that the families of suicidal adolescents and young adults often have poor communication patterns: Family members seldom listen to each other, leading one person to hesitate to speak to another. Such families also tend to impose rigid rules, leaving little opportunity for young people to explore and express their own personalities. Such families as a whole are likely to show long-term patterns of dysfunctionality, including alcoholism, mental illness, parental absence, and incest. Thus, suicidal adolescents are not the only persons in their families who have difficulties. Their difficulties in communicating and forming intimate relationships are often formed within dysfunctional families.

Does Suicide Run in Families? Some families have a history of multiple suicide attempts from generation to generation. How this should be interpreted is a matter of controversy. Some people believe that the disposition to suicide is inherited. There is some support for this position from studies of twins as well as the biology of depression. The theory that has garnered the most support is that some families have a genetic trait that results in a problem with the metabolism of serotonin, a substance that is involved in the transmission of impulses within the central nervous system. People with this genetic problem are more likely than others to be depressed, have large mood swings, engage in antisocial behavior, and abuse drugs as well as make suicide attempts. There has been some success in providing medicinal relief to people who have biological markers associated with

Indicators of Suicidal Tendency Among Young People

- Person has attempted suicide before.
- Other family members have attempted suicide.
- Person undergoes radical behavior changes, such as abandoning favorite interests and activities.
- Person exhibits a sense of hopelessness, apathy, or dread.

- Person talks directly or indirectly about suicide.
- Person's thinking grows narrow and rigid as person ignores shades of meaning and alternative choices, while tending to consider only extreme courses of action.
- Person becomes touchy, unpredictable, and quick to anger.

depression, thereby reducing their suicidal tendencies.

Some observers have pointed out that many depressed and suicidal people are not biologically predisposed to these tendencies. Such people develop their self-destructive inclinations through experiences of loss, frustration, and anxiety about future events. Furthermore, even in suicide-prone families it is likely that the dysfunctional patterns of interaction are key factors. Repeated experiences of rejection and abuse may be the trigger for self-destructive behaviors. It is argued that the key to suicide prevention in all families, whether or not they have possible genetic predispositions to depression, is that family members should learn to live harmoniously with one another and solve everyday conflicts in a competent manner. It is further argued that suicide attempts can become a "family style" of dealing with problems, whether or not a biological component is also present. Although there continue to be different opinions about possible inheritance factors in multisuicide families, it is clear that both medical and counseling approaches can be useful in prevention efforts.

Elderly People at High Risk of Suicide. Throughout much of the world more people in the late twentieth century have lived to advanced ages. Growing old, however, is often perceived as a mixed blessing. Health is the leading concern, but financial worries, the death of loved ones, and ageism also trouble many elderly persons. These problems lead to the high suicide rate among elderly people, especially elderly men. As with young people, however, some elderly people are more at risk of suicide than others. Factors associated with high risk of suicide among elderly people include social isolation, loss of significant relationships because of death or other causes, depression, physical illness, alcohol use, and persistent stress syndrome—being worn down over time physically and emotionally by life pressures that tax persons' coping abilities.

Elderly people who are at high risk of suicide often look sad and dejected. They may be stooped, withdrawn, and fatigued. They may have little eye contact with others and be careless in their grooming habits and dress. Along with loss of appetite, they may also experience sleep disturbances. They may exhibit a tendency to lose the thread of con-

versations and to show a lack of interest, attention, and concentration, sometimes accompanied by restless and agitated behavior, such as hand wringing. Studies indicate that elderly men are less likely to give clear warnings of their suicidal intents than either women or younger adults. Elderly women are more likely than elderly men to have people with whom they can share their feelings and are also more likely to seek help when their situation becomes desperate. Elderly men are more likely than elderly women to keep their feelings to themselves and to try to end their problems with a literally one-shot solution.

Preventing Suicide. Many people have experienced suicidal crises and made strong and enduring recoveries. For example, most of those who have been prevented at the last moment from leaping from San Francisco's Golden Gate bridge have been grateful for their rescue and made no subsequent suicide attempts. There is no guarantee that preventing suicide at one point in time will open the road to a life of renewed purpose and satisfaction, but the many cases of positive outcomes provide a sound basis for hope.

Several approaches can be effective in preventing suicide. First, it is important to recognize and treat depression. Persons who show the warning signs of possible suicide, be they youths or elderly people, should be seen by physicians who are knowledgeable about diagnosing depression. Many family practitioners as well as psychiatrists have this skill. Medications can reduce depression and suicidal feelings in some people. Physicians may recommend individual or family counseling as well. Communities should support suicide education programs in the schools. Such programs may be offered separately or as part of a broader program to improve awareness of mental-health issues and skills. It is also important that communities offer programs to prevent alcohol and drug abuse, especially among youths. Many suicidal, as well as accidental and homicidal, deaths involve the use of alcohol or other drugs. Families should support and make use of crisis telephone services and suicide-prevention centers. Many persons have been helped through suicidal crises by sympathetic counseling and having somebody to listen to them.

Frequently, persons on the verge of a suicide attempt have both prolife and prodeath feelings, the balance of which can be affected by the response of others. It is important to take suicide threats seriously and to listen to person's accounts of their experiences, feelings, and plans without imposing value judgments. If there is reason to believe that a suicide attempt is imminent, it is important to seek immediate help from friends, relatives, clergy, teachers, physicians, or other resource persons. Another form of suicide prevention involves befriending those who are socially isolated—those who are strangers to the community, those who are elderly and limited in their mobility, and those who have recently lost their spouses or companions. Individuals and community organizations that reach out to lonely and depressed people can be highly effective in reducing the impulse to self-destruction.

Helping the Survivors of Suicide. The grief experienced at the death of a family member or friend is often intensified when their lives have been lost through suicide. Some communities have established peer support groups, in which families that have experienced a suicide can share their feelings and encourage one another's recovery. Other communities do not have support groups that specifically deal with suicide, but they do have groups for persons whose family members have died because of other causes. Often grief support groups have experienced counselors as moderators, but it is the mutual help given by all the participants that usually proves most valuable. Many support groups are church-related; others are offered through local mental-health agencies. The family relations and counseling departments of local colleges and universities are also resources for locating and creating peer-support groups.

Stress reactions, depression, and communications difficulties often occur in families that have lost a member through suicide. Family counseling has proven to be effective for many such families, enabling them to resolve their conflicts, build on their strengths, and carry on with their lives.

By being open to discussion, friends and neighbors can help families socially and emotionally recover from the grief of suicidal deaths. Too often, persons are afraid to refer not only to deaths by suicide, but also even to those who have taken their own lives. This contributes to families' sense of social isolation. It is usually far more helpful to acknowledge such deaths for what they are

and to share memories of deceased persons. Suicidal deaths are tragedies, but they are not stigmas unless persons choose to make them so.

—*Robert Kastenbaum*

BIBLIOGRAPHY

Alexander, Victoria. *Words I Never Thought to Speak: Stories of Life in the Wake of Suicide.* New York: Lexington Books, 1991. Draws upon the experiences of people who have lost a loved one through suicide.

Alvarez, A. *The Savage God: A Study of Suicide.* New York: Random House, 1971. History of suicidal thoughts and practices throughout the world.

Conroy, David L. *Out of the Nightmare: Recovery from Depression and Suicidal Pain.* New York: New Liberty Press, 1991. Discusses suicide from the viewpoint of both individuals and society, with particular focus on ways in which self-destruction can be prevented.

Farberow, Norman L., ed. *The Many Faces of Suicide.* New York: McGraw-Hill, 1980. First book to examine the many indirect ways in which people may put themselves at risk short of actual suicide attempts.

Heckler, Richard A. *Waking Up, Alive.* New York: Ballantine Books, 1994. Describes the journey from loss and depression to a suicide attempt, followed by eventual recovery from the self-destructive impulse.

Hendin, Herbert. *Suicide in America.* 2d ed. New York: W. W. Norton, 1995. Examines suicide in relationship to violence, alcoholism, and sexual orientation in young and elderly adults.

Kastenbaum, Robert. *Death, Society, and Human Experience.* 6th ed. Boston: Allyn & Bacon, 1998. Explores the ways in which individual and societal interactions either increase or decrease suicidal behavior.

Quinnett, Paul. G. *Suicide: The Forever Decision.* New York: Continuum, 1992. Suggests ways of overcoming depression and despondency in finding alternatives to suicide.

Richman, Joseph. *Family Therapy for Suicidal People.* New York: Springer, 1986. Emphasizes the role of the family in suicide and suicide prevention.

See also Behavior disorders; Death; Family crises; Grief counseling; Heredity; Postpartum depression.

Supplemental Nutrition Program for Women, Infants, and Children

DATE: Established as the Special Supplemental Nutrition Program for Women, Infants, and Children on September 26, 1972

SIGNIFICANCE: A federally funded nutrition program, the Supplemental Nutrition Program for Women, Infants, and Children aims to help reduce the nutrition-related health problems of pregnancy, infancy, and childhood among low-income families

The Supplemental Nutrition Program for Women, Infants, and Children (WIC) is managed by the Food and Consumer Service of the U.S. Department of Agriculture (USDA). WIC was established as an experimental program in September, 1972,

The Supplemental Nutrition Program was designed to reduce nutrition problems among children of low-income families. (James L. Shaffer)

by an amendment to the Child Nutrition Act of 1966. After a two-year pilot project, the WIC program was made permanent in 1974. In 1994, under the Healthy Meals for Healthy Americans Act, the name of the program was changed from the Special Supplemental Food Program for Women, Infants, and Children to its current name.

WIC provides supplemental foods, infant formula, health care referrals, and nutrition education to families with incomes less than 185 percent of the U.S. poverty income guidelines. WIC serves more than seven million people each month. A study in 1990 showed that women who received WIC during pregnancy had lower health care costs for both themselves and their babies than those who did not. WIC participation has also been linked to lower infant mortality rates, higher birth weights, and fewer premature births.

—David H. Holben

See also Children's rights; Eating habits of children; Foodways; Health of children; Health problems; Poverty; Pregnancy.

Support groups

RELEVANT ISSUES: Aging; Children and child development; Divorce; Health and medicine; Marriage and dating; Parenting and family relationships

SIGNIFICANCE: Support groups provide a valuable resource for dealing with personal crises, medical problems, addictive behavior, and many other challenges of family life

Self-help, support, mutual aid—all are terms used somewhat interchangeably to describe groups in which persons work together on medical, emotional, psychological, or other issues of concern, generally without professional guidance. Although such groups exist throughout the world, the greatest number are in the United States. There were an estimated half a million self-help and support groups in the United States and Canada in the mid-1990's.

History. The support group movement has flourished in the twentieth century, but its roots extend back to the medieval craft guilds that provided aid to their needy members. More recent antecedents existed in the eighteenth and nineteenth centuries in response to pressures and problems engendered by the Industrial Revolution. For example, occupation-based Friendly Societies, such as the Ancient Society of Gardeners, provided loans, funds for burials, and social activities to members; by 1800 there were almost two hundred such groups. In the nineteenth century newly formed trade unions assisted their needy members, while mutual aid societies that helped immigrants to survive and thrive after relocating to the United States grew in size and influence.

In the 1840's the Ladies Physiological Society was founded in Boston and soon spread to other cities. It not only offered information on pregnancy, childbirth, and child rearing but also provided women with compassion and contact with other women while advocating health reforms. These elements of information, support, socializing, and advocacy are the cornerstones of most modern support groups.

In the 1940's an innovative program for treating mental patients—former prisoners of war—was developed in Great Britain. Called the Therapeutic Community, it differed from older treatment models in that patients were not passive recipients, but were made active participants in their treatment—an essential tenet of modern support groups. In the United States two of the earliest examples of the modern self-help or support group movement were the National Committee of Mental Hygiene, founded in 1909 by Clifford Beers, a former patient in a mental asylum, and Alcoholics Anonymous (AA), whose two main founders were Bob Smith and Bill Wilson. The National Committee of Mental Hygiene has evolved into the politically active and successful National Alliance for the Mentally Ill (NAMI), while AA had 90,000 affiliated groups throughout the world in 1995, serving as the model for more than 130 twelve-step groups for a variety of addictions and compulsive behaviors.

A significant step forward in legitimizing support groups, both in the eyes of the general public and in the eyes of government agencies, was the 1987 Report of the Surgeon General's Workshop on Self-Help and Public Health. C. Everett Koop, the activist surgeon general, organized the workshop after having personal and professional contact with self-help groups. He had a positive experience with The Compassionate Friends (TCF) after his son was killed in an avalanche and after he observed, as a pediatrician, that families benefited from discussing their children's illnesses with other families.

Definitions and Divisions of Support Groups. There is no definitive agreement on what constitutes a self-help or support group, but some characteristics and processes apply to the vast majority of these groups: They are voluntary gatherings of peers who share common problems or interests; members meet to discuss relevant experiences, share support, exchange practical information, and teach coping skills; they help members to alleviate isolation, find a sense of belonging, and gain a feeling of empowerment. Most groups have little or no contact with professionals, and they typically do not charge fees. Some researchers differentiate between self-help and support groups by defining self-help groups as more complex systems that are designed to help members change themselves, with support as a byproduct, and by defining support groups as smaller associations that primarily exist to provide support and comfort, with change as a byproduct.

The National Institute of Mental Health distinguishes between three types of groups, depending on the types of populations they serve: persons with mental or physical illnesses, persons with compulsions or addictions, and persons with specific characteristics or interests. Under the first category, there are groups for virtually every disease listed by the World Health Organization (WHO). Offering members mutual support and helping them to deal with stress, many such groups lobby for research funds and work to increase awareness of given diseases among the general public. Many members are persons newly diagnosed with given diseases, while others are family members and friends, especially in cases in which children have birth defects, are mentally retarded, or have died. Groups in the second category help their members to eliminate or control unwanted behavior. A large number of such groups adhere to the general format of Alcoholics Anonymous, following the group's Twelve Steps and Twelve Traditions and including a strong spiritual component. Twelve-step groups follow AA's tradition of not taking political positions, even on matters that affect them. The third category includes groups based on such factors as members' sexual orientation, ethnic heritage, and profession.

Benefits to Families. Support or self-help groups offer a number of unique benefits to families and their members. Significantly, such groups are usually free or require only small donations. The fact that they are nonbureaucratic can be comforting to persons who have been frustrated or made to feel unimportant in their dealings with medical, insurance, government, or other agencies. In the United States, support groups exist outside the government bureaucracy, although in other industrialized societies the government typically provides some support for such groups. Empathy from those who have experienced and survived the same crises or situations is a significant benefit cited by members in research studies. Offering practical advice and the real-life experiences of their members, support groups can decrease the sense of isolation that new members often feel before joining. Persons who feel strange about the situation they face can find a sense of belonging by relating to others in the same situation.

When a medical crisis or addictive behavior disrupts families, it is often difficult for those affected to feel that they are understood by others who have not had the same experience. Even when family members are genuinely supportive and concerned about the troubling situation in which they find themselves, affected persons often find more comfort in the company of others who are "in the same boat" than among those who are not. The unique factor is the experiential knowledge that can only be provided by persons who have "been there." Compared to professional therapy, support groups are more personal, invoking a sense of neighborhood or community that is often lacking in postindustrial societies. Members of support groups are both the consumers and providers of the therapeutic process. It has been noted that those who help others find that they are better able to deal with their own problems, increasing their self-esteem. Furthermore, those who have been helped become helpers and receive the same benefits as those who helped them.

New Forms of Support Groups. In addition to traditional support groups, in which participants meet together face to face, two new types of support groups have arisen that rely on the technological advances of the late twentieth century: telephone conferencing and computer-based groups.

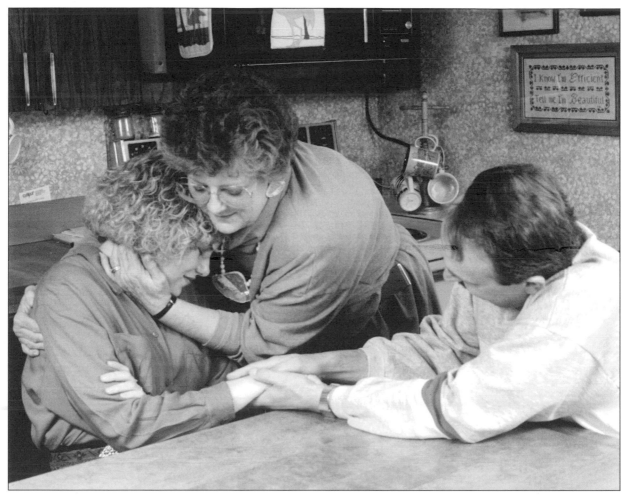

Much of the work done by support group members is informal. (Skjold Photographs)

Support groups that meet through telephone conference calls are useful for persons who live in isolated areas or whose physical condition or caregiving responsibilities preclude their attending regular meetings. Such groups are usually moderated by a professional and are typically of limited duration. A more recent development is the rise of computer-based support groups. In 1997 more than one thousand such groups existed. They take several forms: electronic bulletin boards, news and mail groups, and chat rooms. Groups may be facilitated by professionals or be unmoderated, they may be closed to outsiders or open to anyone, they may operate in real time or allow messages to be saved for later retrieval. Increasing access to computer resources makes it likely that such groups will continue to grow.

There are advantages and disadvantages to telephone- and computer-based groups. The greatest advantage is that persons who are unable to attend regular meetings may be able to participate more easily in these types of groups. For persons with access to computers and modems, the cost of participation in Internet groups is minimal. Disadvantages include the high cost of telephone conferencing and the fact that the cues that are a part of face-to-face discussions are missing. The issue of computer groups also raises the question of security and confidentiality. Participants should be aware that messages sent to many types of groups can be retrieved and distributed by persons outside the group without the knowledge of senders. Finally, the human touch that is so much a part of many face-to-face groups is missing—there is still

Many support groups use billboards to advertise their existence to the general public. (James L. Shaffer)

no way to give or receive a comforting hug electronically.

Two Representative Groups. One of the oldest and best-known family support groups, one that has been the subject of several research studies, is the National Alliance for the Mentally Ill. It is often cited as a model of a non-twelve-step group that combines advocacy on the national level with support for members in its local chapters.

NAMI began in 1979 in Madison, Wisconsin, with a conference attended by approximately three hundred persons representing various groups of family members of the mentally ill in the United States and Canada. By 1995 it had one thousand affiliated chapters in North America. In 1990, 80 percent of NAMI's members were parents of mentally ill persons. NAMI's mission is "to eradicate mental illness and improve the quality of life of those affected by these diseases." Its national office disseminates information on mental illness and its biological basis, advocating increased government funding for research and treatment. On the local level, chapters provide members with comfort and support from others who face the same crises and, by providing education on the biological basis of mental illness, have reduced the feelings of guilt many persons suffer over their children's mental illnesses. A 1994 study determined that one major factor in people's decision to join NAMI is that it provides them with an opportunity to advocate improved care for their mentally ill relatives. This corresponds to the empowerment function of support groups in general.

Unlike NAMI, The Compassionate Friends do not engage in political action or advocacy. It is purely a support group for bereaved parents and siblings. It has a national office, and its affiliates must apply to the national group for recognition and agree to abide by its guidelines. The national office simply responds to letters and calls from bereaved persons and interested professionals and develops new chapters. TCF began in 1969 in Great Britain, with a hospital chaplain as facilitator for six members of two bereaved families. In 1972 the chaplain, Simon Stephens, published *Death Comes Home*, which discusses his experiences in counseling the bereaved. The resulting publicity led to the founding of the first TCF chapter in the United States the same year. TCF's mission statement says it is "a mutual assistance self-help organization offering friendship and understanding to bereaved parents and siblings." TCF charges no dues, and parents compose both the national and local leaderships.

A typical TCF meeting begins with attendees giving their names, the names and ages of their dead children, and brief explanations of the circumstances surrounding their children's deaths. After a presentation by a speaker or a group discussion of a specific topic, members typically meet informally. Two of TCF's stated principles is that members should show friendship and understanding to the bereaved and that the bereaved can help each other positively resolve their grief.

Finding a Support Group. There are many ways to find support groups that meet persons' needs. The appendix to this series lists a large variety of national support groups that either have local chapters or may have information on related groups in specific areas. The bibliography appended to this article lists two directories that have comprehensive listings. Many states have clearinghouses, and most libraries carry the Encyclopedia of Associations, a list of groups that is updated yearly.

Specialized resources for families may be found by searching the Internet, which provides information on chat and discussion groups, lists of relevant toll-free numbers, and links to dozens of support and other groups of interest to families. Many community and college libraries have public Internet access and information on how to search computer databases. Whether persons need help with problems of addiction or abuse, phobias or rare genetic conditions, single parenting or the loss of a loved one, divorce or sexual orientation, a supportive network of persons who share their experience is available to provide help and understanding. —*Irene Struthers*

BIBLIOGRAPHY

Donovan, Joe. *The Self-Help Directory: A Sourcebook for Self-Help in the United States and Canada.* New York: Facts On File, 1994. Lists self-help groups and clearinghouses in the United States and Canada and contains chapters on starting self-help groups and computer-based self-help groups.

Katz, Alfred H. *Self-Help in America: A Social Movement Perspective.* New York: Twayne, 1993. Discusses the leadership, ideology, and growth patterns of twelve-step and other groups and contains a chapter that discusses government policies toward the self-help movement in the United States, Canada, Great Britain, and Germany.

Katz, Alfred H., et al., eds. *Self-Help: Concepts and Applications.* Philadelphia: The Charles Press, 1992. Includes both well-researched, scholarly articles by professionals and some personal accounts from individuals involved in support groups.

Kurtz, Linda Farris. *Self-Help and Support Groups: A Handbook for Practitioners.* Thousand Oaks, Calif.: Sage Publications, 1997. Provides complete, understandable information on groups and their members, detailed examples of several representative groups, a chapter on telephone- and computer-based support groups, and an appendix that lists self-help clearinghouses in seventeen countries.

Reissman, Frank, and David Carroll. *Redefining Self-Help: Policy and Practice.* San Francisco, Calif.: Jossey-Bass, 1995. Argues that membership in self-help groups transforms members from problems into resources and discusses groups for specific populations.

White, Barbara J., and Edward J. Madera, eds. *The Self-Help Sourcebook.* 5th ed. Denville, N.J.: Northwest Covenant Medical Center, 1995. Lists groups by category and in an index and includes chapters on starting a group, being a contact person, and computer-based groups.

See also Al-Anon; Alateen; Big Brothers and Big Sisters of America (BBBSA); Family advice columns; Friend networks; Grief counseling; Parents Anonymous (PA); Parents Without Partners (PWP); Recovery programs; Tough love.

Surrogate mothers

Relevant issues: Health and medicine; Kinship and genealogy; Law; Parenting and family relationships

Significance: Developing technologies for reproduction have created a variety of options for infertile couples, affecting traditional ideas and laws concerning kinship, parenthood, and even the definition of family

Surrogacy existed as long ago as the biblical story of Hagar, who bore a son to Abraham in place of his aged wife Sarah. Surviving evidence seems to indicate that ancient societies basically accepted such arrangements. Laws forbidding or regulating surrogacy were virtually nonexistent prior to the twentieth century. This has changed dramatically, spurred largely by technological developments in human reproduction. Whereas involuntarily childless couples once had only the options of remaining childless or adopting children, reproductive technologies have created other options. Primary among these are artificial insemination, in vitro fertilization, and embryo implantation

Varieties of Surrogacy. Surrogacy falls into two primary categories: biological surrogacy and gestational surrogacy. In the former, surrogates furnish eggs for conception, which are then fertilized by the sperm of husbands of adopting couples or by donors. In the latter, both egg and sperm are furnished to surrogates, who provide only their uterus for carrying children to term and bearing them. This makes possible a number of relationship scenarios. When husbands are infertile, donor sperm can be used to fertilize an egg from their wives, which are then implanted into the wombs of surrogates. In such cases, resulting children are genetically related to the wives but not the husbands. Another possibility is that donors contribute both sperm and eggs, in which case the children are genetically related to neither parent. When only wives are infertile, husbands' sperm can be used to impregnate a surrogate, whereby the resulting children are genetically related to the adopting fathers, but not mothers. Another scenario arises when women can conceive but not carry children to term. In such cases, embryos can be removed from them and surgically implanted into the wombs of surrogates. In such cases, the children are genetically related to both parents, but not to the surrogates. These scenarios mean that children may have three mothers: genetic mothers who furnish eggs, gestational mothers who bear the children, and adoptive or social mothers who actually rear the children. A similar multiplicity of fathers is possible.

Commercial vs. Altruistic Surrogacy. Commercial surrogacy involves contracts between adoptive couples and surrogates in which fees are charged by agencies mediating the agreements. In altruistic surrogacy surrogates, often family members or close friends, agree to bear children for childless couples without compensation. The fees for commercial surrogacy usually range from $30,000 to $50,000, with surrogate mothers receiving about one-fourth of the total. The remainder covers legal and medical fees and fees paid to the agencies involved in the arrangements. The objections against surrogacy have been directed primarily at commercial surrogacy. Altruistic surrogacy tends to be either accepted or ignored. Commercial surrogacy raises a number of social, ethical, legal, and religious issues.

Social Considerations. The impact of surrogacy upon family life is manifold. Surrogacy poses questions about the children born of surrogate mothers and how their self-esteem is affected when they learn that they were conceived specifically to be given away. Some argue that the problems are no different from those of adopted children. There is an important difference, however, in that with surrogacy conception is planned for the specific purpose of transferring children for rearing to persons other than birth mothers. Adopted children can be told that their mothers loved them but, for financial or other reasons, could not keep them. With surrogacy there is no way to maintain that biological mothers loved their children, since the purpose of the conception was to give them away. Another impact of surrogacy upon family life involves the attitude of the community. Surrogate mothers have testified to being unprepared for the contempt, ridicule, and social ostracization they have encountered in their communities. Mothers, children, and even husbands may experience such attitudes.

Since most surrogate mothers are married and have children of their own, surrogacy often places a strain upon their marriages and families. During the period of insemination, which may last from two or three months to a year or more, husbands must abstain from sexual intercourse with their wives. Unless they are unusually supportive and tolerant, this places a strain upon the marriage relationship. Children are also affected when they have surrogate mothers. When they see a little brother or sister given away, their sense of security may be affected, perhaps believing that if their mothers can give one child away, they can also give their other children away, especially if they are "bad." Such thoughts can be devastating to children.

Ethical Issues. One of the first ethical issues raised by surrogacy was whether commercial surrogacy contracts constitute selling babies. Supporters of commercial surrogacy claim that persons do not pay money for children, but for services rendered on behalf of adoptive parents. They refer to the period of gestation as "womb rental." When fathers provide sperm, it is argued that resulting children belong to them and that they cannot buy what is already theirs. There is a fatal flaw in this reasoning, however. Most surrogacy contracts provide for full payment only if a normal, healthy child is born. In cases of miscarriages or stillbirths, mothers receive only a fraction of their fees. This proves that payments are not just for services rendered, since such services are rendered in cases of stillbirths or live births, but rather that payments are for normal, healthy children.

Another issue involves contracts themselves and the ethical permissibility of writing contracts that effactually determine the future of a human life. Supporters argue that surrogate contracts ensure that children will be wanted by parents who will love them and that such children will be in a much better situation than many other children. Opponents argue that there are some things that money cannot buy, and that ownership of a child falls into this category.

There is the further ethical question as to whether surrogacy demeans and degrades womanhood. Feminists are deeply divided over this issue. Some feminists hail surrogacy as a boon to women's freedom and self-determination, arguing that it gives women a choice as to whether or not to bear children for themselves or for others. Career women who want children but do not want to interrupt their careers can have surrogates freely choose to bear children for them. Other feminists argue that this is yet another way of degrading women and eroding their power. Even though no overt coercion is present, they argue that there is still the "coercion" of society's attitude that motherhood is women's ultimate goal and purpose and that this precludes a really free choice.

The operation of agencies which arrange surrogate births raises other ethical questions. Most such agencies employ professional psychologists to "screen" applicants who want to be surrogate mothers. This opens up the possibility that techniques bordering on brainwashing may be used in order to persuade women to become surrogate mothers. Agency lawyers, in order to allay the fears of adoptive parents, tell them and surrogate mothers that they will make surrogates' lives miserable if they consider keeping the babies they bear. Furthermore, some agencies use "closed" surrogacy arrangements, in which adoptive parents and surrogate mothers are not allowed to meet one another until they go to court to finalize the adoption arrangements. Agencies control the flow of information between parents and surrogates.

In vitro fertilization and embryo transplant technologies raise further ethical issues. Now that it is possible to transplant embryos into the wombs of women who have already undergone the menopause, decisions must be made as to whether this is ethically permissible. The question arises whether the aging body is capable of properly nourishing fetuses. In one case, a grandmother gave birth to a child conceived by her daughter's egg and her son-in-law's sperm. Such forms of surrogacy may affect kinship and family relationships. There is at least one known case in which a man who was to undergo a sex change operation wanted to father a child before the operation so that he could be both the father and mother of the child. Reproductive technologies have also made it possible for

While fighting for custody of "Baby M," the daughter she delivered, Mary Whitehead was comforted by Elizabeth Kane, who also had been a surrogate mother. (AP/Wide World Photos)

gay and lesbian couples to have children. Not only genealogical relationships, but even the definition of "family" is challenged by these possibilities.

Legal Issues. Some of the ethical issues involved in surrogacy are also legal in nature. For example, the sale of babies is almost universally illegal. Thus, courts must decide whether commercial surrogacy constitutes the sale of babies, perhaps leading to decisions to outlaw it. If adoptive couples divorce before adoption proceedings are complete, further legal issues are raised. Custody decisions in the courts have generally been guided by the genetic relationship of children to parents, but this could change. In vitro fertilization creates the possibility that children may not be genetically related to either adoptive parent or even to surrogate mothers. It may be necessary to develop guidelines other than genetic relationships to determine child custody.

Another legal issue arises out of the provision often found in surrogacy contracts that if children will be born with serious birth defects, surrogate mothers will undergo abortions. Such contract provisions may be unenforceable in light of the 1973 Supreme Court abortion decision in *Roe v. Wade*, which stipulated that the decision to abort rests solely with women.

A review of two court cases engendered by surrogacy agreements reveals other legal issues. The most widely publicized of these was the 1988 case of "Baby M," in which Mary Beth Whitehead contracted to bear a child for William and Elizabeth Stern for a fee of $10,000. Whitehead changed her mind and attempted to keep the baby. The case was tried in New Jersey, and in 1987 the court ruled that the contract was valid, giving custody of the baby to the Sterns while denying Whitehead visitation rights. After two years of legal maneuvering, the case was appealed to the New Jersey Supreme Court, which ruled that the contract was invalid, voiding the adoption of "Baby M" by the Sterns and restoring Whitehead's parental rights. However, since the child had been in the custody of the Sterns for about two years, the court deemed that it was in the child's best interests to remain with the Sterns.

Another significant case unfolded in California when Anna Johnson agreed to be a gestational surrogate for Mark and Crispina Calvert, the genetic parents, for a fee of $10,000. When Johnson

changed her mind and attempted to keep the baby, the case went before the California Supreme Court. In June, 1993, the court ruled in favor of the Calverts on the grounds that Crispina Calvert, who intended to procreate and rear the child, was the natural mother under California law. The court also ruled that the Johnsons' fee did not constitute the sale of a child but was payment for services rendered.

Legislative and Religious Responses. In the wake of the "Baby M" case seventy-two bills pertaining to surrogacy were introduced in twenty-six state legislatures. As of 1993 thirteen states had enacted laws regarding surrogacy. Of these, twelve outlawed commercial surrogacy and one left the matter unclear. Only four of these states legitimized noncommercial surrogacy, while nine specified that surrogacy contracts were void and unenforceable.

Surrogacy is also an issue in Canada and the United Kingdom. In 1993 Canada's Royal Commission on New Reproductive Technologies called for a ban on all forms of surrogacy, including informal arrangements between family members or close friends. The United Kingdom, in its Surrogacy Arrangements Act of 1985, prohibited any activity by agencies that involved recruiting women for surrogate pregnancies or making arrangements for surrogate births.

The strongest religious responses to surrogacy have come from the Roman Catholic Church. The Instruction on Respect for Human Life in Its Origin and on the Dignity of Procreation, issued by the Vatican in March, 1997, condemned all forms of artificial insemination and surrogate motherhood. The Vatican argued in part that reproductive technology is inherently dehumanizing and does not take into consideration that human beings are a union of body and soul. It argued further that sexual intercourse is both physical and spiritual and that noncoital reproduction diminishes the full significance of human reproduction. The response of other religious groups has ranged from strong opposition to somewhat guarded, conditional acceptance. —*Joe E. Lunceford*

BIBLIOGRAPHY
Alpern, Kenneth D., ed. *The Ethics of Reproductive Technology.* New York: Oxford University Press, 1992. Anthology of articles by authors on all

sides of the ethical issues of surrogate motherhood.

Boling, Patricia, ed. *Expecting Trouble: Surrogacy, Fetal Abuse, and New Reproductive Technologies.* Boulder, Colo.: Westview Press, 1995. Anthology of feminist essays, predominantly by professors of political science, expressing a variety of views on surrogacy.

Field, Martha A. *Surrogate Motherhood.* Cambridge, Mass.: Harvard University Press, 1988. Very readable introduction to most of the pros and cons of surrogacy.

Humphrey, Michael, and Heather Humphrey. *Families with a Difference.* London: Routledge, 1988. Useful survey of literature from Britain on the issue of surrogacy.

Lauritzen, Paul. *Pursuing Parenthood.* Bloomington: Indiana University Press, 1993. Takes the position that surrogate motherhood is morally unjustifiable, while guardedly approving technologically assisted reproduction.

Rae, Scott B. *Brave New Families: Biblical Ethics and Reproductive Technologies.* Grand Rapids, Mich.: Baker Books, 1996. Informed presentation of recent reproductive technologies in general and surrogate motherhood in particular, approached from a conservative Christian viewpoint.

Ragone, Helena. *Surrogate Motherhood: Conception in the Heart.* Boulder, Colo.: Westview Press, 1994. Anthropological study based on personal interviews with various parties to surrogate motherhood.

Rowland, Robyn. *Living Laboratories.* Bloomington: Indiana University Press, 1992. Feminist argument that surrogate motherhood demeans and degrades women.

Saban, Cheryl. *Miracle Child: Genetic Mother, Surrogate Womb.* Far Hills, N.J.: Horizon Press, 1993. Nontechnical, largely first-person account of the process leading to surrogate motherhood.

Wekesser, Carol, ed. *Reproductive Technologies.* San Diego, Calif.: Greenhaven Press, 1996. Anthology with several excellent articles on the pros and cons of surrogate motherhood.

See also Adoption issues; Childbirth; Childlessness; Family: concept and history; Fertility and infertility; *In re Baby M*; Nuclear family; Reproductive technologies; Test-tube babies.

Systematic Training for Effective Parenting (STEP)

DATE: First published in 1976 (revised in 1997)
RELEVANT ISSUES: Children and child development; Parenting and family relationships
SIGNIFICANCE: This parenting education program is designed to strengthen family relationships by teaching parents effective parenting skills

The first Systematic Training for Effective Parenting (STEP) program was developed by Don Dinkmeyer, Sr., and Gary D. McKay. They recognized that although parenting is one of the most important jobs in society, most parents have no training in skillful parenting. To address this, Dinkmeyer and McKay combined the concepts of Rudolph Dreikurs and Thomas Gordon with their own expertise and wrote *Raising a Responsible Child* (1973). The success of this book prompted the development of the STEP program in the late 1970's.

Since then STEP programs have been developed for parents of teenagers (STEP/Teen) parents of children from infancy to age five (Early Childhood STEP), and parents wanting to extend skills learned in one (or more) of the other programs (The Next STEP). In developing Early Childhood STEP and The Next STEP, the first authors were joined by three additional authors: Don Dinkmeyer, Jr., James S. Dinkmeyer, and Joyce L. McKay. The original STEP program was translated into Spanish and published as *PECES: Padres Eficaces Con Entrenamiento Sistematico.* Additionally, the Reverend Michael Bortel developed materials with a biblical focus to accompany STEP and STEP/Teen.

The STEP programs are based on the concept of mutual respect—parents demonstrating genuine respect for children as human beings and children developing and demonstrating genuine respect for parents. Cooperation and individual responsibility for actions are key objectives of the programs. Parenting challenges facing all types of families are addressed through the program materials or through group discussions. STEP materials include parenting handbooks, leaders' resource guides, and video- and audiotapes. Skills are systematically developed through a series of group meetings. Each session focuses on a specific topic and includes discussing information from the parenting handbook, viewing videotapes, listening to audio tapes that demonstrate the skills to be learned, practicing skills, and voluntarily sharing parenting successes and challenges.

The Early Childhood STEP program helps parents develop understanding and positive relation- ships with their children from birth on. Topics in the seven sessions include understanding young children, understanding young children's behavior, building self-esteem in the early years, communicating with young children, helping young children learn to cooperate, applying effective dis-

STEP teaches parenting skills for the purpose of strengthening all relationships within families. (James L. Shaffer)

cipline, and nurturing emotional and social development.

The STEP: Systematic Training for Effective Parenting program is a seven-session course that focuses on communication within families. The topics include understanding oneself and one's children, understanding beliefs and feelings, encouraging one's children and oneself, listening and talking with one's children, helping children learn to cooperate, and applying discipline that makes sense.

The STEP/Teen program is a ten-session series. In addition to developmental topics similar to those in Early Childhood STEP and STEP, this program addresses the unique challenges of raising teenagers. Discussions include growing independence, increased social pressure, dating, cur-

fews, using the car, career plans, sexual activity, and using alcohol, tobacco, and other drugs.

The Next STEP is a six-session follow-up to the basic parenting programs. It helps parents build their own self-esteem, realize they are not perfect and do not have to be, reduce stress in themselves and their children, choose to change, assert their rights, and control situations.

Those interested in more information about any of the STEP programs may contact American Guidance Service, P.O. Box 99, Circle Pines, MN 55014-1796, (800) 328-2560.

—*Carolyn S. Magnuson*

See also Disciplining children; Equality of children; Family unity; Family values; Parenting; Support groups.

Tax laws

RELEVANT ISSUES: Economics and work; Law
SIGNIFICANCE: Tax laws create incentives and have consequences for a range of family decisions, behaviors, and structures

The federal tax code and most state tax codes do more than simply raise revenues for the government. They are intended to carry out a number of additional functions, including the encouragement of certain behaviors (such as charitable giving) and the transfer of resources to the most needy or deserving. In addition to their intended effects, tax codes can generate a number of unintended effects. Since tax codes are largely focused on households, families are directly affected by tax provisions. Two dimensions of tax law that are especially significant for families are the so-called "marriage tax" and the tax allowances for children.

The Marriage Tax. The marriage tax is not a distinct tax formally imposed on marriages but an effect of existing tax laws that can cause a married couple's tax obligation to be higher than that of two single persons with the same income. In other words, this tax is the difference between the tax obligation of married couples and the combined tax that such persons would owe if they were single. Under some circumstances married couples may owe less in taxes than they would if they were single, thereby taking advantage of the marriage subsidy.

The effect of taxing or subsidizing marriage developed from the government's attempt to address different fairness issues. The particular fairness concerns of the tax code have changed over time. As originally devised, federal income tax did not take account of marriage at all. Individuals filed separate tax returns, provided their adjusted income exceeded a certain amount. There was no marriage tax or subsidy, because persons filed the same returns irrespective of their marital status.

Although the tax code treated individuals with similar incomes equally, this approach did not affect married couples equally. By making individuals accountable for their own incomes, the tax code assumed that income would not be shared between spouses. Yet, the graduated nature of the tax rate (with higher marginal rates for higher levels of income) discriminated against one-income marriages. For example, the tax obligation of two spouses earning $25,000 each could be less than that of a couple in which one spouse earned $50,000 and the other nothing, because $50,000 could be taxed in a higher bracket than two $25,000 incomes. This phenomenon—a form of "bracket creep"—was especially pronounced in the mid-1940's, when the top marginal tax rate reached 94 percent.

Changes in the Tax Code. To remedy this disparity between couples, the U.S. Congress altered a basic premise of the tax code in 1948. This change acknowledged that income within households is typically pooled. Based on this logic, married couples were taxed as households rather than as two separate individuals. The new formula essentially imposed a tax obligation equal to twice that owed by a single person earning half the couple's joint income. In this way, couples with the same total income paid the same total tax, irrespective of how they actually apportioned their income between themselves. Thus, it was immaterial whether each spouse earned $25,000 or if one spouse earned $50,000—in both cases the tax obligation would be twice the tax on $25,000. Although this change provided equity between couples, it effectively benefited couples over singles. By calculating the tax rate on only half a couple's income, the tax code tended to place couples in a lower tax bracket than single persons making the same income.

Congress once again altered its approach to taxing couples in 1969, this time establishing separate tax tables for married couples and for singles. By the late twentieth century this approach remained in effect. In many cases married couples in the 1990's had a greater total tax obligation than singles. However, in about the same number of cases couples paid less in taxes than they would have paid as singles. The main determinant of whether couples were forced to pay a marriage tax or allowed to enjoy a marriage subsidy was the apportionment of income between two spouses. This is largely due to the bracket creep effect encountered by combining incomes. Couples with one main income earner tend to receive a marriage subsidy, while couples with two income earners tend to encounter a marriage tax.

Marriage tax reformers have sought to achieve two distinct objectives: to ensure that married couples with the same joint income as individuals pay the same tax and to ensure that one's marital status does not affect one's tax obligation. As a complicating factor, America's tax code has a third objective, to ensure that wealthier persons pay a larger percentage of their income in taxes. Whatever the worthiness of these three principles, they cannot simultaneously be achieved by the same tax code. The aggregation of spouse' incomes required to fulfil the first objective causes tax bracket creep (a result of the third objective), thus making the second objective impossible.

Rising Incidence of the Marriage Tax. An increase in the number of two-income families in the 1980's and 1990's increased the incidence of the marriage tax among families. By the mid-1990's between one-third and one-half of all couples effectively paid a tax for being married. A similar proportion of couples paid less tax than they would have encountered if they were single, and the remainder were not affected either way. The notion of a marriage tax became a potent political issue. In the late 1990's the Republican Party and other forces worked to "repeal the marriage tax."

The marriage tax has been labeled "anti-family" by opponents, who argue that it penalizes persons who choose to marry. Some conclude that the marriage tax therefore discourages marriage. Such arguments are plausible; if the marriage tax was high enough to price people out of the marriage market, marriage rates could be affected. Nevertheless, a number of studies have demonstrated that while a perceived marriage tax causes some couples to delay their marriages, it does not affect the overall rate of marriage.

Marriage-Tax Reform. The main argument for marriage-tax reform concerns the issue of fairness. In general, the principle of tax fairness requires that the tax code treat people in similar circumstances equally, and it should also treat persons in dissimilar circumstances equitably. Yet, equity and fairness are difficult to define, much less to achieve. The tax schedule for married couples may take into account a number of assumptions, not the least of which is that married couples living together in one household have different expenses than two single persons living in separate households. Married couples may also utilize different public services than singles. In other words, fairness does not necessarily require that married couples face the same tax obligations as two single taxpayers.

The marriage-tax reformers' case is stronger when one compares the tax obligation of married couples with that of otherwise identical single, cohabiting couples. In this case, it is difficult to justify imposing a higher tax on married couples. If the marriage tax is defined as unequal treatment of otherwise identical married and unmarried couples, the tax could easily be eliminated by allowing cohabiting couples to file as though they were married. However, many of those who call for marriage-tax reform oppose such a move as weakening the status of marriage.

Tax Provisions for Children. Families that support children have higher living expenses than those that do not. To accommodate this, the tax code has a number of provisions that either reduce taxable income (deductions) or reduce tax obligations (credits) in connection with expenses for children and other dependents. Dependents are generally defined as relatives (or year-round family members) who rely on primary income earners for most of their financial support.

For each dependent, families are entitled to an exemption on their tax returns. Exemptions reduce families' taxable income by a certain amount ($2,650 on 1997 federal tax returns). In effect, exemptions permit families to spend this amount on each of their children tax-free. Whether the dollar figure for these exemptions matches the true expenses of dependent care is a matter of controversy. It is significant, however, that the tax code offers these exemptions at all. Many countries offer no such exemptions, and some actually impose a tax penalty for having more than one or two children.

Georgia congressman Newt Gingrich at a Contract with America rally in Washington, D.C., in early 1995. (Reuters/Mike Theiler/Archive Photos)

When President Bill Clinton delivered one of his weekly national radio addresses in December, 1994, he touted the education tax credits that were a central part of his plan to provide tax cuts to middle-class families. (Reuters/White House/Archive Photos)

In addition to exemptions for dependents, families that itemize their tax returns are entitled to a range of deductions for dependent-related expenses. For example, certain educational, medical, and dental expenses (or portions of them) can be deducted from families' taxable income. By reducing or eliminating the tax on these expenses, the tax code reduces their effective cost to the taxpayers. Presumably, this encourages parents not to skimp on such expenses. In addition, the mortgage interest deduction is an enormously popular, high-value deduction utilized by many families. Proponents argue that it makes the "American dream" of home ownership possible for greater numbers of families.

For those who itemize their deductions and for those who do not, certain forms of income are not subject to taxation. For example, child-support payments received by divorced or separated parents do not figure into their gross income. Alimony payments are taxable, however. Up to a certain amount, inherited money and property is not taxable.

Child Care. Tax law also offers a number of tax credits related to children and families. The earned income credit, formerly known as the earned income tax credit (EITC), is one of the largest of these, providing benefits to the working poor. Originally, the EITC was aimed at helping families beneath the poverty level to meet child-rearing and child-care expenses. It was thus available only to families with children. Since 1994 childless households have also been eligible, although the amount of the credit is lower for those without children. The Earned Income Credit is "refundable"—that is, it takes the form of a cash payment to families too poor to owe income tax.

Since the 1970's the number of mothers with young children entering the labor force has made child-care expenses a particularly salient political issue. The federal government subsidizes child-care expenses through a number of programs, including Head Start and the Child Care and Development Block Grant. Increasingly, the government has turned to tax law as an additional way of defraying families' child-care costs. For example, the Child and Dependent Care Tax Credit is available to parents of children under thirteen years of age. This credit covers child-care costs up to a certain limit and can only be claimed by families in which both parents or single parents work or are looking for work. Some critics have charged that these provisions encourage parents to use child care rather than stay home with their children.

Addressing this criticism in their 1994 "Contract with America," Republican Congressional candidates pledged to pursue a "family tax credit." They argued that a tax credit for families with children could make it financially more feasible for one parent to stay home with the children. After gaining control of Congress after the 1994 elections, the Republicans made the Family Tax Credit a major political issue. In general the party proposed a $500 per child tax credit, financed through a variety of spending cuts. The administration of president Bill Clinton proposed its own $500 dependent-care tax credit, although there was considerable disagreement over the details. Major points of controversy concerned the maximum income families could earn in order to be eligible for the credit. Critics argued that the credit was inappropriate for upper-income households. They also noted that the nonrefundable credit would not apply to the poorest families—in other words, those that do not owe taxes but have the greatest financial difficulty caring for their children.

Tax law continues to serve as a battleground for competing philosophies of child rearing, marriage, work, and societal obligations. The result is a politically influenced, constantly shifting tax code that often generates frustration among families and their advocates. —*Steve D. Boilard*

BIBLIOGRAPHY

August, Jerald David, ed. *The Taxpayer Relief Act of 1997*. Philadelphia, Pa.: American Bar Association, 1998. Discusses various changes to the federal tax code in 1997.

Impact on Individuals and Families of Replacing the Federal Income Tax. U.S. Government Printing Office, 1997. Report from the Joint Committee on Taxation, discussing various ways in which federal income tax affects families and households.

McCaffery, Edward J. *Taxing Women*. Chicago: University of Chicago Press, 1997. Critical assessment of the tax code's alleged bias against women and the resulting effect on family decisions and structures.

Oliver, Philip D., and Peel, Fred W., Jr. *Tax Policy: Readings and Materials.* Westbury, N.Y.: Foundation Press, 1996. Textbook explaining the principles of tax law and their consequences.

Wildavsky, Ben. "Kids' Tax Credit Splits Conservatives." *National Journal* 29 (June 7, 1997). Examines the Family Tax Credit's philosophical appeal to social conservatives and its rejection by free-market conservatives.

See also Child and dependent care tax credit; Domestic partners; Earned income tax credit; Employee Retirement Income Security Act (ERISA); Family businesses; Family economics; Family law; Home ownership; Inheritance and estate law; Intergenerational income transfer; Marriage; Retirement; Social Security; Wealth; Wills and bequests.

Teen marriages

RELEVANT ISSUES: Divorce; Marriage and dating; Parenting and family relationships

SIGNIFICANCE: Teenagers who marry are less likely to complete their formal education and are more likely to experience marriage problems, separation, divorce, single parenthood, financial problems, and poverty

In many parts of the world the average age at first marriage is increasing. However, the yearly number of marriages that include at least one teenager is significant. For some teenagers, custom and tradition dictate that they marry young. For others, teen marriage offers an escape from unpleasant family situations or an opportunity to prematurely play an adult role. Regardless of the reasons behind teen marriage, numerous short- and long-term problems typically accompany it.

Problems Associated with Teen Marriage. Marriages that involve at least one teenager under the age of eighteen are much more likely to fail than are marriages involving adults over the age of eighteen. This is particularly true for white females. Marriage brings with it marital economic, familial, and social responsibilities that require maturity as well as adult cognitive and decision-making skills. Ordinarily, these skills are underdeveloped in teenagers, especially when they fail to complete their formal education. Teenagers also lack maturity. When faced with the responsibilities of developing and maintaining intimate marital

relationships, teenagers frequently fall short, increasing the likelihood that their marriages will end in separation or divorce. Marital stability is further jeopardized when teenage pregnancy and childbirth are simultaneously experienced.

Teen marriage tends to interrupt formal education. Many young girls do not graduate from high school, and even fewer complete any college or vocational training. Their opportunities for good-paying jobs are thus limited, contributing to economic instability. Indeed, teenagers who marry are much more likely than single teenagers, single adults, and adults who marry to experience economic hardship and poverty. This also places their offspring at greater risk of experiencing poverty not only as children but as adults as well.

Incentives for Early Marriage. In spite of such risks, some teenagers choose early marriage. Several factors contribute to their decision. Inadequate parental supervision, for example, increases the likelihood of teen marriage. Lack of parental supervision also increases the likelihood of teenage pregnancy, which in turn increases the likelihood of teen marriage. In the United States in 1981 about 30 percent of pregnant teenage girls married. White teenage girls (40 percent), however, are more likely to marry when pregnant than their African American counterparts (5 percent). African American teenage females are more likely to have been raised in single-parent homes.

Some teenagers choose early marriage in order to escape from an unpleasant family situation. Intense parental conflict, as well as separation and divorce, may cause children and teenagers to experience emotional anxiety and stress. Drug and alcohol use, physical and sexual abuse, violence, financial difficulties, or poverty also increase stress levels within the family. When anxiety and stress are extreme, early marriage might be viewed as an escape from family strife.

Early marriage may also be viewed as an escape from economic instability and poverty. Indeed, married teenagers are more likely than other teenagers to have lived in low-income families or to have experienced poverty at some point in their lives. These teenagers may enter into early marriage in an attempt to improve their financial situation. Yet teen marriage seldom leads to improved economic stability.

Individual personality also plays a role in the

Although average ages of persons who marry have been rising, the overall number of teenage marriages has remained large. (James L. Shaffer)

incidence of teen marriage. Some teenagers have an unusually strong desire to achieve adult status. They tend to take risks that make them appear mature and adultlike. They may drink and smoke in front of their peers. Since marriage marks the transition from adolescence to adulthood, some teenagers marry prematurely in an attempt to achieve adult standing.

Factors Working Against Teen Marriage. Teen marriages have always occurred, but whether or not they are viewed as acceptable and desirable depends upon the time period or the culture in which they occur. Since the 1960's, for example, teen marriage increasingly has been viewed negatively, especially in modern industrial countries like Canada and the United States. This may be attributable to heightened awareness of problems resulting from teen marriage, as well as to economic, social, and educational changes. More and more young women postpone or forgo marriage because educational and job opportunities have increased, enabling them to gain financial security without marrying. Economically independent females are less likely to marry for monetary reasons and are more likely to delay marriage until adulthood than economically dependent females. Birth control is readily available and single motherhood is socially more acceptable than it was previously. Therefore, teenage girls and young women are less likely to participate in "shotgun weddings." The awareness that many married women who work outside the home face a double burden of domestic and job responsibilities decreases some young women's willingness to enter into marriage.

Young men sometimes feel that they bear the bulk of the financial responsibility for the family and delay marriage in order to avoid related financial burdens. It was once thought that married men are more stable, reliable employees than unmarried men. In recent times, however, men are less likely than women to marry for status reasons or to enhance their careers. The increasing social acceptance of couples who live together without marrying also contributes to the increase in the number of delayed marriages.

Historical and Cultural Perspectives. Delayed marriage has not always been viewed as acceptable and desirable. Throughout history there have been periods during which teenagers were expected to marry and to quickly produce offspring. Ancient Hebrew fathers, for example, arranged early marriages for their children in accordance with the scriptural teachings contained in the Talmud. The Talmud specified that daughters were eligible for marriage at age twelve and sons at age thirteen.

During the Middle Ages, early marriage was common among wealthy English families. The marriage of a daughter of a lord or patron frequently represented the final transaction between two families that were entering into a political alliance or financial contract. In short, the daughter was exchanged in marriage for money, land, or political advantage. Typically, marital transactions took place when daughters were between the ages of thirteen and fifteen, although some were younger. Peasant youths, on the other hand, tended to marry when they were in their mid-twenties since there were fewer economic and political considerations to take into account. Later marriage was also typical in colonial America.

Early marriage for females is prevalent in modern Third World countries, in which religious and cultural beliefs and customs promote matrimony between young girls and older men. Latin American culture, for example, places great emphasis on motherhood. Consequently, the average age of marriage for girls is fourteen in some places. Mexico and Colombia are exceptions, where eighteen is the legal marriage age.

The Shiites of the Middle East encourage teenage girls to marry because they believe female sexuality is dangerous and must be controlled. Older males, as husbands, bear the responsibility of controlling their young wives' sexuality in order to maintain sexual purity among both sexes. Other traditional religious beliefs encourage teen marriage. Hinduism, for example, places high value on female virginity and chastity. In order to protect sexual purity, young girls are given in marriage to older males. This practice is widespread. In 1980 the average marriage age for Hindu females in Pakistan and India was nine years old. In 1995 almost 50 percent of Indian females between the ages of fifteen and nineteen were married. Internal and external pressures have caused the Indian government to implement laws that discourage child and teen marriages. Unfortunately, this practice continues, especially in remote rural areas where illiteracy is common and traditional beliefs persist. —*Susan Green Barger*

BIBLIOGRAPHY

Astone, Nan Marie, and Dawn M. Upchurch. "Forming a Family, Leaving School Early, and Earning a GED: A Racial and Cohort Comparison." *Journal of Marriage and the Family* 56 (August, 1994).

Goldscheider, Frances K., and Linda J. Waite. *New Families, No Families.* Berkeley: University of California Press, 1991.

Ingoldsby, Bron B., and Suzanna Smith, eds. *Families in Multicultural Perspective.* New York: Guilford Press, 1995.

Li, Jiang Hong, and Roger A. Wojtkiewicz. "Childhood Family Structure and Entry into First Marriage." *The Sociological Quarterly* 35 (1994).

Luger, Kristin. *Dubious Conceptions: The Politics of Teen Pregnancy.* Cambridge, Mass.: Harvard University Press, 1996.

O'Kelly, Charolette G., and Larry S. Carney. *Women and Men in Society.* 2d ed. Belmont, Calif.: Wadsworth, 1986.

Peters, Edward N. "Too Young to Marry." *America* 174 (June 22, 1996).

Queen, Stuart A., Robert W. Habenstein, and Jill S. Quadagno. *The Family in Various Cultures.* 5th ed. New York: Harper & Row, 1985.

Teti, Douglas M., and Michael E. Lamb. "Socioeconomic and Marital Outcomes of Adolescent Marriage, Adolescent Childbirth, and Their Co-occurrence." *Journal of Marriage and the Family* 51 (February, 1989).

Trent, Katherine. "Family Context and Adolescents' Expectations about Marriage, Fertility, and Nonmarital Childbearing." *Social Science Quarterly* 75 (1994).

See also Arranged marriages; Childbirth; Dysfunctional families; Family economics; Marriage; Poverty; Pregnancy; Puberty and adolescence.

Teen mothers

RELEVANT ISSUES: Children and child development; Parenting and family relationships

SIGNIFICANCE: Teen motherhood remains a focus in family life issues because the timing of their births often makes parenting more difficult and tends to diminish the opportunities for both mothers and their children

Each year nearly one million American girls age nineteen and under become pregnant (about one in ten girls). Of these, approximately 50 percent give birth, 40 percent have abortions, and about 10 percent have miscarriages. In 1994, 59.9 percent of teenagers who had children were eighteen to nineteen years old, 37.6 percent were fifteen to seventeen years old, and 2.5 percent were younger than fifteen. According to the Children's Defense Fund's 1997 yearbook, the average percent of all births to teenagers in the United States was 13.1 percent, with a higher rate for southern states. For example, in 1994 Mississippi led the nation with a rate of 22.1 percent, Arkansas followed with 20.1 percent, and Louisiana was third with 19.2 percent.

Teen Birth Rates. Teen birth rates declined through the 1970's, leveled out in the early 1980's, and then increased sharply between 1986 and 1991. In absolute numbers, more babies were born to teen mothers in the early 1970's than in the early 1980's. The difference in the late 1990's was that the decline affected all but the very youngest girls. The birth rate among teenagers dropped steadily by almost 8 percent between 1991 and 1996. Nevertheless, the modern rate is still above that throughout most of the 1980's.

According to the Children's Defense Fund, 518,389 babies were born to girls ages fifteen to nineteen in 1994, a rate of 58.9 births for every 1,000 girls. Contrary to popular beliefs, the teen birth rate had steadily dropped in the United States for several decades. In 1960 the teen birth rate was 89.1 births per 1,000 fifteen- to nineteen-year-old girls compared to 50.2 per 1,000 in 1986. However, the birth rate rose by one-quarter from 1986 to 62.1 births per 1,000 in 1991. This increase wiped out nearly one-third of the gain made from the earlier decline.

While the teen birth rate has been on the decline, the absolute number of births increased between 1993 and 1994 by 2 percent, as there were more teenagers in the United States. Even with this decline, the birth rate in the United States remains many times higher than that in most European countries. However, patterns of sexual activity are not significantly different. The country with the next highest rate of teen mothers is Great Britain, with half the rate as the United States. According to the United Nations, the teen birth rate to whites in the United States surpasses that of any other industrialized nation. Compared to the

United States, teenage birth rates in Canada have declined considerably since the 1950's. This may be due to improved contraception, legalized abortion, public health insurance, and social assistance benefits, which have enabled poorer women to receive medical care and prescription drugs.

When compared to other industrialized nations, teenagers in the United States use contraception with lesser frequency and consistency, resulting in higher birth rates. The higher rate may also be attributed to teenagers' limited access to sexuality education and health services, more so-cietal ambivalence toward sexuality, and more children and families in poverty.

The decades-long decrease in the teen birth rate is not easily explained. However, the number of teenagers reporting that they engage in sexual intercourse has stopped growing. In fact, in 1995, for the first time in two decades, the percentage of American teenagers having sexual intercourse dropped, and those who engage in sexual intercourse report increasingly that they use contraception. This is particularly encouraging, as the abortion rate for teenagers has also been on the

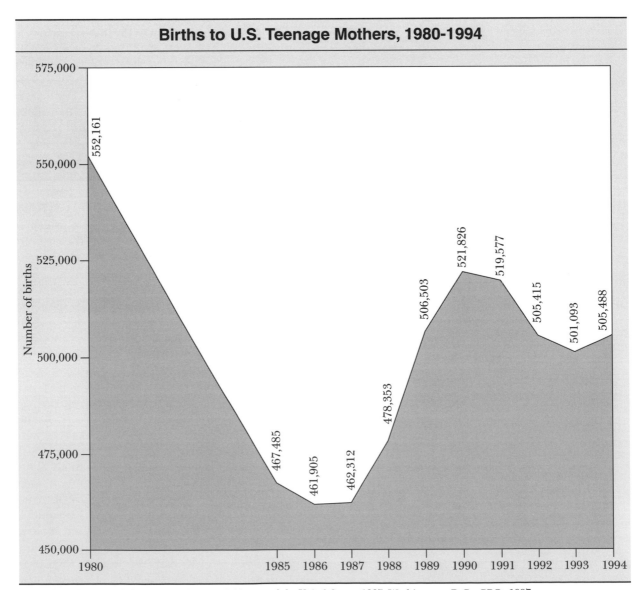

Births to U.S. Teenage Mothers, 1980-1994

Source: U.S. Bureau of the Census, *Statistical Abstract of the United States: 1997.* Washington, D.C.: GPO, 1997.

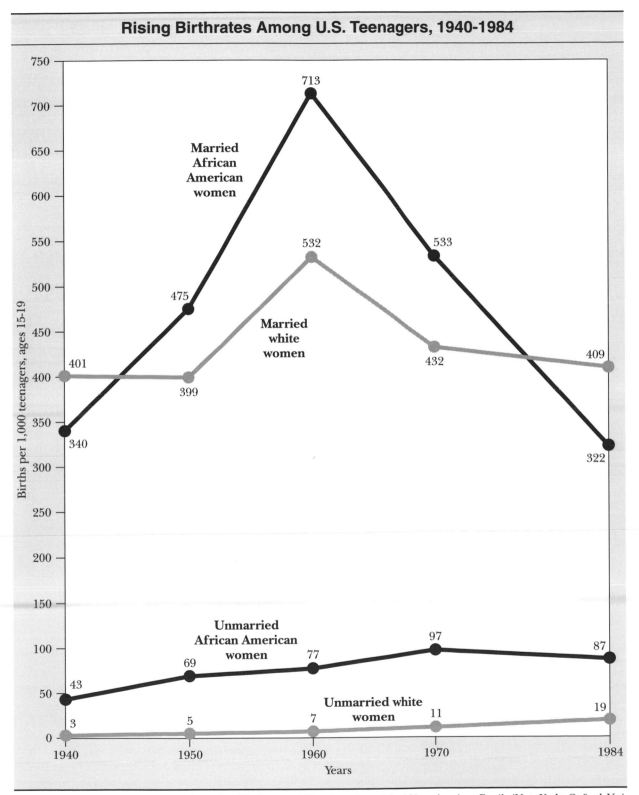

Rising Birthrates Among U.S. Teenagers, 1940-1984

Births per 1,000 teenagers, ages 15-19

Married African American women

713

533

475

Married white women

532

432

401

399

409

340

322

Unmarried African American women

43

69

77

97

87

Unmarried white women

3

5

7

11

19

Years

1940 1950 1960 1970 1984

Source: Donna L. Franklin, *Ensuring Inequality: The Structural Transformation of the African-American Family* (New York: Oxford University Press, 1997)

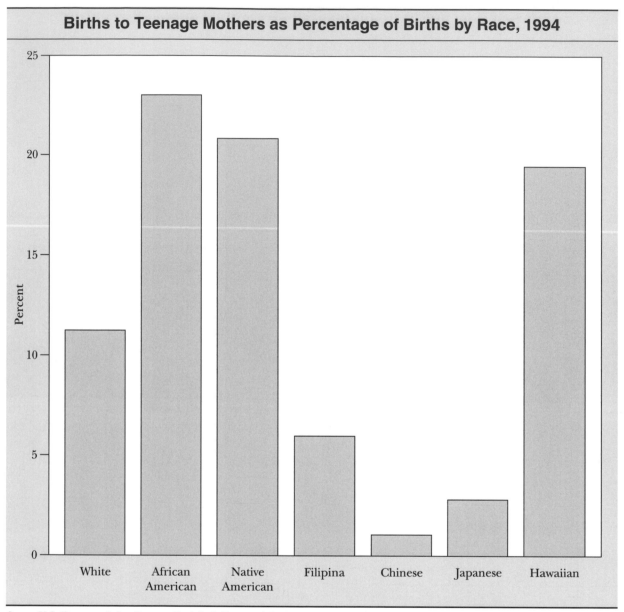

Births to Teenage Mothers as Percentage of Births by Race, 1994

Source: U.S. Bureau of the Census, *Statistical Abstract of the United States: 1997.* Washington, D.C.: GPO, 1997.

decline. The average age at which boys first have sexual intercourse is sixteen and the average age for girls is seventeen, equivalent to the figures in most northern European countries. Some of the decline in the abortion rate among American teenagers can be attributed to comprehensive youth development programs that encourage abstinence, the use of contraception, and consciousness about the dangers of sexually transmitted diseases.

Unwed Teen Mothers. Another change in family life in the United States is the growing number of out-of-wedlock births to teenagers. By the age of twenty about one-fifth of teenage girls are expected to have at least one baby. The number of unmarried teenagers giving birth has been increasing for more than a decade in all age groups. By the late 1980's, 67 percent of all births to teenagers were to unmarried girls, compared to 30 percent in 1970. In absolute numbers, more babies were born to teen mothers in the early 1970's than in the early 1980's. The difference, however, is that raising children in the late 1990's may be more challenging than it was in the 1970's because of changing economic and societal conditions .

In 1960 eighty-nine of every one thousand fifteen- to nineteen-year-old girls gave birth, while in 1994 this figure was only fifty-nine of every one thousand. However, in 1960 five out of six such girls were married, while in 1994 only one in four was married. By the late 1980's, 67 percent of all births to teenagers were to unmarried girls, compared to 30 percent in 1970. The proportion of out-of-wedlock births has continued to grow relative to the number of teen births. The incidence among all age groups in the Untied States was up from 14.2 percent in 1975 to 32.6 percent in 1994. This growing trend is mirrored in Canada, Europe, and other parts of the developed world. Nevertheless, relatively few children are born to unwed adolescent women in Canada as compared to the United States. Of all out-of-wedlock births in Canada, only 20 percent were to women under twenty years of age while 60 percent were to women between twenty and thirty years of age.

Outlook for Teen Mothers. Teenagers from low-income families and those with limited school success are far more likely to get pregnant than those who are more successful in school, come from more affluent families, and have goals and aspirations. Those in the latter category are more likely to have abortions if they do get pregnant. Only half of the teenagers who become parents before the age of eighteen graduate from high school. Teenage mothers are not likely to finish high school and because of this are not likely to fare well in the job market. Teen mothers who live with their parents are more likely to finish high school than those who do not. Adolescent parents have to struggle to provide the economic and human resources that lead to successful child rearing.

With welfare reform, the focus on teen mothers remains of keen interest to society due in part to obstacles associated with premature parenting. Especially among young African American mothers, the link between poverty and poor academic skills is closely tied to adolescent parenting. An unmarried mother who drops out of high school averages ten years on welfare. About half of teenagers who become parents before the age of eighteen

graduate from high school and remain on welfare for an average of ten years.

More than half of families receiving Aid to Families with Dependent Children (AFDC) have been headed by women who had their first child as teenagers. The costs of supporting teen mothers are enormous for parents, their children, and society. A 1996 report, *Kids Having Kids: A Robin Hood Foundation Special Report on the Costs of Adolescent Childbearing*, pegged the public costs of adolescent childbearing at $6.9 billion, which included costs associated with increased medical care, lost tax revenues, additional foster care, welfare payments, food stamps, and corrections. Overall, the costs of teen parenting are estimated at between $13 billion and $19 billion. Efforts to reduce poverty and increase basic academic skills would help reduce these costs.

Given the rate of out-of-wedlock births and adolescents' reliance on welfare, it is tempting to single them out for criticism. However, such criticism may be misdirected. In 1992 unmarried teenagers accounted for 30 percent of out-of-wedlock births, 13 percent of which were among girls under the age of eighteen, while women in their twenties accounted for 54 percent of out-of-wedlock births. Whereas 73 percent of unmarried teenage mothers have gone on welfare within five years of giving birth, 66 percent of unmarried mothers in their early twenties go on welfare.

Children of Teen Mothers. Of the 50 percent of teenagers who give birth, 95 percent of them are expected to keep and raise their children. Children born to unmarried teenage high-school dropouts are ten times as likely to live in poverty when they are eight to twelve years old as those born to mothers who are not unmarried teenage high-school dropouts. About 20 percent of all children live in poor families, while one-half of children born to parents under twenty-five years of age are poor.

The prospects for children of teen mothers tend to be poorer primarily because of poverty. In the short term, while physically able to bear children, teenagers are more at risk of bearing premature babies and those with low birth weight. About one in ten have low birth weight babies, due in part to little or no prenatal care. In addition, children born to teenage mothers are more likely to have poor health, to grow up in father-absent and less supportive households, to suffer from child abuse and neglect, to become runaways, to become teenager parents themselves, to perform poorly academically, to spend time in foster care, and to be less productive in the marketplace.

Effects of Family Life Programs. Since the 1960's family life programs have yielded positive results by increasing low-income families' knowledge of child development and interaction skills. As a result of positive programs, teen parents have increased the likelihood that they will return to school and obtain significantly more education and that their children will progress more positively than children of parents who do not participate in such programs. Teen mothers who did not attend parenting classes are more dependent, more isolated, less interested in activities, more stressed because of child rearing, and more em-

bued with unrealistic expectations of their children than teen mothers who attend such classes. In addition, the Children's Defense Fund has indicated that family-life education may have begun to make a positive change in adolescents' sexual behavior.

Strong agreement exists that children's emotional and cognitive development are enhanced by parents who are actively involved, nurturing, and verbally responsive. While teen parents express empathy and concern for their children, they often lack life experience and knowledge of child development. Because of this they may have inappropriately high expectations of their children. Emotionally, they may not be equipped for the demands of parenting. In comparing adolescent mothers to older parents since the 1980's, it was concluded that teen mothers were less knowl-

When teenagers have children, both their own future prospects and those of their children are likely to be limited. (Hazel Hankin)

Some high schools have worked to discourage pregnant teenagers from dropping out by offering them classes on childbirth and infant care. (AP/Wide World Photos)

edgeable and less aware of what are considered to be normal developmental milestones for infants and children; less forthcoming with quality vocalizations; less sensitive to, aware of, and responsive to their children's needs; less inclined to engage in spontaneous and quality play with their children; less likely to spend time looking at their babies; more ambivalent about being mothers; and more inclined to use physical punishment.

By the mid-1980's evidence surfaced that broad conclusions about teen parenting focusing on age

are complicated by factors such as economic resources and education. Thus, mothers' ages may have less impact on children's development than poor socioeconomic status; poor, little, or no prenatal care; poor nutrition; marital instability; and lack of support systems.

The National Campaign to Prevent Teenage Pregnancy, a nonpartisan, nonprofit, privately supported effort, began in 1996 as an outgrowth of a series of White House meetings to address the issue of teenage pregnancy. The stated goal of this

Many communities try to combat teenage pregnancy through public campaigns. (James L. Shaffer)

campaign was to enlist the media and state and community efforts in order to reduce teenage pregnancy by one-third by the year 2005 and to spread the word about prevention programs that work. The campaign has studied the possible causes of teenage pregnancy, such as reduced social stigma about teenage pregnancy and out-of-wedlock motherhood; the absence of paternal responsibility; the lack of the clear, forceful message that parenthood is for adults only; and the glorification of sex by the mass media.

—Mary Beth Mann

BIBLIOGRAPHY

Bode, Janet. *Kids Still Having Kids: People Talk About Teen Pregnancy*. New York: Franklin Watts, 1992. Collection of narratives by adolescents who confronted unplanned pregnancies.

Children's Defense Fund. *The State of America's Children Yearbook 1997*. Washington, D.C.: Author, 1997. Facts and figures on American families and the state of children in the United States.

Harris, Kathleen Mullan. *Teen Mothers and the Revolving Welfare Door*. Philadelphia: Temple University Press, 1997. Unique study of African American women in Baltimore who spent up to twenty years on welfare after becoming mothers as teenagers.

Horowitz, Ruth. *Teen Mothers: Citizens or Dependents?* Chicago: University of Chicago Press, 1995. Chronicle of a year-long social-services program for teen mothers that provided education so that teen mothers could obtain their general equivalency diplomas (GEDs) and receive job-readiness training.

Lindsay, Jeanne Warren. *School-Age Parents: The Challenge of Three-Generation Living*. Buena Park, Calif.: Morning Glory Press, 1990. Drawing on years of working with teen parents and extensive interviews with their relatives, Lindsay describes the myriad problems associated with unplanned teenage pregnancy.

_____. *Teen Parenting*. Buena Park, Calif.: Morning Glory Press. 1982. Guide designed for teen parents that provides insights into the lives of the teen mothers with whom the author has worked.

Musick, Judith S. *Young, Poor, and Pregnant: The Psychology of Teenage Motherhood*. New Haven: Yale University Press, 1993. Looks at the psychology of adolescent motherhood, describing teenage childbearing in relationship to impoverished girls who desire or are able to do things differently.

Sander, Joelle. *Before Their Time: Four Generations of Teenage Mothers*. New York: Harcourt Brace Jovanovich, 1991. Accessible, in-depth look at teenage parenthood based on interviews with four generations of mothers in one family.

See also Child rearing; Children born out of wedlock; Children's Defense Fund (CDF); Family life education; Infanticide; Poverty; Pregnancy; Pregnancy Discrimination Act; Puberty and adolescence; Unwed fathers; Welfare.

Television depictions of families

RELEVANT ISSUES: Art and the media; Children and child development; Parenting and family relationships

SIGNIFICANCE: Although television's evolving definitions of family may not reflect reality, research has indicated that television itself influences how real-life families view themselves and that it impacts on family interaction patterns

From the beginning of regular network television broadcasting in 1946, family life has been a popular topic for television situation comedies and, to a lesser extent, dramatic series. Most early programs reflected traditional family values. Within the context of a rapidly evolving postwar society, however, it was not long before these values, and even the definition of what constitutes a family, began to change dramatically. Television's power not only to reflect family life, but also to influence it, quickly became apparent. Like other performing arts, television often focuses on unusual situations in an attempt to create interesting plot lines. However, television's pictures and sound provide a level of realism unlike other media. As a result, many viewers believe that families depicted on television represent "normal" or "average" households. Television families have, in many ways, become role models for many real-life families.

The Traditional Family. Television's depiction of the family has changed significantly since the medium's early days. With the exception of a handful of daytime soap operas, relatively few pro-

A top-rated show through the 1950's, I Love Lucy *found much of its humor in the lengths to which husband and wife tried to manipulate each other.* (Arkent Archive)

grams produced during the 1950's and early 1960's made any attempt to dramatize real-life family issues. Family life was more frequently depicted in situation comedies such as *The Adventures of Ozzie and Harriet* (1952-1966), *The Danny Thomas Show* (1953-1971), *The Donna Reed Show* (1958-1966), *Leave It to Beaver* (1957-1963), and *Father Knows Best* (1954-1963). Rather than reflecting real life, these programs made a point of idealizing the family and acted as social role models for families to emulate.

Sitcoms during the 1950's typically depicted a stable nuclear family with the father as the head of the household. Male characters were portrayed as strong and competent, and women were warm and supportive. Children were generally loving and obedient, facing relatively benign issues that taught young viewers moral virtues such as honesty and integrity.

While such shows were quite popular, a handful of comedies took family conflicts to a higher level. *I Love Lucy* (1951-1961), for example, made light of the frequent conflicts between its lead characters, Lucy Ricardo and her husband Ricky. These conflicts often centered around Lucy's efforts to participate in her husband's show business career or to establish a career of her own. Her efforts usually met with disaster, tacitly reinforcing prevailing notions that a woman's proper place was in the home.

During this period, television was rapidly becoming a surrogate family to its viewers. Among the major events signaling the integration of television families into real life was the excitement surrounding the birth of the Ricardos' son Little Ricky on *I Love Lucy* in 1953. It was, in essence, a national family event.

Although most television shows of the 1950's and early 1960's depicted relatively placid households, a handful of shows implied that there was a darker side to family life. The situation comedy *The Honeymooners* (1955-1971), for example, made the husband's warnings to his wife, such as "To the moon, Alice!" and "One of these days, Alice . . . Pow! Right in the kisser!" staples of American idioms. Even the male characters on *I Love Lucy* occasionally clenched their fists in anger, implying their desire to strike their wives.

Modern Traditional Families. The late 1960's and the 1970's signaled a new era in how television

depicted family life. Most television families continued to appear in situation comedies, but the conservative television households of the 1950's and early 1960's were rapidly being replaced by more trendy families, geared specifically toward younger adult viewers. Although television families were still portrayed as basically clean-cut, it was wholesomeness with an edge. Shows such as *Bewitched* (1964-1972), *The Dick Van Dyke Show* (1961-1966), and even cartoons such as *The Flintstones* (1960-1966)—originally targeting adult viewers—continued to portray traditional nuclear families. However, settings were often more fashionable and prosperous. In addition, women were much more likely to be depicted as intelligent and competent. Couples were often portrayed as a team, and in some cases, the women were clearly superior to the men. A recurrent theme in such programs, however, was that while men typically used logic (sometimes flawed) to resolve problems, women relied more on their feminine wiles and intuition.

The Brady Bunch (1969-1974) was one of a tiny number of programs ever to depict a blended family unit. However, it rarely addressed the serious challenges faced by nearly half of all American households—merging two families into one. Producer Norman Lear's situation comedy, *All in the Family* (1971-1983), broke new ground in a different area. Far from the syrupy-sweet families of earlier eras, this controversial "realty-based" show was often fraught with marital and racial conflicts, as well as clashes between young and old, conservatism and liberalism, and the roles of the sexes. A spin-off, *The Jeffersons* (1975-1985), tackled similar issues from an African American perspective. Both series combined criticism of and sympathy for the dominant male characters, reluctant to accept society's changing definition of family. The enduring popularity of these programs indicated that they struck a chord of reality among viewers.

The 1970's also saw a significant number of viewers apparently longing for the perceived simplicity and wholesomeness of earlier eras. *The Waltons* (1972-1981), *Little House on the Prairie* (1974-1983), and *Happy Days* (1974-1984) tapped into viewers' nostalgic notions of family life as warm and supportive. They also answered growing government complaints about television violence. These programs not only complied with the "family viewing hour" concept enacted in 1975, but were also among the top-rated shows of the decade. This swing back toward more conservative depictions of the family continued into the early 1980's. *Family* (1976-1980), *The Cosby Show* (1984-1992), *Family Ties* (1982-1989), and *Eight Is Enough* (1977-1981), for example, all depicted wise, understanding parents, whose children rarely faced serious issues such as drugs, sex, and violence.

The late 1980's saw a backlash to this trend. *Roseanne* (1988-1997), billed as a "reality-based" comedy, depicted a working-class family that bickered constantly and exchanged a steady barrage of stinging wit. The show not only addressed adult issues such as adultery, homosexuality, and workplace discrimination, it also tackled teenage sex, pregnancy, drug use, and other issues faced by young viewers. New networks began to carve niches for themselves by offering even more cynical portraits of family life. Shows such as *Married . . . with Children* (1987-1997) and *The Simpsons* (1989-   ) made light of family conflict. Fathers were frequently buffoons, mothers were nagging, and children possessed the street smarts to outwit nearly any adult. This trend continued throughout the 1990's. To some extent it was followed by the major networks—the National Broadcasting Company, American Broadcasting Company, and Columbia Broadcasting System. However, these networks smoothed some of the hard edges and put a wholesome spin on the genre. Although programs such as *Home Improvement* (1991-   ) followed a format similar to that of their more cynical cousins, conflicts were softened by the depiction of loving and tolerant family members.

The 1990's also saw the emergence of a relatively new genre, the religious-based family program. Dramas such as *Promised Land* (1996-   ) and *7th Heaven* (1996-   ) were clearly designed to appeal to conservative viewers alienated by "reality-based" television fare. Although the religious aspects of these programs were often ambiguous and not central to their plots, the format allowed program creators to communicate moral values rarely depicted on television since the 1960's.

Single-Parent Families. Perhaps because of their perceived ability to generate interesting story lines, single-parent families have often been overrepresented on television. Nearly half of all family-based situation comedies featured single parents.

However, throughout the 1950's, 1960's, and early 1970's, single parents were almost always depicted as widowed, as divorce conflicted with the strong family-values orientation of television during those years.

Male single parents on television were more prevalent than their female counterparts by a wide margin, contradicting the reality that female single parents outnumber males almost nine-to-one. *The Lucy Show* (1962-1974), a spin-off of *I Love Lucy*, was one of the few early programs to feature a female single parent as the lead character. Although versions of this show ran successfully for almost twelve years, only a handful of other programs attempted to depict single mothers.

Hit shows that focused on single-parent households such as *My Three Sons* (1960-1972), *Bachelor Father* (1957-1962), *My Little Margie* (1952-1955), and *The Andy Griffith Show* (1960-1968) usually portrayed middle- or upper-class single fathers. Nearly all of these programs included a surrogate mother figure—usually a housekeeper or governess. This reflected the prevailing notion that men could not be effective parents alone and that child care and homemaking were ultimately the purview of women.

Single parenthood remained a hot topic in the late 1960's and 1970's. Male single parents continued to be a strong presence on network television with hits such as *The Courtship of Eddie's Father* (1969-1972) and *Family Affair* (1966-1971), but women were gaining ground. *The Partridge Family* (1970-1974), *Alice* (1976-1985), and *Julia* (1968-1971), which depicted an African American female single parent, began to validate the notion that female single parents were a social reality. The hit series *One Day at a Time* (1975-1984) went a step further, acknowledging divorce as a reason for single parenthood.

Although television creators began to take a more balanced approach to depicting single parents during the 1980's and 1990's, the male single father remained a strong presence in programs such as *Benson* (1979-1986), *My Two Dads* (1987-1990), *Full House* (1987-1995), and *The Nanny* (1993-   ). Other programs, such as *Cybill* (1995-1998), reflected a trend toward role reversal between single parents and their children. Single parenthood was often portrayed as a symptom of mid-life crisis, and such irresponsible parents re-

Leave It to Beaver *idealized the relationship between Wally Cleaver (right) and his brother, known as the "Beaver."* (Arkent Archive)

quired the supervision of their precocious offspring.

Extended Families. Television reflected the postwar decline in the importance of extended families with a vengeance. Nearly all comedies that featured parents of adult children cast these characters as meddling and intrusive, and most extended family households were depicted as extreme circumstances. Such families usually fell into three categories: rural and unsophisticated (*The Real McCoys*, 1957-1963; *The Beverly Hillbillies*, 1962-1971; and *The Dukes of Hazzard*, 1979-1985), very wealthy (*Bonanza*, 1959-1973; *The Big Valley* (1965-1969) *Dallas*, 1978-1994; and *Dynasty*, 1981-1989, or very strange (*The Addams Family*, 1964-1966 and *The Munsters*, 1964-1966).

One program that successfully broke that mold was *Frasier* (1993-   ), a comedy depicting two snobbish brothers who are both psychiatrists. One, Frasier, hosts a call-in radio show, the other runs his own practice; both are divorced and hopelessly neurotic. Their father, a retired police officer, lives with Frasier and ironically, although less educated, typically uses his street smarts to help his upper-crust sons resolve their problems.

A New Definition of Family. A popular phenomenon of late 1960's, 1970's, and early 1980's television was the appearance of couples without children. *Green Acres* (1965-1971), *The Bob Newhart Show* (1972-1978), *Hart to Hart* (1979-1984), and early episodes of *Mad About You* (1992-   ), for example, validated the notion that the modern family did not require children.

The 1980's and 1990's also saw the emergence of surrogate families. Within this genre of situation comedy, characters shared a household or spent significant time together, acting as a family unit. The actual families of these characters, if shown at all, were generally portrayed as nuisances. A precursor to this trend was the hit sitcom *Three's Company* (1977-1984), which depicted two attractive young women who shared an apartment with a man without engaging in a sexual relationship.

Later programs such as *Cheers* (1982-1993), *Seinfeld* (1990-1998), and *Friends* (1994-   ) were particularly popular among baby boomers and Generation X viewers. This may reflect viewers' own unstable family lives and their need to seek family-like relationships outside the traditional family unit.

Conclusion. Although television depicts a wide variety of family situations, it is remarkably consistent in the way it views specific family traits and habits. For example, television families themselves rarely watch television. Those who do are generally depicted as unsophisticated or dysfunctional.

With relatively few exceptions, most families portrayed on television are white upper-middle-class or better. This may, in part, account for the popularity of those few shows such as *Roseanne* and *Married . . . with Children* that depict family life in lower socioeconomic brackets. Viewers in similar circumstances may feel they can better relate to the characters depicted.

Television generally portrays fathers in one of two ways: workaholics who are rarely home or men with ambiguous careers that allow almost unlimited free time. Although such depictions are probably designed more to create entertaining situations than to serve as social statements, such portrayals can skew viewers' perceptions of real-life fathers.

Early television series often depicted children as innocent and dependent on their parents' wisdom. Since the 1970's, however, television children have become far more precocious and independent. Modern television children are almost invariably smarter than adults. This trend reflects the shift in television's target audience from middle-age adults during the 1950's and 1960's to children, adolescents, and young adults in later decades. At the same time, television exposes young viewers to an increasing amount of adult information, resulting in the development of what media scholar Neil Postman calls the "adult-child."

Television seems to ignore studies indicating that children who are raised in single-parent households are more troubled than those raised in two-parent families. For example, studies have found that children from single-parent families are arrested more often, have more disciplinary problems in school, have a higher rate of tobacco use, and are more likely to run away than children who live with both parents. Nonetheless, television usually portrays single-parent households in a positive or value-neutral light, and children in these television families are no more likely to be troubled than those depicted in two-parent families.

Decreased real-life family interaction and a growing reliance on television as a companion to children and adults alike creates an environment in which television acts as a surrogate family to many viewers. Media expert Christine Nystrom notes that as real-life family interaction declines, television's lessons become increasingly more powerful. This blurring of reality remains at the center of controversies surrounding how societal changes influence television's depiction of the family and how television changes real-life family structures and interaction.   *—Cheryl Pawlowski*

BIBLIOGRAPHY

Brooks, Tim, and Earle Marsh. *The Complete Directory to Prime Time Network TV Shows, 1946-Present.* 4th ed. New York: Ballantine Books, 1988. A compendium of television shows with brief descriptions and comments on their social impact.

Lichter, S. Robert, Linda S. Lichter, and Stanley Rothman. *Prime Time.* Washington, D.C.: Regnery Publishing, 1994. An analysis of how television portrays American culture.

Medved, Michael. *Hollywood vs. America.* New York: HarperCollins, 1992. Medved contends that Hollywood exacerbates social problems and assaults traditional family values.

Postman, Neil. *The Disappearance of Childhood.* New York: Delacorte Press, 1982. Examination of the evolution of the concept of childhood and how the media is erasing the line between childhood and adulthood.

Taylor, Ella. *Prime Time Families.* Berkeley: University of California Press, 1989. Examination of the postwar American family as it is affected by, and depicted on, television.

Winn, Marie. *The Plug-in Drug.* New York: Penguin Books, 1985. Analysis of the impact of the media on children's developing relationships to the real world.

See also Art and iconography; Computer recreation; Entertainment; Film depictions of families; Generation X; Literature and families; Television rating systems.

Television rating systems

RELEVANT ISSUES: Art and the media; Law; Violence

SIGNIFICANCE: Faced with a growing outcry opposing violence on television, television-industry executives and government officials in the United States and Canada have devised their own rating systems for television shows to alert parents to programs containing high levels of violence, sexual content, or rough language

Concern about sex and violence on television is almost as old as the medium itself. Free speech activists argue that any attempt to control television content violates the right to freedom of expression. Parents, politicians, and social scientists, however, say children are being exposed to too much violence, sex, and vulgar language on television, and that steps should be taken to protect children from such programming.

Violence on Television. About five violent acts are committed during an average hour of prime-time evening television programming, and an average of between twenty and twenty-five violent acts occurs each hour on Saturday morning children's programs. By the time children who watch the typical amount of television enter elementary school, they will have seen about twenty thousand murders and more than eighty thousand assaults.

Social scientists have found a link between children's behavior and their television watching habits. Scientists have discovered that children who watch large amounts of television violence may become less sensitive to the pain and suffering of others, may be more fearful of the world around them, and may be more likely to behave in aggressive or harmful ways toward others.

Although scientists are convinced that children can learn aggressive behavior from television, they are also sure that parents can limit some of these effects through careful choice of programs for their children. The implementation of a ratings system for television programming is one means by which the governments in the United States and Canada are trying to provide parents with the information they need to select appropriate programs for their children to watch.

In February of 1996, President Bill Clinton signed into law a massive telecommunication reform bill that contained a provision designed to give viewers the ability to block out television shows with unacceptable content. The 1996 Telecommunications Act requires manufacturers by 1998 to install a tiny computer chip (the V-chip) in all new television sets.

The V-chip (the "V" stands for violence), originally developed in Canada, allows owners to program their television sets to block out undesired programming. The V-chip is designed to be used in conjunction with a television rating system also required by the 1996 act.

The U.S. Television Rating System. The U.S. television rating system, developed by the broadcasting industry and implemented in January of 1997, resembles the well-known Motion Picture Association of America rating system (ratings of G, PG, PG-13, R, and NC-17) developed for the film industry. The U.S. television rating system has six broad rating categories. Children's programming would be labeled either TV-Y (for shows acceptable for all ages) or TV-7 (for shows with some violence or other material unsuitable for children under seven years of age). Other programs would be classified as TV-G (for all audiences), TV-PG (parental guidance suggested), TV-14 (not suitable for children under the age of fourteen), or TV-M (for mature audiences only).

The ratings are made by the producers and distributors of shows. After each television program is rated for its suitability for children, it is transmitted with a special electronic code designating the rating, using the same technology that makes closed captioning for the deaf possible. The V-chip receives these codes and can block programs with ratings unacceptable to the owner of the television set.

The ratings sometimes appear briefly on the television screen. Program ratings are also published in newspaper and other periodical television listings so parents can use them as a guide.

Reaction to Rating System. Child advocates and civil liberties groups have criticized the U.S. television rating system as being intrusive and ineffective. Opponents of the rating system argue that many children have their own television sets and videocassette recorders (VCRs) in their bedrooms. Parents are unlikely to replace their sets with the newer models containing the V-chip, making that technology ineffective.

Child advocates also object to giving the responsibility for rating shows to the same people who produce them. Critics also say the new rating system is not useful because it tells parents nothing about the content of the show. Instead of using broad categories to rate television programs, child advocates say parents should be informed about the actual amount of violence, sexual content, or profanity in each program and be allowed to decide what is appropriate for their children to see.

Some parents groups have urged lawmakers to revise the U.S. television rating system to include the addition of "V" for violence, "S" for sexual content, and "L" for coarse language. There also is support for a revised rating system that incorporates a sliding scale system that ranks programs on a violence intensity scale from one to six.

Canada and Television Violence. Canada also is concerned about the amount of violence and sex in U.S. television programming because Canada gets most of its television programming from the United States. The Canadian Radio-Television and Telecommunications Commission (CRTC), the national regulator for television, radio, and cable television, commissioned two key studies on television violence. Based on the results of the results of these studies, the CRTC concluded that there was a link—although not necessarily a direct one—between television violence and violence in society. There was widespread, national support for the CRTC's stand on

---

Revised TV Ratings, 1997

Y	Suitable for all children.
Y-7	May be unsuitable for children under 7.
TV-G	Suitable for all ages.
TV-PG	Parental guidance suggested.
TV-14	Parents cautioned in letting children under 14 watch.
TV-MA	Suitable for adults only.

New, additional codes:

V	Indicates violence.
S	Indicates sexual content.
L	Indicates offensive language.
D	Indicates language filled with sexual innuendo.
FV	Indicates "fantasy violence" in cartoon and other fantasy programs.

Source: Christian Science Monitor (June 27, 1997)

Television ratings have been designed to help parents select the programs their children are permitted to view. (James L. Shaffer)

television violence. In 1992, the CRTC established a long-term goal of making violence on television socially unacceptable. Canada previously had success with such programs regarding other social issues such as drinking and driving, pollution, and cigarette smoking.

In January of 1994, the Canadian Association of Broadcasters' (CAB) Voluntary Code Regarding Violence in Television Programming went into effect. The CAB code bans the broadcast of gratuitous violence and programs that promote or glamorize violence. The code also requires pay

television services to broadcast viewer advisories and program ratings for all programming that is not suitable for children. The CRTC expects broadcasters to comply with the CAB code as a condition for license renewal or the granting of new licenses. In addition to this voluntary code, the Canadian government also has implemented its own television rating system.

The Canadian Television Rating System. Given the high percentage of U.S. programming distributed in Canada, the Canadian and American governments have worked closely together to develop a uniform television rating system. The classification system approved by the CRTC in June of 1997 incorporates broad categories similar to the categories used by the U.S. television rating system. Canada's television rating system uses the following categories: children (programming for children under age eight), children more than eight years of age (programming for children between the ages of eight and twelve), family (programming intended for the whole family), parental advisory (programming not suitable for children under the age of eight and inappropriate for unsupervised viewing by children between eight and thirteen), more than fourteen years of age (programming with themes or content not suitable for viewers under the age of fourteen), and adults (programming intended for viewers age eighteen and older).

Under this rating system, implemented in September of 1997, Canadian television programs contain on-screen ratings to help identify their content. An icon appears during children's programming, drama, "reality shows," and feature films that helps parents make informed choices as to appropriate viewing for their children.

Canada's television rating system also incorporates the use of the V-chip, and Canadian broadcast distributors are required to make V-chip-equipped television sets available to consumers. Canada's cable industry is responsible for ensuring that all U.S. television programming distributed in Canada is encoded with a V-chip-based rating. English-language pay and pay-per-view services use the new Canadian classification system, and French-language programming services in Canada use the rating system of Quebec's Regie du Cinema.

International Cooperation. The Canadian Radio-Television and Telecommunications Commission has made protecting children from sexual and violent television content a permanent priority of Canada's broadcasting system. The Canadian government, however, has realized that it cannot achieve this goal alone. The entertainment and information marketplace is a global one and will become even more so. This is particularly true for Canada because most of its television programs, films, and videos are imported. To protect children from excessive amounts of violence and sex on television, Canada encourages countries such as the United States, France, Germany, and Sweden to work together to develop an international classification system to regulate violence and sexual content on television. —*Eddith A. Dashiell*

BIBLIOGRAPHY

Berry, Gordon L., and Joy K. Asamen. *Children and Television: Images in a Changing Sociocultural World.* Newbury Park, Calif.: Sage Publications, 1993.

Devore, Cynthia Dilaura. *Kids and Media Influence.* Edina, Minn.: Abdo and Daughters, 1994.

Liebert, Robert, and Joyce Sprafkin. *The Early Window: Effects of Television on Children and Youth.* New York: Pergamon Press, 1988.

Minow, Newton, and Craig L. LaMay. *Abandoned in the Wasteland: Children, Television, and the First Amendment.* New York: Hill & Wang, 1995.

Palmer, Edward L. *Television and America's Children: A Crisis of Neglect.* New York: Oxford University Press, 1988.

See also Film ratings; Television depictions of families.

Test-tube babies

RELEVANT ISSUES: Health and medicine; Parenting and family relationships

SIGNIFICANCE: Test-tube babies are children born through an advanced procedure in reproductive technology called in vitro fertilization-embryo transfer

The term "test-tube baby" is unfortunate because test tubes are not used to conceive babies and because the term conjures up an almost comic image of an infant in a glass tube. In the procedure that may result in test-tube babies, eggs are removed from a woman's ovary with a small needle and combined with a man's sperm in a petri dish—not a test tube—to achieve fertilization. Approximately forty-eight to seventy-two hours later, three or four embryos are transferred to the woman's uterus through the cervix. The hope is that an embryo will attach to the lining of the uterine wall and a normal pregnancy will occur.

The medical profession has termed this complicated procedure in vitro fertilization-embryo transfer. IVF-ET is a form of assisted reproductive technology or ART, a term that can be applied to any advanced therapy directed toward improving an infertile couple's chances for conception.

History. Until IVF-ET was performed successfully in England in 1978, infertility most often was treated by giving a woman fertility drugs that caused multiple eggs to be released from the ovaries each month. More eggs meant a better chance for conception during sexual intercourse, but this would not help every type of infertility.

IVF-ET was the first treatment in which eggs were removed from a female's body by a physician and combined with a male's sperm in the laboratory, thus bypassing the fallopian tubes. Louise Brown, the first in vitro baby, was born to a mother whose tubes were irreparably closed, thus making conception impossible. Her birth gave hope to infertile individuals who could not conceive because of damaged or diseased fallopian tubes. Initially, these were the couples who benefited from IVF-ET, because the eggs bypass the tubes.

After medical experts learned how to inject sperm directly into eggs, IVF-ET also helped individuals whose infertility was caused by insufficient or inadequate sperm. A third group of people who have benefited from IVF are those whose infertility is unexplained. Although other kinds of assisted reproductive technology now exist, IVF-ET is the most common.

Thousands of infertile couples have hoped that they might conceive a child through IVF-ET. Not only does a successful in vitro attempt mean that these couples can raise biological children, but it also means that these couples will have some control over the health of the child in utero, something that is not possible in adoption, the other choice available to infertile people who desire a child.

Stresses. Most people who go through IVF-ET have unsuccessfully undergone various procedures and tests designed to diagnose and cure their infertility. For most, IVF-ET is their last chance for a biological child, and for most, IVF-ET is as emotionally demanding as the treatments they already have been through.

As with any infertility treatment, no guarantee exists that the procedure will work and that a child will be born. Most clinics give couples in which the woman is below thirty-five years of age approximately a 20 percent chance of success with each in vitro attempt. In 1993, 31,900 cycles were at-

In Vitro Fertilization

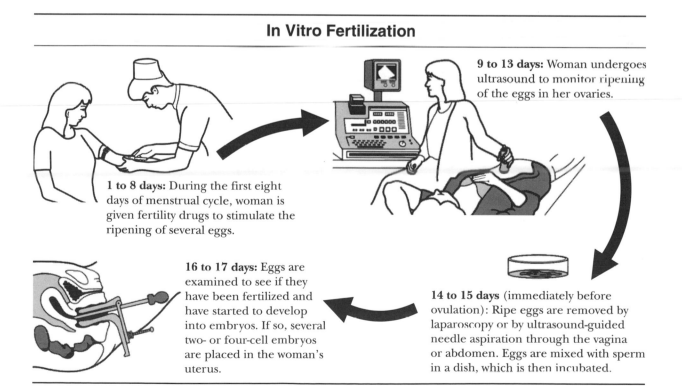

1 to 8 days: During the first eight days of menstrual cycle, woman is given fertility drugs to stimulate the ripening of several eggs.

9 to 13 days: Woman undergoes ultrasound to monitor ripening of the eggs in her ovaries.

14 to 15 days (immediately before ovulation): Ripe eggs are removed by laparoscopy or by ultrasound-guided needle aspiration through the vagina or abdomen. Eggs are mixed with sperm in a dish, which is then incubated.

16 to 17 days: Eggs are examined to see if they have been fertilized and have started to develop into embryos. If so, several two- or four-cell embryos are placed in the woman's uterus.

tempted in the United States and Canada, with approximately 6,350 of these leading to live births. After a failed attempt, a couple may try IVF again. Many couples have tried the procedure ten times or more without success.

The procedure itself is physically demanding. IVF-ET involves a regimented protocol lasting approximately three weeks. On most days during this period, the woman receives one to three injections a day. Side effects experienced from the injections include soreness at the injection site, abdominal bloating, and pelvic discomfort. Egg retrieval, which precedes the fertilization attempt by three days, is the most painful part of the procedure. Although side effects from the retrieval can be serious, they are rare.

Uncertain Results. Just as there is no guarantee that the procedure will result in conception, there is no guarantee that only one child will be born if conception occurs. Because infertility experts have found that pregnancy rates are higher if more than one embryo is placed in a woman's uterus, physicians usually transfer three or four normally developing embryos to the patient with each in vitro attempt. In fact, if a couple produces fewer than three viable embryos, the procedure is often canceled.

Because three or four embryos are placed in the woman's uterus, the chances for multiple births increase to disturbingly high levels: In vitro patients have as much as a 34 percent chance of multiple births, a phenomenon that could put a strain on family life. In addition, couples face a stressful decision if multiple births seem possible. Most clinics provide an elective procedure known as "selective reduction," eliminating one or more of the fetuses or "gestational sacs" through a procedure that does not damage the remaining fetuses in the uterus.

Because IVF-ET is a relatively new procedure, its long-term effects on both mothers and children are unknown. The large doses of drugs such as Lupron, progesterone, Pergonal, and Metrodin that a woman takes during the procedure may produce health risks, especially for women who try the procedure repeatedly. No immediate risks for the child have been associated with this procedure.

Many families also find IVF-ET financially burdensome. The cost of fertility drugs, ultrasound monitoring, minor surgery to harvest follicles, laboratory fees, physicians' fees, and other miscellaneous expenses total approximately $10,000 for each in vitro attempt. Many people must travel long distances to clinics that perform IVF-ET, thus incurring other expenses. Most insurance companies do not pay many of the expenses incurred when a couple goes through this procedure, and most states do not make insurance payment for IVF-ET mandatory. The vast majority of Americans who undergo this procedure must, therefore, pay the costs themselves. In Canada and many European countries, the financial burden is lessened because national health insurance covers IVF-ET.

Social Issues Many people consider this scientific way of bringing human life into the world morally wrong. This view derives in part from the procedure itself and in part from practices related to the procedure, such as cryopreservation (the freezing of embryos for future use). Cryopreservation raises the possibility of sale or destruction of the embryos if the couple does not want to undergo further procedures, either because their goal has been achieved or they have grown weary of the financial and emotional difficulties. In addition, selective reduction violates the moral beliefs of those who consider a fetus to be a human being.

Because of these controversies, some families bear an additional burden because they feel as if they must keep the in vitro fertilization a secret from society at large, friends, family members, and even from the child. Attempting in vitro fertilization is stressful in many ways, but many people are willing to live through it in the hope that their dream of having a biological child is achieved.

—*Cassandra Kircher*

BIBLIOGRAPHY

Brown, Lesley, and John Brown. *Our Miracle Called Louise: A Parents' Story.* New York: Padington Press, 1979.

Lasker, Judith. *In Search of Parenthood: Coping with Infertility and High Tech Conception.* Boston: Beacon Press, 1987.

Olson, Maleia, and Nancy J. Alexander. *In Vitro Fertilization and Embryo Transfer.* Portland: The Oregon Health Sciences University, 1986.

Sher, Geoffrey, et al. *From Infertility to In Vitro Fertilization: A Personal and Practical Guide to Making the Decision That Could Change Your Life.* New York: McGraw-Hill, 1989.

_____. *In Vitro Fertilization: The A.R.T. of Making Babies.* New York: Facts on File, 1995.

Tiltin, Nan, et al. *Making Miracles: In Vitro Fertilization.* Garden City, N.Y.: Doubleday, 1985.

Walters, William A. W., and Peter Singer. *Test-Tube Babies: A Guide to Moral Questions and Present Techniques and Future Possibilities.* Melbourne: Oxford University Press, 1982.

Wiscot, Arthur L., and David Meldrum. *A Guide to In Vitro Fertilization and Other Assisted Reproductive Methods.* New York: Pharos, 1990.

See also Childlessness; Fertility and infertility; Multiple births; Pregnancy; Reproductive technologies; Surrogate mothers.

Time-out

RELEVANT ISSUES: Children and child development; Parenting and family relationships

SIGNIFICANCE: Successful parenting requires that parents use discipline such as time-outs in guiding their children's development

There are two basic behavioral techniques to decrease undesirable behavior in children: positive punishment, such as spanking, and negative punishment, such as the removal of dessert or television watching. While both techniques can be effective, the greater potential for physical abuse associated with positive punishment has led many childrearing authorities to emphasize the use of negative punishment methods.

Time-out can be an effective disciplinary tool, particularly for parents of children from ages two to twelve. When children violate established family rules, such as hitting a sibling, they are sent to a selected location that is quiet, isolated, and distraction-free, such as a chair in the corner of a room. During time-out children are required to stay quietly in such a specified location for a certain amount of time—for example, one minute

---

Time-out Procedures

Childrearing authority Sylvia Rimm has outlined a series of tips for making time-outs work with young children:

- All family members should adhere to the same behavior rules as the children subjected to time-outs.

- One parent should briefly explain to a child that the consequence for unacceptable behavior will be that the child remains in his or her room for ten minutes.

- What constitutes unacceptable behavior should be explained to children, but only the worst behaviors need be enumerated.

- To keep children from opening the doors of their rooms during time-outs, lock the doors from the outside if necessary.

- Every time children behave in ways that have been designated unacceptable, parents should quietly take them to their rooms offering only one-sentence explanations.

- During time-outs parents should—without exception—ignore their children when they slam doors, lose their tempers, bang on walls, throw toys, scream, or talk.

- Clocks used to time time-outs should be set only when children are quiet and behaving properly.

- When the time-out ends after 10 minutes, parents should open the children's doors to let them leave their rooms without any further explanations, apologies, warnings, or discussions—and especially without any hugging

- When parents warn children they will be sent to their rooms they should always follow through.

Source: Family.com website (1998).

---

for each year of the children's age. The time begins when the children are quiet. After time-out from misbehavior, the children are allowed to resume normal activities.

—*Kathleen A. Chara and Paul J. Chara, Jr.*

See also Child rearing; Corporal punishment; Disciplining children; Parenting; Tough love.

Toilet training

RELEVANT ISSUES: Children and child development

SIGNIFICANCE: Toileting is a complex skill that children usually master within the first four years of life

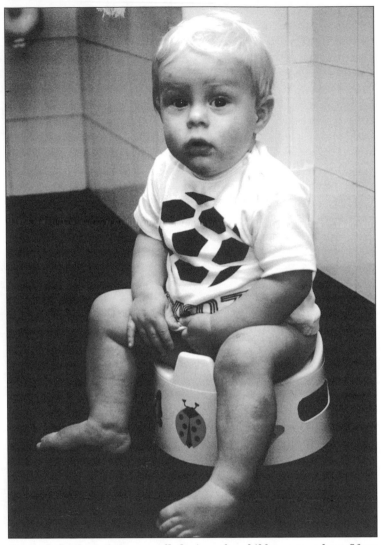

Successful toilet training usually begins after children are at least fifteen months old—almost twice the age of the child in this picture. (Arkent Archive)

Toileting may seem simple, but it is a complex skill. Children must learn to produce both urine and bowel movements in the toilet, stay dry when not on the toilet, clean themselves, dress and undress, initiate going to the toilet without being reminded, and stay dry while asleep. Most children are fully toilet trained—dry all day and night with complete independence in cleaning and dressing—by the age of four.

There has always been disagreement about when and how to toilet train children. Some methods of toilet training lead to more toileting problems later in childhood, and others are stressful or even painful for the child. Some children with developmental delays or physical disabilities need special training methods and supervision to use the toilet successfully.

Historical Debate over Toilet Training. The training methods of different cultures and times in history show tremendous variety. Children in many ancient and modern traditional cultures, usually in warm climates, do not wear diapers or restrictive clothing when they are infants. Parents simply clean up the mess where it happens to fall. Children accompany their parents everywhere and learn to use the toilet by imitation and encouragement from the parent. Children begin to wear trousers or other clothing after they have learned to use the toilet successfully, usually by the age of three or four.

In European history, toilet training recommendations have ranged from sitting the child on the toilet at three months to giving no training at all. Some have recommended punitive methods such as tying the child on the toilet, forcing food or drink, striking or shaming the child, or forcing the child to smell or touch the remains of an accident. Others recommended gentleness, patience, and indulgence of accidents.

Freudian Approaches. A major controversy about the effects of toilet training began in the early 1900's with Sigmund Freud. By talking to his adult patients with mental illness about their childhood experiences, Freud came to believe that toilet training could cause mental problems later in life. He theorized that children who were toilet trained early and punished for failure might develop an anal retentive personality, excessively concerned with dirt, neatness, and order, with little emotional expression. Children who were toilet trained too permissively or with too much physical contact during toileting were believed to develop anal expulsive personalities: messy, prone to tantrums and hysteria, and thoughtless of other people's needs.

Freud also believed that toilet training contributed to sexual development by providing the first occasion for boys to fear castration and girls to develop penis envy and feel inferior. Freud's theories shocked many people at the time, and parents began to worry about the permanent harm they could inflict on their children with the "wrong" toilet training. Opposed to Freud was the behaviorist approach, which held that toileting was simply a learned behavior and that, with the right training methods, children could learn to use the toilet at any age the parent chose.

Neither of these schools of thought had any evidence to support its position. Freudian ideas dominated popular advice on child care in the United States from the 1940's through the 1960's.

Later Approaches. During the 1960's, T. Berry Brazelton and other researchers studied the variety of actual toilet training practices around the world. They found that toilet training before the age of thirteen months, when children first gain voluntary control over the sphincters (muscles) that control urination and bowel movements, was not very effective and sometimes led to problems such as bed-wetting and encopresis (soiling outside the toilet). Children who were punished during toilet training often developed toileting problems and also sometimes had nightmares, tantrums, and other behavior problems later in childhood.

These researchers found no ill effects of starting toilet training at any time after thirteen months up through age three. Children who were not toilet trained by age four usually had developmental or physical disabilities.

Also during the 1960's and 1970's, Nathan Azrin and other behavioral researchers learned that young children could begin to use the toilet without the use of any punishment, shame, or scolding. In addition, they found that children and adults with disabilities who previously were thought to be "untrainable" could be toilet trained using positive methods. Many other researchers learned about methods of toilet training that worked for real families, as well as the most effective ways to deal with toileting problems.

Successful Toilet Training. By the early 1980's, most researchers concluded that there is no one best method of toilet training and that children cannot learn complete toileting independence overnight. All successful toilet training methods have three things in common: timing, consistency, and a positive approach.

Two kinds of timing seem to be important for toilet training. First, training should begin only when the child is ready, which the child may indicate by showing awareness of being wet or interest in watching parents and older children in the bathroom. Some children show these signs of readiness as early as fifteen months; others never do. Nearly all children can begin toilet training successfully by the age of twenty-four months even if they do not indicate readiness.

The second type of timing is in visiting the toilet. Children need the toilet after meals, every two or three hours between meals, and before bedtime or long car trips, just as adults do. Encouraging the child to sit on the toilet at these times for a few minutes each visit usually produces results.

Consistency in time and place and the parents' reaction to success and failure also are important. The more consistent the time of the child's meals and visits to the toilet are, the faster children will learn to use the toilet independently. There should be a child-sized potty in the bathroom. Training pants help children to recognize when they are wet more quickly than diapers do and should be worn every day once toilet training starts, although diapers can be used at night. Parents and caregivers should consistently be happy about success and calm about failure.

A positive approach includes small treats or special activities to celebrate successes, giving children encouragement and affection whether or not they succeed, and discussing toileting with the child in a calm and encouraging manner. There are picture books for toddlers that show children using the potty. These books can introduce discussions by parents with their children about toileting.

Toileting Problems. Children who have conditions that cause developmental delay such as Down syndrome and prenatal brain damage or those who have physical disabilities may have difficulty with toileting. Sometimes mild developmental delays or health problems are first discovered because of problems with toilet training. Children with these extra challenges usually need special toilet training methods and take more time to complete training. Special methods include using positive reinforcement, setting timers to remind children to use the bathroom, sensors in clothing or bedding that alert the child to wetness, biofeedback, medication, and surgery to tighten the urinary or anal sphincter or to reshape an incomplete bladder or colon. Even children with very severe disabilities usually learn some level of toileting skill, although many still need reminders and physical assistance for many years.

Children with normal development also can have toileting problems. These included enuresis (urinating outside the toilet), usually at night; fear of the toilet, urine, or feces; encopresis and hiding or playing with feces; and frequent tantrums and accidents. It is normal for children under the age of four to have any of these problems occasionally, stressful as they are for parents. Older children or those who have more frequent problems should visit a pediatrician to rule out physical causes. Toileting problems sometimes occur along with other behavior problems, and in these cases family therapy may be helpful.

Nighttime enuresis, or bed-wetting, is the most common toileting problem experienced by older children and adults. The cause of most bed-wetting is probably neurological and may be inherited; it is rarely caused by mental illness, as many once believed. Drug and behavioral treatments have proved effective in solving this common problem.

—*Kathleen M. Zanolli*

BIBLIOGRAPHY
Brazelton, T. Berry. *Toddlers and Parents*. New York: Delta, 1974.
Faull, Jane. *Mommy, I Have to Go Potty!* Seattle: Parenting Press, 1996.
Frankel, Alona. *Once Upon a Potty*. Hauppage, N.Y.: Barron's, 1979.
Schaefer, Charles. *Toilet Training Without Tears*. New York: Signet, 1989.

See also Behavior disorders; Brazelton, T. Berry; Child rearing; Childhood fears and anxieties; Disciplining children; Freudian psychology.

Tough love

RELEVANT ISSUES: Children and child development; Parenting and family relationships

SIGNIFICANCE: As a method of child rearing, tough love requires that parents not intervene to prevent their children from experiencing the unpleasant consequences of their actions and requires that children learn from painful mistakes

Tough love encompasses acts that are undertaken because recipients need them. Frequently, shielding recipients or avoiding encounters would be easier. Tough love allows persons to fail, hopefully under controlled conditions, and facilitates learning. The concept of tough love paralleled the rise in drug use in the late 1960's and 1970's and also roughly paralleled the rise in the number of single-parent families. Both of these social phenomena seem to be connected to a decrease in the amount of attention given to children and the increased likelihood that they will encounter undesirable influences during adolescence.

Parents and others who care for children have learned that young people need practice in making decisions. They have also realized that children may make poor choices with serious consequences. Tough love is applied when caregivers stop protecting children. Practioners of tough love believe that although the consequences of an action may be unpleasant, it is better to allow young people to make painful mistakes. Practitioners of tough love hope that adolescents and young adults will learn from their experiences and not repeat their mistakes if the consequences are drastic.

Tough love is one of several options usually available to persons and involves saying yes or no when the opposite response would be far more easily given. Whereas the clear parental instinct is to protect children, tough love requires restraint. Tough love means allowing children to fail in the expectation that learning will occur. This is necessary for normal development. Tough love is an ongoing process that taxes persons' abilities to love one another. It requires maturity on the part of givers and tests the bonds between givers and receivers. Watching young children ride bicycles without training wheels for the first time makes parents nervous. Sheltering children by holding them as they learn to ride their bicycles may seem the better alternative in the short run but it can inhibit normal development. Watching children cross the street alone for the first time is similarly

Helping a child ride a bicycle without training wheels for the first time can be a difficult task for a parent. (Dick Hemingway)

upsetting for parents, but preventing them from doing so inhibits independence.

In applying tough love it is necessary to control the environment so that the chances of injury are minimized. As children grow, this becomes more and more difficult to achieve. However, the importance of tough love increases with the age of recipients, as does the effort required to administer it.
— *L. Fleming Fallon, Jr.*

See also Child rearing; Child safety; Disciplining children; Family caregiving; Love; Parenting; Time-out.

Townsend movement

DATE: Launched in September, 1933

RELEVANT ISSUES: Aging; Economics and work; Sociology

SIGNIFICANCE: A movement to design an old-age pension plan, the Townsend movement attempted to end the Great Depression of the 1930's and bring about a general economic recovery

In response to his own desperate situation and the general collapse of the American economy during the Great Depression, Francis Everett Townsend (1867-1960) developed a plan that was intended to assist elderly Americans directly and to stimulate an economic recovery throughout the United States. In September, 1933, Townsend announced a pension plan that would eliminate the economic distress being experienced by senior citizens and provide the U.S. economy with an influx of capital. He proposed that all Americans age sixty and older who had been citizens for at least five years receive $200 monthly for the remainder of their lives on the condition that they spend it within thirty-five days of receiving it. To finance this twenty-billion-dollar pension scheme, a 2 percent sales tax on all transactions would be imposed. Townsend maintained that his plan would restore confidence in the American economy and family-based values.

Within ninety days of his announcement, Townsend's proposal was transformed into a major social movement. Local and regional Townsend clubs were established and *The Townsend National Weekly* began publishing in 1934. Although his plan was denounced by economists and officials in the administration of President Franklin D. Roosevelt, Townsend continued to attract support during 1935. Townsend entered into an anti-Roosevelt coalition with the Share Our Wealth Society, founded by Louisiana governor Huey P. Long, and the National Union for Social Justice of the reactionary, anti-Semitic priest Charles E. Coughlin. Their Union Party failed to achieve a credible level of support in the 1936 election. The movement collapsed with the gradual economic recovery of the late 1930's.   —*William T. Walker*

See also Aging and elderly care; Poverty; Social Security.

Tribes

Relevant issues: Economics and work; Kinship and genealogy

Significance: Named linguistic groupings, tribes are complex, usually mobile, warlike, territorially expansionistic, pastoral-based peoples that control and fulfill social, economic, and political functions for multiple lineages and clans

The term "tribe" is derived from the Latin *tribus,* referring to political groups that had numerous dispersed communities in which sodalities—nonkin corporate groups—interacted socioeconomically, politically, and legally with one another. Task-oriented sodalities were an effective way of integrating men of comparable age, regardless of exogamous lineage, clan, or moiety affiliation.

Anthropologists first regarded tribes as homogeneous societies that exhibited social institutions but lacked complex political structure. However, tribes were later classified as political and legal entities that based their laws on status rather than on contractual rights. The term "tribe" generally applied to small-scale, sociopolitical, autonomous, and egalitarian groups that coalesced primarily for offense or defense against other contiguous groups that likewise attempted to defend or acquire winter or summer pasturage for large herds of horses. Consequently, tribes invariably came together in early spring and late fall, when the land supported large numbers of domesticated grazing animals.

Major decisions of movement, warfare, and external confrontation were made by councils that attempted to achieve a consensus of opinion. Leadership was seldom hereditary; most leaders were selected because of their demonstrated accomplishments, bravery, ability to make decisions and resolve conflicts, their oratory skills, and persuasiveness. Throughout history nomadic tribes were often the principal agents for maintaining trade between agriculturally based urban centers.

Such highly mobile pastoral tribes were generally located in the higher latitudes of Asia, in grassland areas of North America, and in the higher elevations of Western and Central Europe and the Middle East. Where edible plant growing seasons were usually less than sixty days, people had to live off the by-products of domesticated animals. The brilliant military achievements and leadership of such Mongol tribal leaders as Genghis Khan (c. 1162-1227), who ruled the largest land empire, exemplifies the destructive advantage that highly mobile, pastoral tribes had over more sedentary agriculturally based societies.

In Africa tribes usually had relatively large populations that were supported by agricultural and even diverse subsistence activities. One such tribe, the Nuer, supported itself by agriculture, cattle raising, fishing, and hunting. Most tribes have given way to industrialization. For example, through much of the twentieth century the Bakh-tyari were a large tribe that annually migrated with more than one million animals between Iran and Iraq. However, warfare and intolerance toward this pastoral, nomadic people altered its way of life.

A modern use of the term "tribe" has been applied to and even used by some counterculture groups in the United States and the British Isles. Membership may be determined by certain initia-tion rites, totemic symbols, ritual costumes, hair styles, a strict sense of territorialism, and even jargon that emphasizes selective membership and recognizes members' obligatory economic and social rights and responsibilities. —*John Alan Ross*

See also Ancestor worship; Clans; Coats of arms; Extended families; Lineage; Moiety; Native Americans; Rites of passage.

Native Americans, more than any other North American peoples, maintain tribal forms of community organization. (James L. Shaffer)

Twins

RELEVANT ISSUES: Children and child development; Health and medicine; Parenting and family relationships

SIGNIFICANCE: Parenting twins can present many challenges, and twins are valuable in studies of human behavior, intelligence, disease, and mental illness

An interest in twins goes back as far as recorded history. In myth and literature, they are considered to be special human beings. In some cultures, twins are believed to be a bad omen and one twin may be killed to ward off evil. In other cultures, twins are considered to be a good omen and an occasion for rejoicing.

It was not until the late 1800's that scientists recognized that there were two types of twins. Identical twins develop from the fertilization of one ovum by one sperm. The fertilized egg divides into two separate individuals who have the same genetic makeup and are of the same sex. Fraternal twins result from the fertilization of two ova by two

The Two Main Types of Twins

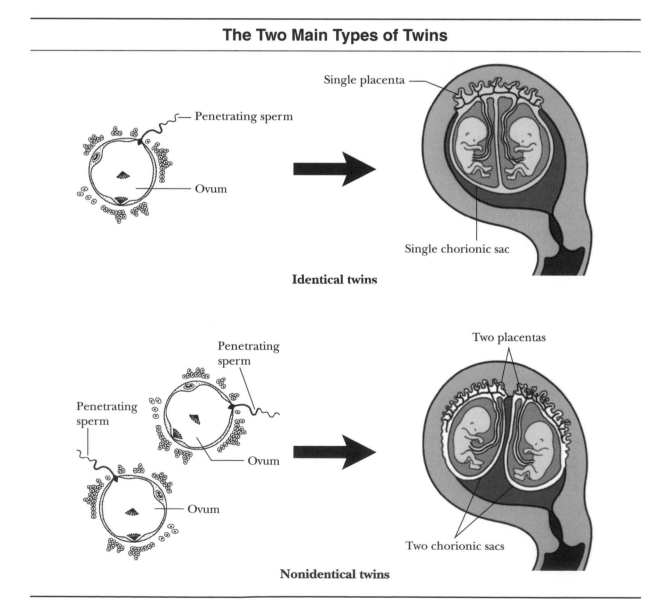

Identical twins

Nonidentical twins

Thanks to extraordinary measures made possible by modern medical science, the Pennsylvania twins in this picture were delivered ninety-four days apart in 1996. The girl (foreground) was delivered four months prematurely, weighing only twenty-three ounces. The boy remained in their mother's womb another three months and was delivered after nearly reaching full term. (AP/Wide World Photos)

Research has shown that the way parents treat twin children can affect how twins themselves relate to each other as adults. (Dick Hemingway)

separate sperm. This is the most common type of multiple birth. Fraternal twins are no more genetically similar than brothers and sisters in the same family.

Mothers who are themselves a twin or who have twins on both sides of their family have a greater chance of producing twins. Advances in fertility treatments such as fertility drugs and in vitro fertilization enhance the chances of twin or multiple births. The age and ethnic origin of the mother also affect the probability of twin births.

Demographics. The *Journal of the American Medical Association* reported in March 1997 that between 1980 and 1994, the rate of twin births in the United States increased by 42 percent. Twin births also increased in Canada during that time. In the 1992-1994 period, the rate of twin births in the United States was 24 per 1,000 live births, about 2 percent of all births. Twin births were defined as individual live births rather than sets of twins.

With increasing maternal age, the rate of twin births increases: Twins are more likely to be born to mothers who are 25 years of age or older. In 1994, the twin birth rate among non-Hispanic white mothers was 24.5 (rates are expressed per thousand births), among non-Hispanic African American mothers 28.3, and among Hispanic mothers 18.6. The rate of twin births ranged from 19.8 in Idaho and New Mexico to 27.7 in Connecticut and Massachusetts. After adjusting for maternal age, race, and Hispanic origin, the rates of twin births for Connecticut and Massachusetts remained significantly higher than the overall rate for the United States. This state variation might result from maternal age, ethnic distribution, the use of fertility drugs and in vitro fertilization, and the insurance benefits available for fertility treatments.

Twins are at greater risk than single-born children for pre-term birth, low birth weight, mortality at birth, and long-term disability. Preterm and low birth weight twins still show impairment of locomotor, speech, language, and emotional development at four years of age. Twins have more disease and poorer health than single-born children. In a privileged social environment, however, these risks are minimal.

The crowded conditions in the womb impede the development of twins and often result in early birth. This situation is considered to be a major contributing factor to biological difficulties for twins at birth. There is some evidence that many humans may start their first weeks of life in the uterus with a twin who fails to survive.

Twin Studies. The first twin study was published in 1875 by Sir Francis Galton. Since that time, the study of twins has been important in efforts to determine the influence of heredity and environment on human behavior, mental abilities, and physical well-being.

Human identical twins provide especially valuable subjects for study. Because their genetic makeup is the same, it can be assumed that differences between twins stem from their environment. If identical twins are more like one another on a given trait than fraternal twins, that is evidence for the influence of heredity on that trait. If identical twins reared apart have similar traits, this is even clearer evidence of a genetic contribution to that trait. On the other hand, weak correlations between identical twins reared apart indicate strong environmental influences on that characteristic.

Twin studies have shown a genetic link to diseases such as cancer and obesity, mental disorders such as schizophrenia, behaviors such as bedwetting, and sexual preference. Recognizing these genetic links can enhance understanding of the various aspects of human behavior and can assist scientists in designing treatments for specific diseases and mental disorders.

Identical twins have greater similarities than fraternal twins in personality characteristics such as emotionality, sociability, and impulsiveness. If one twin cries a lot, for example, the identical twin is much more likely to cry a lot than a fraternal twin. Thomas Bouchard, an intelligence researcher, estimated that the chances that IQ is inherited is between 75 and 80 percent. His conclusion was based on research with identical twins reared apart.

Rearing Twins. When twins are born, emotional, economic, and social adjustments must be made by all members of the family. Parents of twins are subject to greater stress than parents of single-born children. Twins are more biologically vulnerable, and impose greater economic demands simply because there are two of them. Parents have to deal with increased time pressures, conflicts between twins, and their competing needs. Sibling jealousy can result when other chil-

Celebrations of Twins

Twins have at least two annual events. Over one weekend every July, Cassville, Wisconsin, stages Twin-o-Rama, celebrating twins and all multiple births. In early August, Twinsburg, Ohio, puts on the Twins Day Festival—an event that attracts nearly 100,000 visitors every year. Twinsburg is reputedly the only city named after twins—Aaron and Moses Wilcox, early settlers in the region.

dren get less attention from parents because of the time demands of twins.

When compared to single-born children, twins receive fewer verbal interchanges, fewer directions, and less follow-through from their parents. Twins have shorter mother-child interactions and are more likely to be interrupted. They receive less praise and affection from parents, who also show less sensitivity when a twin is in distress. The increased stress level experienced by parents probably is why they tend to be less involved with their twins. All these factors may contribute to the slight lag in the language and verbal skills of twins.

Most parents indicate a desire to treat their twins fairly but also as individuals. Treating twins fairly does not mean they are treated the same: Different treatment in at least some respects is important to the development of their individual identities. Practices such as dressing twins alike, giving them similar names, or insisting that they share all their toys do not support their individuality. Some evidence suggests that parents tend to treat their genetically similar children more alike than they treat their genetically dissimilar children.

Twin Relationships. Twins develop a strong cohesive relationship with each other and often play together and exclude other siblings. In frightening situations or times when they need nurturance, however, they turn to their mothers rather than each other. One twin is likely to be more dominant than the other throughout their lives.

The speech of twins may evolve into sounds that are intelligible only to the co-twin. This has been referred to as the private language of twins. Development of this special language can cause twins to seek less contact with others and may lead to social isolation for them.

Studies have indicated that the way parents treat twins has definite effects on their relationship to each other as adults. When parents treat them as individuals, they are usually well adjusted and successful. If parents treat them as objects or as a unit rather than individual people, they do not have a deep relationship as adults.

When twins receive little nurturing as children, they often mother each other. When this happens, they come to rely heavily on each other for comfort and tend to think of themselves as a single unit. This overly close relationship creates anxiety for them when they are separated. It also interferes with the development of healthy relationships with other people. When parents designate one as "bad" and the other as "good," they tend to become distrustful of one another.   —*Davia M. Allen*

BIBLIOGRAPHY

Bornstein, Marc H. *Handbook of Parenting. Vol. I: Children and Parenting.* Mahwah, N.J.: Lawrence Erlbaum, 1995.

Bouchard, Thomas J., Jr., and Peter Propping, eds. *Twins as a Tool of Behavior Genetics.* Chichester, England: John Wiley & Sons, 1993.

Child Study Association of America. *And Then There Were Two: A Handbook for Mothers and Fathers of Twins.* New York: Child Study Press, 1973.

Farber, Susan L. *Identical Twins Reared Apart: A Reanalysis.* New York: Basic Books, 1981.

Lytton, Hugh. *Parent-Child Interactions: The Socialization Process Observed in Twin and Singleton Families.* New York: Plenum Press, 1980.

Powledge, Tabitha M. "The Inheritance of Behavior in Twins." *Bioscience* 43 (July-August, 1993).

Watson, Peter. *Twins: An Uncanny Relationship?* New York: Viking Press, 1982.

See also Birth order; Genetic disorders; Heredity; Literature and families; Multiple births; Parenting; Reproductive technologies; Siblings.

Uniform Child Custody Jurisdiction Act (UCCJA)

DATE: Enacted by the states between 1968 and 1983

RELEVANT ISSUES: Divorce; Law

SIGNIFICANCE: Conflicts between courts of different states resulting in prolonged child-custody battles led the American states, in the best interests of children, to adopt this act

Because of differing state judicial decisions favoring one parent over another who have undergone divorce, children were often shifted from one state to another by parents seeking a favorable custodial arrangement. A climate fostering jurisdictional competition and parental kidnapping was created. To reduce this divisiveness, the National Conference of Commissioners on Uniform State Law proposed the Uniform Child Custody Jurisdiction Act (UCCJA) in 1968 to promote cooperation between courts of different states, deter child abductions, and ensure that the best interests of children were foremost in court proceedings. North Dakota was the first state to adopt the act in 1969 and the District of Columbia, Massachusetts, and Texas were the last in 1983.

The UCCJA supersedes inconsistent provisions of previous laws and provides for the recognition and enforcement of out-of-state custody decrees, with limited ability to modify such decrees. Furthermore, UCCJA specifications apply to custodial decrees granted by other countries if all affected persons are given a fair opportunity to be heard. The impact of this act has been to remove some of the reasons for bitter custody battles. Consequently, the well-being of children of divorced parents has been enhanced, as such children are less likely to be the subjects of intrastate jurisdictional conflicts. —*Kathleen A. Chara and Paul J. Chara, Jr.*

See also Child abduction; Child custody; Divorce; Family law; Parental divorce; Parental Kidnapping Prevention Act (PKPA); Uniform Marriage and Divorce Act (UMDA); Visitation rights.

Uniform Marital Property Act (UMPA)

DATE: Recommended for enactment on July 22-29, 1983

RELEVANT ISSUES: Divorce; Law; Marriage and dating

SIGNIFICANCE: Whereas the common law gave husbands more control than wives over property, legal trends in the late twentieth century were directed toward equal rights over property

The Uniform Marital Property Act (UMPA), authored by the National Conference of Commissioners on Uniform State Laws, divides property into two classes: marital property and individual property. Property and income acquired during marriage is presumed to be marital property regardless of who acquires the property or earns the income. Property acquired before a marriage is individual property. Property acquired by one spouse during a marriage by gift or inheritance can still be individual property depending on how it is acquired.

UMPA provides that each spouse has a present undivided one-half interest in all marital property. Upon death, divorce, sale, or other event, each spouse gets one-half of all marital property. Individual property, however, belongs entirely to the individual owner, and this person retains control over it. Under UMPA, management and control of marital property is normally the right of both spouses. Exceptions are when marital property is held in the name of only one spouse. Individual property is controlled totally by the individual owner.

Spouses and prospective spouses may alter most rules of UMPA by agreement, such as in reclassifying property. A court will examine such an agreement, however, to see if it is unconscionable or made voluntarily. Such agreements must be preceded by a fair and reasonable disclosure between spouses of all their financial obligations. No agreement can adversely affect the support rights of children. —*David E. Paas*

See also Inheritance and estate law; Prenuptial agreements; Wills and bequests.

Uniform Marriage and Divorce Act (UMDA)

DATE: Enacted in 1979
RELEVANT ISSUES: Divorce; Law
SIGNIFICANCE: The rise of contested child custody cases, stimulated by no-fault divorce laws, led to the creation of the Uniform Marriage and Divorce Act, which set evaluation standards for custody decisions

The Uniform Marriage and Divorce Act (UMDA) established legal criteria for what a decision maker should consider when determining child custody arrangements following a divorce. The UMDA directs the court to consider "all relevant factors," including the wishes of children and their parents, children's interactions with parents and significant others, children's adjustment in diverse social settings, and the mental and physical health of all involved parties. The act further stipulates that parental behaviors irrelevant to a child's welfare should not be considered by the court.

The UMDA shifted the basis of custody decisions from the fitness of the mother to the best interests of the child. This has led more fathers to seek custody and more professionals to become involved in determining custody arrangements. While the UMDA established uniform criteria for making custody decisions, it failed to prioritize which information should be most important in those decisions. As a result, child custody evaluators could gather reams of documentation with no clear method to determine what is most pertinent in assigning custody. Nevertheless, the UMDA provided a good foundation upon which subsequent legislation and judicial action, such as the Uniform Child Custody Jurisdiction Act, has been built.

—*Kathleen A. Chara and Paul J. Chara, Jr.*

See also Child custody; Divorce; Family courts; Family law; Marriage laws; Parental divorce; Uniform Child Custody Jurisdiction Act (UCCJA).

United Nations Convention on the Rights of the Child

DATE: Issued on November 20, 1989
RELEVANT ISSUE: Children and child development
SIGNIFICANCE: This convention established a universal standard for the care and development of children

The United Nations Convention on the Rights of the Child advanced the work of the United Nations on behalf of children that began in 1959 with the Declaration of the Rights of the Child and was continued by the International Year of the Child in 1979. The convention affirms the family as the fundamental unit of society. Upon adoption by member states, this convention establishes legal requirements regarding the treatment of children. The convention is a lengthy document of 54 articles that outlines in detail the rights of children. Some are rights to which all members of society are entitled, such as the right to life, protection against discrimination, freedom of expression, freedom of conscience, and freedom of religion. The specific needs of children are identified in detail. Among them are protection against physical or mental abuse, access to health care and social security, the right to education, the right to rest and leisure, protection from economic exploitation, and exclusion from military service for children under the age of fifteen. Special provisions exist for adopted, refugee, disabled, and minority children and children separated from their parents. A Committee on the Rights of the Child was created to oversee countries' observance of these provisions. This convention became international law in 1990 and was adopted by 155 countries by the end of January, 1994. —*Joseph L. Nogee*

See also Child Abuse Prevention and Treatment Act (CAPTA); Child safety; Children's rights; Educating children.

Unwed fathers

RELEVANT ISSUES: Parenting and family relationships; Sociology
SIGNIFICANCE: Because most of the increase in child poverty from the 1960's to the 1990's was

related to the increase in children born to unwed mothers, policymakers became interested in identifying the men who were fathering these children and in trying to get unwed fathers more involved in their children's lives

Single-parent families typically involve two parties: mothers and children. Many of these single-parent families are headed by women who have not been married. In 1990 about 30 percent of all births in the United States were to unmarried women. Many of these women have relied on public assistance to support their families. In 1989 a majority of the families receiving Aid to Families with Dependent Children (AFDC) were headed by never-married mothers, and never-married mothers were much more likely than divorced mothers to be long-term welfare recipients. Until the mid-1980's mothers themselves were the focus of attention. However, as the support of children has traditionally been the obligation of fathers, media attention and public interest began to turn to the men who had produced the children of unwed mothers.

Stereotypes About Unwed Fathers. During the mid-1980's articles and reports on unwed fathers began to appear in the scholarly and popular media. Organizations such as the National Urban League and the Children's Defense Fund (CDF) initiated campaigns to promote sexual responsibility and a sense of paternal obligation among young men. Despite this increased interest in unwed fathers, however, information on this group has been scant, and popular images of them frequently tend to be based largely on stereotypes. A widely viewed 1986 prime-time documentary produced by Bill Moyers featured an unwed African American father who boasted of fathering several out-of-wedlock children with several women, all of whom were receiving public assistance. Research on unwed fathers, however, has indicated that the reality is somewhat more complicated than this kind of stereotype suggests.

Who are the unwed fathers? Robert I. Lerman, an economist at American University, has done extensive research on unwed fathers. He found that most unwed fathers in the 1980's did not marry or live with the women who had borne their children. However, they also did not generally father numerous children with a variety of partners.

Although about 45 percent of unwed fathers in Lerman's study had more than one child, only about 12 percent had more than two children.

Young unwed fathers generally had lower levels of education than other young men, and unwed fathers were more likely to have engaged in criminal behavior. African American men were more likely than white men to be unwed fathers, since about one out of every four African American men aged twenty-three to thirty was an unmarried father in 1988.

Unwed fathers were not completely uninvolved in the lives of their children. About 60 percent visited their children at least once per year during the first two years. However, visits tended to drop dramatically as the children grew older. Over one-third of unwed fathers reported paying child support to their children, although the amounts of payments were generally quite low.

Legal Obligations and Rights of Unwed Fathers. Many state and federal laws have been enacted to increase unwed mothers' chances of receiving financial support from the biological fathers of their children. For example, the 1974 Social Service Amendment Act (Public Law 93-647) made the states solely responsible for collecting child support from fathers whom they labeled "deadbeat dads." The 1984 Child Support Enforcement Amendments (Public Law 98-378) established specific guidelines for the collection of support monies and levied sanctions (punishments) against deadbeat dads when collections were considered delinquent.

The legislation that is considered to have had the greatest impact on families since the inception of the Social Security Act in 1935 was the Family Support Act of 1988. The Family Support Act, spearheaded by Senator Daniel Patrick Moynihan, created sweeping changes in the welfare system. The act was designed to make all parents, including unwed fathers, meet their parental obligations and responsibilities to their children

The legal rights of unwed fathers have been argued in a number of cases. *Stanley v. Illinois* (1972) was an early landmark case that involved Peter Stanley, who had fathered his children out of wedlock but lived with them and their mother for eighteen years. Even though Stanley had provided for the family during the time he lived with them, he was considered an unfit parent under Illinois

Studies have found that at least 60 percent of unwed fathers maintain some involvement in their children's lives. (Mary LaSalle)

law, which stipulated that unwed fathers were unfit as parents. Upon the mother's death, the children became wards of the state. Stanley fought the custody ruling by the state and noted that he had not been notified of nor had he received an unfit-parent hearing. As a result of Stanley's case, the court acknowledged that unwed fathers have rights to due process and equal protection under the law. Six years later the U.S. Supreme Court offered modifications to *Stanley* in the case of *Quilloin v. Walcott* (1978). The Court held that although an unwed father should be notified and given an opportunity to have a hearing, he cannot veto an adoption of his biological child without a fitness hearing.

Services and Programs. Most public and private social services and community programs are designed specifically for women and their children. There are few programs that provide emotional and or financial assistance to unwed fathers. Many of the programs that should provide services to fathers have been developed based on stereotypes, myths, and lack of understanding. Much of this information comes from the mothers of children and has limited foundation in empirical research. As a result, the majority of available programs and services are based on matricentric approaches (needs of the mothers), resulting in very few if any programs for fathers, particularly unwed fathers.

Many of the programs for unwed fathers involve academic, parenting skills, substance abuse, and job readiness training. Few include information on budgeting information, nutritional issues, and nurturing skills. Numerous programs for unwed fathers, especially programs for teenage unwed fathers, have emerged throughout the United States and Canada. In addition, there are a number of support self-help groups, such as DADS Charitable Services, which provides a telephone crisis line, periodic meetings, paralegal services, shelters for fathers, and a national forum for fathers' support groups.

One issue with which many of the programs must deal is that many of the fathers who have children out of wedlock are not teenagers. According to a 1996 report in the *Beloit Daily News*, two-thirds of the babies born to teenage mothers in 1993 were fathered by adult males who were up to six years older than the mothers. The Guttmacher Institute considered fathers' ages in out-of-wedlock births and came to the similar conclusion that most of the fathers were older males. Some of the implications are that programs must be designed to target not only the needs of teenage fathers but also those of adult males. However, even with program support, many unwed fathers experience difficulties in establishing meaningful relationships and interactions with their children—especially in instances in which they are married adults with families. In situations such as this it is difficult to establish or attempt to foster relationships with the out-of-wedlock children. —*Glenn Canyon*

BIBLIOGRAPHY

Blankenhorn, David. *Fatherless in America: Confronting Our Most Urgent Social Problem.* New York: Basic Books, 1995.

Brown, Robin, ed. *Children in Crisis.* New York: H. W. Wilson, 1994.

Garfinkel, Irwin, and Sara McClanahan. *Single Mothers and Their Children: A New American Dilemma.* Washington, D.C.: Urban Institute Press, 1986.

Lerman, Robert I., and Theodora J. Ooms, eds. *Young Unwed Fathers: Changing Roles and Emerging Policies.* Philadelphia: Temple University Press, 1993.

See also Amerasian children; Child support; Children born out of wedlock; Fatherhood; Fatherlessness; *Gomez v. Perez*; Men's roles; Paternity suits; Single-parent families; Teen mothers.

Vanier Institute of the Family (VIF)

DATE: Founded in 1965

RELEVANT ISSUES: Education; Parenting and family relationships

SIGNIFICANCE: This Canadian organization disseminates information about families to the general public and collaborates with various organizations on issues important to families

The Vanier Institute of the Family (VIF), a Canadian nonprofit organization, was formed in 1965 by Governor-General Georges Vanier and his wife Pauline, whose purpose was to promote the well-being of Canadian families. The organization considers families to be the "building blocks" of any society and is inclusive in its respect for all types of families, accomplishing its work through research, publications, public education, advocacy, and support for various public and community organizations. Different types of memberships and membership rates are available, such as individual and organizational memberships.

Themes of research change over time depending on changing trends in Canadian society. For example, in 1983 research themes included child care, health care, the informal economy, family mobility, and learning and the family. In 1997 the institute concentrated on workers with family responsibilities, the diversity and policy implications of modern families, childhood poverty, demographic change and societal aging, family and the economy, and new reproductive technologies.

The institute interprets government, academic, and statistical publications for the lay public, presenting information in an easy-to-read, nonbiased, and timely manner. Their newsletter, *Transition*, is published four times a year in English and French and provides information on Canadian life, family trends, and demographics. In addition to publishing information on such subjects as job security, youth crime, work and family, and grandparenting, it contains conference announcements, opin-

ion pieces, and book reviews. The institute also publishes and sells various other publications on family-related topics.

The Vanier Institute of the Family provides "one-stop-shopping" for statistical information on Canadian families, both at the national and provincial/territorial level. The institute is a key resource on family issues in Canada, responding in one year to at least four hundred requests for interviews from the media. Additionally, it works on various projects in collaboration with other organizations and individuals, including with educators on educational supplements and with media professionals and researchers to determine the impact of the media on families. The institute also provides critiques of social policy to the government.

The institute is instrumental in educating persons about family life. It was at the forefront in Canada during the 1994 International Year of the Family. The awards the institute has received are indicative of the service it has provided over the years. In 1995 it received the international award of "Distinguished Service to Families" from the National Council on Family Relations and the "Family Service Canada Leadership Award" from Family Service of Canada. In 1996 it received the "Distinguished Leadership and Service to Families Award" from the American Association for Marriage and Family Therapy (AAMFT).

—*Áine M. Humble*

See also Child care; Educating children; Family demographics; Grandparents; Health problems; National Council on Family Relations (NCFR); Poverty; Reproductive technologies; Work.

Vengeance in families

RELEVANT ISSUES: Kinship and genealogy; Parenting and family relationships; Violence

SIGNIFICANCE: Vengeance, the intense wish or intention to get even or to avenge an injury, is a dysfunctional form of family communication that may be transferred to future generations

Literature, fiction, music, cinema, and real life are abundantly filled with examples of vengeance wished for, held in the mind, nurtured in the heart, and acted upon. A large body of descriptive literature exists on vengeance. The largest body of information on vengeance appears to be in the anthropology of duels, feuds, and vendettas. Duels still occurred in the U.S. South after Reconstruction. Hot tempered men might still bristle over an insult or injury in the twentieth century, but they no longer resort to the elaborate etiquette of the duel. World literature and drama provide extensive information on revenge. The causes of conflict and vengeance in families have played a smaller and less-defined role in literature. Abusive, vindictive, revengeful family backgrounds are more common among families seeking therapeutic help. Vengeance within families as a driving emotion or way of being represents a love and hate, life and death force and is a psychological dynamic yet to be fully examined and understood.

Concept of Vengeance. Vengeance may be understood as the intense, compelling wish or intention to get even—right or wrong—or to avenge an injury. Vengeance may be best understood on a continuum from harmless retaliatory fantasies or actions to the delivery of death and destruction. Revenge, or the hope of revenge, may seek to restore persons' self-esteem and is a conflict motive with which individuals and families struggle.

Family vengeance is as potent as love, hate, pride, and shame and holds the power to preserve or destroy. The more violent instances of vengeance appear to be the result of unrestricted,

In Mark Twain's novel Adventures of Huckleberry Finn *(1884), Huck spends several weeks with a southern family that destroys itself in a family feud so old that no one remembers how it started.* (Edward W. Kemble, illustrator in *Huckleberry Finn,* 1884)

1334 • <small>Vengeance in families</small>

relentless ego-driven rage precipitated by an actual or perceived injury to the self. Such rage may defy self-containment or may be successfully negotiated through life situations. In instances in which revenge defies self-containment, vengeful feelings, emotions, or fantasies may erupt into dangerous, violent behaviors.

Types of Vengeance. Like other feelings and emotions, vengeance may be expressed, resolved, and adaptive or may be unexpressed, unresolved, and maladaptive for families. The dynamic of vengeance is as complex as it is experienced, expressed, or understood in the lives of individuals or family systems. In social interactions, people seldom say what emotions they are experiencing. In order to interpret emotions, people note outer cues indicating persons' inner state. Although a driving wish to get even or exact justice in response to a perceived injury, adaptive vengeance does not actually require a life for a life in order to be satisfied. Adaptive vengeance does not compel one to a destructive action or to a lifetime of bitterness, but diminishes in intensity with the passage of time.

Maladaptive vengeance or nonadjusted vengeance is defined as a driving wish in which the compulsion to get even overrides and consumes persons' lives. The compulsion results in a constricted life orientation or the expressions of harmful, dangerous behaviors toward others or the self. Unlike adaptive vengeance, maladaptive vengeance strengthens and feeds itself with the passage of time.

Maladaptive or unadjusted vengeance might involve acts that are socially disapproved or outright illegal. One key feature of maladaptive vengeance is that it appears to gain strength with the passage of time. The commitment to right a wrong can make a return to adequate family functioning appear to be disloyal and unattainable. The pledge to never forget until justice has been done can become a pledge to refuse to adapt or recover.

For example, mourners who view other people as responsible for a loved one's death may wish to harm such putative perpetrators or see them pay somehow for their terrible deed. Simultaneously, mourners may sense that their desires for revenge are improper and that they are engaging in unkind thinking. Those who blame others and seek revenge may have a more difficult time recovering, adapting, or adjusting to daily life routines than those who blame others and do not desire revenge. In *Beyond Grief: Studies in Crisis Intervention* (1979), Erich and Elizabeth Lindemann indicate that the desire for revenge in families mourning loved ones can keep survivors focused on their loss and make it difficult for them to reduce their ties to their lost loved ones. This occurs when family members feel an ongoing responsibility to avenge the death of a loved one.

Vindictiveness and Conflict. Adversarial relationships and expressions of conflict are viewed by families as normative, as is the imposition of severe punishment in order to deter or prevent future violence or retributive justice. Vengefulness occurs subsequent to a self-perceived injury rather than as a defense against perceived threat or danger. Conflict differs significantly from one family to another and with respect to the duration and intensity of the conflict. Vengeance in families may be viewed as a very different state of mind that has certain salient characteristic features distinguishing it from other mental states associated with aggression, rage, hate, hostility, spite, pride, and shame. Vengeance is often more cruel, lustful, and insatiable—hence the "thirst for vengeance." Vengeance is often postponed and indirect.

Vindictiveness may be viewed as a neurotic solution, compulsive in nature, which has the power, if unaddressed, to become a way of life, fueled by the need for triumph. Vindictiveness or revenge may be conceptualized as self-protection and as the restoration of the pride of persons who have been injured. The aim of vindictiveness and revenge is to humiliate, frustrate, or exploit. Vindictiveness may be satisfied by the open expression of aggression through long-suffering, self-effacing presentation or the tyranny of detachment.

Key aspects of revenge and vindictiveness that may be represented in the bond between family members are the emotions of pride and shame. Pride generates and signals a secure bond, just as shame generates and signals a threatened or injured bond. These two emotions have a unique status relative to social and family relationships. Individuals and families feel pride when they experience success and acceptance and shame when they err and suffer rejection. Shame is the emotion that occurs when individuals feel too close or too far from others and appear frequently in disguise. When too close, they feel exposed or violated; when too far, they feel invisible or rejected. The need for the right degree of communication and human connection is so primitive that individuals often take it for granted.

Shame leads directly to anger, insult, and aggression when not acknowledged. When shame is not expressed, silence reigns, and there is no acknowledgment of one's humiliation. The lack of acknowledgment of humiliation creates a shame-rage spiral. A continuing shame-rage spiral leads to madness and revenge, whether for individuals or groups. Shame-rage spirals may be brief or they may last for hours, days, or a lifetime as bitter hatred or resentment. The emotion of shame can be directly acknowledged by referring to one's inner states of insecurity or feelings of separateness or powerlessness.

Unacknowledged, shame is the underlying cause of revenge-based cycles of conflict. The identification of shame-anger sequences in the causation of conflict may help solve the problem of the causation of revenge in families. Threats to the social and familial relationship give rise to violent emotions, shame, and rage. Unless these feelings are resolved, the stage is set for cycles of insult, humiliation, and violent revenge. Alienation or damaged familial social bonds may be viewed as a basic cause of destructive conflict. Individuals and families who understand each other both cognitively and emotionally are apt to trust and cooperate. Secure social and family bonds ensure clear boundaries that help keep vindictiveness and revenge in check and make disagreements productive, even during competition or conflict.

The successful resolution of maladaptive vengefulness depends upon the modification of individuals' self-perception and the acceptance of ordinariness and imperfection. Adaptive families experience, tolerate, and integrate effects and emotions in order to understand conflict and vengeance. The ability of families to recognize the emotional source of conflict and repair the broken social bond in order that both sides can achieve cognitive and emotional understanding allows them to trust and cooperate. Families and their individual members may then live as ordinary, imperfect human beings without a need to seek revenge for perceived injuries.

—*Lessie L. Bass*

BIBLIOGRAPHY

Boris, J. "Identification with a Vengeance." *International Journal of Psychoanalysis* 71 (1990).

Lindemann, Erich, and Elizabeth Lindemann. *Beyond Grief: Studies in Crisis Intervention.* New York: Jason Aronson, 1979.

Parkes, C. M., and R. S. Weiss. *Recovery from Bereavement.* New York: Basic Books, 1983.

Scheff, Thomas J. *Bloody Revenge: Emotions, Nationalism, and War.* Boulder, Colo.: Westview Press, 1994.

See also Bonding and attachment; Cycle of violence theory; Domestic violence; Emotional expression; Generational relationships.

Vietnamese Americans

RELEVANT ISSUES: Parenting and family relationships; Race and ethnicity

SIGNIFICANCE: Large numbers of Vietnamese refugees fled to North America after the Vietnam War, disrupting their lives and forcing them to adapt to mainstream American culture

In order to understand Vietnamese American family customs, it is important to examine briefly the historical background of Vietnamese immigration to North America. Technically, the Vietnamese were not immigrants at all, but refugees. Refugees are people who leave their native land and are afraid to return because of persecution and the threat of death. The Vietnamese sought safety in North America, a direct result of U.S. involvement in the war between North and South Vietnam.

Background. When the United States ended its military involvement in Vietnam in 1974, it left behind many Vietnamese citizens who had been connected to the United States in some way. During the period immediately preceding the fall of Saigon on April 30, 1975, about 100,000 Vietnamese were evacuated. Many of this "first wave" were people who feared that their involvement with the Americans would lead to persecution or death under North Vietnamese Communist rule. Most of this first group of refugees were educated urban-dwellers, about half of whom were Roman Catholic.

Within two years after the fall of Saigon, the second wave of Vietnamese began leaving Vietnam. Many left by boat in order to escape ethnic and religious persecution as well as deprivation. Of this group, many were ethnic Chinese. Others were Montagnards who had allied themselves with American intelligence during the Vietnam War. Other minority groups fleeing Vietnam included the Cham and the Khmer, as well as the Hmong from nearby Cambodia. The second wave of refugees was generally less educated than earlier immigrants, and they were often from the countryside.

A final group of refugees were the Amerasians, the children of American military personnel and (usually) Vietnamese women. The Amerasians,

The number of Vietnamese living in the United States before 1970 was almost nil. By 1990, however, their numbers had risen to nearly 600,000. (James L. Shaffer)

called *bui doi* (dust of life), were subjected to harassment and discrimination in Vietnam under Communist rule. While many were killed, many other Amerasian children lived homeless in the streets. Eventually, some 68,000 settled in the United States under a special program for Amerasians.

To speak of Vietnamese Americans as a homogenous group is clearly an error. The refugees brought with them different customs, biases, and prejudices. Moreover, while their refugee status allowed them to enter North America more easily than other immigrant groups, it was also a source of trauma and pain. Many expected the move to be temporary and that they would soon return to Vietnam. Many had left family members behind, thinking that they would return or that they would be able to send for their families after they were settled.

Demographics. When the Vietnamese refugees came to the United States, they were settled by voluntary agencies who found sponsors for each family to help with the transition to life in the United States. As a result, the Vietnamese people were deliberately scattered throughout the country, the reasoning being that they would assimilate more quickly if they were on their own in the midst of mainstream American culture. What the well-intentioned voluntary agencies failed to consider is the importance of family in Vietnamese culture. Since most refugees had left their extended families behind, they needed to establish communities where other Vietnamese could take the place of the larger family. Therefore, once the refugees were initially settled in the United States, many moved a second time to be nearer to family members and other Vietnamese people.

Many Vietnamese subsequently moved to California. The 1990 census showed that 45 percent of the Vietnamese American population lived in California, where the city of Westminster, in Southern California, has become the center of Vietnamese culture and economics in the United States. In the 1990's Westminster boasted some 1,500 Vietnamese businesses. Texas had about 11 percent of the Vietnamese American population, followed by Washington with 4.8 percent, Virginia with 3.5 percent, and Louisiana with 2.9 percent. Florida and Pennsylvania also had significant Vietnamese America populations.

Most Vietnamese Americans live in established Vietnamese communities in urban areas. They represent 8 percent of the total Asian American population and numbered around 593,213 in 1990. Of these, 31 percent arrived before 1980, 49 percent arrived between 1980 and 1990, and 20 percent are native born. In 1990 most Vietnamese Americans lived in family units headed by a father and a mother, although about 16 percent lived in female-headed households.

Cultural Identity. For the Vietnamese, family is the most important foundation of their society. The trauma and disruption caused by war and flight forced the refugees into situations in which their cultural norms shifted. In response to the fact that many Vietnamese were deprived of their families, "adopted" kin groups grew up in Vietnamese communities, and family members moved to be closer to other family members arriving in North America.

When the Vietnamese refugees arrived in North America, they quickly looked for work in order to survive and as a matter of self-respect. Among immigrant groups, Vietnamese Americans have a high employment rate. Nevertheless, many found themselves in jobs of lower socioeconomic status than the ones they left behind in Vietnam. In addition, Vietnamese women often found work more easily than did their husbands, largely because they looked for lower-status jobs. Nevertheless, the Vietnamese American self-perception is that they are hard-working, tenacious survivors; most adapted to their changed circumstances fairly quickly.

Religion, Holidays, and Ceremonies. One way that Vietnamese Americans maintain their cultural identity is through the observance of their religions. Many of the early refugees were Roman Catholics, and Vietnamese Americans have demonstrated leadership in the Roman Catholic Church. The majority of Vietnamese are Buddhists, and Buddhism affects the way most Vietnamese Americans view life. For the Buddhist, all life is suffering and the end to suffering comes only with the suppression of desire, which can be accomplished by following the Eightfold Path, which includes right speech, right action, right intention, right views, right livelihood, self-discipline, self-mastery, and contemplation. Confucianism is also a strong tradition among Vietnamese Americans. This phi-

Vietnamese American sisters in a New York City high school. (Hazel Hankin)

losophy has at its core the attention to social and familial order. A hierarchical system, Confucianism teaches the importance of filial piety.

There are a number of other smaller religious sects among the Vietnamese, including Taoism, Cao Dai, and Hoa Hao, which also exert influence on the Vietnamese American community. In each case, however, the buildings housing the various religious institutions often serve as meeting places and community centers for Vietnamese Americans.

Vietnamese Americans also preserve their cultural identity through the observance of Vietnamese holidays and traditions. By far the most important festival for Vietnamese Americans is Tet Nguyen Den, the Lunar New Year. It usually falls on three days at the end of January and the beginning of February. Tet is a family holiday, and all

members of the family express appreciation and respect for one another. During Tet people give each other gifts, wear their best clothing, prepare special foods, and honor their ancestors. For Vietnamese Americans, this holiday is the cultural, social, and spiritual high point of the year.

The Family and Cultural Change. As family structure is the underpinning of Vietnamese culture, persons think of themselves in relation to the other members of their nuclear and extended family. The father is traditionally the head of the family, while the mother must ensure harmony within the family unit. Children are valued and considered treasures. They are responsible for taking care of their parents in old age. Much of this structure arrived intact with the refugees. Yet, because so many refugees left members of their families behind and because so many men found that

This Canadian poster inviting Vietnamese-speaking victims of domestic abuse to seek help reflects the fact that the special stresses endured by immigrant families can make them prone to dysfunction. (Dick Hemingway)

their wives must work in order to help support their families, family structure and identity shifted as Vietnamese Americans grew into the American mainstream culture.

Children and adolescents have been placed under pressure by the tension between traditional and North American culture. Since they often learn English more quickly than their parents, young people find themselves having to translate and solve problems for their parents, leading to a role reversal that would not be typical in Vietnamese society. In addition, young people are subjected to the same pressures that other young North Americans face: drugs, alcohol, and gangs. Although much has been made of gangs among Vietnamese American youths, most scholars think that this has been exaggerated. In spite of the difficulties encountered by young Vietnamese, it seems clear that most young people still value education as do their families. As a group, Vietnamese Americans excel in school and continue their education past high school.

Vietnamese Americans continue to work toward stability within the mainstream culture. Many Vietnamese incorporate American ways without disregarding Vietnamese ways. In spite of the difficulties that Vietnamese Americans have experienced in their new home, the family remains the source of support and stability for their culture.

—*Diane Andrews Henningfeld*

BIBLIOGRAPHY

Bandon, Alexandra. *Vietnamese Americans.* New York: New Discovery Books, 1994.

Freeman, James. *Hearts of Sorrow: Vietnamese-American Lives.* Stanford, Calif.: Stanford University Press, 1989.

Ng, Franklin, ed. *Asian American Encyclopedia.* 6 vols. New York: Marshall Cavendish, 1995.

Nguyen, Qui Duc. *Where the Ashes Are: The Odyssey of a Vietnamese Family.* Reading, Mass.: Addison-Wesley, 1994.

Rutledge, Paul James. *The Vietnamese Experience in America.* Bloomington: Indiana University Press, 1992.

Tran, De, Andrew Lam, and Hai Dai Nguyen, eds. *Once Upon a Dream: The Vietnamese-American Experience.* Kansas City, Mo.: Andrews and McMeel, 1995.

See also Amerasian children; Chinese Americans; East Indians and Pakistanis; Family size; Filipino Americans; Holidays; Japanese Americans; Korean Americans; Pacific Islanders; Southeast Asian Americans; War brides.

Violence Against Women Act

DATE: Enacted on September 13, 1994
RELEVANT ISSUES: Violence; Sociology
SIGNIFICANCE: This act provides federal protection to the victims of gender-motivated violence

The Violence Against Women Act of 1994, Title IV of the Violent Crime Control and Law Enforcement Act of 1994, was the result of four years of testimony before Congress and was drafted in response to what its chief legislative sponsor, Senator Joseph R. Biden, called a "national tragedy." In a 1991 report, for example, the Senate concluded after an investigation of the subject that violence perpetrated by men was at the top of the list of dangers to women's health in the United States, that every fifteen seconds a woman is battered, and that every six minutes a woman is raped.

Signed into law by President Bill Clinton in 1994, the act authorized $1.6 billion in grants over six years to assist state and local law enforcement officers and prosecutors in their efforts to reduce violent crimes against women, including domestic violence. The act also created a federal right to be free from gender-based violence and allowed victims of gender-motivated violence to bring suit for damages. Additionally, the act assured that protective orders against domestic violence obtained in one state would be given "full faith and credit" in other states. Finally, the act increased penalties for federal rape convictions.   —*Timothy L. Hall*

See also Cruelty as grounds for divorce; Dating violence; Domestic violence; Emotional abuse; Family Violence Prevention and Services Act; Marital rape; Shelters.

Visitation rights

RELEVANT ISSUES: Children and child development; Divorce; Law; Parenting and Family Relationships
SIGNIFICANCE: When families separate, reasonable visitation rights of noncustodial parents—

most often men—must focus on the needs of children, the physical proximity of both parents, and parents' efforts to be fair to all family members

Since 1980, when President Jimmy Carter held the first White House Conference on the Family, political and legal definitions affecting child care, health care, education, welfare reform, employment, and cultural values have moved to the forefront of public policy and debate. All of these topics influence parents' visitation rights. Since the divorce rate of American families has constantly increased over the last four decades, legislators have been forced to address and restructure laws concerning child custody, child support, and visitation rights.

Until the 1970's domestic courts awarded mothers custody of minor children in more than 95 percent of all divorce cases. However, since 1980, after a cultural revolution in the 1960's and 1970's developed different definitions of family that included communal care and dual parenting and nurturing of children, fathers have increasingly petitioned for and been granted joint and even sole custody of their children.

Myth of the Deadbeat Dad. A common description of noncustodial fathers is that they are "deadbeat dads," those who never pay child support and live luxurious lives while mothers and children barely survive in virtual poverty. All surveys of divorced fathers indicate that the majority want to be a viable part of their children's lives through visitation, decision making, and financial support. Most courts agree that fathers should receive visitation rights even when they do not support their families financially. Unmarried fathers receive even fewer visitation rights than do divorced fathers. However, statistically, fewer unwed fathers request custody or visitation rights than do divorced fathers. In cases in which the courts suspect or have established evidence of abuse, fathers are usually allowed only supervised visits in which every minute of the father-child interaction is monitored.

The typical divorced father ends up becoming a weekend father, usually seeing his children every Saturday or every other weekend regardless of whether he has overnight or restricted visitation privileges. Common complaints of custodial mothers include: "He spoils their dinner with treats and sends them home," or "Anybody can be a daddy for a few hours," or "When he sees them, he tries to buy their love by spending money on frivolous things." Most fathers make valiant efforts to plan action-packed Saturdays and indulge their children, because they see them so seldom. Spending money on children seems to be an unconscious attempt to make up for lost time since the last visit. Weekend time with fathers is usually more exciting than daily time with mothers, because many children do not see their fathers for weeks at a time. Thus, it is understandable why custodial mothers have difficulty with their children's glowing reviews of time spent with their fathers.

These negative feelings, whether warranted or unfounded, often cause mothers to interfere with fathers' visitation arrangements, complicating matters and limiting the frequency of visits. Hostility toward noncustodial fathers is the cause of many mothers' efforts to undermine established visitation formulas. Some mothers often hinder or prevent fathers' visitation rights as a way to vent their anger for problems in the former marriage or to assert themselves in areas in which they felt powerless before divorce.

Even though visitation laws have changed so that fathers are included more often in the visitation equation, courts, without cost-prohibitive monitoring, cannot guarantee that laws and visitation orders are obeyed. In most surveys fathers blame mothers, and mothers even agree that they are often the obstacles to fathers' ability to visit and communicate with their children. Custodial mothers who do not receive timely child support payments or women who still hurt from earlier marital problems or continue to deal with postmarital disagreements may feel justified in denying fathers their visitation rights.

Problems with Visitation Rights. In monitoring situations in which families are fairly functional, most researchers in family and marital counseling agree that children experience better psychological, social, and emotional development when they have access to both parents after divorce. Research supports the premise that in addition to visitation rights, noncustodial fathers are more consistent in paying child support when they are encouraged to be a larger part of their children's lives. Fathers are more likely to pay child support

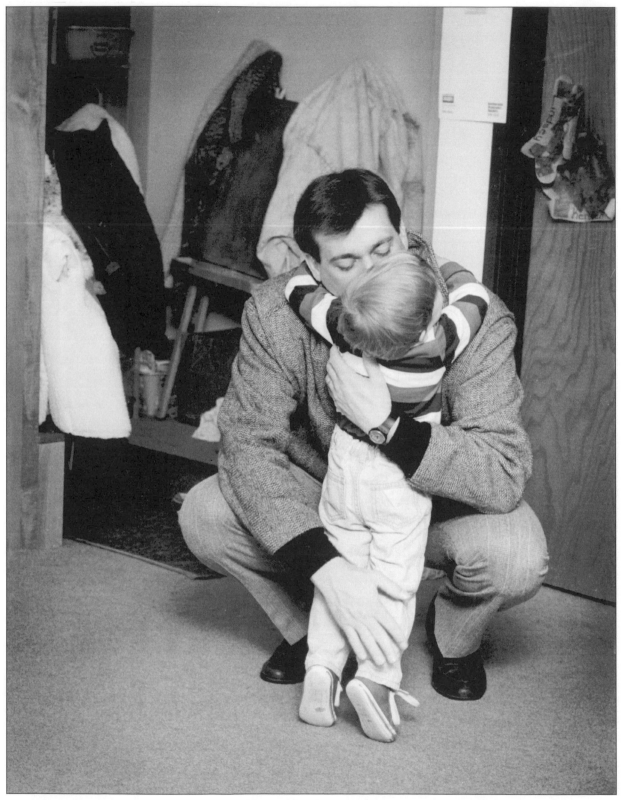

Many divorced fathers see their own children only when court orders permit them. (James L. Shaffer)

when they visit their children regularly. Encouraging fathers to participate in child rearing becomes more difficult when custodial mothers or noncustodial fathers remarry and stepfathers and stepmothers enter into the new family equation. Stepfathers often resent having to disrupt the new family's plans because of the birth father's visitation schedule.

According to the Federal Bureau of Investigation (FBI) and the National Hotline for Missing and Exploited Children, the majority of kidnapped children in the United States are taken by noncustodial parents. Acting out of frustration, revenge, or confusion, parents kidnap their own children when they feel that they have no other choice, especially when they have no control over visitation arrangements. Custodial parents have more support from the courts when changing visitation schedules because they already gained legal approval at previous hearings. Parents most likely to abduct their own children are those who have been turned down for sole or joint custody by the courts, have been denied visitation rights by the courts, or have had visitation rights denied by custodial parents.

In Ontario, Canada, custody and access to children are evaluated by assessors. Although the use of such assessors is not mandatory unless courts are petitioned with dual requests for sole custody or if there is a question of one parent's fitness to care for children, such assessors are usually trained social workers who are skilled in child development, generally knowledgeable about family law, and capable of being impartial. They study mothers' and fathers' financial status, living arrangements, and ability to care for children following divorce. The courts are not bound by assessors' opinions and recommendations; however, when child custody is contested, assessors' evaluations become a valuable tool to help decide if custody shall be shared or if one parent shall be granted sole custody. —*Thomas K. McKnight*

BIBLIOGRAPHY

Brownstein, Gila. *Paralegal Guide to Child Support*. New York: John Wiley and Sons, 1997.

Dabbagh, Maureen. *The Recovery of Internationally Abducted Children: A Comprehensive Guide*. Jefferson, N.C.: McFarland & Co., 1997.

Goldstein, Joseph, ed. *The Best Interests of the Child: The Least Detrimental Alternative*. New York: Simon and Schuster, 1996.

Lyster, Mimi E. *Child Custody: Building Agreements That Work*. Berkeley, Calif.: Nolo Press, 1996.

Mason, Mary A. *From Father's Property to Children's Rights: The History of Child Custody in the United States*. Columbia, Md.: Columbia University Press, 1994.

See also Child custody; Child support; Divorce mediation; Family law; Grandparents; In-laws; Legal separation; Parental divorce; Parental Kidnapping Prevention Act (PKPA); Stepfamilies; Uniform Child Custody Jurisdiction Act (UCCJA).

Volunteerism

RELEVANT ISSUES: Economics and work; Sociology

SIGNIFICANCE: As fiscal restraint guides modern governments in the United States and Canada, there has been increased interest in the unpaid work of men, women, and teenagers in and for their communities and the lasting social contribution of their labor

On Monday afternoon, seventy-six-year-old Anita reads to preschool children in an impoverished urban school. Each week the Smith family purchases five or six extra grocery items that they take with them for their shift at the food bank. John, an accountant by profession, has promised to get the swim team's financial records in shape before the next fund-raising event. A grandmother and her granddaughter stand quietly before a Salvation Army kettle in a local shopping mall, where they collect donations for families who cannot afford to buy their children Christmas presents. Deep in suburbia, Judy stuffs her station wagon full of ketchup and hot dogs as she prepares to make hot lunches at the local school. Sam and Mike, two teenagers, spend one Saturday afternoon a month working at a soup kitchen. Jack, Sally, and their three school-aged children open their home every Tuesday night to lead and host a Bible study for adults and children in their church. Since his retirement, Joe has kept his carpentry skills finely tuned by assisting with the building of a community playground.

What do these people have in common? They are volunteers, willing to give of their time and talents without any direct financial remuneration.

The Gift of Time. Each year more than 90 million Americans—the young, the middle-aged, and the elderly—volunteer their skills or services. In total, they offer more than 20 billion hours of free labor, which could never be repaid monetarily by those who benefit from their services. They are motivated by a desire to help out, assisting the local hospital, the homeless shelter, the art gallery, or neighbors. Volunteers report that giving of themselves to others or to projects they deem worthy makes them feel good about themselves and offers them a personal opportunity to "give back" to society or to those who are less fortunate. While the nature of volunteering has changed over time, fiscal restraint in the public sector has placed even greater demands on the unpaid, voluntary labor of men, women, and teenagers.

Many of the services performed by volunteers are essential to the health and well-being of individuals and communities. In rural communities volunteers drive ambulances and fire engines. In urban settings they staff food banks and soup kitchens. Hospitals, churches, civic libraries, and amateur sports organizations are very dependent

More than 90 million Americans do at least some volunteer work in a typical year. (James L. Shaffer)

upon the unpaid labor of members of the public.

The lives of typical children in the United States—boys and girls—highlight the role of volunteers. Children go to school where countless volunteers, most of whom are mothers, raise funds for school events, assist on the playground, accompany classes on field trips, distribute hot lunches, and staff extracurricular activities, such as science programs or drama classes during noon recess. After school, these same children are involved in myriad sports programs run almost exclusively by volunteers, who coach the children, transport their teams, raise funds for uniforms, and organize interteam competitions. On weekends and in the evenings most churches and synagogues offer age-specific programs for children ranging from Boy Scout and Girl Scout troops to Hebrew training or Roman Catholic catechism. If seasonal events are taken into consideration, such as Christmas programs or summer camps, the work performed by volunteers for the average child becomes colossal.

The lives of typical adults in the United States, men or women, also highlight the role of volunteers. Adults rely on neighbors to sit for their cats while they are on vacation. When they need X rays at the local hospital, they are directed to the unit by volunteers. If they participate in a professional association, play tennis at a club, or go to a church picnic, they reap the benefits of volunteer labor. Several times during the year they open their doors to volunteers collecting money for organizations such as the Heart and Lung Association. When they go to the nearby shopping mall on Saturdays, countless dads and Big Brothers wash cars or sell apples to raise money for Little League or soccer teams. Neighbors and coworkers may ask for sponsorship in events such as walk-a-thons or purchase chocolate bars for their children's schools. Volunteers are everywhere.

Changing Pattern of Volunteer Work. While it may not often occur to many, U.S. culture is heavily dependent on the services and skills of volun-

Student Volunteers

A study released in 1997 by the U.S. Department of Education's National Center for Education Statistics found that among teenagers who were *asked* to volunteer to do community service, 93 percent actually did so. This figure contrasted with the 24 percent of teenagers who volunteered to do community service without being asked. The study, conducted in 1996 among eight thousand students in grades six through twelve, also produced these observations:

- The more activities in which students were involved, the more apt they were to volunteer to do community service.

- Students whose parents were involved in community service were more likely to volunteer themselves than students whose parents were not so involved.

- Students in private schools—especially religious schools—were more likely to do community service than those in public schools.

- The students most likely to be involved in community service were girls with good grades from English-speaking homes who were active in other types of activities.

Source: Christian Science Monitor (May 5, 1997).

teers. In fact, most people volunteer from time to time. They serve on committees for local charities, baby-sit for neighbors' children, prepare food for the sick or bereaved, teach a children's class in Sunday school, offer reassurance as part of crisis telephone services, or perform yard work for senior citizens.

Volunteer work has changed. Americans are likely to make short-term volunteer commitments, offering to perform work more directly related to their specific skills and training. Rather than allowing organizations to "choose" what tasks they perform, volunteers demand that their volunteer jobs match previous levels of training and expertise. Although volunteers come from all educational and income categories, a large proportion of college-educated and higher-income persons participate in the volunteer sector.

Many organizations offer training to volunteers, equip them for the unique demands of their agencies and offer job descriptions. Thus, the volunteer stakes for both individuals and organizations have reached new levels. While the pool of volunteers may have changed (particularly since a large proportion of married women are in the paid labor force) and the expectations placed upon vol-

Retired persons have made significant contributions to education by serving as volunteers in classrooms. (James L. Shaffer)

unteers have increased, the need for volunteers continues to grow. Not surprisingly, many volunteers experience exhaustion and burn-out.

If all this community spirit seems too good to be true, there is a cost to be paid. Volunteers have become a "stopgap" in an economy that is downsizing and demanding of the labor force high levels of skills and job experience. Thus, many young people find themselves with little option but the volunteer labor force in order to gain the work experience required by the labor market. Moreover, as the skills and expertise given and demanded of volunteers reaches unprecedented levels, one by-product is competition between the volunteer labor force and paid workers. Driven by their desire for profit, organizations are often inclined to use the expanding services of volunteers at the expense of their nonspecialized labor. A

prime example of this situation involves hospital volunteers.

Foster mothers are another case in point. These women care for children who have been removed from their biological parents as a result of abandonment, neglect, or abuse. From the point of view of the state, foster mothers provide love, nurturance, and care to children who are in need of emotional and physical support. In this way, foster homes become a temporary family to dislocated children. Foster families volunteer to shelter and nurture children who are temporarily under the care of the state, although mothers actually perform most of the volunteer activities.

Motivation for Volunteering. Susan is a young woman in her early twenties who was graduated from a local college with a bachelor of arts degree. Each week Susan spends between six and ten hours at the Shelter for Battered Wives, a local community feminist initiative seeking to empower women who have sought refuge from the fear and reality of violence directed against them by their male partners. Susan wants to help women gain control over their lives and to maximize their choices for a life free from abuse. Her motivation for volunteering at the shelter has political as well as social implications. In essence, Susan wants to eradicate abuse in the lives of individual women and to help produce a society where women and men can live in harmony. Some would say these are radical objectives.

Joshua grew up in a foster home, where he experienced firsthand the volunteer efforts of a family that treated him as "their own." Anxious to reciprocate some of the care and compassion he had received as a troubled youth, Joshua decided to become a Big Brother. As a Big Brother he wants to give back, repay a debt, as it were. In the beginning, it was Joshua's social worker who suggested volunteer work as a way to build up his self-esteem. Once he became a Big Brother, Joshua began to see what a difference he could make in another boy's life. He became a friend *par excellence*. In so doing, Joshua receives as much as he gives.

Brenda turned fifty on her last birthday and soon said good-bye to her youngest child who left home to go to college. During the day Brenda is employed as an office manager for a law firm. Less occupied on evenings and weekends than she was previously, she was intrigued by a newspaper advertisement recruiting volunteers for the regional hospital in her local area. Volunteering gives Brenda the sense of satisfaction that she can share her skills with others in an environment that is less pressured than her normal office setting. Besides, Brenda gets to meet other volunteers, many of whom are middle-aged women like herself. Having been "blessed" in her life, Brenda sees volunteering as a way to give back to society and to

fill the void of an "empty nest."

William is an enterprising young accountant who moved to an urban area to accept a promotion in an expanding business. Desiring to make contacts and to be accepted into the new community, William volunteered to monitor the expenditures of the United Way and to assist in some of its fund-raising ventures. Before long, William's enthusiasm was noticed by others, and he accepted a position as the treasurer of the local community board. With specific skills and expertise to share, the nonprofit organization is delighted to have William as part of its team. On the other hand, he is interested in both advancing his career and helping those less fortunate than himself.

Volunteering, then, offers benefits to volunteers and recipients of volunteer service. In this way, volunteering is bidirectional: It is both individualistic and altruistic. Part of the irony associated with

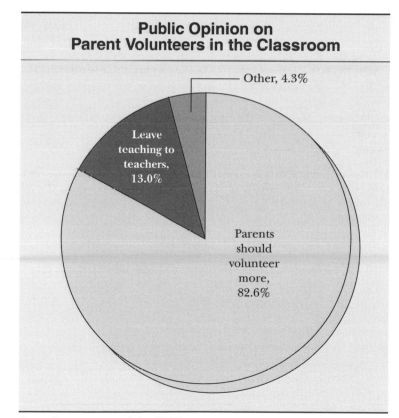

Public Opinion on Parent Volunteers in the Classroom

Other, 4.3%

Leave teaching to teachers, 13.0%

Parents should volunteer more, 82.6%

Source: Parentsroom website (1998)

Note: In early 1998 Parentsroom conducted an informal poll among visitors to its website, asking them if parents should volunteer more in their children's classrooms. This chart summarizes responses. Percentages are rounded to the nearest 0.1%.

volunteering is that its very success reduces the pressures on government to provide an adequate social safety net.

Habitat for Humanity International: A Case Illustration. It is a steamy, sunny Saturday on the outskirts of Birmingham, Alabama. Several people arrive by car, while others arrive on foot. There is a bustle of activity. Everyone seems to be carrying tools—a hammer, a saw, or a level. Judging by the crowd that has assembled, however, it is clear that this is not a typical work site of a construction crew. Many women, several children, and even entire families have come to work. This is the modern equivalent of an Amish barn raising: home construction under the auspices of Habitat for Humanity International (HFHI).

Founded by Millard Fuller, a millionaire entrepreneur who converted to radical Christianity later in life, Habitat for Humanity is a volunteer-based home construction and community development organization. Fuller's vision, which he calls "the theology of the hammer," is very basic: By hitting the nail with the hammer and constructing homes for those for whom home-ownership would never be otherwise possible, volunteers put into practice Christian love and social action.

Several high profile public figures have donated their physical labor to constructing homes for Habitat for Humanity, with Jimmy and Rosalyn Carter being the most celebrated examples. Habitat volunteers come from all walks of life and are motivated by the desire to serve others and to eliminate poverty in an explicitly Christian framework.

In 1996, Habitat for Humanity completed its fifty thousandth dwelling, constructed totally by volunteer labor. Habitat homes are modestly priced (approximately $35,000 in 1996). Purchasers must make a down payment of $100 and volunteer their labor for both their own and others' homes.

Understanding the Voluntary Sector. Sociologist Robert Wuthnow argues that young Americans learn to perform volunteer work, as boys and girls watch caring and nurturing take place in their home environment. He contends that religious settings offer both opportunities for volunteer activities and an ideology that is favorable to both caring for the needy and supporting community agencies. Seen in this way, "learning to care" involves a reconfiguration of the nurturance people

received as children. In essence, individuals model what they have received.

American families thus become the social setting that introduces children to the giving of themselves to others. At this initial stage, volunteering becomes a way to express the debt that is owed to others. Wuthnow believes that volunteering offers an important step for youth as they bridge the chasm between acts of kindness in the family and institutional gestures of goodwill. However, young children and teenagers also learn that volunteering is a gendered activity. Through his research, Wuthnow claims that mothers pass on nurturing roles while fathers are models for concerns about social justice.

—*Nancy Nason-Clark and Danielle Irving*

BIBLIOGRAPHY

Horne, Laura. "Building Straw Houses on a Firm Foundation." *Christianity Today* 41 (February 3, 1997). Article that expands upon the "theology of the hammer," Habitat founder Millard Fuller's title for how to put Christian faith into social action.

Husock, Howard. "It's Time to Take Habitat for Humanity Seriously." Policy Review 75 (January/February, 1996). Discusses the policies and guidelines for Habitat for Humanity's construction projects and selection of homeowners.

Kennedy, John W. "Habitat Builds Fifty Thousandth Home." *Christianity Today* 40 (October 28, 1996). Short article that gives an overview of the tremendous growth and vision of Habitat for Humanity.

Nason-Clark, Nancy. *The Battered Wife: How Christians Confront Family Violence.* Louisville, Ky.: Westminster/John Knox Press, 1997. Documents through survey data, interviews, focus groups, and community consultations what happens when abused religious women in Canada seek help from their faith community, describing the strong informal support network of religious women who offer others both practical and emotional support.

Wuthnow, Robert. *Acts of Compassion: Caring for Others and Helping Ourselves.* Princeton, N.J.: Princeton University Press, 1991. Impressive study of how Americans struggle to reconcile their enthusiasm for individualism with their generosity and altruism and a compelling argument for compassion in the postmodern world.

_____. *Learning to Care: Elementary Kindness in an Age of Indifference.* New York: Oxford University Press, 1995. Sociological investigation into the motivation and rewards teenagers derive from volunteering in their communities.

See also Big Brothers and Big Sisters of America (BBBSA); Communities; Family caregiving; Family values; Foster homes; Habitat for Humanity International (HFHI); Settlement houses; Shelters; Support groups.

War brides

RELEVANT ISSUES: Law; Marriage and dating; Race and ethnicity

SIGNIFICANCE: Despite war-related problems, foreign brides, fiancés, and children of servicemen entered the United States in large numbers between 1943 and 1975

War brides were non-American immigrants who were married or engaged to American servicemen stationed or assigned in a foreign country during, or as a result of World War II, the Korean War, or the Vietnam War. Estimates of the number of war brides from World War II vary widely from 115,000 to one million, depending on whether children and other dependents are included, on the chosen time period, and on who is included as a war bride. World War II war brides came from almost sixty nations. The first and largest single group came from Great Britain. Others came later from Japan, the Philippines, Korea, Thailand, Vietnam, and China.

War Brides and Immigration Law. The military at first discouraged overseas marriages and engagements because it was feared that they would not last and that they would divert servicemen's attention from the task at hand: fulfilling their military duties and responsibilities. Evidence from World War I suggested otherwise, as 6,400 of the 8,000 marriages between foreign women and American servicemen were permanent. Eventually, the military had to accept the inevitable. Secretly at first, and then by U.S. Congressional legislation, war brides and fiancés were transported to the United States during and immediately following World War II, from 1943 to 1952.

Although war brides were at first subject to the same naturalization process as other immigrants, they were exempt from quota limits. Most of those who came during World War II were wives and children of husbands who had been wounded or released from enemy prisoner of war camps. After the war, laws were passed with the intent of providing more orderly means for war brides to enter the United States. Asian war brides faced special problems because of the Oriental Exclusion Act of 1924. However, race and gender were removed as a bar to immigration to the United States after passage of the McCarran-Walter Act of 1952. The number of Asian war brides increased dramatically from 1952 to the end of the Vietnam War in 1975.

British War Brides. The first and largest contingent of war brides, fiancés, and children, approximately seventy thousand persons from Great Britain, entered the United States during the mid-1940's. During wartime they were secretly transported on ships carrying wounded servicemen, former prisoners of war, and enemy prisoners. After the war ended, considerable resentment was directed toward the transportation of war brides to the United States, because they occupied space that could have been filled by returning servicemen. At first, most military brides were ineligible for army transport, because only officers and noncommissioned officers in the top three enlisted ranks were allowed to use military transportation. The alternative for those in the lower four ranks was expensive commercial transportation until 1944, when they too became eligible for transportation at the army's expense.

The foreign wives of military husbands did not automatically receive U.S. citizenship. Rather, war brides were eligible for visas only and had to meet the same naturalization requirements as other immigrants. War brides were advantaged by not being included in immigration quotas established for their native countries. Children were admitted without restriction as long as fathers had been more than twenty-one years of age when the children were born and had lived in the United States for more than ten years.

Responding to pleas and pressures, Congress approved Public Law 271, the War Brides Act of December 28, 1945, the single most important piece of legislation pertaining to World War II war brides. The visa requirement was waived. If husbands of war brides were serving in the armed forces or had been honorably discharged, their wives and minor children could become U.S. citizens provided they applied for citizenship during the three-year life of the act and passed a medical examination. As had been the case earlier, war brides were nonquota immigrants.

One problem remained. Public Law 271 was directed at war brides and children only. It did not apply to alien fiancés or, indeed, fiancés of American servicewomen. Congress responded again by passing Public Law 471, the Fiancées Act, on June 29, 1946. Foreign women and men engaged to present or former members of the armed forces whose status was identical to those included in Public Law 271 could obtain passport visas allowing them to enter the United States as temporary visitors for three months. If their marriages occurred during those three months, Public Law 271 applied. Otherwise, fiancés, with some exceptions, were compelled to leave the United States or be deported. In fact, the U.S. Attorney General now possessed the power to require prospective American spouses to provide a bond, usually five hundred dollars, to cover all possible deportation expenses. Public Law 471 was in effect for eighteen months, until December 28, 1947.

Plans were made to provide thirty ships to transport sixty thousand British war brides, grooms, and children by the end of June, 1946. An additional sixteen thousand came from Australia and New Zealand. The first official contingent of 452 war brides (thirty of whom were pregnant), 173 children, and one war groom left England on January 26, 1946. The youngest bride was sixteen years old and had an eighteen-month-old daughter, while the oldest was forty years old and had a seventeen-year-old daughter from a previous marriage. Their American spouses had been wounded, were hospitalized in the United States, or had been deployed there. Of the seventy thousand World War II British war brides who entered the United States, most came from lower-middle-class backgrounds. Most also had completed their education at age fourteen. Their average age was twenty-four. British war brides were less likely than those from other nations to settle in a single ethnic community, in large part because of the absence of a language barrier. They were well received. Yet, many retained a strong bond with their homeland and were never completely assimilated into American society.

Brides from Germany and Austria. War brides came in much smaller numbers from other European nations, including from World War II enemy countries Germany and Austria. American servicemen were warned against marrying German women. Order Number 1067, issued in April, 1945, by the Allied Chiefs of Staff, made it clear that Germany was occupied as a defeated nation, not for liberation. Fraternization with German officials and the German population was strongly discouraged. Yet, Order 1067 was seldom enforced and almost universally ignored. German women who kept company with Americans were often referred to as "Ami whores" by other Germans. The term was applied both to German prostitutes and to German women employed by Americans. The tension created by opponents of fraternization was reduced when American military personnel who had participated in liberating the Nazi prisoner of war camps or who had fought against the Germans were sent home and replaced by troops who had not experienced wartime conditions.

Restrictions on fraternization were lifted in Austria in August, 1945, and in Germany the following October. A year later the ban on American servicemen marrying Austrian and German women was lifted. By the end of December, 1946, twenty-five hundred soldiers had applied to marry German women. Marriages, however, could not take place until American soldiers were within thirty days of completing their overseas tours of duty.

Asian War Brides. Initially, all Asians—whether allies, such as the Chinese, or enemies—were subject to prewar immigration laws and quotas. During World War II Congress passed Public Law 199, the Magnuson Act, which repealed the 1882 Chinese Exclusion Act but set a quota of just 105 Chinese immigrants annually. To be eligible for citizenship, aliens were required to have a preponderance of white, African, or Chinese blood or a preponderance of any two of the three. Eventually, Chinese wives of American citizens were given nonquota status through an act passed on August 9, 1946. Most of the six thousand Chinese war brides married Chinese American soldiers.

The most significant legislation assisting all Asian war brides, the McCarran-Walter Act, was passed by Congress on June 27, 1952. It repealed the Oriental Exclusion Act of 1924 by eliminating both race and gender as a barrier to immigration.

From 1947 to 1975 more than 165,000 Asian war brides entered the United States. Most were Japanese (66,000) and Filipino (52,000), although 28,000 Koreans, 11,000 Thais, and 8,000 Vietnamese were also admitted.

Asian war brides experienced prejudice and discrimination from both native-born Americans and from their own countrymen, including women who lived in the United States. As one Korean author expressed it, they were "caught in the shadows between the Korean and American communities" and would never be able to become members of Korean American society. Because of the difficulty in learning the English language, Asian war brides relied heavily on their American husbands. Isolation and the depression it provoked was the most common concern expressed by Asian war brides. Living on military bases magnified their loneliness. Yet, most chose to remain in the United States rather than return to their native countries. —*John Quinn Imholte*

BIBLIOGRAPHY

Gimbel, John. *The American Occupation of Germany: Politics and the Military.* Stanford, Calif.: Stanford University Press, 1968.

Hibbert, Joyce. *The War Brides.* Toronto, Canada: PMA Books, 1978.

Moore, John Hammond. *Over-Sexed, Over-Paid, and over Here: Americans in Australia 1941-45.* St. Lucia, Queensland: University of Queensland Press, 1981.

Shukert, Elfrida Berthiaume, and Barbara Smith Scibetta. *War Brides of World War II.* Novato, Calif.: Presidio Press, 1988.

Virden, Jenel. *Goodbye Piccadilly: British War Brides in America.* Urbana, Ill.: University of Illinois Press, 1996.

See also Amerasian children; Children born out of wedlock; Chinese Americans; Filipino Americans; Japanese Americans; Korean Americans; Mail-order brides; Military families; Vietnamese Americans.

Watson, John B.

BORN: January 9, 1878, near Greenville, S.C.
DIED: September 25, 1958, New York, N.Y.
AREA OF ACHIEVEMENT: Behavioral psychology

SIGNIFICANCE: The father of behaviorist psychology, Watson was one of the most influential psychologists of the twentieth century.

Watson graduated from the University of Chicago with a Ph.D. in psychology in 1903. He remained there for five more years and then took a position at The Johns Hopkins University. In an important article titled "Psychology as the Behaviorist Views It" (1913) Watson defined psychology as the science of behavior. In particular, he argued for an objective psychology based on observable events and behaviors. He emphasized the importance of the environment in shaping behavior. Complex behaviors could be explained in terms of simple stimulus-response (S-R) units. Watson is especially well remembered for a series of experiments that involved conditioning a fear response in an infant known as "Little Albert." These early classical conditioning experiments lay the groundwork for the anxiety-reducing technique known as "systematic desensitization."

Watson's stellar academic career ended prematurely in 1920 when he was asked to resign because of a divorce. Shortly thereafter, he married Rosalie Raynor and became a successful executive with a large advertising agency. For several years he continued to write popular articles and books on behaviorism. His influential books include *Behavior: An Introduction to Comparative Psychology* (1914), *Psychology from the Standpoint of a Behaviorist* (1919), *Behaviorism* (1925), and *Psychological Care of the Infant and Child* (1928). —*Russell N. Carney*

See also Addams, Jane; Childhood fears and anxieties; Motherhood; Skinner, B. F.

Wattleton, Faye

BORN: July 8, 1943, St. Louis, Mo.
AREA OF ACHIEVEMENT: Health and medicine
SIGNIFICANCE: As president of Planned Parenthood from 1978 until 1992, Wattleton not only changed the organization's image but also made it better known to the American public

Born in St. Louis, Missouri, on July 8, 1943, Alyce Faye Wattleton was the only child of a factory worker and a minister. She was raised to believe that she should help others and to value a sense of achievement. In 1964 she received a bachelor's

Faye Wattleton at a press conference in 1983. (Library of Congress)

degree in nursing from Ohio State University. Earning her room and board by working part-time at a children's hospital, Wattleton was first exposed to battered children. After teaching at the Miami Valley Hospital School of Nursing for two years, she won a full scholarship in 1966 to Columbia University, completing her master's degree in maternal and infant health care. Specializing in midwifery, she became aware of the suffering associated with unintended pregnancies and the trauma associated with illegal abortions. When she became assistant director of the Montgomery County Combined Public Health District in Dayton, Ohio, she successfully expanded local prenatal health care services. In January, 1978, Wattleton was appointed to the presidency of Planned Parenthood, the world's oldest and largest voluntary reproductive health care organization. Wattleton, an African American, was the youngest president in the history of Planned Parenthood. —*Frances R. Belmonte*

See also Planned Parenthood Federation of America (PPFA); Pregnancy; Sanger, Margaret.

Wealth

RELEVANT ISSUES: Aging; Economics and work
SIGNIFICANCE: Household wealth can be an important basis for a lifestyle of comfort, especially in old age

Wealth includes financial assets as well as a family's personal property, such as clothing, jewelry, household furnishings and appliances, and automobiles and other vehicles. A major component of wealth for most families is their house. About two-thirds of families in the United States and Canada own their own homes. In 1992, the median value of owner-occupied houses was about $80,000, meaning that half the houses were worth that much or more.

Forms of Family Wealth. Very few families can pay cash for such an expensive purchase, so they normally borrow most of the price on a mortgage loan, secured by the property. Repaying the loan (typically by fixed monthly installments) becomes an important form of "forced saving." Such saving can be an important preparation for old age. Many elderly couples have paid off their mortgage and can either live in their house rent-free, sell it for a sizable lump sum, or borrow against it.

Household wealth also includes many types of financial assets. Cash assets such as currency and checking deposits are low in risk and high in convenience, but they pay little or no income. Banks offer time and savings deposits and certificates of deposit. In the mid-1990's, these paid around 6 percent interest and were federally insured against loss of principal.

Many households invest their savings in securities—stocks, bonds, and related items—that are bought and sold at fluctuating prices. Corporate stocks are ownership claims against a corporation. At the discretion of the management, they may pay dividends, which are returns to investors in the form of cash or additional shares of stock. Many investors hope to sell their stocks for more than they paid, and in the long run stock prices have tended to increase. By 1995 about 15 percent of families in the United States reported owning stocks.

Many households invest in such securities indirectly, by buying shares in investment companies, most of which are mutual funds, meaning they are owned by the investors. Investment companies use the money they obtain from investors to buy a diversified portfolio of many different securities, thus offering less risk than owning stock in a single company.

Aging and Retirement. Some financial assets are specifically aimed at providing for retirement. Many companies provide pension programs that can be viewed as part of the employees' wealth. In addition, many employees open their own retirement accounts. For a time, U.S. families were able to defer income tax liability on savings put into Individual Retirement Accounts (IRAs), which were subject to special regulations. In 1995, about 43 percent of United States families reported owning some type of private retirement account.

In the United States and Canada, as in most developed countries, the proportion of the population over the age of sixty-five is steadily increasing. When elderly people have ample retirement income, they are able to maintain their own homes and independent lifestyles. If they lack such resources, their care often becomes a problem for their adult children. As late as the 1940's, it was still common for elderly persons to move back in with their children in their later years. By the 1990's, such arrangements seemed unusual.

The floor of the New York Stock Exchange, where millions of Americans invest their savings. (AP/Wide World Photos)

Unincorporated Businesses and Farms. Very different types of wealth are involved in self-employment and unincorporated business. In the past, many families in the United States and Canada lived on farms. The farm house, barn, equipment, and livestock were a form of wealth as well as essential inputs for farm production and farmers' livelihood. By 1990, only about 2 percent of families in these countries lived on farms.

There are many forms of unincorporated businesses, and the net worth of each is part of the personal wealth of the owner. Many retail stores and service firms are unincorporated. In the mid-1990's, 80 percent of United States millionaires were working, and two-thirds of these were self-employed. Such financial success was particularly associated with firms in the computer software and biological technology industries.

Small businesses are often family businesses. A motivation for keeping the firm unincorporated may be the founder's desire to pass the business along to other family members. Not every child, however, is happy about being co-opted to fill a role in the family firm, and family members are not necessarily the best managers.

Wealth, Capital, and Productivity. The tangible wealth of the U.S. economy—all the land, buildings, machinery, and stocks of consumer and producer goods on hand—was worth about $30 trillion in 1992. This wealth was an important source of national productivity. Nations with a lot of tangible capital per worker are able to pay high wages and give most families a comfortable living. Such capital increases only through saving and investment, as opposed to consumption. In the 1980's and 1990's, the level of saving in the United States was relatively low, causing productivity to increase at a slow rate.

Some economists believe that saving follows the life cycle. When young adults first set up their own families, they go into debt to buy a car, a house, and other tangible property. In their later working years, they save a lot, paying off the mortgage and acquiring life insurance and pension-fund assets. At retirement, however, they shift to a pattern of net dissaving, living off their accumulated wealth.

Inequality of Wealth Ownership. There were about sixty-eight million families in the United States in 1992. The total net worth of all households was about $20 trillion, so average wealth per family was about $300,000. Wealth was very unequally distributed. In 1995, families with incomes over $100,000 (the top 6 percent) owned 44 percent of the household net wealth.

In the early twentieth century many social critics believed that inequality in property ownership was a major cause of poverty and income inequality. In the late twentieth century, however, nearly four-fifths of earned incomes in the United States and Canada represented income from one's own labor. Corporate executives, athletes, entertainers, doctors, and lawyers could all aspire to personal incomes of $100,000 a year or more on average, regardless of their wealth.

Despite talk of the "idle rich," data on the 5 percent of U.S. families getting the largest incomes indicated that 94 percent received some labor income. In contrast, among the 20 percent of families receiving the lowest incomes, only 54 percent reported labor income. The differences in property income nevertheless were very large: 96 percent of the high-income families received some, compared with only 30 percent of the low-income families.

Wealth Transfers and Taxation. There are many ways in which a high-income, high-wealth family can pass economic advantages on to children. Probably the most common is by giving them a good education and good medical attention. Parents also can transfer wealth to the children directly through gifts or bequests. Because the children have not "earned" these benefits by any productive efforts of their own, they may appear unfair. This is one reason why such wealth transfers are taxed.

The U.S. federal government taxes estates and gifts at rates from 18 to 55 percent; however, these taxes do not apply to transfers to a surviving spouse, do not include life insurance death benefits, and apply only to transfers above $600,000 to other beneficiaries. Individual states levy additional inheritance taxes. Such taxes are criticized insofar as they create serious problems for maintaining unincorporated businesses. Prudent owners of such firms usually carry large life insurance policies to cover such taxes. The tax burden is blamed for the fact that less than half of all family businesses survive to the second generation.

Although children born and reared in a wealthy family have potential economic advantages, the psychological effects may be damaging, depending on the family's lifestyle and values. Some wealthy families, such as the Rockefellers and Kennedys, developed a family tradition of high achievement and public service. For some children, however, the option of living in luxury and idleness can be corrupting. The offspring of a wealthy family can be attractive prey for fortune-hunting potential marriage partners. A prenuptial agreement may be used to safeguard property of one marriage partner. Sensational crimes have shown the seamy side of wealthy family life, involving such people as Claus von Bülow, who was acquitted in 1985 of trying to murder his heiress wife, and Lyle and Erik Menendez, who were convicted in 1996 of murdering their wealthy parents.

—*Paul B. Trescott*

BIBLIOGRAPHY

"Family Finances in the U.S.: Recent Evidence." *Federal Reserve Bulletin* 83 (January, 1997).

Gilder, George. *Wealth and Poverty.* New York: Basic Books, 1981.

Stanley, Thomas J., and William D. Danko. *The Millionaire Next Door: The Surprising Secrets of America's Wealthy.* Atlanta, Ga.: Longstreet Press, 1996.

Thorndike, Joseph J., Jr. *The Very Rich: A History of Wealth.* New York: American Heritage, 1976.

Wolff, Edward N. *International Comparisons of the Distribution of Household Wealth.* New York: Clarendon Press, 1987.

See also Alimony; Corporate families; Employee Retirement Income Security Act (ERISA); Family businesses; Family economics; Family life cycle;

Inheritance and estate law; Intergenerational income transfer; Political families; Poverty; Prenuptial agreements; Retirement; Social capital; Tax laws; Uniform Marital Property Act (UMPA); Wills and bequests.

Weddings

RELEVANT ISSUE: Marriage and dating

SIGNIFICANCE: Weddings represent one of the most important rites of passage in modern society, marking the blending of two families and the establishment of the nucleus of a new one

Few events stir the emotions more than beautiful wedding ceremonies. Whether simple or elaborate, in churches, synagogues, mosques, or outdoors, weddings express the quintessence of a couple's love and dreams and the pride and hope of families and friends.

Although exotic locations are not uncommon—marriages have been recorded on top of the Empire State Building in New York, on hot air balloons, at Disney World, and even at the drive-through window of a McDonald's restaurant—most weddings in the United States and Canada take place under religious auspices. This is also true of weddings in most cultural traditions around the world, and has always been so. The actions and words of priests, rabbis, and ministers and the solemnity of the holy setting express the belief that couples' union is divinely sanctioned and that the vows brides and grooms make to each other are sacred.

Basic Elements of the Wedding Service. In Christian tradition the wedding ceremony contains elements derived from two sources that predate Christian times: the *sponsalia*, or ceremony of betrothal, and the *nuptioe*, or marriage ceremony itself. The former contained the trothplight, the joining of hands, and the giving and receiving of rings and other gifts, such as the promise of a dowry. The principal features of the latter were the veiling of brides, the "giving away" of brides to bridegrooms by parents or guardians, the declaration of the completion of the wedding contract, and the bringing of brides to their new homes.

In Roman Catholicism and Protestantism, the essential requirement for the fulfillment of the marriage ceremony is the free consent of both parties, made in the presence of a priest or minister and two witnesses. It should be noted, however, that in the United States the state actually authorizes marriages.

Although denominational practices vary, Protestant ceremonies in general follow The Book of Common Prayer with its elevated Elizabethan language. The wedding service begins with words of welcome, followed by scriptural readings and a homily or sermon. This is followed by the declaration of intent, the blessing of the congregation upon brides and grooms, the question "Who gives this bride away?", the vows, the presentation of rings, the announcement that the couple is now husband and wife, and a prayer. Sometimes a thanksgiving, Holy Communion, and an agape meal (Love Feast) may be added. The ceremony concludes with the benediction, or blessing, which dismisses the congregation.

Roman Catholic wedding ceremonies take place during a Mass held especially for the wedding (although weddings may take place without a Mass). The ceremony begins with the entrance and rite of welcome, followed by an opening prayer. The liturgy of the word that follows includes readings from the Old and New Testaments selected from an approved list, a responsorial psalm, and a Gospel reading. After the homily comes the rite of marriage, the wording of which may vary. It includes the consent and the vows, the exchange of rings, and the prayer of the faithful. The Liturgy of the Eucharist and the Nuptial Blessing follow. If there is a Mass, the service ends with a Blessing and Dismissal. If there is no Mass, it ends with the Lord's Prayer and a Blessing.

Jewish wedding ceremonies vary according to the three main branches of Judaism: Orthodox, Conservative, and Reform Judaism. There are, however, many elements common to all. The wedding service usually takes place under a Huppah (canopy), which symbolizes the couple's new home. The groom places a ring on the forefinger of the bride's right hand, and declares, "Behold, thou art consecrated to me with this ring according to the laws of Moses and Israel." The giving of the ring and its acceptance in the presence of witnesses makes the wedding binding in the eyes of Jewish law.

During Orthodox and Conservative services, the *Ketubah*, or marriage contract, is read and then

Robert Altman's film A Wedding *(1978) captured the interactions among members of a big wedding party, their relatives, and guests, illustrating the complex role weddings play in family relationships.* (Museum of Modern Art, Film Stills Archive)

handed to the bride. The *Ketubah* describes the obligations that the couple has entered upon. In former times it was a legal document serving as evidence of the validity of the marriage. Reform Judaism does not use the *Ketubah*. During the ceremony the bride and groom drink from the same glass of wine. At the end of the ceremony it is customary for the bridegroom to break a thin wineglass by smashing it under his foot. For many, the broken glass is a reminder of the trials of the Jewish people, especially the destruction of the temple in Jerusalem in 70 C.E., or simply a reminder of the frailty of life and the reality of sorrow.

Wedding Rituals and Their Origins. Many of the rituals that accompany the modern wedding have their roots in ancient times. When the groom carries his bride over the threshold, for example, it is a distant echo of the "marriage by capture" that was the practice in some ancient tribal cultures. The modern best man was originally the groom's friend who helped carry out the abduction. The honeymoon is also an echo of marriage by capture, since the man had to hide away with his bride in order to evade the pursuit of her family, anxious to reclaim their "property."

Some customs, such as the wedding cake, were originally fertility symbols. Ancient Romans would bake a cake made of wheat or barley and break it over the bride's head as a symbol of her fertility. In medieval Europe sprigs of orange blossoms were carried to express the hope of fertility. By the eighteenth century this had become a bouquet of flowers—the modern bridal bouquet. The throwing of rice and flower petals has the same origin, although in modern America it is usually just a way of wishing the couple good luck. In some cultures eggs or dates and figs are thrown at the couple.

The practice of giving an engagement ring goes back to the times when marriage by purchase was customary. The suitor would make part of the payment to the bride's family in the form of "earnest money." The marriage ring is an ancient symbol, but it did not always carry the symbolism of love and unity that it possesses to modern eyes. In marriage by capture, a ring was placed around the ankle of the bride-to-be to prevent her escape.

It is unknown when wedding rings were first worn. They were probably made of a strong metal, such as iron, so that they would not break. The practice of placing the ring on the third finger of the left hand goes back to the belief held in ancient times (and disproved by modern science) that a vein ran from this finger directly to the heart.

Ethnic Wedding Practices. In some Latino weddings, thirteen gold coins, representing the groom's gift to his bride, are blessed by the priest during the wedding ceremony and passed between the hands of the newlyweds several times before being retained by the bride. Also during the ceremony a large rosary or white rope is sometimes wound around the couple's shoulders in a figure-eight to symbolize their union.

At some African American wedding ceremonies, the bridal couple "jump over a broom" to symbolize the beginning of their new life. The ritual dates back to the era of slavery and before to an African tribal marriage ritual of placing sticks on the ground to represent the couple's new home. In modern ceremonies, the jumping of the broom symbolizes the sweeping away of the old and the welcoming of the new. It is performed either at the wedding ceremony after the minister pronounces the couple husband and wife or at the reception. The broom is often decorated with bows and flowers and other trinkets in wedding colors. Sometimes guests at the reception participate by tying ribbons around the broom before the ritual begins.

Weddings and Family Conflict. A wedding is a testing time for all involved, because it signifies a profound shift in the dynamics of each family. For the couple, it represents the end of childhood and dependence, a break with old family ties. This can be especially difficult for both sets of parents, a situation that the old adage, "Think of it not as losing a son but gaining a daughter" (or vice versa), is clearly meant to address. The new situation can be experienced as a loss or an opportunity for transformation, as new relationships emerge within an extended family. Perhaps modern parents have a greater opportunity to adjust to the independence of their children than those of previous generations. Over the last few decades there has been a steady rise in the age at which men and women marry in the United States, and it is far less common now that newlyweds go directly from living with their parents to their new homes together. Most have had some experience with independence or semi-independence, because they have gone to college or been employed.

Family tensions in planning the wedding can come from almost any source, from the compilation of the guest list to the type of reception held. Sometimes apparently minor things, such as the color and style of a dress, can prompt arguments. Because a wedding is such a significant event, some family members may have very definite ideas of what is appropriate at each stage of the ceremony and reception and may be unwilling to compromise. There is a Jewish saying that no *Ketubah* is ever signed without quarreling. The wedding may also spark conflicts that are not directly about the wedding itself, but about other family relationships, including the parents' own marriage.

Weddings are typically organized to offer special roles to as many members of the involved families as possible. (James L. Shaffer)

The key moment in a wedding comes when the couple exchanges vows. (James L. Shaffer)

The potential problems are magnified when the wedding is between two people of different faiths, in which case the meetings between the families and the ceremony itself must be planned with special care. In this situation, the couple will also have to make decisions about the faith in which their children are to be raised, which may present another challenge to the families involved.

Conflicts can also become opportunities for strengthening all relationships within a family. Ideally, the wedding day should be a time in which all the disparate elements of a family come together in a ceremony of love and unity. For example, a wedding offers a chance for family members who have not seen each other for years to become reacquainted. It is an opportunity for a family to reaffirm the solidity of its ties or to restore them if they have been broken.

Recent Trends in Weddings. For centuries the wording and general format of wedding ceremonies, hallowed by religious tradition and authority, remained largely unchanged. In the 1960's and 1970's, as a result of liberalizing trends in Western society, it became fashionable for some couples to discard or modify traditional forms in favor of a ceremony, often written by the bride and groom themselves, that expressed their feelings and their goals together in a more direct and personal way than formal ceremonies permitted. Such "new" or "personal" weddings, as they became known, often included poetry and other inspirational, yet non-biblical, readings; a wide range of music, both popular and classical; and personal statements read by brides and grooms. Many of these weddings also included greater guest participation in the ceremony.

A popular wedding tradition is the best man's offering of a toast to the newly married couple. (Hazel Hankin)

As part of the changes set in motion by the Second Vatican Council (1962 to 1965), the Roman Roman Catholic Church made some changes to the wedding service liturgy in 1969, offering a choice of thirty biblical passages instead of the standard readings from the Gospels and Epistles. Some Protestant denominations, such as the Lutherans and Episcopalians, modernized the language used in wedding ceremonies and gave couples a wider range of choice in what is said and done during the service.

These trends have continued; small but significant changes in the wording of the wedding ceremony are increasingly common. For example, changing attitudes toward marriage prompted by the rising divorce rate (it is estimated that one marriage in two ends in divorce) are reflected in the frequent emendation "As long as we both shall love" for the traditional "As long as we both shall live." Some couples believe this to be a more realistic vow, a recognition that a marriage loses its validity when the love that sustains it is lost. Moreover, the traditional pronouncement of "man and wife" is often amended to read "husband and wife," in keeping with the societal trend toward more equal relations between the sexes. For the same reason, the question "Who gives this bride away?" is often omitted, since many brides do not consider themselves to be anyone's property in the first place.

There has been a growing flexibility regarding who pays for the wedding. Traditionally, the bride's family was expected to meet all costs, but the social system that produced such an arrangement—the need of the family to "marry off" its daughter—has long been swept away. It has become more common for expenses to be divided between the two families concerned. Many couples who have been financially independent for some years prefer to pay many of the wedding expenses themselves, and this change sometimes results in a situation in which costs are shared between three economic units: the bride's family, the groom's family, and the couple themselves.

—*Bryan Aubrey*

BIBLIOGRAPHY

Diamant, Anita. *The New Jewish Wedding*. New York: Summit Books, 1985. Attempts to provide an alternative vision of the modern Jewish wedding in America. Examines the trend toward a dynamic synthesis of modern sensibilities and Jewish tradition.

Fielding, William J. *Strange Customs of Courtship and Marriage*. Philadelphia: Blakiston Press, 1942. Concise and readable review of all the rituals and traditions that contribute to or underlie wedding celebrations in the United States.

Kirschenbaum, Howard, and Rockwell Stensrud. *The Wedding Book: Alternative Ways to Celebrate Marriage*. New York: Seabury Press, 1974. Describes the elements that make up the "new" or "personal" wedding and serves as a handbook for those who, instead of following traditional forms, wish to write their own wedding ceremony.

Klausner, Abraham J. *Weddings: A Complete Guide to All Religious and Interfaith Marriage Services*. New York: NAL/Penguin, 1986. Reproduces texts and wedding ceremonies from Episcopal, Presbyterian, Methodist, Unitarian, Friends (Quaker), Roman Catholic, Jewish, Orthodox Christian, Carpatho-Russian Orthodox, Muslim, and interfaith weddings and provides detailed explanations of each wedding stage.

Seligson, Marcia. *The Eternal Bliss Machine: America's Way of Wedding*. New York: William Morrow, 1973. Insightful, humorous, and sometimes quirky view of weddings, written on the premise that the American way of wedding is a glaring reflection of the American way of life.

See also Arranged marriages; Civil marriage ceremonies; Couples; Dowry; Family gatherings and reunions; Marriage; Marriage laws; Matchmaking.

Welfare

RELEVANT ISSUES: Economics and work; Law; Parenting and family relationships; Sociology

SIGNIFICANCE: Government assistance has played a major role in the lives of many poor North American families, and this assistance has generated much controversy between those who want to abolish it and those who insist that abolishing it will cause deeper poverty

"Welfare" is usually defined as government support for low-income people, although the term is sometimes extended to refer to government assistance to any members of a society. Until the middle of the twentieth century, most help for poor families in the United States and Canada came from private charities, such as religious organizations. Local governments sometimes had programs for the poor such as poorhouses, institutions in which the poverty-stricken would receive food and be forced to work. Some towns and cities also provided assistance to the "deserving poor," such as widows or the physically disabled, who remained in their own homes. In general, however, support for the disadvantaged was seen as creating dependence and as an inappropriate use of the taxpayers' money.

Origins of Family Welfare Programs. The crisis of the Great Depression of the 1930's and the enormous expansion of central governments that followed World War II brought federal welfare into existence. The Depression plunged America into a state of social turmoil and widespread unemployment. In the United States the administration of President Franklin D. Roosevelt attempted to pull the country out of its economic difficulties by a variety of reforms.

In 1935 the U.S. Congress passed the Social Security Act, the foundation of the U.S. welfare system. The core of this act was the Social Security system, a program to collect money from workers and employers in order to pay the workers when they later retired or became disabled. The act also contained provisions for public assistance, or welfare.

Not all poor people could receive public assistance. The concept of the "deserving poor" continued to determine who would be eligible for government support. The 1935 act designated three categories of people as deserving: children in families without a parent capable of working, who could receive assistance under the Aid to Dependent Children (ADC) program; the blind and disabled, who were eligible for the Aid to the Blind (AB) and Aid to the Disabled (AD) programs; and elderly people not eligible for regular Social Security payments, who qualified for the Aid to the Aged (AA) program.

The children supported by ADC were primarily those in households with widowed or abandoned mothers, and these mothers were not expected to be able to support families. Although the money in theory went to the children, since minors must live with adults, ADC became a family support program, oriented primarily toward families with only one parent. In the 1950's Aid to Dependent Children was changed to Aid to Families with Dependent Children (AFDC), because parents came to be seen as essential to the lives of their children. However, AFDC continued to be designed to support families with mothers, but not with fathers.

The states administered AFDC money and set payment levels. The federal government matched the amount each state paid recipients, so that costs were shared by the central government and the states. States were required to give assistance to needy families, but the amount of such assistance varied greatly from state to state. During the 1960's an expanded AFDC program, AFDC-UP (unemployed parent) was added in about half the states. In those states that participated in AFDC-UP, families with two parents could receive assistance as long as the fathers were seeking employment, in a job-training program, or disabled.

AFDC was supplemented by a variety of other forms of public assistance. The Medicaid program, approved by Congress in 1965, paid for medical care for welfare recipients. President John F. Kennedy began a modest demonstration food stamp program in 1961. Food stamps were vouchers that could be used only to purchase food. Under President Lyndon B. Johnson, the food stamp program was greatly extended in 1964. Finally, 1974 legislation made food stamps available in every county in the United States, whereby food stamps became the most widely used form of noncash assistance. Also in 1974, Section 8 of the Federal Housing and Community Development Act of 1974 established rent subsidies as a major housing program for low-income families.

In 1972, Aid to the Blind, Aid to the Disabled, and Aid to the Aged were combined into Supplementary Security Income (SSI). While the states and the federal government shared responsibility for most other welfare programs, SSI payments were made by the federal government to eligible people. AFDC and SSI together accounted for most of the cash assistance to needy families.

Welfare support for families in Canada also came into existence as part of the nation's social security system, which was created in 1945. The Family Allowances Act, a part of this system, established monthly payments to support all dependent children under the age of eighteen. Other financial assistance programs were established by the various Canadian provinces. The Canada Assistance Plan, developed by the Canadian government in 1966, created a consolidated program for sharing welfare costs between the provinces and the central government. Under this plan the Canadian federal government agreed to pay 50 percent of the costs of provincial and municipal assistance. The administration of most welfare programs was left to the provinces, whereby each province could establish its own criteria for welfare eligibility and its own assistance levels.

Extent of Welfare Reliance. Not all poor families have received welfare. In the United States during the mid-1990's, only about 43 percent of families below the official poverty level received cash public assistance payments. About 27 percent of poor families received no assistance at all, meaning that they did not participate even in noncash programs such as food stamps. The 1990 U.S. Census makes it possible to determine which fami-

In 1961 the federal government launched the food stamp program to put into the hands of the poor a form of currency that could be used only to purchase food. (Ben Klaffke)

lies received public assistance. Although the link between single-parent family structure and welfare eligibility has been weaker in Canada than in the United States, the trends have generally been similar in the two countries. Approximately 60 percent of families receiving U.S. public assistance income were whites and approximately 30 percent were African Americans. People of other racial groups, such as Asian Americans or Native Americans, made up the remaining 10 percent. About 8 percent of all families received welfare. More than 50 percent of the families that received public assistance income were headed by single women.

Among whites 6 percent of all families and 4 percent of dual-parent families received public assistance income, while 25 percent of families headed by single women received public assistance. Among African Americans 21 percent of all families, 9 percent of dual-parent families, and 35 percent of families headed by single women received public assistance income. Among Hispanics of both races, 14 percent of all families, 8 percent of dual-parent families, and 36 percent of families headed by single women received some form of public assistance.

These figures demonstrate that even though the majority of welfare recipients were white, minority families were much more likely to be on welfare. This is a result of the fact that minority families were much more likely than white families to be poor. Since AFDC is the major form of public assistance and AFDC is primarily available to single-mother households, it is understandable that families headed by women make up such a large proportion of families on welfare. This connection between welfare participation and family structure became one of the sources of a major debate: Did welfare encourage the maintenance of single-parent households?

Welfare and Single-Parent Families. As the number of American welfare recipients increased following 1960, the number of single-parent families, the overwhelming majority of which were headed by women, also increased. Some of the increase in single-parent families was caused by divorce, but much of it was also a result of growing numbers of children born to mothers who had never been married. From 1960 to 1990, the number of children born out of wedlock in the United States grew from 5 percent of all births to 30 percent. By 1992, a majority (58 percent) of children in families receiving AFDC were children born out of wedlock.

Some critics of the welfare system argued that welfare was one of the major causes of the increase in children born to unmarried mothers. Testifying before the U.S. Senate in April, 1995, the social critic Charles Murray argued that welfare payments to single mothers essentially paid unmarried women to have children. He maintained further that dual-parent families were beneficial to children and that welfare was therefore not in the interests of America's children.

Other experts argued that welfare was not the reason a growing number of children were being born to single mothers. They pointed out that

Total Social Welfare Expenditures Under U.S. Public Programs, 1980-1993

Year	Total	Social insurance	Public Aid	Health and medical programs	Veterans programs	Education	Housing	Other social welfare	All health and medical care
1980	493	230	73	27	21	121	7	14	100
1985	732	370	98	39	27	172	13	14	171
1989	957	468	129	57	30	239	18	17	240
1990	1,049	513	147	61	31	258	19	18	274
1991	1,159	561	181	66	33	277	22	20	313
1992	1,264	617	208	70	35	292	21	22	354
1993	1,364	657	221	75	37	332	20	23	381

Source: U.S. Bureau of the Census, *Statistical Abstract of the United States: 1997.* Washington, D.C.: GPO, 1997.
Note: Figures, in billions of dollars, encompass all federal, state, and local programs.

even though more single women were having children, the average size of AFDC families appeared to have decreased over time. In 1970 the average AFDC family included 4.0 people while in 1993 it included 2.9 people. Moreover, they maintained that welfare benefits were not generous enough to encourage women to choose single parenthood as a lifestyle.

The sociologist William J. Wilson offered one of the most influential views on the relationships among poverty, welfare, and family structure. Wilson maintained that marriage had declined in low-income communities, particularly in inner cities, because the absence of jobs had undermined men's abilities to contribute to family incomes. Single-parent families, however, could receive income in the form of public assistance, making the one-parent family the best available option.

Welfare, Families, and Employment. When Aid to Dependent Children was created in 1935, the parents of children who received this aid were generally not expected to work, because so many of them were widowed mothers. As the number of families receiving welfare increased and American women entered the labor force in large numbers, these expectations changed. In the United States it was not until 1962 that welfare recipients, especially single mothers, were first encouraged to work. That year the Social Security Act was amended to establish cost sharing between the federal government and the states in providing job counseling to welfare recipients. Five years later, in 1967, women in the United States were required to register for the Work Incentive (WIN) program. Although Canada was generally less concerned than the United States with pushing welfare recipients into jobs, the Province of Ontario established its own Ontario Work Incentive program in 1979, modeled on the U.S. effort. WIN in both the United States and Ontario provided wage supplements to women who left the welfare roles to go to work.

One of the most radical ideas for overhauling the U.S. welfare system came from Republican president Richard M. Nixon, whose 1969 Family Assistance Plan contained the proposal that all families with children be provided with a guaranteed income. Since many American lawmakers objected to simply guaranteeing money to all, Nixon's advisor Daniel Patrick Moynihan added a provision to the plan requiring that people must work to receive the guaranteed income. William Safire, a Nixon speech writer, labeled this work requirement "workfare." Although the guaranteed income plan failed, the term "workfare" became a permanent part of the American political vocabulary, used to describe the practice of forcing aid recipients to work.

During the 1980's opposition to traditional welfare and support for some form of workfare increased. The 1988 Family Support Act was a major piece of workfare legislation that created the Job Opportunities and Basic Skills Training (JOBS) program, which required states to provide job skills training, counseling, and placement to welfare recipients. The Family Support Act of 1993 required that welfare parents with children over the age of three seek work and also barred states from using federal matching grants to establish child-care programs. In both the United States and Canada, the lack of affordable child care has seriously impeded welfare parents' ability to work, because neither country has provided public day care for needy working parents.

Families and Welfare Reform. By the early 1980's, popular perceptions that government had grown too large and that welfare rolls were swollen with those unwilling to work led to calls for reduced federal involvement in assisting poor families. In Canada Prime Minister Brian Mulroney attempted to scale back federal spending on public welfare. In the United States, the Republican Ronald Reagan was elected president in 1980 after promising to reduce the role of government in people's lives. During his eight years in office, President Reagan removed nearly a half million families from welfare and reduced the benefits received by hundreds of thousands of additional families by tightening AFDC eligibility standards. His government also cut one million people from the food stamp program. Beyond this, President Reagan promised a "new federalism," under which many federal programs, including AFDC, would be transferred from the federal to state and local governments.

President Reagan's Republican successor, President George Bush, continued the criticism of welfare. Yet the biggest steps toward shrinking welfare assistance to families and handing welfare responsibilities over to state governments were taken by

Government cuts in welfare programs are invariably met by public protests. (Dick Hemingway)

Democratic president Bill Clinton. In August, 1996, President Clinton signed a new welfare bill. Under the new policy the federal government would no longer guarantee assistance to needy families, and it would no longer pay the states a matching share of the money needed to help families who qualified for assistance. Instead, the federal government would provide blocks of money, known as block grants, to the states. Each state could use its block grant to set up its own welfare program. The central government merely required that the states limit the amount of time recipients can remain on welfare and require that recipients work. In general, welfare recipients would not be allowed to receive assistance for more than a total of five years. Further, each state had to certify within a specified period of time that a certain percentage of their welfare recipients were either working or in job-training programs. Critics of the new welfare policy argued that many American families would lose income and that many children would be pushed deeper into poverty.   —*Carl L. Bankston III*

BIBLIOGRAPHY

Bane, Mary J., and David T. Ellwood. *Welfare Realities: From Rhetoric to Reform.* Cambridge, Mass.: Harvard University Press, 1994. An examination of welfare policy and its effects that recognizes the existence of welfare dependency but attempts to find ways of improving welfare rather than abolishing it.

Murray, Charles. *Losing Ground: American Social Policy, 1950-1980.* New York: Basic Books, 1984. An influential work that maintains that welfare actually increased poverty, because it involved paying people not to work and not to form two-parent families.

Patterson, James T. *America's Struggle Against Poverty, 1900-1980.* Cambridge, Mass.: Harvard University Press, 1981. A history of antipoverty programs in the United States.

Quadagno, Jill. *The Color of Welfare: How Racism Undermined the War on Poverty.* New York: Oxford University Press, 1994. Historical examination of welfare policy in the United States that argues that the public perception of welfare as a minority issue kept Americans from adopting adequate welfare policies.

Wilson, William J. *When Work Disappears: The World of the New Urban Poor.* New York: Vintage, 1996. A detailed examination of the impact of joblessness on family life and welfare dependency.

See also Aid to Families with Dependent Children (AFDC); Child Welfare League of America (CWLA); Children born out of wedlock; Children's Bureau; Day care; Family economics; Family Protection Act; Fatherlessness; Feminization of poverty; McKinney Homeless Assistance Act; Poverty; Single-parent families; Social workers; Tax laws; Teen mothers.

Widowhood

RELEVANT ISSUES: Aging; Marriage and dating; Parenting and family relationships

SIGNIFICANCE: Because the majority of marriages end in the death of one partner, families must learn to adjust to death and to assist bereaved and often frail members

The majority of marriages in modern societies end in the death of one partner. Widowhood is a predictable and significant life event, one that affects nearly all families. More often than not, the survivor is a woman (widow), and she has an average of more than ten years to live without her husband. Men who are widowed (widowers) are fewer in number and are more likely to remarry than are widows.

Because widowhood generally occurs in late middle to old age, the surviving spouse is often frail and thus dependent on other family members for physical and emotional care. Daughters and daughters-in-law may find themselves "sandwiched" between a widowed parent, on one hand, and their own young adult offspring and young grandchildren, on the other, each involving some sort of emotional or financial responsibility.

Effect of a Spouse's Death. The death of a spouse is extremely stressful for the survivor, whether or not the death is expected. Family and friends generally gather to follow prescribed rituals associated with death, assisted by professionals such as clergy and morticians. The shock of the death itself and the necessity of making arrangements for death rituals leaves most families exhausted. Survivors often report difficulty in sleeping and in conducting acts of daily living, and they may get panic attacks in which they have difficulty

The majority of widowed persons are women, who live an average of ten years after losing their husbands. (AP/Wide World Photos)

breathing. These dramatic physiological and psychological responses to bereavement generally disappear after a few months.

After a partner dies, the survivor has to adjust to a new life. Changes that people report include doing household and social things by oneself, which may provide an opportunity to learn new skills. For example, a widower may find himself doing more cooking and household work, and a widow may drive herself to social events.

Most widowed people prefer to live alone, but this is an adjustment that takes some time. Some enjoy the freedom of living alone and organizing their lives independently. A minority report continued ongoing feelings of loneliness and isolation.

Most survivors, while married, were part of social groups composed of couples. Being suddenly single may make the person feel like a "fifth wheel." Many widows and widowers find themselves making new friends among people in similar circumstances. Having a very good friend in which the widowed person can confide seems to help considerably in coping with grief and bereavement and in formulating new patterns of interaction.

Economic Difficulties. Widowhood for women often means a dramatic loss of income. A widow rarely has an income as large as the one she had while her spouse was alive. Employed women generally earn less than men, and retired women have less retirement income than men because they earned less while working. Partly because of lower incomes, widows are less likely to own their homes than are widowers.

Approximately one-fourth of single parents of children under eighteen years of age in Canada and the United States are widowed. They have the responsibilities of being both mother and father to their children, of helping children deal with grief over the death of a parent, and of earning a living and doing household work without the help of a partner. Other family members, such as the widowed person's parents or siblings, may be needed for assistance in child rearing.

Some widows report that a new sense of self develops over time, as confidence in their new skills grows. Morale and the overall feeling of well-being appears to fall at the time of death of the spouse but returns to previous levels in two to three years. Morale is higher among those widowed persons with good health and higher levels of income and education.

Loneliness brought on by death of an intimate partner is natural. It persists for a long period of time more often among widowers than among widows, partly because women are more involved with their kin than are men.

Widowed Persons in Families. Offspring may take a more prominent part in the lives of their widowed parent than they did when the parents were both living. Emotional support is the most

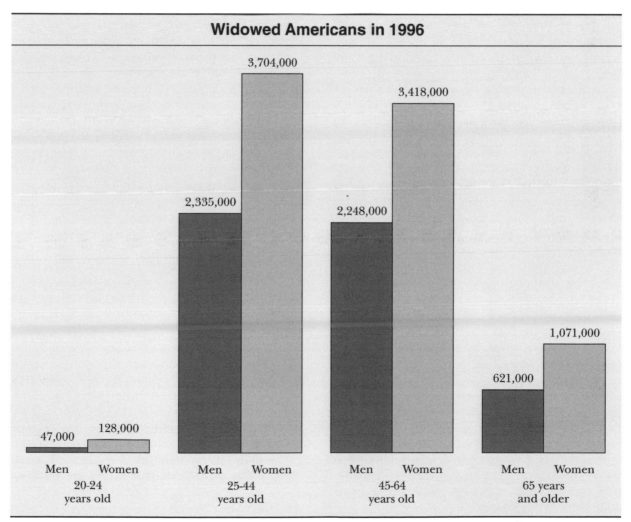

Widowed Americans in 1996

3,704,000

3,418,000

2,335,000

2,248,000

1,071,000

621,000

128,000

47,000

| Men | Women | Men | Women | Men | Women | Men | Women |
| 20-24 years old | | 25-44 years old | | 45-64 years old | | 65 years and older | |

Source: U.S. Bureau of the Census, *Statistical Abstract of the United States: 1997.* Washington, D.C.: GPO, 1997.
Note: Numbers rounded to nearest 1,000.

frequent type of assistance given. This includes visits, having meals together, talking on the telephone, and going to social or religious events. Older widowed people often share in family life by looking after grandchildren or great-grandchildren, giving gifts, and telling stories that are part of the heritage of the family.

Frail, elderly North Americans often prefer to have a spouse look after them. Upon widowhood, survivors most often want an offspring to be their caregiver. Because the surviving person more often is a woman, she wants her daughter to assist with personal care, such as providing help with activities of daily living such as bathing and household work. If a daughter is not available, a daughter-in-law often helps. Sons or sons-in-law are likely to arrange for hired helpers, to provide assistance with financial matters, and to give advice. If families or friends cannot give needed services, formal care by public agencies or hired private helpers may be sought.

Caregiving responsibility for frail elderly widowers generally is assumed by middle-aged offspring who are employed, have partners themselves, and have children and grandchildren. Some people, particularly daughters or daughters-in-law, feel pressure and stress because of the demands made on them by different generations.

Siblings are an important source of support for widows and widowers, and sibling relationships often become stronger after the death of one sibling's spouse, particularly when it occurs in old age. Older widows and widowers are less likely to have wide support networks because they no longer have coworkers (if retired), and many of their friends may have died. Siblings may be the best source of support left to them.

Social Supports for Widowed Persons. Widowed people depend on friends and family for some needs, but they also can join self-help groups, such as Widow-to-Widow programs. These provide peer support and may assist in the transitions from married to single status. Two factors make participation in self-help groups more common among widows than among widowers: First, there are more widows than widowers, and second, women tend to discuss their personal situations more than do men.

Some widowed persons are assisted by their religious beliefs. Religious behavior usually does not change as a result of being widowed, but for people with a faith and a religious community, morale in widowhood tends to be higher.

Widowed persons in rural areas or small towns may have more difficulty getting services than residents of urban areas. Social services such as home health care or transportation may not be offered in every small town because there is not enough demand for them.

Much of what is known about widowed people comes from information provided by whites. People of other races, as well as those from religions or ethnic backgrounds different from the dominant culture, need to be studied more to see what similarities and differences they have.

Remarriage. Remarriage occurs for the majority of widowers and a minority of widows. Men are more likely to remarry because the ratio of widowers to widows is imbalanced, with more female than male survivors. By the age of sixty-five, the majority of women are widowed, but the majority of men are still married. It is not until the age of eighty that widowers outnumbered married men.

Remarriage appears to succeed best when the widowed person has waited a year or so to remarry, when the couple's children favor the remarriage, and when the couple lives in a different house or apartment from the one in which either of them lived before remarriage. Remarriage provides companionship and a sexual partner, and most remarried couples report that they are very happy and satisfied.

People in same-sex or heterosexual cohabitational relationships who experience the death of a partner may have many of the same feelings and need to make many of the same adjustments as people who were married. A surviving partner who was not formally married to the person who died, however, may not have the same sources of social support. Such people are also not often entitled to the same death benefits through transfer payments or inheritance that widowed people can get. Because more people now live in long-term, intimate partnerships outside marriage, more information needs to be gathered about their adaptation processes.   —*Carol D. H. Harvey*

BIBLIOGRAPHY

Connidis, Ingrid Arnet. *Family Ties and Aging.* Toronto: Butterworths, 1989.

Harvey, Carol D. H., and Howard M. Bahr. *The Sunshine Widows: Adapting to Sudden Bereavement.* New York: Lexington Books, 1980.

Lopata, Helena Znaniecka. *Current Widowhood: Myths and Realities.* Thousand Oaks, Calif.: Sage Publications, 1996.

_____, ed. *Widows: Vol. II. North America.* Durham, N.C.: Duke University Press, 1989.

Matthews, Anne Martin. *Widowhood in Later Life.* Toronto: Butterworths, 1991.

See also Aging and elderly care; Dating; Death; Family life cycle; Funerals; Gender longevity; Life expectancy; Midlife crises; Remarriage; Sandwich generation; Social Security; Wills and bequests.

Wills and bequests

RELEVANT ISSUES: Economics and work; Law
SIGNIFICANCE: Wills and bequests are used to control persons' wealth after they die

Free alienability allows the current owner of property to transfer it by sale, gift, or will without any legal restrictions. The law, however, recognizes restrictions on alienability. Some of these restrictions can be severe and keep property tied up for many years. Many such restrictions serve useful purposes, such as providing for a spouse and children.

Entailment refers to legal devices invented in English common law to keep land in the hands of a family. An entailment, therefore, restricts alienability. Entailment gave rise to primogeniture, by which land automatically went to the eldest son upon the death of the father. Even without primogeniture, other legal devices such as trusts and life estates can be used to keep property within a family or other group. A will as written by the current owner cannot affect transfer of property covered under such devices upon the current owner's death.

How Property Passes at Death. Wills and family bequests are part of a larger probate system in which title to property passes to another person upon death of the current owner. Property can pass in a number of ways when the owner dies. The deceased may have left a valid will directing where property should go. Such a person is said to have died testate, a term coming from the last will and testament.

If there is no will or a court refuses to probate a will because it fails to meet one or more legal requirements, then the person dies intestate. Such a person's property passes to the people designated in the state's intestacy statute, which essentially is a backup will written by the state to apply to anyone who dies intestate.

Determining who gets property when someone dies intestate has changed dramatically over the centuries. In England, land went to the eldest son under the rule of primogeniture. Personal property, however, was divided among all the children. This difference arose because the common law courts of the king determined title to land, but the courts of the Roman Catholic Church decided title to personal property.

Persons Who Inherit Wealth. In the American colonies before the Revolutionary War, primogeniture was common in a small number of colonies, particularly in the South, where society and land ownership resembled England more closely. Other colonies divided all property among the children. Modern intestacy laws usually give property first to the surviving spouse, then to all the children in equal shares.

Whether a person dies testate or intestate, there is a legal proceeding called probate in which a court decides who gets title to property. Probate is very important when the property is land, a business, or a large investment. It is difficult or impossible for an heir to sell, use, or deal with property inherited from someone without a legal determination of title.

Property can also pass automatically upon death, with the interest of the deceased in the property automatically transferred to someone else without the need for probate or a will. Many people own property as joint tenants with rights of survivorship. If one joint tenant dies, his or her interest in the property automatically and immediately is transferred to the surviving joint tenants. Property that can be owned as joint tenants includes homes, cars, bank accounts, and investments.

Women presented special problems for the writers of wills until the passage of the Married Women's Property Acts in the nineteenth century. Until these acts went into effect, married women lacked the legal capacity to execute a contract. Husbands generally controlled the property of their wives. Only unmarried women could enter into contracts or control their own property. Leaving property to a woman in a will carried a substantial risk that her husband would dissipate the property. The problem was solved initially by wills that gave women something less than full legal ownership. Widows were given only life estates in property. Trusts and other devices were used to give daughters and other women property without the risk of a husband using the property.

Trusts and Similar Devices. Once the Married Women's Property Acts were passed, it was not necessary to leave property to a woman in a trust or other complicated legal form. Trusts nevertheless have remained popular parts of the wills of the wealthy. Spendthrift and caretaker trusts are used

to provide gifts for people unable or unwilling to take care of themselves. Such individuals may include minors, people in financial trouble, and adults unable to care for themselves.

Trusts also are used to perpetuate family dynasties. The will of the founder of the dynasty may put all assets into a trust, with current income going to the support of the next living generation. The principal assets of the trust, however, are not available for current use and must be kept intact for future generations. Entire family fortunes thus can be made secure for the future.

The use of trusts and similar devices is still largely limited to the wealthy. Drafting a will with a trust is complex and expensive. Trustees must be appointed and paid for their services.

Trusts and other devices are usually limited to the wealthy. Many estates have little more to pass along than a family home. (James L. Shaffer)

Public Policy Concepts on Alienability. Entailments of land served a useful purpose in monarchies such as England. Where power and influence were tied to land, people found ways to keep land within the family. The landed aristocracy of England also faced a powerful king and central government. Entailments were used as a counterbalance to this centralized power.

Entailments of land were always known to have negative effects as well. They created a land monopoly that was often economically inefficient. Changes in agriculture and industry, for example, often made land more valuable in the hands of new owners. Dynasties based on land became less important after the Industrial Revolution created other forms of wealth and power than land.

Land monopolies and land dynasties were never popular in America. The republican form of government of the United States rejected aristocracy and its accompanying entailment of property. The principles of equal rights and individual merit established a climate unsuited to the entailment of property to new generations.

English law created the Rule Against Perpetuities to limit entailments. The rule allowed land to be tied up in one family for two generations into the future but no longer. American law attempted even more severe restrictions on entailments. The market had to be kept free and open for transfers of property by sale, gift, or will.

Legal attempts to restrict entailments, however, have not been successful in all cases. Once a person has accumulated wealth, there is a natural desire to keep such wealth concentrated in a family. This concentration allows the maximum use of power and influence. Family pride also affects how wealth is distributed, because people naturally want to leave property to their offspring. Parents also are anxious for the well-being of children. All these factors have contributed to evasions of the laws that favor free alienability of property. Modern equivalents of entailments, such as the trust, have been used to keep property within families.

Restrictions on Alienability. People with little or no wealth also are able to create restrictions on the free alienability of their property. Spouses are legally required to leave at least some property to each other. Community property laws in some states require that a surviving spouse receive half of all property acquired during the marriage. Joint

tenancies and similar devices also tie up property. Such devices are sometimes referred to as the poor person's will, because they are often easier to create than a formal written will.

The law recognizes the social and economic utility of many restrictions on free alienability. Such restrictions provide for the care of spouses and minor children when a person dies.

Free alienability of property, however, is the norm in American society. Nobody is required to create a trust, joint tenancy, or other device. The old English entailments have been abolished or substantially restricted by statute and court decision. With the exception of spouses, it is possible to write a will that leaves property as the deceased wishes. As it turns out, most people who write wills continue to leave property to their immediate family.

—*David E. Paas*

BIBLIOGRAPHY
Friedman, Lawrence M. *American Law.* New York: W. W. Norton, 1984.
_____. *A History of American Law.* New York: Simon & Schuster, 1973.
Posner, Richard A. *Economic Analysis of Law.* 4th ed. Boston: Little, Brown, 1992.

See also Guardianship; Inheritance and estate law; Intergenerational income transfer; Living wills; Prenuptial agreements; Primogeniture; Tax laws; Uniform Marital Property Act (UMPA); Wealth; Widowhood.

Wilson, William G.

BORN: November 26, 1895, East Dorset, Vt.
DIED: January 24, 1971, Miami Beach, Fla.
AREA OF ACHIEVEMENT: Health and medicine
SIGNIFICANCE: As a cofounder of Alcoholics Anonymous (AA), Wilson played a substantial role in developing the twelve-step recovery program, the model for subsequent recovery organizations

William (Bill) Griffith Wilson was the son of quarry worker Gilman Wilson and his wife Emily Griffith Wilson. The Wilson family had a history of alcoholism, and Gilman Wilson deserted the family when Bill was ten years old. Bill Wilson was later placed in the care of his mother's family when Emily Wilson left for Boston.

Wilson grew up insecure and overly competitive. In 1914 he enrolled at Norwich University in Vermont. At the age of twenty-one he took his first drink and quickly became a heavy drinker. In 1918 he married Lois Burnham. Upon returning from noncombatant service in France, he briefly attended the Brooklyn Law School, but he ultimately became a successful stockbroker. After the 1929 market crash, Wilson found himself in debt, unable to find steady work, and increasingly dependent on alcohol. Attempts to break his dependency failed until he was influenced by the Oxford Group, an evangelical movement stressing personal confession of guilt and restitution.

After his spiritual conversion, Wilson discovered that sharing his experiences with Robert H. Smith, a fellow alcoholic, enabled both of them to control their dependency. As "Bill W" and "Dr. Bob S," they founded Alcoholics Anonymous (AA) in 1935 and organized the Alcoholic Foundation as a trusteeship for the organization in 1938. Wilson also published *Alcoholics Anonymous* (1939), a compendium of individual alcoholics' experiences in recovery, followed by *Twelve Steps and Twelve Traditions* (1953), which outlined the organization's philosophy and procedure. Wilson placed the foundation under an elected General Service Board in 1954 but remained active. By 1971 AA had some 500,000 members in 85 countries.

Many researchers consider alcoholism to be a family disease. Research findings indicate that alcoholism seems to be prevalent along family lines. Although conclusive evidence has yet to be found, studies have shown that between 50 and 80 percent of all alcoholics have had a close relative who suffered from alcoholism. One reason that families should participate in recovery programs is that such programs foster an awareness of addiction and provide a means for overcoming it.

—*Ralph L. Langenheim, Jr.*

See also Al-Anon; Alateen; Alcoholism and drug abuse; Dysfunctional families; Family counseling; Recovery programs; Support groups.

Wisconsin v. Yoder

DATE: Ruling issued on May 15, 1972
RELEVANT ISSUES: Education; Religious beliefs and practices

SIGNIFICANCE: This Supreme Court decision limited the right of states to enforce compulsory education laws when such laws conflict with the right of parents to decide their children's religious upbringing

Wisconsin v. Yoder pitted the state of Wisconsin, which required all children to attend school up to the age of sixteen, against members of the Old Order Amish community, which allowed their children to attend public schools only through the eighth grade. Since Amish beliefs require their members to withdraw completely from the world at large, only a minimum amount of education is thought necessary for adherents to participate fully in Amish community life. Wisconsin saw the refusal of Amish parents to allow their children to attend school beyond the eighth grade as a violation of its compulsory education law and brought suit to force those parents to comply. After reversals for both sides in various state courts, the case came before the U.S. Supreme Court.

The Court, in deciding for the parents, ruled that a state's obligation in matters of education could not override parents' fundamental right to the free exercise of religious belief. Writing for the six-member majority, Chief Justice Warren Burger warned that "only those interests of the highest order and those not otherwise served can overbalance claims to the free exercise of religion." In this case, "enforcement of the State's requirement of compulsory formal education . . . would gravely endanger if not destroy the free exercise of [Amish] religious beliefs" and thus the Amish way of life.

The Yoder decision was significant in that it strongly affirmed the primacy of parents' role in directing the religious upbringing of their children: "The primary role of the parents in the upbringing of their children," wrote Burger, "is now established beyond debate as an enduring American tradition." —*Robert C. Davis*

See also Educating children; Home schooling; Mennonites and Amish; Public education; Religion.

Women's roles

RELEVANT ISSUES: Economics and work; Marriage and Dating; Parenting and family relationships

SIGNIFICANCE: The diverse roles played by women as mothers, wives, breadwinners, and more within the evolving notion of family and shifting social relations have been the subject of intense popular, political, and religious debate

A key concern in sociology is the manner in which societies establish prescribed roles or patterns of behavior for specific categories of individuals. One area of investigation is the extent to which these roles are inherent and to what degree they are learned. Gender is one crucial factor in determining prescribed behavior within the family. There appears to be a crosscultural notion of family, but how that family is constituted and what roles women play are diverse. The American and European tradition of roles for women within the family includes a strict division of labor, in which women are wives and mothers. However, these roles are evolving, and by the latter part of the twentieth century women had come to play the role of breadwinners and to exercise greater leadership.

Multifaceted Understanding of the Family. In North America, the understanding of family has evolved throughout the twentieth century and has been affected by economic class and cultural heritage. The nuclear family, consisting of a husband, wife, and children living under the same roof, has been the most prevalent definition of family. This configuration dominates the historical understandings of women's role. However, economic circumstances and cultural norms influenced by diverse groups of immigrants have led to alternative conceptions of the family, which include extended family members such as grandparents, aunts, uncles, and cousins. Within a household of extended family members gender remains a significant determinant of behavior, but women's roles are likely to be shared.

Because of greater social acceptance, more liberal divorce laws, and a growing number of women who believe that they could survive without a man in the family, the latter part of the twentieth century saw the rise of single-parent households led by women. Under these conditions, gender roles within the family have been rendered somewhat irrelevant as mothers play both traditional male and female roles. In addition, the end of the twentieth century was marked by a greater acceptance of alternative lifestyles, which have created new family configurations. Lesbian households, for example, have offered some women an opportunity to alter the connection between gender and circumscribed roles. Despite these alternative conceptions of what constitutes a family, the romanticized notion of the heterosexual, nuclear family and its associated gender roles has remained prevalent.

Child Raising. While giving birth and breast-feeding infants is a role women play in the family because of biology, these activities have traditionally been extended to relegating women through adolescence and adulthood to the primary care of children. Motherhood has entailed the physical care of children, including feeding, bathing, and grooming, as well as emotional formation in the form of modeling tenderness and care. In the tradition of a strict division of labor within the family, these mothering activities encompass much of women's time through their children's school-age years. A strict notion of separate gender spheres helped to maintain conformity to this role through the 1960's. Women were responsible for home life while men left the home to undertake paid labor. This meant that the bulk of daily parenting was left in the hands of mothers. Fathers' duties included family leadership and decision making, the disciplining of the children, and coordinating leisure activities on weekends and holidays.

Gender was also the deciding factor in how children were raised. While women cared for all their children, they also served as models of prescribed gender behaviors for their daughters. Gender identification with the activities and behavior of same-sex parents was a source of great pride. As children grew into adolescence, their activities, play, and chores were often determined by gender. In this manner, children's experience of family served to reproduce gender roles for the next generation. While numerous efforts were made to diminish gender stereotyping, it remained a determining factor in child raising through the end of the twentieth century.

Social institutions such as the justice system and religious organizations supported definitive roles within the family. For example, numerous Christian denominations invoked the Bible and church doctrine to argue that it was proper and perhaps divinely inspired for men to be the "head" of families while women were their "heart." Through the 1960's most states maintained laws that prohibited married women from serving on juries, because it was believed that such service would remove them from their primary duty in the home and from child care. In numerous overt and covert ways society made it clear that the responsibility for raising children belonged to mothers.

Beginning in the 1970's a combination of consciousness raising, which revealed that men could and should be more involved parents, and economics, which drove more women to work, caused an erosion in women's strict child-raising responsibility. By the end of the twentieth century, mainstream popular expectations had shifted to the opinion that men and women should share more or less equally in the development of their offspring. One indication of this shift in popular culture was the transformation of the fictional roles of mothers and fathers depicted on television and in film. In the 1950's virtually all women depicted on television were in stable heterosexual married relationships, whereby they stayed at home to tend to the house and children. In the 1980's and 1990's the pendulum had swung the other way, as almost all women featured on television had careers or career goals. However, a subtle bias toward maternal parenting remains and is often revealed in child-custody battles in which women receive custody of their children more often than men because both parties often consider it best for mothers to be primary caregivers. In addition, the rhetoric surrounding legislation to support child tax credits often appears to support a nostalgic return to women's primary role as mothers and housewives.

Domestic Management. In addition to child raising, the notion of separate gender spheres saw women as unpaid home laborers. While men were considered the leaders of their households, women managed and maintained them. The domestic role of women included preparing meals, housecleaning, doing the laundry, and shopping. Strict gender demarcation existed for these responsibilities. Men often maintained the yard and were responsible for vehicle upkeep, although such activities seldom required daily attention. Men's primary role was as paid laborers outside the home.

The post-World War II economic boom combined with more sophisticated mass marketing techniques created an opportunity for exploitation of gender roles in the development of household appliances and other consumables. Advertisements for food, toiletries, and other small-ticket items were geared toward women, because it was understood that women made the routine purchase decisions in the home. Advertisements for big-ticket items, such as automobiles, were geared to men, because it was understood that they made the major purchase decisions in the home. Advertisements for appliances targeted women by claiming that such appliances provided greater convenience, but these advertisements also promoted rigid gender roles by glamorizing domestic labor. During the 1960's many women began to ask questions about the limitations of the roles dictated to them by their gender. These concerns in part gave rise to a fresh wave of feminism.

The language of roles was an important element in the rise of a feminist criticism of gender inequalities in the family. While men's and women's roles were often described as complementary within the family, women began to ask why power and influence were primarily ascribed to men. When feminists employed the theme "the personal is political," they saw the family as a metaphor for the power relationships in society at large. The gender inequalities at home were mirrored in government, business, and religion. Understanding how social acceptance could create artificial limitations, many women refused to accept the idea that women's roles were natural or divinely ordained.

While feminism may have provided an intellectual undercurrent to change, it was primarily economics that drove women to seek paid employment outside the home in the latter part of the twentieth century. As the real wages of men plateaued, women had to work if families were to achieve much-desired middle-class lifestyles. Despite their participation in paid labor, women were not able to extricate themselves from the role of domestic management. The popular expectation was that women would work full-time jobs and then go home to perform traditional household duties such as cooking and cleaning. In the 1980's and 1990's this phenomenon became known as the "second shift." Women worked double duty by laboring like their male counterparts while trying

Women have traditionally served as models of prescribed gender behavior for their daughters. (James L. Shaffer)

to fulfill their mothers' roles as housewives. A very stressful "superwoman" complex resulted, which placed a premium on finding free time to accomplish everything expected of women. New roles and old roles intersected.

Bread Winner. Demographics indicate that in the 1970's dual-earner families became the norm rather than the exception in North America. Nevertheless, lingering notions persisted that husbands were families' sole providers. For the middle class, the fact that women worked was indicative that their husbands' careers were unsuccessful. Women were not to labor for money, but rather to provide unpaid domestic work. Often, middle- and upper-class women who found these roles too confining found outlets for their energies in volunteer work in the community, particularly in church organizations, schools, and hospitals. Such work did not challenge husbands' responsibility to economically provide for their families. Sometimes middle-class women worked part-time for a living, but their wages were referred to as "pin money," money that was used to buy luxuries or extras. If women had part-time or even full-time jobs, they often rationalized that this was a temporary condition. The romanticized norm for the middle class through much of the twentieth century had been that families should have a single male income provider. Poor families, on the other hand, rarely had the luxury of creating a purely domestic role for women.

According to resource theory, the impact of the shift toward dual incomes should have been significant in equalizing power relations within the family. However, traditional roles die hard. The necessity and desirability that wives should work outside the home has resulted in role conflicts and turmoil within the family. The ability to earn money was more than simply the role given to men within the equal partnership of marriage. Male income was emblematic of male power and status within the family. In cases of marital conflict, men often held the trump card because they brought home the paycheck. Women who had never worked outside the home were left in a dependent position, because they needed a man to earn a living. Even divorced women were urged to remarry because of financial concerns. The ability of both men and women to earn incomes has greatly mitigated female dependence and had

thus altered the balance of power in families at the close of the twentieth century. A number of factors contribute to lingering biases favoring male breadwinners, however. The glass ceiling and the wage gap between the genders continue to give men an edge over women in earning ability.

Creating Family Itself. One persistent role that women have continued to play within the family, despite economic upheaval and social change, is that of builders of the very essence of family and family relationships. Women have consistently been at the core of creating kinship groups. Women have been largely responsible for planning and managing family gatherings, entailing that they have maintained their traditional roles of cooking, cleaning, scheduling, and inviting. A common metaphor for this role is that women "knit together the fabric of the family." Married women often find themselves responsible for remembering and celebrating occasions such as birthdays and anniversaries, even when they involve their in-laws. In this role women develop and employ communications and bonding skills that are not expected of men or that men are reluctant to develop in the family context.

Women's role of binding the family together in conjunction with their responsibility as families' primary caregivers has created new burdens for North American women as the baby-boom generation has begun to age at the end of the twentieth century. In addition to being wives and mothers, women are often daughters of living but aging parents. Women are the primary providers of elder as well as child care, care they often extend to their in-laws. As medical advances have allowed people to live longer, increasing longevity has sometimes been accompanied by women's heightened care-giving responsibilities, which has affected their financial and psychological well-being and impinged on their time. Women are again caught in the middle of multiple role demands to provide income for their families while caring for their children, husbands, and parents. Given the outlook of an aging population, the issue of elder care will continue to be of concern well into the twenty-first century. —*Maurice Hamington*

BIBLIOGRAPHY

Benokraitis, Nijole V. *Marriages and Families: Changes, Choices, and Constraints.* Englewood

Cliffs, N.J.: Prentice Hall, 1996. Comprehensive sociological text that provides an overview of modern literature on families and the roles of family members, while analyzing modern trends.

Bird, Gloria W., and Keith Melville. *Families and Intimate Relationships*. New York: McGraw-Hill, 1994. Provides a broad background to the sociological understanding of family roles, paying particular attention to their history and evolution.

Coontz, Stephanie. *The Way We Never Were: American Families and the Nostalgia Trap*. New York: Basic Books, 1992. Analyzes the myths and traditions surrounding families, including lingering romanticization of the single-earner households of the 1950's.

Friedan, Betty. *Beyond Gender: The New Politics of Work and Family*. Washington, D.C.: Woodrow Wilson Center Press, 1997. Feminist scholar Friedan demonstrates how, largely because of changing economics, the concerns of women in families in the 1990's have shifted from those which sparked the resurgence of the feminist movement in the 1960's.

Higginbotham, Elizabeth and Mary Romero. *Women and Work: Exploring Race, Ethnicity, and Class*. Thousand Oaks: Sage Publications, 1997. Collection of articles that broadens the perspectives about the intersection of work and women's roles beyond white, middle-class concerns by including issues of race and social class.

MacKinnon, Alison. *Love and Freedom: Professional Women and the Reshaping of Personal Life*. New York: Cambridge University Press, 1997. Addresses the social crises over the roles of women at the end of the twentieth century, given the demands on women to be wives and paid laborers.

Weston, Kath. *Families We Choose: Lesbians, Gays, Kinship*. New York: Columbia University Press, 1997. Analyzes male and female roles in increasingly prevalent nontraditional family associations.

See also Cult of True Womanhood; DINKs; Dual-earner families; Equalitarian families; Family: concept and history; Feminist sociology; Gender inequality; Marriage; Menopause; Men's roles; Mommy track; Mother-daughter relationships; Mother-son relationships; Motherhood; Parenting; Pregnancy.

Work

RELEVANT ISSUES: Children and child development; Economics and work; Parenting and family relationships

SIGNIFICANCE: The two most important spheres in people's daily lives, work and family, involve conflicts or compatibilities that have a significant impact on families' emotional, social, and economic life

The historical shifts in North America from an agricultural economy to a manufacturing economy and finally to a service-oriented economy has changed not only the nature of work, but also the structure and functions of the family unit. It is a myth that the traditional role of men is to be breadwinners who perform work outside the home while women act as wives and mothers who perform family duties inside the home. To understand modern family life and the transformation that has led to it, it is necessary to understand the links between the roles persons play in the family and in the economy. These links can be analyzed from several perspectives: the impact of the economy and its historical transformation on family life, the influence of economic well-being on family happiness, the influence of the family on labor-force participation and work commitment, and the interdependence of work and family roles.

Economic Transformation. There are two aspects of the economy's impact on family life: historical economic shifts and families' economic well-being. The former concerns the structure and functions of families and how these have changed in the course of history, while the latter examines family incomes and their impact on lifestyles, happiness, children's education, and occupational opportunities.

In agricultural economies extended families are well suited to the conditions of society. In extended families more than two generations of common kin live together, either in the same house or in adjacent dwellings. All able-bodied family members are economic assets. Therefore, the more children in the family, the more labor power the family possesses. The home and the workplace are typically in close proximity to each other; hence, work and family roles are integrated. In such a context, families rarely sense tension between work and family roles. Husbands and wives work side by side on their farms, and as soon as their children are old enough, they also participate. Work hours often last from dawn until dusk. Steven Mintz and Susan Kellogg's *Domestic Revolution* (1988) pointed out that in such economies the talents of children better suited to other types of work have often gone largely untapped. Thus, in preindustrial societies occupational mobility from one generation to the next has played no major role.

Industrialization ushered in a new system of production in which mechanical rather than human or animal power was used to produce commodities. The utilization of these new forms of power meant that workers had to be concentrated in common work locations, giving rise to the factory mode of production. In shifting the production of commodities from the home to the factory, industrialization produced a labor force of people who worked for wages. The emergence of wage laborers created new social distinctions: Society became composed of those who worked for pay and those who were unemployed, men who performed paid labor in industry and women who performed unpaid labor in the home, and women and men who performed sexually segregated labor in the workplace. The shift of production from the home to the workshop to the factory transformed men into wage laborers, who left home each day to work at manufacturing jobs. Working predominantly in blue-collar positions, men could increasingly contribute to their families both as the producers of products and as earners who could pay for products. In contrast, the decline of domestic production left women to perform the invisible and socially devalued tasks of housekeeping and child rearing.

Impact on the Family. These distinctions affected both the structure and function of the family. A new family system emerged in which the family group consisted only of parents and their dependent children living apart from other relatives. This new system of the nuclear family was better adapted to the conditions of industrialized economies for several reasons. Life in industrialized societies was dynamic: It offered and sometimes required geographical mobility, impelling workers to go where the jobs and promotions were. Extended families, with their many members, became hindrances to mobility. Unlike agricultural societies, industrial societies offered people a chance to achieve new and often higher social status. The education, values, and incomes of socially mobile people were very different from those of people in traditional extended families in agricultural societies. Furthermore, in industrialized societies, schools, hospitals, welfare agencies, day-care centers, and other social institutions arose to assume many of the functions that were once the responsibility of the family in agricultural societies.

In industrialized societies children gradually ceased to be assets and became economic liabilities. Parents could derive no economic benefit from their children in return for the vast expense of clothing, feeding, and educating them. Almost as soon as the young were able to earn a living, they left home and prepared to form their own separate families. Couples in industrialized societies therefore found it convenient to restrict the size of their households. Finally, people in modern industrialized societies were increasingly concerned with self-fulfillment. Individual desires became more important than traditional obligations, and people expected personal freedom in choosing their mates and places of residence.

During the middle decades of the twentieth century the U.S. economy experienced an important shift from producing goods to providing services. During the 1950's more than 50 percent of the salaried labor force was employed in service-producing industries. Most of the new service-oriented jobs were white-collar positions requiring little physical effort in such branches as health, education, banking, and insurance. This economic phase, known as postindustrialization, opened up job opportunities for women that had been unavailable to them in preceding decades. By creating new work opportunities for women, postindustrialization raised new work-family issues that were previously unknown in agricultural or industrial societies, such as dual-career households and the concomitant need for child-care centers.

Economic Well-Being of Families. Researchers who focus on the relationship between family income and family life have traditionally assumed that economic and occupational success bring higher-quality family life. The traditional view is that marital happiness is highest among families that are moderately successful in economic and occupational terms, as opposed to those that are least or most successful. The reasoning behind this view is that the least successful families lack sufficient economic resources to support their families, whereas many of the most economically successful families have difficulty in performing family roles because of their extensive effort and involvement directed toward work.

Levels of family income depend on the number of working family members and their incomes. How families provide for themselves economically has important implications for family formation, stability, and happiness. Couples usually coordinate their marriages and careers, deciding not to marry until they are able to support themselves. Families also require adequate employment and incomes to ensure stability and cohesion. Lacking them, they are deprived of motivation and encouragement, especially the motivation to have children. Thus, unemployment or underemployment may result in a vicious circle in which employment instability increases family instability and vice versa. Children from prosperous families enjoying relatively high social status generally have higher educational aspirations and levels of achievement and are therefore able to enter occupations promising higher prestige, income, and power.

Work and Family. Some researchers have studied the economic well-being of families by examining how job characteristics—schedules, work hours, and satisfaction—influence family life. Empirical studies have shown that these influences are complex and sometimes inconsistent. Overall, daytime work schedules, limited work hours, and higher job satisfaction decrease family work conflicts and strains. Greater work involve-

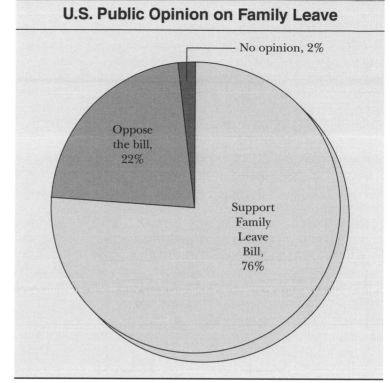

U.S. Public Opinion on Family Leave

No opinion, 2%

Oppose the bill, 22%

Support Family Leave Bill, 76%

Source: CNN/*USA Today*/Gallup Poll
Note: In 1994 a cross-section of Americans were asked if they supported the federal Family Leave Bill that required employers to give new parents twelve weeks of unpaid leave to care for their new babies.

ment, including rigid work schedules, ambiguous job descriptions, and pressures to work harder and better can impinge on family life.

The average length of the working week has generally decreased in postindustrial societies. How many hours persons work partially depends on their gender and family status. Married men tend to work longer hours than unmarried men, whereas unmarried women tend to work longer hours than married women. Furthermore, because of their lower earnings young fathers tend to work longer hours than older fathers, while more young mothers are employed than older mothers. Working long hours is likely to produce more work-family conflicts and strain, contributing to divorce.

In addition to the hours persons work, their work schedules also affect their family life. Family members who work evening or night shifts or on weekends experience high levels of work-family conflict and strain. Some studies reveal interesting differences between husbands and wives in dual-career families. Although weekend work reduces the time that husbands spend on housework and child care, it does not reduce the amount of time wives spend on these activities. This and other differences may be related to the traditional societal expectation that women should perform most household and child-care duties.

Finally, job satisfaction can strongly affect family life. This relationship, which is called "spillover," can be positive or negative. Positive spillover occurs when persons satisfied with and stimulated by their jobs bring home high levels of energy and satisfaction. In contrast, work problems and stress drain and preoccupy individuals, making it difficult for them to participate adequately in family life. Some experts challenge the concept of negative spillover by arguing that people "make up," or compensate, for their unsatisfactory jobs by deriving greater satisfaction from other areas of life. However, evidence tends to give more weight to the existence of the spillover effect than to the compensation effect.

Influence of the Family on Work Commitment. Another aspect of the link between family and work involves how family environments prepare children for their future careers. The family functions in several ways to provide children with a sense of their social identity. Family value systems shape gender socialization; the family occupies a position within the stratification of society, which influences children's identity; and cultural influences, such as religion and ethnicity, shape families' beliefs, practices, and opportunities. The existence of functional families, in which children have appropriate role models from whom they can learn and practice disciplined work habits, is crucial for their futures. Although children's self-image is subject to many other sources of influence throughout the course of their development, the first impressions, illuminated through the intimacy of their families, carry considerable weight.

At home, boys and girls acquire characteristics and tendencies that are specific to their genders. Mothers who serve as family caretakers and fathers who work outside the home are powerful role models for their children. The division of labor according to traditional gender lines exemplifies two divergent types of identities for boys and girls: Girls are expected to identify with their mothers and boys with their fathers. If parents believe in

traditional sex-role stereotypes and act these out in everyday life, they will likely reward their sons for being leaders, encouraging competitiveness, autonomy, aggressiveness, and independence. In contrast, they will likely discourage their daughters from behaving similarly. Traditionally, girls are rewarded for being gentle, caring, nurturing, and supportive of others, and they typically internalize these characteristics as a normal part of female identity.

Traditional Sex-Roles and Work. The different socialization of females and males inclines women to seek and choose only the typically low-paying jobs that society deems acceptable for them, forcing them to conform to the family roles considered appropriate for women. On the other hand, women who violate traditional family values by entering occupations traditionally reserved for men encounter hostility, harassment, and ostracism. Because of family socialization, men and women tend to embrace different values that affect their work lives, such as how important it is to have authority on the job or make money. At work, gender-role socialization encourages men to expect a sexual division of labor that guarantees them better jobs, greater promotion opportunities, higher positions of authority, and higher pay than women. At home, the sexual division of labor relieves them of day-to-day domestic chores.

While some scholars agree that women occupy certain jobs because these jobs are somehow more compatible than others with the gender socialization women have experienced in their parental homes, two other theories may also explain occupational segregation by gender. The first holds that jobs dominated by women allow them to accommodate their work to their family demands, enabling them to concentrate on their supposedly greater interest in being wives and mothers and to mold their work responsibilities to fit this interest. In contrast, the second theory holds that women's presumed greater interest in family life is an excuse for assigning them the worst jobs. While there is little evidence that women's jobs can be easily accommodated to family responsibilities, there is evidence that family roles are an excuse for assigning undesirable jobs to women.

Social Class and Work. Parents' social-class position, because it profoundly affects their child-rearing practices, thereby influences their chil-

Women who enter occupations traditionally reserved for men often encounter hostility and social ostracism. (Hazel Hankin)

Twelve Leading Occupations of U.S. Women, 1997

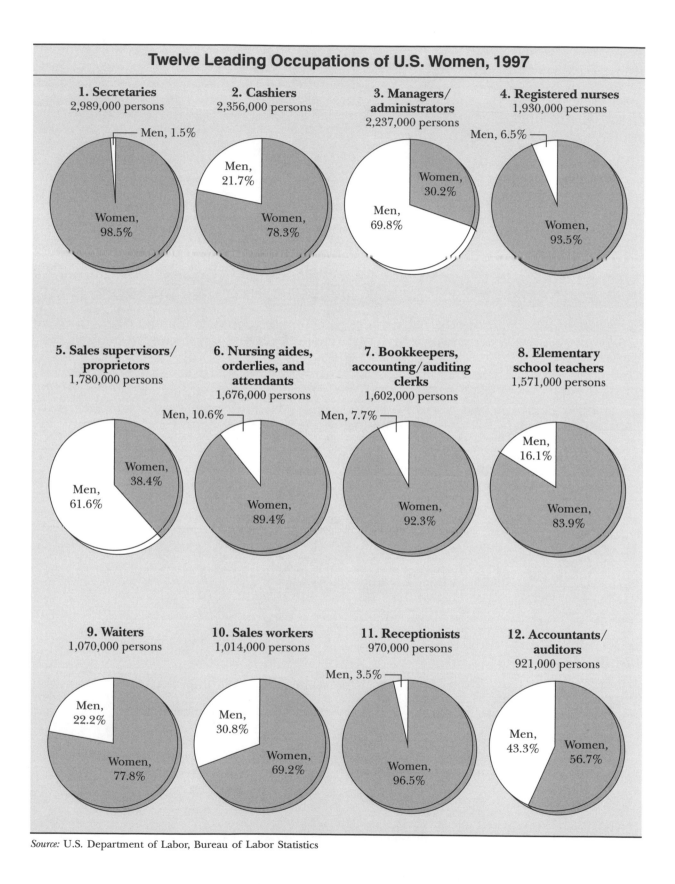

1. Secretaries
2,989,000 persons

Men, 1.5%
Women, 98.5%

2. Cashiers
2,356,000 persons

Men, 21.7%
Women, 78.3%

3. Managers/ administrators
2,237,000 persons

Women, 30.2%
Men, 69.8%

4. Registered nurses
1,930,000 persons

Men, 6.5%
Women, 93.5%

5. Sales supervisors/ proprietors
1,780,000 persons

Women, 38.4%
Men, 61.6%

6. Nursing aides, orderlies, and attendants
1,676,000 persons

Men, 10.6%
Women, 89.4%

7. Bookkeepers, accounting/auditing clerks
1,602,000 persons

Men, 7.7%
Women, 92.3%

8. Elementary school teachers
1,571,000 persons

Men, 16.1%
Women, 83.9%

9. Waiters
1,070,000 persons

Men, 22.2%
Women, 77.8%

10. Sales workers
1,014,000 persons

Men, 30.8%
Women, 69.2%

11. Receptionists
970,000 persons

Men, 3.5%
Women, 96.5%

12. Accountants/ auditors
921,000 persons

Men, 43.3%
Women, 56.7%

Source: U.S. Department of Labor, Bureau of Labor Statistics

dren's future careers and work habits. Studies have shown that family values differ from class to class. For example, the higher the parents' social class, the more likely they are to value characteristics associated with self-direction and the less likely they are to value characteristics associated with conformity to external authority. Consequently, upper- or upper-middle-class children are more likely to seek challenging jobs that demand discretion and decision-making ability. By contrast, the children of working-class or lower-class families are more likely to have jobs at which they perform routine tasks. Furthermore, to the extent that access to high-status jobs depends upon advanced educational credentials, these jobs tend to be reserved for the upper socioeconomic classes, despite the availability of free public education and financial aid. At lower economic levels, children tend to face more pressure to cut short their formal education in order to earn a living. For example, professions such as law are often beyond

the reach of members of lower-class families, because law-school applicants must first earn bachelor's degrees at four-year colleges and then incur the financial burden of an additional three to four years of full-time schooling. Children of Americans who earn less than the median family income usually cannot afford law schools.

Families' ethnic and religious background can affect children's work and occupational choices to the degree that families' subcultural traditions or socialization practices influence their orientation toward education or work. For instance, many Protestant families have seen work as the purpose of life. More than prayer and good deeds, work, for them, assures salvation. Despite varying work values among U.S. families, the majority of Americans view work as central to their identity, self-esteem, and life goals.

The importance of early childhood socialization for subsequent self-development has been extensively discussed by social scientists. Role models

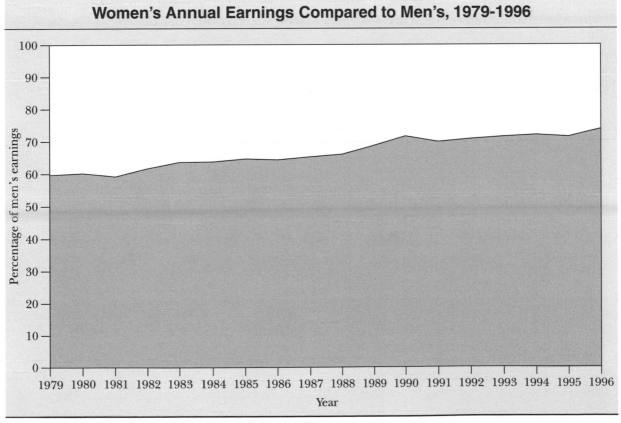

Women's Annual Earnings Compared to Men's, 1979-1996

Source: U.S. Department of Labor, Women's Bureau (April, 1998)

and supportive family relationships not only become the models for subsequent relationships, but they also teach individuals who they are and what they might expect to do in the working world. Parental influence on children's development extends beyond behavior to work attitudes and work habits. For example, dissatisfied housewives are likely to encourage their daughters to find jobs. The influence of families on work attitudes becomes critical when families are dysfunctional, a condition afflicting many single-parent families. Most single-parent households are headed by women, but single fathers require much interest and attention as well. The problems of single-parent families are not limited to economic hardship. In both the work and the family spheres single parents are vulnerable; because they lack adequate social supports to handle work-parenting conflicts, they are unprepared to tackle the job of being parents and workers simultaneously, and their children lack satisfactory role models.

Work and Family Interdependence. The interdependence of work and family roles is illustrated by the concept of the work-family cycle, which provides a means for mapping the increasing variety of ways in which men and women coordinate work and family roles over the life course. Studies have shown that women have greater problems integrating work and family life than men, because it has traditionally been assumed that women are available during the day to care for their children. In other words, working women face the simultaneous role demands of work and family, whereas men face only sequential role demands—that is, they have no family responsibilities until they get home from work. This situation is more burdensome for working mothers and wives than for working husbands and fathers.

The interdependence of work and family operates both at the economic and the individual levels. At the economic level, the interaction of labor and consumption highlights the interdependence of work and family. Goods and services are produced, and families consume them. They purchase these goods and services with their earnings from work. By the same token, labor performed by family members is rewarded with wages and other benefits. On the individual level, the interdependence of work and family can be understood by examining the performance of multiple roles.

Experts use role conflict—that is, the degree to which work demands contradict family demands—to analyze interdependence at the individual level.

Many studies reveal that while the performance of multiple roles has a positive effect on women's and men's mental and physical health, conflicts between these roles have a negative effect both on their physical and mental health and their actual performance of these roles. For example, some studies report high rates of coronary heart disease among clerical workers, especially those who are married and have children. Stress caused by depression and work is high among women experiencing role conflicts, especially those with small children. Role stress is a major psychological problem of employees who perform multiple roles. This stress is mainly the result of overload and interference. Overload occurs when the pressure of multiple roles places so many demands on persons' time and energy that they fail to perform, while interference occurs when the demands of one role conflict with those of others.

There are a variety of ways to deal with the stress people suffer from performing multiple roles: coping strategies, sequential work-family roles, and symmetrical family-work role allocation. Through coping strategies, individuals manipulate the demands associated with their multiple roles in order to construct workable patterns of relationships and activities. In sequential work-family role strategies—the most common type of labor-force participation for women—mothers adjust their working lives to accommodate family demands, especially childbearing. Finally, symmetrical work-family role allocation enables mothers and fathers who work outside the home and share the family work to modify gender-based norms and reduce differentiation by exchanging specialized tasks, whereby wives adopt a greater share of traditional male duties and husbands assume a greater share of traditional family duties.

Dual-Career Families and Role Strains. The conflicts between family and work roles are greatly intensified when both husbands and wives have demanding and competitive careers. Such typical high-status positions as those held by business executives, physicians, and lawyers require high levels of commitment, long work hours, and couples' full devotion to each other. Dual-career problems resulting from such occupations have significantly

Within typical dual-earner families, women face the simultaneous demands of work and family, while men do not face family responsibilities until after they return home from work. (James L. Shaffer)

increased during the past generation in industrialized nations. The stresses and strains that accompany dual careers result from the competing demands of simultaneously maintaining a career and a full family life. These stresses cause many spouses to accept more traditional careers or jobs. One spouse's career will be affected by the other's, and men as well as women may have to pass up job offers or accept less desirable jobs in the interests of preserving family cohesion.

Women are more often affected than men when such work-family decisions are posed, for women, more often than men, accept less desirable jobs or leave the workforce entirely in order to maintain their spousal and family relationships. Moreover, the constraints of the job market and the work environment override many decisions made by spouses. Husbands are more likely than their wives to be offered good jobs at higher salaries; they are also less likely to feel the responsibility for child care that their wives have generally been socialized to accept. Finally, dramatic differences in levels of success between husbands and wives committed to their careers can lead to marital problems.

—*Max Kashefi*

BIBLIOGRAPHY

Cheal, David. *New Poverty: Families in Postmodern Society.* Westport, Conn.: Greenwood Press, 1996. Provides a critical examination of the relationship between employment and marital status, focusing on children in poor families.

Dunn, Dana. *Workplace/Women's Place: An Anthology.* Los Angeles: Roxbury Publishing, 1997. Examines a wide range of issues pertaining to women and work, including job stress, tokenism, hiring and pay discrimination, and occupational segregation.

Goldsmith, B. Elizabeth. *Work and Family: Theory, Research, and Application.* Newbury Park, Calif.: Sage Publications, 1989. Collection of research papers investigating the nature of the work and family interchange, including cross-cultural and transnational studies.

Mintz, Steven, and Susan Kellogg. *Domestic Revolution: A Social History of American Family Life.* New York: Free Press, 1988. Discusses changes in the economy and their effects on family structure, while focusing on collective family economy as an interdependent unit of work organization.

Parcel, L. Toby, and Elizabeth G. Menaghan. *Parents, Jobs, and Children's Lives.* New York: Aldine De Gruyter, 1994. Explores dangers and advantages of maternal employment, particularly focusing on children's verbal and cognitive development and thereby on their later occupational opportunities.

Reskin, Barbara, and Irene Padavic. *Women and Men at Work.* Thousand Oaks, Calif.: Pine Forge Press, 1994. Addresses men's and women's everyday experiences on the job and their progress in the world of work, with up-to-date evidence on gender inequality and work.

Voydanoff, Patricia. *Work and Family Life.* Newbury Park, Calif.: Sage Publications, 1987. Extended analysis of the interdependence of work and family and its implications.

See also Corporate families; Day care; Dual-earner families; Earned income tax credit; Family businesses; Family-friendly programs; Gender inequality; Mommy track; Retirement.

Youth sports

RELEVANT ISSUES: Children and child development; Education; Parenting and family relationships

SIGNIFICANCE: Family participation in youth sports offers the chance for children to develop confidence, self-discipline, and healthy habits against a backdrop of fun and physical activity

A 1988-1994 government study of 4,063 U.S. children found that 26 percent spent more than four hours a day in front of the television. Instilling in children a love of sports and physical activity is a gift that will only grow in value, and the benefits far outweigh any potential risks. Youth sports have been shown to boost self-esteem, promote the skills needed to work toward a desired goal, encourage respect for others, and teach the joy of

Studies have indicated that girls who participate in sports have higher self-esteem than those who do not. (Hazel Hankin)

cooperation. According to the World Health Organization (WHO), "Health and sport are closely linked, and physical exercise is every bit as important to the mind as it is to the body."

For girls, sports is even more important. In an era in which being in good shape has more to do with appearance than actual physical fitness, sporting activities give young women a chance to use their bodies for something other than attracting boys. In 1972 Title IX of the Educational Amendment Act prohibited sex discrimination in any educational program or activity receiving federal funds. As a result, schools were required to establish teams and leagues for female students. Studies have shown that girls who participate in sports have higher self-esteem than their peers who do not participate in sports. They are also far less likely to experience the pitfalls of youth—truancy, drug and alcohol use, and teen pregnancies.

Parent-Child Relationships. It is important that parents recognize the difference between playing and competing, especially for children under the age of six. Children instinctively look for ways to have fun, whereas most games taught to children by adults are competitive in nature. Structured team play can inhibit athletic development and remove the joy of playing.

Rainer Martens, known for his research on children and competitive play and considered by many to be the father of modern sports psychology, believes that competitive sports are part of "the process of social evaluation." At ages three and four, kids are primarily interested in their own performance, how far they can throw, or how high they can jump. It is not until they reach five or six that they start measuring themselves against other children. Eventually they learn to keep score. According to Martens, competing and comparing themselves with others is universal among children and can help them discover their abilities.

Youth sports activities offer parents the perfect opportunity to spend quality time with their children. While many parents choose to coach or assist with training and equipment, just watching from the bleachers can provide a valuable boost to the child athlete's self-esteem. Nevertheless, it is important to remember that children see themselves through their parent's eyes and can easily discern disappointment. Parents who scream at coaches, deride the children on the opposing team, and punish their own children for poor performance on the field do far more damage than a simple mark in the loss column. Some parents also make the mistake of trying to live vicariously through their children. Just because a father lettered in three sports in high school does not mean that his son has the talent or the inclination to follow in his father's footsteps.

Competition. Twenty million children ages six and older participate on organized sports teams. This can be a positive experience, but it can just as easily become a negative one if the emphasis changes from cooperation to winning. Being a good sport is a vital aspect of all youth sports—for both children and parents. Sporting activities have traditionally been considered a positive method of channeling aggressive behavior in children and adults. Unfortunately, the decline of sportsmanship and fair play in the professional ranks has trickled into the amateur arena, leading to an increased emphasis on aggressive, victory-at-all costs sports play. Pushing children in this manner teaches them at a young age that if they are not the big winners, they must be the big losers. As an antidote, children should be taught to "play fair" instead of "play tough." Children learn behavior

The Largest U.S. Youth Sports Organizations in 1998

Organization	Founded	Age range	Youth participants
Pop Warner Football	1929	5-15	300,000+
Little League Baseball	1939	5-12*	c. 2,000,000
American Youth Soccer Organization (AYSO)	1964	5-18	560,000+

Source: American Youth Soccer Organization; Little League Baseball; Pop Warner Football
*"Classic" Little League, excluding leagues for older children

Since the creation of the American Youth Soccer Organization (AYSO) in 1964, soccer has become one of the most popular youth team sports in the United States. (R. Kent Rasmussen)

patterns from the adults around them, and it is up to the parents and coaches to set a good example.

There is competition off the field as well. For lower- and middle-class families, playing well in high school means more than just winning. With the rising cost of college, more and more families have turned to sports scholarships as a way to finance higher education. Some parents spend well over $10,000 per child per year to produce a child athlete, using money that would have been better invested in a college savings fund.

In 1997 fourteen-year-old figure skater Tara Li-

pinksi became the youngest World Champion in the history of the sport. A year later, she proved it wasn't a fluke by winning a gold medal at the Winter Olympics in Nagano, Japan, at age fifteen—before she was old enough to vote or even obtain a driver's license. However, for every young Olympian, there are thousands of children who never make it beyond the local level of competition. Being pushed into a sport before developing the necessary coordination and emotional maturity leads to frustration in preadolescent athletes. This, coupled with children's intense need to please their parents can turn defeat into devastation. In extreme cases, children literally become an "investment" after parents have devoted considerable time and financial resources into making them stars.

Family Participation. Youth sports benefit the entire household, not just the children who actively compete. Training and proper nutrition can be a family affair, motivating parents and siblings who might not otherwise maintain healthy lifestyles. Exercise should not be an artificial obligation but a natural part of family life. Studies have shown that many adult health problems, such as high cholesterol, high blood pressure, and obesity, are due in part to sedentary lifestyle habits ingrained in childhood.

While family participation is important, sports should not become families' sole leisure activity. Nonsporting siblings may resent spending every Saturday afternoon at the ballpark. Group activities also ensure that the brothers and sisters of child athletes do not feel left out. The all-inclusive sports lifestyle can quickly become expensive. According to the Georgia Youth Soccer federation, in the late twentieth century the average parent spent almost $500 a year on registration fees, cleats, driving expenses, and meals to subsidize a six-year-old's participation in a sport. Parents of traveling team members spent almost another $3,400.

Social Aspects. For many families, actual sporting activities are only part of the social picture. Groups of parents who spend week after week in the bleachers sharing coaching tips and comparing schedules often develop friendships that go beyond the ball field. For families with more than one child participating in more than one sport, these friendships can be a blessing, as practice and playing schedules leave little time for everyday socializing. The downside to this sort of social circle is that it can place undue stress on the children doing the actual playing. They may feel pressure to "make the team"; or worse, they may continue in a sport that is no longer fun, just so that the family can remain part of the sporting social circle.

Overall, Martens sums up the positive side of sports participation: "There are 30 million children and probably as many adults who are sometimes involved in competitive sports," he says.

> Some may be pushed into them by peer pressure and, thus, may experience more stress than they should and won't get the benefits they might. However, it seems plain that most people compete at games voluntarily because it gives them pleasure. Not for all and not all of the time, but often and for many people, sport is a major source of joy and therefore, on balance, is useful to them and to society.

—*P. S. Ramsey*

BIBLIOGRAPHY

Bingham, Mindy, and Sandy Stryker, with Susan Allstetter Beufeldt, Ph.D. *Things Will Be Different for My Daughter.* New York: Penguin Books, 1995.

Galton, Lawrence. *Your Child in Sports.* New York: Franklin Watts, 1980.

Geist, Bill. *Little League Confidential.* New York: Macmillan, 1992.

Hopper, Chris. *The Sports-Confident Child.* New York: Pantheon Books, 1988.

Simon, Nissa. *Good Sports: Plain Talk About Health and Fitness for Teens.* New York: Thomas Y. Crowell, 1990.

Wolff, Rick. *Good Sports: A Parent's Guide to Youth Sports.* Champaign, Ill: Sagamore Publishing, 1997.

See also Child safety; Community programs for children; Competition during childhood; Favoritism; Puberty and adolescence; Recreation.

Zablocki v. Redhail

DATE: Ruling issued on January 18, 1978
RELEVANT ISSUES: Divorce; Law; Marriage and dating
SIGNIFICANCE: The U.S. Supreme Court ruled that a Wisconsin law prohibiting the marriage of residents failing to comply with court-ordered child-support payments and obligations unconstitutionally interfered with the right of personal choice in marriage and family life

On September 27, 1974, Roger Redhail was denied an application for a marriage license by Thomas Zablocki, the clerk of Milwaukee County, on the grounds that Redhail had not complied with state family law. The Wisconsin Family Code made Redhail's ability to marry dependent on his payment of child support from a previous relationship and on assurances that minor children were not and would not become wards of the state.

Redhail, unmarried, unemployed, and poor, had not paid court-ordered child support, and his illegitimate daughter had received benefits under the Aid to Families with Dependent Children program since her birth. He challenged the law. On August 31, 1976, a federal district court said that the Wisconsin law violated the equal protection clause of the Fourteenth Amendment to the U.S. Constitution. The Supreme Court agreed and ruled that the state significantly interfered with the fundamental right to marry, the most important relation in family life and a liberty protected by the Fourteenth Amendment. Individuals, including "deadbeat dads," may make personal decisions relating to marriage without unjustified governmental interference. —*Steve J. Mazurana*

See also Aid to Families with Dependent Children (AFDC); Antimiscegenation laws; Child support; Family law; *Loving v. Virginia*; Marriage; Marriage laws; Poverty; Privacy; Welfare.

Zero Population Growth movement

RELEVANT ISSUES: Demographics; Sociology
SIGNIFICANCE: Since the 1950's the movement to curb population growth has had a considerable effect on making family planning universally available and advancing the economic and social status of women

The major premise of the population movement is that the resources of the world are finite and cannot support indefinitely a steadily increasing number of people. In 1997 global population was 5.9 billion and projected to increase over the following decade at the rate of 100 million a year. 90 percent of this increase, it was argued, would occur in the developing world. At 1990's rates of growth, the world's population could double by 2050. The negative effects of supporting such rapid growth include loss of forests and agricultural land; pollution and waste; a heightening of competition for scarce resources; urban problems of congestion, unemployment, and social dysfunction; and economic and political instability. Advocates of population control say that unless population growth is slowed, it will be impossible to address these and other critical social and environmental problems.

Early Population-Control Strategies. Serious efforts to curb world population growth began in the 1950's, when it became clear that decreased infant and child mortality after World War II were leading to a population explosion that could threaten the welfare of everyone on the planet. Early landmarks in the population movement were the founding in 1952 of the Population Council by John D. Rockefeller III and the International Planned Parenthood Federation (IPPF). Also in 1952, India became the first nation to announce a governmental policy to reduce fertility.

From the 1950's to the 1970's the population movement grew rapidly. In 1958 a U.S. presidential committee recommended that economic aid

One effect of the Zero Population Growth movement in North America has been a trend toward smaller families. (James L. Shaffer)

be tied to countries' efforts to curb population growth. Although that recommendation was rejected by President Dwight D. Eisenhower, the late 1960's saw Congress pass legislation that earmarked funding for population control measures in the developing countries. In the 1960's organizations tackling the population problem included the Rockefeller Foundation, the U.S. Agency for International Development (AID), the United Nations Population Fund (UNPF), and the World Bank.

In 1974, at the World Population Conference held in Bucharest, Romania, representatives of 136 countries attempted to reach a consensus on the need to curb population growth. Many developing countries refused to support the movement, however, and were joined by the Soviet Union, China, and some Roman Catholic countries. In spite of this, family planning programs throughout the developing world increased over the next few years. Ten years later, at the Second World Population Conference in Mexico, positions were reversed. The developing world, including China, endorsed the goal of population control, but the United States, influenced by a conservative domestic agenda, declared itself neutral. Support from AID to IPPF and the UNPF was halted, until this decision was reversed by President Bill Clinton's administration in 1993.

In the 1980's the population movement began to emphasize, in addition to family planning, the advancement of the role and status of women. This trend continued into the 1990's and featured prominently at the third United Nations International Conference on Population and Development in Cairo, Egypt, in 1994. Studies show that programs that improve women's health, social status, educational opportunities, and economic well-being are effective ways to lower fertility rates.

Population-Control Movement in the United States. In the United States, the largest organization concerned with the impact of rapid population growth is Zero Population Growth (ZPG). Founded in 1968 as a nonprofit organization, ZPG carries out a wide range of educational and advocacy activities in communities across the nation. ZPG advocates a variety of measures to reduce population pressures, including adoption of a national population policy, access to safe and affordable contraceptives, reproductive choice, school-based sexuality education and health care services, enhanced educational and employment opportunities for women, and international support for basic education and voluntary family-planning programs.

ZPG and similar U.S. organizations hope to stimulate grassroots involvement in an effort to bring population control back into the forefront of public debate, where it has not been since the 1950's and 1960's. In the earlier period there was widespread agreement that the U.S. population was growing too fast. In the 1950's women of child-bearing age had an average of 3.35 children, but this rate had fallen to 2.45 children by 1970. By the

1970's the rationale for family planning, which was first supported by the federal government in 1964, shifted from population control to the need to provide poor women with more control over their reproductive lives and also to reduce the amount of tax dollars that went to welfare payments. This continued to be the focus as the fertility rate fell further during the 1980's, reaching a record low of 1.82 in 1987. It subsequently rose slightly to 2.05 in 1992.

ZPG points out that the United States remains one of the world's fastest-growing industrialized nations. According to a moderate projection made by the U.S. Bureau of the Census in 1994, the U.S. population could increase by 50 percent to more than 390 million by 2050. The lowest projection was that by 2050 the United States would have 1.9 births per woman, producing a peak population of 293 million in 2030 followed by a decrease to 285 million in 2050. The highest projection assumed 2.6 births per woman and a population of 522 million by 2050, more than double the figure in the late twentieth century.

Immigration and Abortion. Two social issues that have provoked divisive debates in the United States in the 1990's play a key role in population issues. The first is immigration, which adds at least 800,000 people annually to the U.S. population. Many population experts wish to restrict immigration, but others say that the only long-term solution is to alleviate the conditions that compel people to emigrate to the United States. Foremost among these are population growth, economic stagnation, environmental degradation, poverty, and political repression.

The second divisive issue is abortion. From the 1950's to the 1970's the population movement in the United States, aware that family planning and contraception had only recently found general acceptance, pursued a cautious, conservative approach to abortion and abortion research. During the 1980's and 1990's, however, support for abortion became more open, and population experts became unanimous in favoring women's right to safe, legal access to abortion, both in the United States and worldwide. They pointed out that nearly half of the estimated fifty-five million unwanted pregnancies that end in abortion every year are illegal procedures carried out mostly in the Third World. The World Health Organization

(WHO) reported that illegal abortions account for the deaths of 200,000 women each year.

Future of the Population Movement. Since 1960 family planning has prevented more than 400 million births in the developing world and should prevent a cumulative 4.6 billion by the end of the twenty-first century. Reduction in fertility has been most marked in Asia and Latin America. However, during the 1990's the population movement stood at a crossroads. The traditional approach, whereby the chief goal was to promote contraception and family planning as a means of curbing population growth, was supplemented and to a certain extent overshadowed by a concern for the improvement of every aspect of women's lives. Advocates of this approach sometimes viewed the traditional emphasis on birth control to be coercive and not necessarily in the best interests of the women concerned.

The new approach was particularly apparent at the third United Nations Conference on Population in Cairo in 1994. Delegates called for measures that would approach family planning in terms of overall health care for women and which would also address issues such as women's education, women's rights, women's status in the family and the community, and women's economic independence. The Cairo Conference did not neglect demographic concerns, however, aiming to stabilize world population at 7.27 billion by 2015. If this goal is not achieved, the population could reach 12.5 billion by 2050, which many experts consider unsustainable.   —*Bryan Aubrey*

BIBLIOGRAPHY

Back, Kurt W. *Family Planning and Population Control.* Boston: Twayne, 1989.

Berelson, Bernard, et al., eds. *Family Planning and Population Programs.* Chicago: University of Chicago Press, 1966.

Demerath, Nicholas J. *Birth Control and Foreign Policy.* New York: Harper & Row, 1976.

Ehrlich, Paul R., and Anne Ehrlich. *The Population Explosion.* New York: Simon & Schuster, 1990.

Harkavy, Oscar. *Curbing Population Growth: An Insider's Perspective on the Population Movement.* New York: Plenum Press, 1995.

Piotrow, Phyllis. *World Population Crisis: The United States Response.* New York: Praeger, 1973.

Ward, Martha C. *Poor Women, Powerful Men: America's Great Experiment in Family Planning.* Boulder, Colo.: Westview Press, 1986.

See also Abortion; Birth control; Family demographics; Family size; Fertility and infertility; Planned Parenthood Federation of America (PPFA); Reproductive technologies.

Important Legislation and Court Decisions

c. 1000	The theory of monogamous and indissoluble marriage as the ideal is firmly rooted in Christian Europe, although divorce and common-law marriage are still widely practiced.
1543-1563	The Roman Catholic Church at the Council of Trent bans informal marriages by requiring the participation of a priest and other witnesses.
1563	The archbishop of Canterbury compiles the various biblical and canonical injunctions against marriage between kin; his tables become the foundation for related future Anglo-American legislation.
1576	English Poor Law requires that parents of children born out of wedlock pay for their children's maintenance.
1601	English Poor Law Act obligates fathers to support their children up to the age of twenty-one.
1620	English Privy Council authorizes London children to be bound as apprentices against their will and shipped to Virginia.
1641	The Massachusetts Bay Colony adopts the "Body of Liberties," which forbids husbands from abusing their wives except in the case of self-defense, forbids the government from depriving men of their wives or children without some "express law of the country established by the General Court and sufficiently published," prescribes capital punishment for rebellious children over sixteen years of age, allows children to defend themselves from excessively severe punishment, and forbids parents from choosing their children's mates.
1642	The Massachusetts Bay Colony requires fathers to teach their children reading, the knowledge of "Capital Laws," and the principles of religion.
1646	Virginia enacts a "binding out" statute enabling local authorities to remove children from their homes without parental consent. "Body of Liberties" is amended to require bringing rebellious sons to court to confirm wanton rebelliousness.
1647	The Massachusetts legislature orders towns of at least fifteen families to provide public elementary education, primarily for the purpose of teaching reading and religious doctrine, and solidifies the practice of family-based education.
1661	Maryland becomes the first American colony to enact a ban on interracial marriage.
1662	A Virginia law states that a person will be deemed slave or free depending on the status of his or her mother; another law prohibits whites from having sexual relations with blacks.
1681	Maryland requires special juries to oversee the property interests of orphans.
1696	Maryland extends jurisdiction of orphan's courts to cover all orphans, even when they are covered by a father's will.
1704	Lord Holt rules in *Hutton v. Mansell* that mutual promises of marriage may be proven by circumstantial, rather than direct, evidence.
1719	In *Holt v. Ward Clarencieux*, minors are exempted in breach-of-promise of marriage, setting a long precedent in American marital law.
1753	English Marriage Act makes religious ceremonies compulsory and establishes fixed formal requirements, including registration and parental consent; only Quakers, Jews, and members of the Royal family are exempt.
1764	The Pennsylvania Supreme Court rules in *Davey v. Turner* that a married woman must give her legal consent to the sale or transfer of property held with her husband.

1773	The first grant of petition of divorce is awarded to a woman in Massachusetts on the grounds of adultery by her husband.
1780	The Pennsylvania legislature decrees that the children of slaves are required to serve their owners as indentured servants until the age of twenty-eight, a decree that is characteristic of the gradual abolition of slavery in the northern states.
1785	A Virginia statute legitimizes the offspring of voided marriages, making them capable of inheriting property.
1791	The first ten amendments to the Constitution take effect, including the First Amendment guaranteeing religious freedom and the Ninth Amendment which says that a listing of certain rights in the Constitution "shall not be construed to deny or disparage others retained by the people." These amendments form the basis of later battles over parental rights.
1803	Abortion is made a statutory crime in England.
1809	In *Fenton v. Reed* the New York Supreme Court upholds the doctrine of the validity of common-law marriage.
	In *Prather v. Prather* a South Carolina equity court denies full parental custody to an adulterous father, leading to the doctrine of the "best interests of the child."
1812	In *Commonwealth v. Bangs*, the Massachusetts Supreme Court upholds the legality of "pre-quickened" abortion.
1818	In *Wightman v. Coates* Massachusetts chief justice Isaac Parker rules in favor of a woman suing for breach of promise when her suitor refuses to marry her after a long engagement; this ruling established the validity of the prevailing economic doctrine of laissez faire in marriage law.
1819	The Louisiana Supreme Court allows that the incipient rights of slave marriages, while dormant during servitude, nevertheless exist in case of manumission.
1830	Congress makes abortion a crime, although only after the "quickening" of the fetus.
1839	In *Ex Parte Crouse*, the Pennsylvania Supreme Court upholds the right of the state to remove children from households deemed unsuitable.
	Justice Thomas Noon Talfourd introduces the "tender years" doctrine as the first major challenge to paternal dominance.
1842	Massachusetts law limits children twelve and under to a ten-hour workday.
	In *Mercein v. People* the New York Supreme Court replaces the authority of common law with the natural rights argument that favors mothers, arguing that "by the law of nature, the father has no paramount right to the custody of his child."
1848	The New York state legislature enacts the Married Woman's Property Act, allowing women to control property received by gift, grant, or bequest.
	The Maine state legislature requires that couples wait a prescribed period of time after being examined by a public official before being wed, a process that by 1906 was adopted by all states except New York and South Carolina.
1851	The Massachusetts legislature makes adoption a legal procedure in which the court is responsible for determining parental fitness and in which the rights of the natural family are dissolved; this legislation becomes the model for adoption policy in most states.
1852	The Massachusetts legislature passes the first compulsory school attendance law.
1853	New York City passes a truancy law, linking family relief to school attendance.

1857	The English Matrimonial Causes Act becomes the foundation of divorce proceedings in most Canadian provinces.
1860's	Married women are allowed to own property and keep their wages throughout the United States.
1860	New York State enlarges its Married Woman's Property Act to include the woman as joint guardian of her children along with her husband, with equal rights and duties.
	The Massachusetts Supreme Court in *Reynolds v. Reynolds* holds that violations which go to the "essence" of the matrimonial agreement constitute fraud and might serve as the basis for annulment.
	The U.S. Congress passes the Morrill Act, declaring polygamy illegal in all American territories.
1864	In *Denslow v. Van Horn* the Iowa Supreme Court rules that juries should know the premarital behavior of women involved in breach-of-promise suits.
1866	Congress passes the Civil Rights Act, ensuring the rights of former slaves. The act is vetoed by President Andrew Johnson, who argues that "if Congress can abrogate all state laws of discrimination between the two races . . . may it not also repeal the state laws as to the contract of marriage between the two races?"
1869	Confirming a long trend toward full recognition of civil marriage contracts, the Pennsylvania Supreme Court upholds the validity of a secret marriage followed by the birth of a child.
1870	The U.S. Supreme Court in *Stikes v. Swanson* holds that slave marriages had always been valid.
	William Whitmore publishes *The Law of Adoption* as a guide to a Massachusetts legislative committee considering revision of adoption law, calling for greater statutory uniformity and special care that natural families not be undermined by adoption.
1879	In *Reynolds v. United States* the U.S. Supreme Court holds that the federal antibigamy law does not violate the free exercise of religious rights of Mormons.
1881	In *Chapsky v. Wood* the Kansas Supreme Court supports the rights of surrogate parents over a biological father, invoking the best-interests-of-the-child rule.
1882	U.S. Congress passes the Edmunds Act, making mere cohabitation rather than marriage with more than one woman a crime.
	New York passes the Factory Act, prohibiting work by children under the age of thirteen.
1886	In *McPherson v. Ryan* the Michigan Supreme Court holds that private espousal statements alone do not constitute proof of a marriage commitment.
1888	The U.S. Supreme Court observes in *Maynard v. Hill* that marriage is more than a mere contract.
1890	New York State enacts the first law assuming full responsibility for the "insane poor."
	Mormon president Wilford Woodruff renounces polygamy, leading to Utah statehood four years later.
1892	The National Conference of Commissioners on Uniform State Laws is founded, the goal of which is to develop uniform divorce legislation and coordinate other law-reform efforts.
1896	In *Plessy v. Ferguson* the U.S. Supreme Court establishes the "separate but equal rule," reinforcing the de facto practice of segregation.
1898	The U.S. Supreme Court rules in *United States v. Wong Kim Ark* that a man born in California to Chinese parents is a U.S. citizen.
1899	Illinois enacts the first juvenile court law.
	The first juvenile court in America is established in Chicago on the premise that rehabilitation is possible.

1900	By the turn of the century, every state prohibits marriages between blood relations, at least as far as first cousins, marking the rise of state intervention in an area previously self-regulated.
1906	The Pennsylvania Supreme Court in *Commonwealth v. Fisher* upholds the legality of the juvenile court system.
1907	Indiana passes the first mandatory sterilization act, authorizing the sterilization of "criminals, idiots, imbeciles, and rapists" in state institutions. Designed to prevent the infection of society, twenty-seven states by 1931 had passed similar legislation.
1911	Missouri and Illinois become the first states to supply aid from state funds to mothers of dependent children. The idea spreads to seventeen other states by 1913.
	The U.S. government creates the Children's Bureau within the U.S. Bureau of Labor. Investigations soon show the need for greater protection of maternal and infant health.
1912	Arizona and North Dakota follow the "Norwegian model," legitimizing all offspring of natural parents and providing for full support and education; no other states follow.
1913	Wisconsin becomes the first state to require that persons undergo medical tests "by a competent physician, who should decide whether they are proper candidates for parentage."
1916	Congress passes the Keating-Owen Act, banning interstate commerce in products made by children under fourteen years of age in factories and under sixteen years of age in mines.
1917	Minnesota creates the first state board to safeguard the interests of illegitimate children.
1918	The U.S. Supreme Court in *Hammer v. Dagenhart* declares the Keating-Owen Act unconstitutional in relying on interstate commerce as a means of regulating child labor.
1921	Congress passes the Sheppard-Towner Maternity and Infancy Protection Act, providing states with federal matching funds to establish prenatal and child-care centers.
1923	Suffragist Alice Paul proposes the Equal Rights Amendment (ERA): "Equality of rights under the law shall not be denied or abridged by the United States or by any State on account of sex."
	The U.S. Supreme Court in *Meyer v. Nebraska* strikes down a state law limiting the teaching of foreign languages in public schools as a violation of the Constitution's "liberty" guarantee, which includes the right "to marry, to establish a home and bring up children."
1924	Congress passes a constitutional amendment banning child labor, but the states fail to ratify it.
	Congress tightens immigration, implementing quotas favoring northern and western Europeans.
1925	The U.S. Supreme Court in *Pierce v. Society of Sisters* rules that an Oregon law requiring children to attend public school unreasonably interferes with parents' liberty to direct the education of their children.
1927	The U.S. Supreme Court in *Buck v. Bell* holds that the involuntary sterilization of a mentally handicapped woman is constitutional.
1929	Under pressure from the American Medical Association (AMA), Congress terminates the Sheppard-Towner Maternity and Infancy Protection Act, which provided states with federal matching funds to establish prenatal and child-care centers.
1932	Some states needing revenue begin "quickie divorces."
1933	Section 213 of the National Economy Act prohibits more than one member of a family from working for the federal government, substantially reducing the number of government jobs for women.
	Congress passes the National Recovery Act, which contains provisions prohibiting child labor for children under sixteen years of age.

1933-1935	The Federal Emergency Relief Administration (FERA) supplies shelter, food, medical care, money, and jobs to the homeless.
1935	Congress passes the Social Security Act, which establishes Aid to Dependent Children (ADC), a program designed to assist low-income families by providing maternal and child health services and various child welfare services.
	Congress creates the National Youth Administration to employ students and other needy youth.
	FERA is replaced by a variety of programs targeting individual needs.
	The U.S. Supreme Court in *Shechter Poultry Corporation v. United States* declares the National Industrial Recovery Act unconstitutional, thus abolishing the prohibition against child labor.
1936	The U.S. Court of Appeals, in *United States v. One Package*, gives doctors the right to prescribe birth control devices.
1938	Congress passes the Fair Labor Standards Act (FLSA), regulating working hours and pay and establishing child-labor rules.
1942	The Lanham (Community Facilities) Act, passed in 1940, is amended to establish child-care centers in forty-one states.
1943	In *West Virginia State Board of Education v. Barnette*, the U.S. Supreme Court rules that the free exercise of religion clause prohibits schools from compelling Jehovah's Witness children to participate in flag salute ceremonies.
	Congress provides funds for the Emergency Maternal and Infant Care Program for the families of men in the four lowest grades of enlisted personnel in the military.
1944	The Serviceman's Readjustment Act creates the Veteran's Administration (VA) program, which guarantees mortgage insurance, and expands the Federal Housing Authority (FHA), which encourages veterans to enter the housing market.
1946	The U.S. Supreme Court in *United States v. Cleveland* upholds the convictions of traveling polygamous Mormons as having transported women across state lines "for immoral purposes."
	Congress passes the War Brides Act to allow for the immigration of foreign wives.
	Congress passes the National Mental Health Act, which eventually provides funding for mental health work among families.
1947	In *Everson v. Board of Education* the U.S. Supreme Court rules that state reimbursement of parents for costs of transportation to parochial schools does not violate the establishment of religion clause.
1948	Congress allows income splitting on joint tax returns.
	The U.S. Supreme Court bans real estate agreements in which individuals agree not to sell property to persons of certain races, religions, or nationalities.
1950	Aid to Dependent Children (ADC) becomes Aid to Families with Dependent Children (AFDC), the cornerstone of the modern welfare system; state welfare agencies are required to notify law enforcement officials when welfare benefits go to a child who has been abandoned by a parent.
1951	Congress passes the Federal Youth Correction Act, establishing the youth authority approach in federal corrections administration.
1953	The U.S. Department of Health, Education, and Welfare is created.
	In *McGuire v. McGuire* the Supreme Court of Nebraska holds that courts will not intervene in marital support cases while couples are living together, except in cases of "gross neglect."

1954	In *Brown v. Board of Education* the U.S. Supreme Court outlaws school segregation, leading to racial integration and the decline of community schools.
1958	Congress passes the National Defense Education Act, providing federal aid for mathematics, science, and foreign language instruction.
1960	Sex discrimination is banned in the Canadian Bill of Rights.
	The Legal Aid Society establishes a pilot program in which New York City juveniles are represented in juvenile courts by lawyers.
1962	The U.S. Supreme Court in *Engel v. Vitale* bans daily prayer in the classroom as a violation of the constitutional guarantee of separation of church and state, leading many teachers to avoid discussion of morals in the classroom.
1963	The U.S. Children's Bureau enables states to require physicians to report suspected cases of child abuse; all states enact these reporting laws within three years.
	Congress passes the Community Health Centers Act, which deinstitutionalizes more than 400,000 mentally ill people.
	In *Abington School District v. Schempp* the U.S. Supreme Court holds that recitations of the Lord's Prayer and Bible reading in public schools violates the establishment of religion clause.
1964	Congress enacts the Head Start program to provide preschool education for impoverished children.
	Congress passes the Civil Rights Act, banning discrimination because of a person's color, race, national origin, religion, or sex; Title VII prohibits sex discrimination in employment.
1965	In *Griswold v. Connecticut* the U.S. Supreme Court strikes down a ban on contraception and affirms couples' right to privacy.
	Congress passes the Elementary and Secondary Education Act, providing funds for Head Start and aid to low-income students (Title I), while requiring parental involvement.
	Immigration and Nationality Act amendments increase immigration and allow for family unification.
1966	Congress passes the Adult Education Act, and the Smithsonian Institution launches the Reading Is Fundamental (RIF) program for distributing books to needy children.
	New York State passes a law widening the grounds for divorce to include cruel and inhuman treatment, abandonment, confinement in prison, or agreed upon separation for more than two years.
1967	The U.S. Supreme Court rules in *In re Gault* that juveniles are entitled to due process of law.
	The U.S. Supreme Court in *Loving v. Virginia* strikes down a Virginia statute preventing interracial marriages, arguing that "the freedom to marry, or not marry, a person of another race resides with the individual and cannot be infringed by the State."
	The U.S. Supreme Court in *Griswold v. Connecticut* holds that a state law forbidding the use of birth-control devices, even by married couples, is unconstitutional, articulating the constitutional right to marital privacy.
	Congress passes the Age Discrimination in Employment Act, supporting the right of older Americans to earn an "adequate income."
1968	Congress enacts the Fair Housing Act, barring discrimination in the sale or rental of housing; no enforcement mechanism is provided.
	In *People v. Sorenson* the California Supreme Court rules that a sterile husband contracting to consent to the artificial insemination of his wife is legally bound as the father of the child so produced.

1968 (cont.)	Congress passes the Juvenile Delinquency Prevention and Control Act to assist courts, correctional systems, and schools in dealing with juvenile delinquency.
1969	The Canadian Government liberalizes abortion laws.
	Congress passes the Child Protection and Toy Safety Act, banning many dangerous toys.
	Republican governor Ronald Reagan of California signs the Family Law Act, the first U.S. no-fault divorce law; forty-five states adopt some form of no-fault divorce by the mid-1970's.
1970	The Uniform Marriage and Divorce Act establishes the "best interests of the child" standard in resolving custody cases.
	Congress passes the Education of the Handicapped Act, providing for teacher training and the education of the handicapped.
1971	The U.S. Supreme Court in *Swann v. Charlotte-Mecklenburg Board of Education* declares forced school busing to be constitutional.
	The U.S. Supreme Court in *Reed v. Reed* holds as unconstitutional a state law automatically preferring fathers over mothers as executors of children's estates.
	The U.S. Supreme Court in *Stanley v. Stanley* rules that unwed fathers should be presumed fit custodians of their children whether they are divorced, separated, or widowed.
	The Pennsylvania Supreme Court in *McKeiver v. Pennsylvania* holds that trial by jury is not a constitutional right in juvenile courts.
1972	The U.S. Supreme Court decides in *Eisenstadt v. Baird* that unmarried people have the right to use contraceptives as part of privacy rights.
	The U.S. Supreme Court rules in *Yoder v. Wisconsin* that Amish parents and religious groups have the right to determine their own style of education.
	The U.S. Supreme Court in *Lindsey v. Normet* affirms the right to housing without discrimination.
	Congress enacts the Ethnic Heritage Studies Program.
	The U.S. Supreme Court decriminalizes vagrancy.
	Title IX of the Education Amendments prohibits sexual discrimination in institutions of higher education that receive public funds; among its other results, the legislation produces a large expansion in women's athletics programs.
	Congress passes the Child Development Act, but President Richard Nixon vetoes it.
	Michelle Triola Marvin, former live-in companion of film actor Lee Marvin, files a suit seeking half of the $3.8 million Lee Marvin had earned during their seven-year relationship. The suit is dismissed, but the California Supreme Court reverses earlier judicial decisions in 1976, remanding the suit to lower courts for trial. In 1979 a California judge orders Marvin to pay $104,000. Appeals lead to the 1981 decision of a California appellate court that he is not required to pay the money, the award having "no basis whatsoever, either in equity or in law."
	The U.S. Supreme Court in *Pennsylvania Association for Retarded Children (PARC) v. Commonwealth of Pennsylvania* upholds a lower court ruling that denying schooling to handicapped children is unconstitutional.
	The U.S. Supreme Court in *Stanley v. Illinois* holds that the fathers of children born out of wedlock cannot be presumed to be unsuitable parents.
1973	The U.S. Supreme Court holds in *Frontiero v. Richardson* that the dependents of female military personnel are eligible to receive the same monetary benefits as the dependents of male personnel.

1973 (cont.)	In *Roe v. Wade* the U.S. Supreme Court strikes down a Texas statute outlawing abortions, in effect legalizing abortion. The decision generates intense political controversy over women's reproductive rights.
	Congress passes the Comprehensive Employment and Training Act (CETA), providing grants to local agencies for training displaced homemakers and preparing them for future jobs.
	In the custody case of *Watts v. Watts* a New York court finds in favor of the father, challenging nearly a century of judicial presumption in favor of mothers.
1974	Congress passes the Child Abuse Prevention and Treatment Act, establishing the Center on Child Abuse and Neglect and offering funds to states that develop laws requiring medical, educational, and other professional authorities to report suspected physical abuse.
	Congress passes the Family Educational Rights and Privacy Act, assuring parental access to their children's school records.
	In *Geduldig v. Aiello* the U.S. Supreme Court holds that a temporary disability insurance plan excluding pregnancy does not violate Fourteenth Amendment guarantees of equal protection.
	Amendments to the Fair Labor Standards Act (FLSA) restrict children working in agriculture to those twelve years of age and older.
	The National Conference of Commissioners on Uniform State Laws (NCCUSL) and the American Bar Association (ABA) promulgate the Uniform Marriage and Divorce Act, setting the age of marital capacity at sixteen and the age of marriage without parental consent at eighteen; the act also includes no-fault divorce provisions; forty-five states already possess some kind of no-fault provision.
1975	With the addition of Part D to Title IV of the Social Security Act, the Office of Child Support Enforcement (OCSE) is established, the purpose of which is to monitor state child-support programs, to locate absent parents, to establish paternity in never-married cases, and to require mothers to assist states in tracking down their children's absent fathers.
	Congress passes the Education for All Handicapped Children Act to protect the rights of children with disabilities and to guarantee the rights of their parents to participate on school committees.
	The U.S. Supreme Court in *Stanton v. Stanton* holds that the traditional idea that "generally it is the man's primary responsibility to provide a home and its essentials" can no longer be used to justify different legal treatment based on gender.
	In cases of harm to the child of either parent, the U.S. Court of Appeals in *United States v. Allery* allows an exception to the common-law rule that one spouse cannot serve as a witness against another in criminal trials.
1976	In *General Electric v. Gilbert* the U.S. Supreme Court holds that a company insurance plan is not discriminatory by virtue of excluding disabilities related to pregnancy; the impact of this case leads to the passage of the Pregnancy Discrimination Act of 1978.
	An appeals court rejects the Federal Communications Commission (FCC) plan for a television "Family Hour."
	Congress passes the Equal Credit Opportunity Act, making it unlawful for a creditor to discriminate against an applicant on the basis of race, age, sex, or marital status.
	The U.S. Supreme Court in *Planned Parenthood of Central Missouri v. Danforth*, disallows parental notification requirements and other limitations on abortion.
	In an important euthanasia case, the New Jersey Supreme Court rules that Karen Anne Quinlan, a young woman in a "persistent vegetative state," has a constitutional right through her guardian and family to refuse life-sustaining treatment.

1977	The U.S. Supreme Court in *Carey v. Population Service*, decides that minors have a right to use contraceptives.
	The U.S. Supreme Court in *Beal v. Doe* rules that states do not have to use public funds to pay for abortions.
	The U.S. Supreme Court in *Maher v. Roe* holds that the state has no obligation to pay for an indigent woman's nontherapeutic abortion.
	Democratic president Jimmy Carter asks Congress to curb the tax advantage of unmarried cohabiting couples.
1978	Congress passes the Indian Child Welfare Act, allowing tribes to exercise limited authority in preventing the adoption of Native American children by non-Native Americans.
	The U.S. Supreme Court affirms a Federal Communications Commission (FCC) decision banning George Carlin's "seven dirty words" during peak radio hours.
	Congress passes the Pregnancy Discrimination Act (PDA), providing a standard for employer practices toward pregnant women.
1979	In *Bellotti v. Baird*, the U.S. Supreme Court rules that teenagers do need parental consent to obtain abortions.
	In *Parham v. J.R.* the U.S. Supreme Court supports the right of parents to commit their children to mental institutions.
	In *Colautti v. Franklin* the U.S. Supreme Court affirms a lower court ruling that voided a Pennsylvania state law requiring physicians to exercise life-saving efforts on fetuses that "may be viable."
	In *Orr v. Orr* the U.S. Supreme Court holds that a state law authorizing courts to impose alimony obligations on husbands but not on wives violates equal protection of the law.
	In *Caban v. Mohammed* the U.S. Supreme Court holds that a state law requiring the permission of the mother but not the father to offer an illegitimate child for adoption violates equal protection of the law.
	In *Califano v. Westcott* the U.S. Supreme Court holds that a federal law awarding welfare benefits to families with an unemployed father (but not an unemployed mother) violates equal protection of the law.
	The Department of Health, Education, and Welfare establishes the Office of Domestic Violence.
	The New York Supreme Court rules in *Callahan v. Carey* that the state and city must provide "clean bedding, wholesome food and adequate supervision and security" to the homeless.
	With the introduction of the Family Protection Act, Congress hopes to provide incentives that shift the public burden of family support away from the federal government and toward state agencies and private industry.
1980	The U.S. Supreme Court in *Harris v. McRae* upholds the decision that Medicaid cannot be used to pay for abortions.
	In *Wengler v. Druggists Mutual Insurance* the U.S. Supreme Court holds that a state workers' compensation law providing death benefits to widows but not to widowers violates equal protection of the law.
	The Washington State Supreme Court allows a troubled teenager to remain in alternative residential placement, arguing that the interests of the child and the state warrant the "relatively minor degree of intrusion on the constitutional rights of parents."
	Congress passes the Adoption Assistance and Child Welfare Act.

1980 (cont.)	California pioneers court preference for joint custody as in the best interests of the child in divorce proceedings; by 1988 thirty-six states follow California's lead.
1981	The Reagan administration closes the Office of Domestic Violence.

Congress consolidates educational programs, cancels some "Great Society" requirements for parental involvement, and cuts federal education funding by more than 40 percent.

In *H.L. v. Mattheson* the U.S. Supreme Court upholds the constitutionality of a state law that requires minors seeking an abortion to notify their parents "if possible" prior to the abortion.

In *Kirchberg v. Feenstra* the U.S. Supreme Court holds that a state law giving husbands complete control over the disposition of marital property violates equal protection of the law. |
| 1982 | The U.S. Supreme Court in *Plyler v. Doe* holds that the state cannot refuse public schooling to illegal aliens.

Congress authorizes Medicare coverage for the hospice care of terminally ill patients.

The U.S. Supreme Court in *Santosky v. Kramer* rules that when the state moves to dissolve parental rights there is a critical need for procedural protections and there must be more than a preponderance of evidence. |
| 1983 | The U.S. Supreme Court in *City of Akron v. Akron Center for Reproductive Health* strikes down a state law requiring a twenty-four hour waiting period before women may obtain an abortion and mandating that physicians must tell their patients that a fetus is a "human life from the moment of conception."

In *Planned Parenthood v. Ashcroft* the U.S. Supreme Court upholds the constitutionality of a state law requiring the presence of a second physician to attempt to save the life of fetuses in abortions performed after viability and requiring a pathology report for all abortions.

In *Newport News Shipbuilding v. EEOC* the U.S. Supreme Court holds that an employer's refusal to pay the medical costs associated with pregnancy for the spouses of male employees while paying all medical costs for the spouses of female employees violates federal law.

In *Lehr v. Robertson* the U.S. Supreme Court holds that a state law allowing the adoption of an unmarried father's child without notice to him does not violate due process or equal protection of the law.

The National Conference of Commissioners on Uniform State Laws proposes a Uniform Marital Property Act, which would make spouses equal co-owners of all property acquired during marriage, except gifts of inheritance. |
| 1984 | Congress passes the Child Support Enforcement Amendments, requiring states to adopt nonbinding mathematical guidelines for setting child support and, in some cases, giving women the means for collecting late child-support payments through wage withholding.

Berkeley, California, becomes the first U.S. city to offer benefits to the domestic partners of municipal workers.

Congress passes the Child Abuse Amendments of 1984, placing the nontreatment of severely disabled infants under the laws of child abuse and neglect. |
| 1985 | The Family and Medical Leave Act (FMLA) is introduced in Congress, sparking a national debate on the question of pregnancy in the workplace. |
| 1986 | In *Thornburgh v. American Counsel of Obstetricians and Gynecologists*, the U.S. Supreme Court holds as unconstitutional a state abortion law imposing informed consent and reporting requirements and requiring that physicians attempt to preserve the life of fetuses. |

1986 (cont.)	The U.S. Supreme Court in *City of Renton v. Playtime Theaters* upholds zoning regulations as a means of controlling the location of adult theaters in neighborhoods.
	The Drug-Free Schools and Communities Act provides federal funding to schools for antidrug programs.
1987	Congress passes the Stewart B. McKinney Homeless Assistance Act, providing emergency shelters and job training to the homeless.
	In *California Federal Savings and Loan v. Guerra* the U.S. Supreme Court holds that the special treatment of pregnancy in the workplace does not necessarily undermine the doctrine of equality.
	The California Supreme Court in *In re Amber B.* undermines the testimony of experts in sexual abuse cases involving young children by deeming the use of anatomical dolls scientifically unreliable.
1988	Congress passes the Civil Rights Restoration Act over the veto of President Ronald Reagan, restoring the ability to enforce provisions of Title IX of the Education Amendments of 1972.
	President Reagan signs amendments to the Fair Housing Act, adding disability and familial status as protected classes.
	The Canadian Supreme Court in *Queen v. Morgenthaler, Smoling, and Scott* strikes down a federal abortion law as unconstitutional.
	A national minimum drinking age of twenty-one and the Office of National Drug Control Policy headed by William J. Bennett is established.
	Congress passes the Family Support Act, designed to enforce child-support orders, to promote self-sufficiency among female welfare recipients, and to require that mathematical formulas be applied in most cases.
	Likening surrogacy contracts to "baby bartering," the New Jersey Supreme Court in *In re Baby M* declares that such contracts are void and establishes the principle that "a sperm donor simply cannot be equated with a surrogate mother."
1989	In *Brashci v. Stahl Associates* the New York Court of Appeals rules that the term "family" should not be "rigidly restricted to those people who have formalized their relationship" through marriage certificates or adoption orders.
	The Canadian Supreme Court in *Brooks, Allen, and Dixon v. Canada Safeway* rules that discrimination on the basis of pregnancy amounts to sexual discrimination.
	In *Webster v. Reproductive Health Services* the U.S. Supreme Court upholds a ban on abortions performed by state employees or in public facilities and a requirement that physicians perform a test to determine the viability of fetuses.
	In *Michael H. v. Gerald D.* the U.S. Supreme Court holds that a state law creating the presumption that a child born to a married woman living with her husband was the child of the marriage did not violate due process or equal protection of the law.
	Washington State extends its statute of limitations to child-abuse cases.
1990	The Displaced Homemakers Self-Sufficiency Assistance Act is passed by Congress.
	The Individuals with Disabilities Education Act is amended to define the rights of parents.
	The U.S. Supreme Court in *Maryland v. Craig* allows children to testify in court cases via closed-circuit television.
	The U.S. Supreme Court in *Osborne v. Ohio* holds that child pornography is not protected under the First Amendment, which guarantees freedom of speech.

1990 (cont.)	Washington State passes the Community Protection Act, which pioneers legislation permitting states to indefinitely detain dangerous "sexual predators" in mental facilities after their release from prison.
	The U.S. Supreme Court in *Ohio v. Akron Center for Reproductive Health* requires teenagers to notify one parent before obtaining an abortion.
	The Family and Medical Leave Act is approved by the House and Senate but vetoed by President George Bush; more than half of the states have enacted some kind of job-protected leave for workers who must stop work for medical reasons.
	Congress grants the Labor Department the authority to raise penalties on child labor.
	Congress passes a $22.5 billion child-care assistance package.
1991	The U.S. Supreme Court in *Rust v. Sullivan* upholds the constitutionality of federal guidelines forbidding government-funded family planning agencies from providing abortion information or counseling; President George Bush vetoes legislation allowing such agencies to discuss abortion in their counseling.
	In *Farrey v. Sanderfoot* the U.S. Supreme Court holds that a lien on a homestead granted to a former wife in divorce proceedings in order to secure the value of her interest in this portion of the marital estate is not avoidable in bankruptcy.
	The Minnesota Court of Appeals grants guardianship of a thirty-five-year-old woman left brain-damaged by an auto accident to her lesbian lover; according to the court, the two "are a family of affinity, which ought to be accorded respect."
1992	In *Planned Parenthood v. Casey* the U.S. Supreme Court upholds most of the restrictions that the Pennsylvania legislature has imposed on women seeking abortions, including a twenty-four-hour waiting period and parental consent; but it rules unconstitutional a provision requiring that women notify their spouses of their intent to obtain an abortion. The case is regarded as a significant setback for abortion rights, although it reaffirms the principle of the 1973 *Roe v. Wade* decision.
	In *Ankenbrandt v. Richards* the U.S. Supreme Court holds that the domestic relations exception to the diversity jurisdiction of federal courts, which prevents federal courts from issuing divorce, alimony, and child-custody decrees, does not apply to a woman's child-abuse claim against her former husband and his female companion.
	Congress passes the Child Support Recovery Act, authorizing courts to impose federal criminal penalties on parents who fail to meet child-support obligations for a child living in another state.
	The District of Columbia approves legislation granting benefits to the domestic partners of city employees.
	Congress passes the National Literacy Act to coordinate federal, state, and local efforts to boost literacy among children and adults.
	The U.S. Supreme Court bars the personal use of RU-486, the abortion pill developed in France.
	The Tennessee Supreme Court in *Davis v. Davis* rules that "preembryos" formed in vitro but not yet implanted in the prospective mother do not have the rights of a fetus.
1993	The Hawaii Supreme Court rules that gay marriages should be legal unless a lower court shows compelling state interest to the contrary.
	Congress passes the Family and Medical Leave Act, requiring companies with fifty or more employees to grant workers up to twelve weeks of unpaid leave each year to care for a new baby or a family member who is seriously ill.

1993 (cont.)	Janet Reno becomes the first woman to serve as attorney general of the United States; her unmarried and childless status again raises the issue of the disadvantages facing women who try to combine marriage and children with public careers.
	The New York appeals court in *Alfonso v. Fernandez* finds New York City's condom distribution program unconstitutional without a provision for parental choice.
1994	Congress rescinds half of fiscal 1995 funding for drug education in schools. President Bill Clinton vetoes this recision bill in 1995, leading to the restoration of all but $16 million in funding.
	California voters pass Proposition 187, which denies school and health benefits to noncitizens, including children, although courts block its implementation.
	The murder of seven-year-old Megan Kanka by a released sex felon leads the New Jersey legislature to pass "Megan's Law," which requires that communities be notified when dangerous sex offenders move into an area.
	A California Superior Court jury awards Gary Ramona $500,000 in damages in finding that two psychotherapists had implanted false memories of childhood sexual abuse in the mind of his adult daughter.
	A federal judge in New Jersey declares the notification clause of "Megan's Law" unconstitutional.
	In *J. E. B. v. Alabama* the U.S. Supreme Court holds that a state attorney's use of peremptory challenges to exclude males from a jury in a paternity suit violates equal protection of the law.
	The Elementary and Secondary Education Act is reauthorized with provisions for character development and requirements for parental involvement.
1995	President Bill Clinton vetoes the Balanced Budget Act, which contains tax relief for the "marriage penalty" and cuts welfare spending by $81.5 billion.
	The U.S. Supreme Court in *Vernonia School District v. Acton* rules that schools may randomly test student athletes for drugs.
	A parental rights bill is introduced in the U.S. Senate and House of Representatives.
	The conviction of George Franklin (1990), which had been based on "recovered memories" of abuse, was overturned by a U.S. District Court in San Francisco.
	Congress passes provisions for requiring television manufacturers to include a V-chip, an electronic device that allows parents to block access to undesirable programming.
1996	In April the head of the National Labor Committee tells a congressional hearing that television star Kathie Lee Gifford's Wal-Mart clothing line is made in sweatshops, sparking a national debate over the responsibility of Americans in protecting children in other countries from sweatshop labor.
	A New York appeals court loosens restrictions on divorced parents moving out of state with children, leading to similar rulings in other states.
	President Bill Clinton vetoes a bill that would ban the partial-birth abortion procedure.
	Congress passes the controversial Defense of Marriage Act, which denies federal recognition of same-sex marriages.
	Congress passes the Personal Responsibility and Work Opportunity Act, ending the federal guarantee of cash assistance to poor children, and turns most federal responsibilities over to the states.

—*John Powell*

Time Line

The following Time Line, concentrating on U.S. history from the seventeenth century to the late 1990's, presents some of the changes undergone by families over the centuries, emphasizing shifting values that have particularly affected women and children.

451-450 B.C.E.	Free consensual marriages are known at the time of the earliest Roman law codes and become common by the second century B.C.E. Divorce by mutual consent is usually punished only when the dissolution is deemed unjustifiable.
c. 400 B.C.E.	The Hippocratic Oath includes the injunction against giving to "a woman an instrument to produce abortion."
c. 360 B.C.E.	Plato in *The Republic* and *The Laws* suggests the need to regulate fertility that corresponds to the economic means of the community and provides stability among plotholders by limiting heirs to one per family.
c. 340 B.C.E.	Aristotle in *Politics* argues for forced miscarriages "before sense and life have begun in the embryo" as a means of regulating family size.
c. 50 C.E.	"Monstrous offspring we suppress," writes Seneca, "and we drown infants that are weakly or abnormal."
c. 90	The Stoic Musonius Rufus views nonprocreative sex and marriage negatively.
c. 100	Plutarch hails marriage as an ordering force and a brake on sexual passions.
c. 130	Soranus says that virginity is healthy and that women in Rome "usually are married for the sake of children, and not for mere enjoyment," sometimes leading to the divorce of a loved but barren wife.
c. 150	According to Galen of Pergamum, sexual intercourse is necessary for health.
c. 200	Child abandonment in Rome is described as murder, but it is not officially condemned; Tertullian wonders why one would want children who were encumbrances and "perilous to the faith."
318	The Emperor Constantine declares that a father's murder of his children is a crime.
c. 400	Child murder is criminalized in the Roman Empire; Augustine condemns any means of contraception and declares any sexual intercourse for pleasure as a venial sin.
529	Justinian outlaws the enslavement of foundlings.
542	Justinian extends penalties to divorce by mutual consent in the Byzantine Empire; the right to terminate marriages is so firmly entrenched and the opposition so strong that Justinian's successor repeals the penalties. Indissolubility of marriage and sacramental marriage are proposed by leading church figures but slow to sway people's minds.
c. 1000	The theory of monogamous and indissoluble marriage as the ideal is firmly rooted in Europe, although divorce is still widely practiced.
1522	Martin Luther declares that procreation is "the purpose" for which women exist.
1543-1563	The Roman Catholic Church at the Council of Trent bans informal marriages by requiring the participation of a priest and other witnesses at weddings.

1563	The Archbishop of Canterbury compiles the various biblical and canonical injunctions against marriages between kin; his tables become the foundation for future Anglo-American legislation.
1576	English Poor Law requires that parents of children born out of wedlock pay for their maintenance.
1601	English Poor Law Act obligates a father to support his children until they are twenty-one years old.
1614	Pocahontas, a Native American, marries John Rolfe.
1620	English Privy Council authorizes London children to be bound as apprentices against their will and shipped to Virginia.
1641	The Massachusetts Bay Colony adopts the Body of Liberties, which forbids husbands from abusing their wives except in the case of self-defense, forbids the government from depriving a man of his wife or children without some "express law of the country established by the General Court and sufficiently published," prescribes capital punishment for rebellious children over sixteen years of age, allows children to defend themselves from excessively severe punishment, and forbids parents from choosing their children's mates.
1642	The Massachusetts Bay Colony requires fathers to teach their children to read and impart to them knowledge of "Capital Laws" and the principles of religion.
1646	Virginia enacts a "binding out" statute, enabling local authorities to remove children from their homes without parental consent; Body of Liberties amended to require bringing a rebellious son to court to confirm wanton rebelliousness.
1647	The Massachusetts legislature orders towns of at least fifteen families to provide public elementary education, primarily for the purpose of teaching reading and religious doctrine and solidifies the practice of family-based education.
1648	First Orphan's Court in America established in Virginia.
1661	Maryland becomes the first American colony to enact a ban on interracial marriage.
1662	A Virginia law states that a person will be deemed slave or free depending on the status of his or her mother; another law prohibits whites from having sexual relations with blacks.
	Congregational synod adopts the Half-Way Covenant, allowing the grandchildren of full communicants to be baptized, even though their parents could not demonstrate conversion.
1681	Maryland requires special juries to oversee the property interests of orphans.
1682	Pennsylvania requires parents to ensure that their children are educated; the British crown disallows the law.
1696	Maryland extends jurisdiction of orphan's courts to cover all orphans, even when they are covered by a father's will.
1699	Cotton Mather publishes *A Family Well-Ordered*, an early parenting handbook.
1704	Lord Holt rules in *Hutton v. Mansell* that mutual promises of marriage may be proven by circumstantial, rather than direct, evidence.
1719	In *Holt v. Ward Clarencieux*, minors are exempted in breach-of-promise of marriage, setting a long precedent in American marital law.
1729	The first orphan home in the United States is established at the Ursuline Convent in New Orleans.

1739	George Whitefield establishes Bethesda orphanage in Georgia.
1753	English Marriage Act makes religious ceremonies compulsory and establishes fixed formal requirements, including registration and parental consent. Only Quakers, Jews, and members of the Royal Family are exempt.
1762	Jean Jacques Rousseau publishes *Emile*, stressing that nature "wants children to be children before they are men" and encouraging education suited to the particular nature of each child.
1765-1769	William Blackstone publishes *Commentaries on the Laws of England*, defining marriage as a civil contract rather than as a sacramental observance, thus justifying public control.
1773	The first grant of petition of divorce is awarded to a woman in Massachusetts on the grounds of adultery by her husband.
1774	Ann Lee immigrates to the American colonies, bringing with her the Millennial Church (Shakers), which prohibits sexual intercourse and marriage.
1780's	This decade witnesses the sharp rise in the publication of romantic novels, reflecting an increasing expectation of affection in marriage.
1780	The Pennsylvania legislature decrees that the children of slaves are required to serve their owners as indentured servants until the age of twenty-eight, a decree characteristic of the gradual abolition of slavery in the northern states.
1785	A Virginia statute legitimizes the offspring of a voided marriage, making them capable of inheritance.
1789	William Blake publishes *Songs of Innocence*, undermining the traditional Christian insistence on the innate wickedness of children.
1790	Connecticut Supreme Court reporter Jesse Root voices central assumptions of Republican family values in declaring that the idea that "one man should be joined to one woman in a constant society of cohabiting together, is agreeable to the order of nature" and necessary for social order.
1791	The first ten amendments to the Constitution take effect, including the First Amendment guaranteeing religious freedom and the Ninth guaranteeing that a listing of certain rights in the Constitution "shall not be construed to deny or disparage others retained by the people." These form the basis of later battles over parental rights. Secretary of the Treasury Alexander Hamilton produces *Report on Manufactures*, recommending the employment of women and children in manufacturing.
1793	The Pennsylvania courts in *Respublica v. Kepple* hold that parents cannot bind out their children except as apprentices.
1797	The Society for Relief of Poor Widows with Small Children is founded by Isabella Graham in New York City.
1803	Abortion is made a statutory crime in England.
1807	William Wordsworth publishes *Ode: Intimations of Immortality*, in which he asserts the essential innocence of children and their closeness to God.
1813	Connecticut requires basic education for factory-employed children.

1816	Tapping Reeve publishes *Law of Baron and Femme*, the first American book on domestic relations.
1818	Hanna Barnard publishes *Dialogues on Domestic and Rural Economy*, regarded as the first housekeeping manual.
1825	The New York House of Refuge is founded as the first U.S. institution for juvenile delinquents.
1826-1830	James Kent, chief justice of the New York Supreme Court, publishes *Commentaries on American Law*.
1828	*Ladies' Magazine* is published in Boston to instruct middle-class women about their duties in the home.
1830	Congress makes abortion a crime, although only after the "quickening" of the fetus.
1831	Alexis de Tocqueville arrives in America, observing that family life is becoming increasingly child centered, that marriage is becoming more intimate, and that children are granted greater freedom in controlling their lives.
1832	Charles Knowlton publishes *Fruits of Philosophy*, offering the first widely available explanation of contraception and reproduction. Public outrage leads to a conviction on obscenity charges. Nevertheless, more than 10,000 copies are sold before the end of the decade.
1834	The New York Moral Reform Society is established, which seeks to halt prostitution and family diversity.
1836	America's first widespread elementary curriculum, *McGuffey's Readers*, emphasizes patriotism, parental respect, and Christian principles.
1837	Timothy Walker publishes *Introduction to American Law*, advocating greater freedom for women and children.
1839	Michael Ryan publishes *The Philosophy of Marriage and Its Social, Moral, and Physical Relations*, clearly pointing to sexuality in children.
1841	Catherine Beecher publishes *Treatise on Domestic Economy*, an influential book on homemaking and housekeeping.
1842	Massachusetts law limits children twelve years of age and under to a ten-hour workday.
1845	Margaret Fuller's *Women in the Nineteenth Century* considers the position of women in American society.
1847	A. M. Mauriceau publishes *Married Woman's Private Medical Companion*, openly espousing contraception and promoting marriages of love rather than of convenience.
1848	The first Women's Rights Convention at Seneca Falls, N.Y., calls for expanded civil rights for women, including greater custody rights. The New York state legislature enacts the Married Woman's Property Act, allowing women to control property received by gift, grant, or bequest.
1850	The average number of children born to women during their fertile years drops to 5.42, resulting in a decline of average family size by 25 percent from the beginning of the century. Around this time there is a great surge in the publication of juvenile literature, which will last throughout the century.
1851	The Massachusetts legislature makes adoption a legal procedure in which the court is responsible for determining parental fitness and in which the rights of the natural family are dissolved. This legislation becomes the model for adoption policy in most states.

1852	Harriet Beecher Stowe publishes *Uncle Tom's Cabin: Or, Life Among the Lowly*, which humanizes African Americans through its portrayal of slave family life.
	Joel Bishop publishes *Commentaries on the Law of Marriage and Divorce*, seeking to bring order to the multitude of judicial and statutory law that had developed since Reeve's *Law of Baron and Femme* in 1816.
	Massachusetts legislature passes the first compulsory school attendance law.
	Brigham Young publicly announces the adoption of polygamy in the Utah territory.
1853	Charles Loring Brace founds the New York Children's Aid Society, which in its first twenty-five years placed some 40,000 homeless or destitute city children into farm homes, where "food and cost to the family is of little account."
	New York City passes a truancy law, linking family relief to school attendance.
	Stephen Pearl Andrews publishes a series of letters, *Love, Marriage, and Divorce*, in the *New York Tribune*, in which he elevates the sovereignty of individual choice.
1855	Henry Wright publishes *Marriage and Parentage*, criticizing marriage as a means of economic or social advancement and arguing that romantic love is the only true source of marital happiness.
	William Alcott publishes *Physiology of Marriage*, contending that excessive sexual relations produces weak children and debilitated parents.
1856	Margaretha Meyer Schurz establishes the first kindergarten in the United States in Watertown, Wisconsin.
1857	The English Matrimonial Clauses Act becomes the foundation of divorce proceedings in most Canadian provinces.
	Tom Brown's School Days is an American and British best-seller, promoting the idea that "sports builds character."
1860's	Married women are allowed to own property and keep their wages throughout the United States.
1860	New York State enlarges its Married Woman's Property Act to include the woman as joint guardian of her children along with her husband, with equal rights and duties.
1861-1865	Approximately 600,000 men die during the American Civil War, particularly affecting gender balance and family life in the South.
1862	Editors of the revised edition of Reeve's *Law of Baron and Femme* (1816) observe that innovations are already underway in the laws governing married women.
	U.S. Congress passes the Morrill Act, declaring polygamy illegal in all American territories.
1866	U.S. President Andrew Johnson vetoes the Civil Rights Act, arguing that "if Congress can abrogate all state laws of discrimination between the two races . . . may it not also repeal the state laws as to the contract of marriage between the two races?"
1867	The number of divorces granted in the United States reaches 10,000 annually.
1868-1869	Louisa May Alcott publishes *Little Women*, a novel that follows the adventures of four sisters into womanhood.

1870	James Schouler publishes *Law of Domestic Relations*.
1871	Joel Bishop publishes *Commentaries on the Law of Married Women*, a sustained defense of common law that champions judicial decisions as most effective and least disruptive in encouraging social change.
1872	The New York Society for the Suppression of Vice is established, leading the late nineteenth century drive against contraception.
1873	The first public kindergarten opens in Saint Louis, Missouri.
1874	The New York Society for the Prevention of Cruelty to Children, first designed to look after exploited street children, is founded.
1876	Baptist minister Russell Conwell publishes *Women and the Law*, arguing that women enjoy favored legal status in the courts.
	Eliza Duffey publishes *The Relation of the Sexes*, the main purpose of which is to convince women that they are not obligated to have children.
	William Whitmore publishes *The Law of Adoption* as a guide to a Massachusetts legislative committee considering revision of adoption law, calling for greater statutory uniformity and special care so that natural families are not undermined by adoption.
1879	In *Reynolds v. United States* the U.S. Supreme Court holds that the federal antibigamy law does not violate Mormons' free exercise of their religious rights.
1880	The U.S. Commerce Department reports that one in sixteen U.S. marriages fails, leading to the formation of the National Divorce Reform League. The U.S. Census Bureau reports that an estimated 17 percent of all children ages ten to fifteen are employed outside the home.
1881	The New England Divorce Reform League (later the National League for the Protection of the Family) assumes control of the various groups that organized during the 1870's to lobby for more restrictive divorce laws.
	Dr. John H. Kellogg publishes *Plain Facts for Old and Young*, urging parents to acknowledge sexual feelings in their children.
1882	New York passes the Factory Act, prohibiting work by children under the age of thirteen.
1888	Massachusetts attorney Frank Gaylor Cook, calling for reform of nuptial law, publishes "Marriage Celebration in the United States" in the *Atlantic Monthly*, arguing that the "widest diversity of race, religion, and sentiments" among the populace undermines traditional respect for "statutory forms" of marriage law.
1889	The first U.S. national survey of divorce and marriage laws reveals a 150 percent increase in divorce since 1870 and decries the scarcity of data in most states.
	Ladies' Home Journal begins publication, glorifying motherhood.
	The American Pediatric Society is founded, further delineating childhood as a distinct stage of life.
1890	New York State enacts the first law assuming full responsibility for the "insane poor."
	Mormon president Wilford Woodruff renounces polygamy, leading to Utah statehood four years later.
1891	The Women's Athletic Association is established by students at Bryn Mawr College to formalize sports competition among college women.

1892	Kate Douglas Wiggin publishes *Children's Rights*, demonstrating the sentimentalization of children and urging a more realistic view of childhood.
	The National Conference of Commissioners on Uniform State Laws is founded, with the goal of developing uniform divorce legislation and coordinating other law-reform efforts.
1896	In *Plessy v. Ferguson* the U.S. Supreme Court establishes the "separate but equal" rule, reinforcing the de facto practice of segregation.
1897	The National Congress of Mothers, which later becomes the National Parent Teachers Association (PTA), is founded in Washington, D.C.
1898	Charlotte Perkins Gilman publishes *Woman and Economics*, questioning the ideal of womanly "innocence."
1899	Sigmund Freud in Vienna, Austria, publishes *The Interpretation of Dreams*, in which he develops the idea of the "Oedipus Complex," which maintains that the sexual feelings developing in childhood toward the parent of the opposite sex may lead to personality disorders in adults.
	The National Federation of Consumers' Leagues is founded, in part to end child labor.
	Lelia Robinson publishes *The Law of Husband and Wife, Compiled for Popular Use*, which emphasizes the role of economic dependence in legal decisions regarding women.
	The first juvenile court in America is established in Chicago on the premise that rehabilitation is possible.
1900	By the turn of the century every state prohibits marriages between blood relatives up to first cousins, marking the rise of state intervention in an area that was previously self-regulated.
1904	Stanford sociologist George Eliot Howard publishes *History of Matrimonial Institutions*, representing the social scientist as a new source of authority in the development of matrimonial law. Howard argues that matrimony can only be successful when it unites two competent individuals who have carefully considered their choice.
	National Child Labor Committee founded, the first children's rights organization to bring about effective federal legislation regulating child labor.
1907	Novelist Theodore Dreiser inaugurates a national home placement campaign, allowing families to receive children without a written instrument, through indenture, or through adoption. The effort is largely unsuccessful in locating free placements.
1909	Bessie Locke founds the National Kindergarten Association to spread the idea of schools for young children.
	President Theodore Roosevelt convenes the first White House Conference on the Care of Dependent Children, which establishes the principle that poverty alone should not justify the removal of children from parents.
1910	The U.S. Census shows that almost 15 percent of the total population of the United States are foreign born.
1911	Missouri and Illinois become the first states to grant aid to mothers of dependent children from state funds, an idea that spreads to seventeen other states by 1913.
	The U.S. government creates the Children's Bureau within the U.S. Bureau of Labor, the investigations of which soon show the need for greater protection of maternal and infant health.

1912	Arizona and North Dakota follow the "Norwegian model," legitimizing all offspring of natural parents and providing for full support and education; no other states follow.
1913	Wisconsin becomes the first state requiring persons to undergo medical tests "by a competent physician, who should decide whether they are proper candidates for parentage."
1914	Margaret Sanger founds the National Birth Control League (later the Birth Control Federation of America), coining the term "birth control." President Woodrow Wilson announces the first national Mother's Day.
1915	William Healy, director of the Juvenile Psychopathic Institute, publishes *The Individual Delinquent*, in which he reluctantly admits that no single factor can be cited to explain the causes of juvenile delinquency.
1916	Congress passes the Keating-Owen Act, banning interstate commerce in products made by children under the age of fourteen in factories and under the age of sixteen in mines.
	Arthur Calhoun publishes *Social History of the American Family*, summarizing the fundamental shift in the basis of family law, based upon the primacy of the individual.
1918	The Maternity Care Association of New York offers prenatal care to poor women.
	John D. Rockefeller establishes the Laura Spelman Rockefeller Memorial with an endowment of $73 million. In 1923 the organization turns its attention to child study and parent education.
1919	The Voluntary Parenthood League is formed by Mary Ware Dennett.
	The International Labour Organisation (ILO) is founded and passes first convention against child labor.
1921	The American Birth Control League (the predecessor of Planned Parenthood) is founded by Margaret Sanger.
	Congress passes the Sheppard-Towner Maternity and Infancy Protection Act, providing states with federal matching funds to establish prenatal and child-care centers.
	The Lucy Stone League is launched to promote the right of women to keep their own names after marriage.
1922	Margaret Sanger publishes *Women, Morality, and Birth Control*.
	Congress, the Children's Bureau, and organized labor all support a federal anti-child-labor amendment, strongly opposed by factory owners and farmers.
1923	Alice Paul proposes the Equal Rights Amendment (ERA), which reads: "Equality of rights under the law shall not be denied or abridged by the United States or by any State on account of sex."
	The Women's Division of the National Amateur Athletic Federation is formed by Lou Henry Hoover and others active in athletics to promote sports for women at the school and college level.
1924	One American marriage in seven ends in divorce.
	Congress passes legislation restricting immigration, implementing quotas favoring northern and western Europeans.
1925	Vassar College launches the School of Euthenics, which emphasizes the care and promotion of the family.

1925 (cont.)	Smith College offers the Institute to Coordinate Women's Interests as a means to explore ways for women to combine family and career.
	Psychologist Lewis Terman publishes results of a thirty-year study of gifted persons, suggesting that giftedness evolves from childhood to adulthood without high incidence of emotional problems.
1926	Virginia Collier publishes *Marriage and Careers*, asserting that the question is "no longer, should women combine marriage with careers, but how do they manage it and how does it work?"
1927	Boston reformer Mirian Van Waters publishes *Parents on Probation*, arguing that "a new sense of chivalry" must be developed in which the natural rights of parents are subordinated to the "welfare of children."
1929	Under pressure from the American Medical Association (AMA), Congress terminates the Sheppard-Towner Act.
1930	The White House Conference on Child Health and Protection is held.
	Hollywood's Motion Picture Production Code is created by Will Hays.
1931	The motion picture *Blonde Venus* emphasizes the danger to the family of economically emancipated women.
1932	Some states needing revenue initiate "quickie divorces."
	Emily Mudd begins the Marriage Council of Philadelphia, devoted to marital counseling.
1933	Section 213 of the National Economy Act prohibits more than one member of a family from working for the federal government, substantially reducing the accessibility of government jobs to women.
	Congress passes the National Recovery Act, which contains provisions prohibiting labor by children under sixteen years of age.
1934	The Grandmothers Clubs of America are founded. The Production Code Administration is formed by Will Hays, with Joseph Breen as director.
1933-1935	The Federal Emergency Relief Administration (FERA) supplies shelter, food, medical care, money, and jobs to the homeless.
1935	Congress passes the Social Security Act, which establishes Aid to Dependent Children (ADC), a program designed to assist low-income families; maternal and child health programs; and various child welfare services.
	Congress creates the National Youth Administration to employ students and other needy youth.
	The Federal Emergency Relief Administration (FERA) is replaced by a variety of programs targeting individual needs.
	The U.S. Supreme Court in *Shechter Poultry Corporation v. United States* declares the National Industrial Recovery Act unconstitutional, thus abolishing the prohibition against child labor.
1936	The right of doctors to prescribe birth control devices becomes legal in *United States v. One Package Containing 120, More or Less, Rubber Pessaries to Prevent Conception*.
1938	Congress passes the Fair Labor Standards Act (FLSA), which regulates work hours and pay and establishes child-labor rules.
	The National Council on Family Relations is established.

1940	The White House Conference on Children in a Democracy, while recognizing that many causes of delinquency are rooted in economic factors, recommends that possible youthful offenders should remain under close scrutiny to prevent them from becoming criminals.
1941-1945	The induction of sixteen million men into the military during World War II leads to a 57 percent increase in female employment, initiating a permanent shift toward women in the workplace and altering perceptions of their competence. In 1942, only 13 percent of Americans object to women working outside the home.
1942	The Planned Parenthood Federation of America evolves out of activities begun by Margaret Sanger's American Birth Control League.
	The Lanham (Community Facilities) Act, passed in 1940, is amended to establish child-care centers in forty-one states.
	The American Association of Marriage Counselors (AAMC) is founded as a network for professionals and for the purpose of devising standards for the practice of marriage counseling.
	The All-American Girls Professional Baseball League is founded by Philip K. Wrigley.
1944	The Serviceman's Readjustment Act creates the Veteran's Administration (VA) program, which guarantees mortgage insurance, and expands the Federal Housing Authority (FHA), which encourages veterans to enter the housing market.
1945	Paul Popenoe popularizes the profession of marriage counseling with his monthly article "Can This Marriage Be Saved?" in *Ladies' Home Journal*.
1946	The beginning of the baby boom, initiating a long-term rise in the birth rate after low fertility during the depression and war years.
	For the first time, a majority of American families own their own homes.
	Benjamin Spock publishes *The Common Sense Book of Baby and Child Care*, whose health-care admonitions are especially welcome to the last generations of parents, who routinely fear life-threatening or debilitating diseases such as polio and meningitis. By 1976, twenty-eight million copies are sold, making it the second-best-selling book of the century after the Bible.
	Congress passes the War Brides Act to allow for the immigration of foreign wives.
	Congress passes the National Mental Health Act, which eventually provides funding for mental health work among families.
1948	Congress allows income splitting on joint tax returns.
	The United Nations Universal Declaration of Human Rights holds that "Parents have a prior right to choose the kind of education that shall be given to their children."
1949	William J. Levitt uses production-line techniques to build inexpensive single-family homes, initiating the flight to the suburbs.
1950	Aid to Dependent Children (ADC) becomes Aid to Families with Dependent Children (AFDC), the cornerstone of the modern welfare system. State welfare agencies are required to notify law-enforcement officials when welfare benefits go to children who have been abandoned by their parents.
	The words "damn" and "hell" are first used on television by Arthur Godfrey.

1951	Congress passes the Federal Youth Corrections Act, establishing the youth authority approach in federal corrections administrations.
	I Love Lucy, one of many programs portraying American families, debuts on television.
1952	Congress holds its first hearings on television violence.
1953	The U.S. Department of Health, Education, and Welfare is created.
	Simone de Beauvoir's *The Second Sex* is published in the United States.
1954	In *Brown v. Board of Education* the U.S. Supreme Court outlaws school segregation, leading to racial integration and the decline of community schools.
	Frederick Wertham publishes *Seduction of the Innocent*, arguing that crime comics cause juvenile delinquency. Comic-book publishers adopt a voluntary code to prevent obscenity, vulgarity, and horror.
1955	Rudolf Flesch attacks schools for abandoning phonics in *Why Johnny Can't Read*.
	A U.S. Senate subcommittee investigates the causes of juvenile delinquency and establishes in its final report of 1957 the complexity of causes, thus resisting a complete ban on crime comics and other media expressions.
1956	La Leche League International is founded in a Chicago suburb to promote knowledge about the benefits of breast-feeding infants.
	Peak of the post-war "baby boom."
1958	In the wake of Soviet successes in space, the National PTA successfully lobbies for education legislation designed to help the U.S. catch up with the Soviets. The National Defense Education Act provides federal aid for math, science, and foreign-language instruction.
	Nathan Ackerman publishes *The Psychodynamics of Family Life*, which urges psychiatrists to treat patient mental disorders as a part of family process dynamics.
	The American Association of Retired Persons (AARP) is formed.
1959	The Mental Research Institute (MRI), founded in Palo Alto, California, by Don Jackson, pioneers family treatment.
1960	The Association of American Foreign Service Women begins to obtain greater recognition and training for wives of diplomats overseas.
	Sex discrimination is banned in the Canadian Bill of Rights.
	The Legal Aid Society establishes a pilot program in which New York City juveniles are represented in juvenile courts by lawyers.
	The National Conference on Day Care is held in Washington, D.C., and sponsored by several federal government agencies.
	The birth control pill ("the Pill") is introduced in the United States.
1961	Planned Parenthood of Canada is organized by Barbara and George Cadbury.
	Family Process becomes the first journal in the newly emerging field of family therapy.
	Actress Yvette Mimieux becomes the first woman to bare her navel on television.

1962   The U.S. Supreme Court in *Engel v. Vitale* bans daily prayer in the classroom as a violation of the constitutional guarantee of separation of church and state, leading many teachers to avoid discussion of morals in the classroom.

1963   Betty Friedan publishes *The Feminine Mystique*, articulating the grievances of middle-class women of the 1950's.

        The U.S. Children's Bureau enables states to require that physicians report suspected cases of child abuse. All states enact reporting laws within three years.

        The Report of the Presidential Commission on Women, while recognizing the expanding role of married women in the economy, contends that women's primary responsibility is in the home and recommends that they be trained for marriage and motherhood.

1964   Congress enacts the Head Start program to provide preschool education for impoverished children.

        Title VII of the Civil Rights Act prohibits sex discrimination in employment.

        A Department of Labor study finds that there are almost one million children without adequate adult supervision during significant portions of the day in the United States, sparking the child-care debate of the late 1960's and 1970's.

1965   Congress passes the Elementary and Secondary Education Act, providing funds for Head Start and aid to low-income students (Title I), while requiring parental involvement.

        Daniel Patrick Moynihan's report, *The Negro Family: The Case for National Action*, argues that the African American family is threatened by the growing absence of black men and the dominant role of black women. Controversy ensues about whether the report is accurate and whether it reflects racist and sexist views.

        Immigration and Nationality Act amendments increase immigration and allow for family unification.

1966   Patricia Maginnis creates the Association to Repeal Abortion Laws in California.

        James S. Coleman of the University of Chicago issues a report in which he argues that families have more impact on students than schools.

        Louis Raths publishes *Values and Teaching*, urging teachers to help students "clarify" their values without being judgmental.

        Congress passes the Adult Education Act and the Smithsonian Institution launches the Reading Is Fundamental (RIF) program for distributing books to needy children.

        The founding statement of the National Organization for Women (NOW) rejects the notion that "home and family are primarily woman's world and responsibility," calling for "an equitable sharing of the responsibilities of home and children."

        New York State passes a law widening the grounds for divorce to include cruel and inhuman treatment, abandonment, confinement in prison, or agreed upon separation for more than two years.

1967   Congress passes the Age Discrimination in Employment Act, supporting the right of older Americans to earn an "adequate income."

1968   Students at McGill University in Quebec illegally publish the *Birth Control Handbook*.

        The Motion Picture Association of America launches its movie ratings system.

1968 (cont.)	Congress enacts the Fair Housing Act, barring discrimination in the sale or rental of housing; no enforcement mechanism is provided.
	The Roman Catholic Church introduces the Marriage Encounters counseling program.
	The National Conference for Repeal of Abortion Laws is established and becomes the National Abortion Rights Action League (NARAL).
1969	The Canadian government liberalizes Canada's abortion laws.
	Midnight Cowboy becomes the first X-rated film to be widely distributed.
	The NOW chapter in New York forms New Yorkers for Abortion Law Repeal.
	Congress passes the Child Protection and Toy Safety Act, banning many dangerous toys.
	Republican governor Ronald Reagan of California signs the Family Law Act, the first U.S. no-fault divorce law; forty-five states adopt some form of no-fault divorce by the mid-1970's.
1970	The White House Conference on Children is held to address issues involving children and working mothers.
	The Uniform Marriage and Divorce Act establishes the "best interests" standard in resolving custody cases.
	The National PTA merges with the National Congress of Colored Parents and Teachers.
	Congress passes the Education of the Handicapped Act, providing for teacher training and the education of the handicapped.
1971	The Association for Intercollegiate Athletics for Women is launched to challenge the male-dominated National Collegiate Athletic Association (NCAA).
	All in the Family airs, featuring the first gay character on American television.
1972	The surgeon general's report on violence cites the influence of television.
	Congress enacts the Ethnic Heritage Studies Program.
	The U.S. Supreme Court decriminalizes vagrancy.
	Title IX of the Education Amendments prohibits sexual discrimination in higher education institutions receiving public funds; among its other results, the legislation produces a large expansion in women's athletics programs.
	Congress passes the Child Development Act, but President Richard Nixon vetoes it.
1973	The U.S. Supreme Court decides in *Frontiero v. Richardson* that the dependents of female military personnel are eligible to receive the same monetary benefits as the dependents of male personnel.
	In *Roe v. Wade* the U.S. Supreme Court strikes down a Texas statute outlawing abortions, in effect legalizing abortion. The decision generates intense political controversy over women's reproductive rights.
	The Comprehensive Employment and Training Act (CETA) is passed in Congress, providing grants to local agencies to train displaced homemakers and prepare them for future jobs.

1973
(cont.)   Joseph Goldstein, Anna Freud, and Albert Solnit publish *Beyond the Best Interests of the Child*, establishing the concept of a "psychological parent" who ought to retain custody regardless of biological relationship.

David and Vera Mace establish the Association of Couples for Marriage Enrichment (ACME), building upon their pioneering work as marriage counselors in England in the 1950's and the United States in the 1960's. This ushers in a rapid period of growth for the marital/family enrichment movement.

An international agreement sets the minimum working age at fifteen.

The Children's Defense Fund is established.

1974   President Richard Nixon signs the Child Abuse Prevention and Treatment Act, establishing the Center on Child Abuse and Neglect and offering funds to states developing laws that require medical, educational, and other professional authorities to report suspected cases of physical abuse.

Congress passes the Family Educational Rights and Privacy Act, assuring parental access to their children's school records.

The Women's Sports Foundation is started to expand opportunities for women in athletic pursuits.

Little League Baseball is opened to women by Congressional action.

Amendments to the Fair Labor Standards Act (FLSA) restrict children working in agriculture to those twelve years of age and older.

The Canadian Association for the Appeal of the Abortion Laws (CARAL) forms; it becomes the Canadian Abortion Rights League in 1980.

The National Conference of Commissioners on Uniform State Laws and the American Bar Association (ABA) promulgate the Uniform Marriage and Divorce Act, setting the age of marital capacity at sixteen and age of marriage without parental consent at eighteen. It also includes no-fault provisions; forty-five states already possess some kind of no-fault provision.

1975   The Office of Child Support Enforcement is established with the addition of Part D to Title IV of the Social Security Act.

Title IX takes effect, but high schools and colleges are given three additional years to comply with requirements for providing equal athletic opportunities.

Congress passes the Education for All Handicapped Children Act to protect the rights of children with disabilities and to guarantee the rights of their parents to participate on school committees.

NOW sets up a Task Force on Battered Women/Household Violence.

Phyllis Schlafly founds Eagle Forum to oppose the Equal Rights Amendment (ERA) and abortion.

1976   An appeals court rejects the Federal Communications Commission (FCC) plan for a television "Family Hour."

Congress passes the Equal Credit Opportunity Act, making it unlawful for creditors to discriminate against applicants on the basis of race, age, sex, or marital status.

The first national survey of U.S. high-school students shows that almost half have tried marijuana before graduation.

1977	Bare breasts are first shown on U.S. network television in *Roots*.
	The American Association for Marriage and Family Therapy is recognized by the Department of Health, Education, and Welfare as an accrediting body for degree programs in marriage and family therapy.
	Democratic president Jimmy Carter asks Congress to curb the tax advantage of cohabiting couples who are not married.
1978	Congress passes the Indian Child Welfare Act, allowing tribes to exercise limited authority in preventing the adoption of Native American children by non-Native Americans.
	The U.S. Supreme Court affirms the Federal Communications Commission (FCC) decision banning George Carlin's "seven dirty words" during peak radio hours.
	The White House Conference on Families, called by President Jimmy Carter, eventually recommends ratification of the Equal Rights Amendment (ERA), the right to abortion, and sex education in the schools as a means of strengthening family life. Opposition from the "pro-family" movement makes implementation of these proposals impossible.
1979	*Children's Legal Rights Journal* begins publication.
	National Coalition for Parental Involvement in Education is founded.
	The U.S. divorce rate peaks at 5.3 per 1,000 persons.
	Marijuana use among high-school students peaks at almost 60 percent by the twelfth grade.
	The Department of Health, Education, and Welfare establishes the Office on Domestic Violence.
1980	California pioneers the court preference for joint custody in divorce proceedings as in the best interests of the child. By 1988, thirty-six states followed suit.
	23 percent of all households in the United States consist of one person living alone.
1981	The Ronald Reagan administration closes the Office of Domestic Violence.
	Congress consolidates educational programs, cancels some "Great Society" requirements for parental involvement, and cuts federal education funding by more than 40 percent.
	Betty Friedan's *The Second Stage* is published, emphasizing the role of motherhood.
1982	The National Institute of Mental Health links social violence with television.
	Congress authorizes Medicare coverage for hospice care of terminally ill patients.
1983	The National Conference of Commissioners on Uniform State Laws proposes a Uniform Marital Property Act, which would make spouses equal co-owners of all property acquired during marriage, except gifts of inheritance.
1984	Antiabortion women advocates in Canada create Real, Equal, Active, for Life (REAL), claiming to speak for the "real" women of the nation.
	Berkeley, California, becomes the first U.S. city to offer benefits to the domestic partners of municipal workers.
	The Reagan administration ends U.S. financial contributions to international birth control programs.

1985	Sociologist Lenore Weitzman publishes *The Divorce Revolution*, contending that no-fault divorce penalizes women and leading to the establishment of the California State Senate Task Force on Family Equity.
	The Parent and Teacher Association launches the Big City project to increase parental involvement in urban schools.
	The Family and Medical Leave Act (FMLA) is introduced in Congress, sparking a national debate on the question of pregnancy in the workplace.
	At the prompting of the Parents Music Resource Center and the National Parent and Teacher Association, the Recording Industry Association of America institutes a voluntary labeling system to warn parents of the contents of recordings.
	Child Advisory and Protection Newsletter begins publication as a clearinghouse for policy and program information for lawyers dealing with child-protection issues.
1986	Randall Terry creates Operation Rescue to close down abortion clinics.
	The Drug-Free Schools and Communities Act provides federal funding to schools for anti-drug programs.
1987	Congress passes the Stewart B. McKinney Homeless Assistance Act, providing emergency shelters and job training for the homeless.
1988	Congress passes the Civil Rights Restoration Act over the veto of President Ronald Reagan, restoring the ability to enforce provisions of Title IX of the Education Amendments of 1972.
	The National Day of Rescue, sponsored by Operation Rescue, leads six thousand demonstrators to target forty-five abortion clinics in twenty-seven states, resulting in two thousand arrests.
	The national minimum drinking age of twenty-one and the Office of the National Drug Control Policy headed by William J. Bennett are established.
	The Courage to Heal, a "survivor's manual" for victims of childhood sexual abuse, suggests that many victims of abuse never gain memories of their trauma, opening the door to a wide range of unsubstantiated claims against parents.
1989	The National Center for Family Literacy is founded.
	Judith Wallerstein argues in *Second Chances: Men, Women, and Children a Decade After Divorce* that the long-term emotional and psychological effects of divorce on children are worse than previously imagined.
	The United Nations General Assembly unanimously adopts the Convention on the Rights of the Child, guaranteeing certain fundamental rights for all children, including health care, education, and protection from abuse.
	Washington State extends its statute of limitations to child-abuse cases.
1990	Supported by experts on domestic-partnership law, nontraditional families begin registering with the California secretary of state's office to gain legal status as unincorporated nonprofit groups.
	Former University of Colorado football coach Bill McCartney forms The Promise Keepers (PK), a largely evangelical Christian movement assisting men in keeping their promises to wives, families, and God. By 1996 more than one million people participate annually in PK rallies around the United States.

1990 (cont.)	George Thomas Franklin is convicted of a 1969 murder on the basis of testimony by his adult daughter, who had a sudden "recovered memory" of his abuse and murder of her childhood friend.

Washington State passes the Community Protection Act, pioneering legislation permitting states to detain dangerous "sexual predators" in mental facilities indefinitely after their release from prison.

The Family and Medical Leave Act is approved by the House and Senate but vetoed by President George Bush. More than half of the states have enacted some kind of job-protected leave for workers who must stop work for medical reasons.

Congress passes a $22.5 billion child-care assistance package. |
| 1991 | The national PTA passes a resolution on the rights and responsibilities of parents.

The International Labour Organisation (ILO) introduces the International Program for the Elimination of Child Labor.

American television's first lesbian kiss occurs on *L.A. Law*. |
| 1992 | The Child Support Recovery Act authorizes courts to impose federal criminal penalties on parents failing to meet child support obligations for children living in another state.

Vice President Dan Quayle publicly criticizes the decision of television character Murphy Brown to become a single mother, sparking national debate over marriage and parenthood.

The Vatican, in a statement to U.S. Catholic bishops, endorses discrimination against homosexuals in housing, employment, health benefits, and military service as a means of promoting the traditional family.

Presidential nominee Bill Clinton, speaking at the Democratic National Convention, speaks of an American family that includes "every traditional family and every extended family, every two-parent family, every single-parent family, and every foster family. Every family."

The American Psychological Association links television violence to real violence. Time-Warner drops a rap artist after the public outcry over the song "Cop Killer."

Adults accused by their children of sexual abuse form the False Memory Syndrome Foundation in Philadelphia.

An episode of the television show *Seinfeld* dealing with masturbation is boycotted by some advertisers. |
| 1992-1993 | The New York City diversity curriculum touches off widespread public protest, inspiring a parental rights movement. |
| 1993 | Women who are prospective cabinet appointees in the new Clinton administration are prevented from holding office because they have employed undocumented immigrants in their homes and have not paid Social Security taxes on their wages; a national debate ensues about the role of women in public life and the special demands made upon them when they have young children.

Television networks agree to finance a study on television violence.

Congress passes the Family and Medical Leave Act, requiring companies with fifty or more employees to grant workers up to twelve weeks of unpaid leave each year to care for new babies or seriously ill family members. |

1993
(cont.)

Janet Reno becomes the first woman to serve as attorney general of the United States; her unmarried and childless status again raises the issue of the disadvantages facing women who try to combine marriage and children with public careers.

The first Take Our Daughters to Work Day is organized by the Ms. Foundation for Women.

Paul Hill murders a physician who performs abortions at a Florida clinic; the episode symbolizes rising violence by the radical wing of the antiabortion movement.

The Of the People organization based in Arlington, Virginia, begins promoting parental rights amendments to various state constitutions.

The Agriculture Department reports that virtually all federally-funded school lunches exceed recommended fat levels.

The National PTA endorses a requirement for teacher preparation in parent/family involvement.

1994

The United Nations Population Conference is held in Cairo, Egypt.

Congress rescinds half of fiscal 1995 funding for drug education in schools. In 1995 President Clinton vetoes the Congress rescission bill, leading to the restoration of all but $16 million in funding.

California voters pass Proposition 187, denying school and health benefits to noncitizens, including children, although courts block its implementation.

Former education secretary William Bennett tells a meeting of the Christian Coalition that divorce has been more damaging to the family than the gay rights movement.

The murder of seven-year-old Megan Kanka by a released sex felon leads the New Jersey legislature to pass "Megan's Law," requiring that communities be notified when dangerous sex offenders move into an area.

International Confederation of Free Trade Unions launches a campaign to end child labor.

The American Medical Association (AMA) announces that recovered memories of childhood sexual abuse are "of uncertain authenticity" and "should be subject to external verification."

International conference on parental involvement held in Oakland, California.

1995

The Christian Coalition introduces its "Contract with the American Family," which opposes the U.N. Convention on the Rights of the Child (1989) and calls for a parental rights act.

President Bill Clinton vetoes the Balanced Budget Act, which contains tax relief for the "marriage penalty" and cuts welfare spending by $81.5 billion.

The Center for Media Education petitions the Federal Trade Commission to prevent telemarketers from targeting children through the Internet.

Parental rights bills are introduced in the U.S. Senate and House of Representatives.

Presidential candidate Bob Dole attacks Hollywood for its "depravity."

A survey by the U.S. Conference of Mayors notes that 24 percent of the requests by homeless families have gone unmet.

1995 (cont.)	The cable television industry conducts Voices Against Violence Week, while continuing programs depicting violence.
	Congress passes provisions requiring television manufacturers to include a V-chip, an electronic device that allows parents to block access to undesirable television programs.
1996	The Whitewater scandal and other issues raise questions about the role and character of First Lady Hillary Rodham Clinton; she becomes the target of two congressional probes and sets off renewed national debate about the proper role of the president's wife.
	Religious and conservative groups rally against same-sex marriage proposals just before the Iowa Republican presidential caucuses.
	The International Labour Organisation (ILO) and its employer members meet in Geneva to adopt a resolution against child labor.
	The head of the National Labor Committee tells a congressional hearing that television star Kathie Lee Gifford's Wal-Mart clothing line is made in sweatshops, sparking a national debate about the responsibility of Americans in protecting children in other countries from sweatshop labor.
	The Southern Baptist Convention, America's largest Protestant denomination, calls for a boycott of the Walt Disney Company for promoting "anti-Christian" and "anti-family" values in extending benefits to same-sex partners of employees and supporting gay and lesbian activities in their parks.
	President Bill Clinton vetoes a bill that would have banned the partial birth abortion procedure.
1997	The four major broadcast networks institute a voluntary six-category rating system for television programs.
	The Food and Drug Administration (FDA) announces preliminary approval of RU-486, a drug that induces abortion up to seven weeks after conception.
1998	Most televisions are required to be equipped with the V-chip.

—John Powell

Support Groups

This appendix presents a varied list of resources of interest to families and persons studying families. It is divided into four sections: General Support Groups; Support Groups for Addictive Behavior; Adoption, Pregnancy, and Other Reproductive Issues; and Diseases and Disabilities, Physical and Mental.

Where available, fax numbers, toll-free (800) telephone numbers, e-mail addresses, and Internet addresses are provided in addition to groups' mailing addresses and telephone numbers. Several Internet-based groups that have links to a variety of sites of interest to families are also included. The following are examples of topics covered in each section:

General Support Groups: aging, interracial families, parenting, men's groups, single parents, stepfamilies, missing children and adults, family violence, grief, and divorce. This section also includes references to two clearinghouses that list a large number of self-help groups and provide information on setting up self-help groups that are not yet available in specific areas.

Addictive Behavior: alcoholism, drug abuse, and emotional and sexual addictions.

Reproductive Issues: pregnancy, infertility, adoption, family planning, multiple births, and breast-feeding.

Diseases and Disabilities: Sudden Infant Death Syndrome (SIDS), acquired immunodeficiency syndrome (AIDS), Alzheimer's disease, groups that grant wishes for terminally ill children, and groups that deal generally with birth defects, childhood disabilities, and genetic disorders. Groups that deal with specific rare diseases are not covered in this appendix.

GENERAL SUPPORT GROUPS

A Way Out
(800) A-WAY-OUT
Counsels parents who have abducted or are considering abducting their children, and offers free professional mediation to parents involved in child-custody disputes.

American Divorce Association of Men International (ADAM)
1519 S. Arlington Heights Road
Arlington Heights, Ill. 60005
(708) 364-1555, Fax: (708) 364-7273
Works for divorce reform. Provides divorce counseling and mediation, meetings, investigative services, referrals to lawyers, and information on self-representation in court.

American Self-Help Clearinghouse
c/o Northwest Covenant Medical
25 Pocono Road
Denville, N.J. 07834
(201) 625-7101, TTY: (201) 625-9053
Publishes *The Self-Help SourceBook*, which lists several hundred self-help groups and self-help clearinghouses and gives information on how to start a self-help group. The publication is inexpensive and updated every other year.

Americans for Indian Opportunity
681 Juniper Hill Road
Bernalillo, N.Mex. 87004
(505) 867-0278, Fax: (505) 867-0441
Helps Native Americans, Eskimos, and Aleuts set up local self-help groups and promotes communication among various tribes and with non-Native Americans.

Association for Couples in Marriage Enrichment
P.O. Box 10596
Winston-Salem, N.C. 27108
(800) 634-8325, (910) 724-1526
Sponsors marriage enrichment retreats and seminars and communication training. Refers callers to couples in their area who lead marriage enrichment programs.

Association of MultiEthnic Americans
P.O. Box 191726
San Francisco, Calif. 94119
Internet: http://www.ameasite.org
Provides legal and educational information on and for multiracial families; web site provides links to other sites of interest to multiracial and interracial families.

Batterers Anonymous
1850 N. Riverside Avenue, Number 220
Rialto, Calif. 92376

(909) 355-1100

Self-help program for men who are abusive to women, this organization attempts to replace physical and emotional abuse with positive alternatives.

Black Community Crusade for Children

25 E Street NW

Washington D.C. 20001

(202) 628-8339

National group that promotes the African American community tradition of self-help and works with African American leaders on specific goals for children.

Boys Town National Hotline

(800) 448-3000, (800) 448-1833

Trained counselors provide short-term crisis counseling, referrals to local resources, and emergency intervention for issues such as family conflicts, suicide, pregnancy, abuse, runaways, and substance abuse.

Center for Loss in Multiple Birth

P.O. Box 1064

Palmer, AK 99645

(907) 746-6123

Peer support for parents who have lost a multiple-birth child during pregnancy or after birth. Newsletter includes resources for dealing with multiple-birth loss and names of parents willing to share experiences.

Center on Work and Family

232 Bay State Road

Boston, Mass. 02215

(617) 353-7225, Fax: 617-353-7220

Works for the well-being of families by encouraging responsiveness to families in the workplace and in the community.

Child Care Action Campaign

330 7th Avenue, 17th Floor

New York, N.Y. 10001

(212) 239-0138, Fax: (212) 268-6515

Advocacy and education on problems relating to child care; works with community groups on plans for better services.

Child Care Aware

2116 Campus Drive SE

Rochester, Minn. 55904

(800) 424-2246, (507) 287-2220

Fax: (507) 287-2411

Puts parents in touch with local referral services related to child care. Callers can listen to recorded information, talk to staff members, or have information mailed to them.

Childhelp/IOF Foresters National Child Abuse Hotline

(800) 4-A-CHILD, TDD: (800) 2-A-CHILD

Trained counselors provide children and adults with crisis intervention, information and literature, and referrals for persons with concerns about child abuse. Through AT&T language line, translation in 140 languages is possible.

Children of Aging Parents

1609 Woodbourne Road

Levittown, Pa. 19057

(800) 227-7294, (215) 945-6900

Fax: (215) 945-8720

National information and referral service for caregivers of elderly persons. Offers workshops, seminars, and conferences. Organizes and promotes caregivers' support groups.

Children's Hospice International

1850 M Street NW, Suite 900

Washington, D.C. 20036

(800) 242-4453, (703) 684-0330

Provides information on children's hospices and referrals to local hospices. Provides medical and technical assistance, research, and education for affected children and their families.

Christian Family Movement

P.O. Box 272

Ames, Iowa 50010

(515) 232-7432, Fax: (515) 232-7432

e-mail: office@cfm.org

Promotes Christian family life.

Clearinghouse on Women's Issues

P.O. Box 70603

Friendship Heights, Md. 20813

(202) 362-3789, Fax: (202) 638-2356

Provides information on issues related to discrimination on the basis of race, sex, age, or marital status, especially in the form of public policies affecting the status of women.

Coalition for Asian-American Children & Families

120 Wall Street, Third Floor

New York, N.Y. 10005

(212) 809-4675, Fax: (212) 344-5356
e-mail: cacf@cacf.org
Internet: http://www.cacf.org
Advocates for social policies and programs that support Asian American families and children. Works to empower Asian Americans, publishes a newsletter, and sponsors symposia on cultural sensitivity for service providers.

Committee for Mother and Child Rights
210 Olc Orchard Drive
Clear Brook, Va. 22624
(541) 772-3652, Fax: (541) 772-5677
Support and information for mothers who have lost custody of their children or are involved in custody disputes.

Compassionate Friends
P.O. Box 3696
Oak Brook, Ill. 60522
(708) 990-0010, Fax: (708) 990-0246
Self-help organization for parents and siblings of a child who has died, with chapters throughout the United States. Offers phone support as well as meetings.

Covenant House Nineline
346 W. 17th Street
New York, N.Y. 10011
(800) 999-9999, (212) 727-4000
Fax: (212) 989-7586
Provides telephone crisis intervention, referrals, and information to homeless, runaway, and other troubled youth and their families. Connects runaways to their families and to referral agencies, arranges transportation home or to a safe shelter, and provides a message relay service so that runaways can let their families know they are safe. Also offers immediate short-term help for runaway and homeless youth, transitional living arrangements for homeless young mothers and their children, and a substance abuse intervention program.

Dads Against Discrimination
P.O. Box 8525
Portland, Oreg. 97207
(503) 222-111
Offers legal and mediation referrals and information on family law. Provides a shelter service for fathers barred from their homes by restraining orders.

Dakota Women of All Red Nations
P.O. Box 423
Rosebud, S.Dak. 57570
Grassroots organization that establishes local groups to work on such problems as sterilization, women's health, adoption and foster care, education, juvenile justice, and legal issues.

Eldercare Locator
National Association of Area Agencies on Aging
1112 16th Street, Suite 100
Washington, D.C. 20036
(800) 677-1116, (202) 296-8130
Fax: (202) 296-8134
Federal government service providing information on state and local resources for community-based services for the elderly.

Facts for Families
Internet: http://www.aacap.org/factsfam/
An Internet site sponsored by the American Academy of Child and Adolescent Psychiatry. Offers articles on topics such as adoption, sleep disorders, adolescent development, and teen suicide. Articles are in English, French, and Spanish.

Family History Department of the Church of Jesus Christ of Latter-day Saints
50 E. North Temple
Salt Lake City, Utah 84150
(801) 240-2331, Fax: (801) 240-5551
e-mail: fhl@byu.cdu
Promotes research on family and local history; preserves genealogical data and research. Has a large reference library.

Family Research Coalition of America
200 S. Michigan Avenue, Suite 1600
Chicago, Ill. 60604
(312) 341-0900, Fax: (312) 341-9361
e-mail: hn1738@handsnet.org **or** family@class.org
Works to promote and increase the quality of family resources and programs to strengthen families and improve the lives of children. Has African American and Latino caucuses.

Family Research Council
801 G Street NW
Washington, D.C. 20001
Internet: http://www.frc.org
(202) 393-2100, (800) 225-4008
Fax: (202) 393-2134

Studies and offers support on such issues as parental absence, community support for single parents, and the effects of the tax system on families.

Fathers Rights and Equality Exchange (FREE)
701 Welch Road, Suite 323
Palo Alto, Calif. 94304
(415) 853-6877
e-mail: free@vix.com
Provides educational programs, referrals, support, and advocacy for noncustodial fathers.

Flying Solo
Internet: http://www.flyingsolo.com
An Internet site focusing on two broad areas: divorce and separation and the elderly and disabled. Includes a media library with additional sources of information.

Focus on the Family
8605 Explorer Drive
Colorado Springs, Colo. 80920
(719) 531-3400/3341, Fax: (719) 548-4525
Promotes Judeo-Christian values and strong families.

Genealogical Institute
P.O. Box 22045
Salt Lake City, Utah 84122
(801) 250-6717, Fax: (801) 250-6717
e-mail: eakle@xmission.com
Publishes and distributes how-to-do-it genealogical materials; conducts training in genealogy and conducts research; operates a speakers' bureau and publishes a journal.

Grandparents Anonymous
1924 Beverly
Sylvan Lakes, Mich. 48320
(810) 682-8384
Assists grandparents seeking legal visitation rights after situations such as divorce, custody disputes, or the death of a son or daughter.

Grandparents Raising Grandchildren
P.O. Box 104
Colleyville, Tex. 76034
(817) 577-0435
Provides support, legal advice, and lobbying for grandparents who are primary caregivers for grandchildren.

Grandparents Rights Organization
555 S. Woodward Avenue, Suite 600
Birmingham, Mich. 48009
(810) 646-7191, Fax: (810) 646-9722
Advocacy group supporting legislation that benefits grandparents and children when grandparents have been denied visitation.

Gray Panthers
P.O. Box 21477
Washington, D.C. 20009
(800) 280-5362, Fax: (202) 466-3133
Activist group that combats ageism (discrimination against people based on age). Advises and organizes local groups.

Heartbeat
2015 Devon Street
Colorado Springs, Colo. 80909
(719) 596-2575
Support and help to persons who have lost loved ones to suicide from persons who have resolved their grief. Education aimed at preventing suicide among survivors.

Helping Other Parents in Normal Grieving (HOPING)
P.O. Box 30480
Lansing, Mich. 48909
(517) 483-3873, Fax: (517) 351-1404
Support for parents who have lost babies through miscarriage, stillbirth, or infant death, from trained parents who have had a similar experience.

Hospicelink
190 Westbrook Road
Essex, Conn. 06426
(800) 331-1620
Provides information on hospices and palliative care, making referrals to local hospices, palliative care units, and bereavement support services.

House of Ruth
5 Thomas Circle NW
Washington, D.C. 20005
(202) 667-7001, Fax: (202) 667-7047
Provides emergency shelter for women and children in crisis, transitional housing, counseling, food, job training, help for pregnant women and new mothers who have been substance abusers, and help for women and children leaving situations of domestic violence. Has a twenty-four-

hour hotline for victims of abuse. Offers help to children who are homeless, abused, or at risk.

I Am Lost Hotline
(800) I AM LOST

Hotline for parents who want to register missing children, lost children who want help, and people who think they have seen a missing child and want to file a report. Also offers counseling for parents of missing children.

Incest Survivors Anonymous
P.O. Box 17425
Long Beach, Calif. 90807
(310) 428-5599

A program for adult and teenage victims of incest and other forms of sexual abuse, based on the Twelve Steps and Twelve Traditions of Alcoholics Anonymous.

Indian Youth of America
609 Badgerow Building, P.O. Box 2786
Sioux City, Iowa 51106
(712) 252-3230, Fax: (712) 252-3712

Works to improve the lives of Native American children by preventing the break up of Native American families, providing information on the rights of Native Americans under the Indian Child Welfare Act, helping social service agencies to find appropriate placements for Native American children, counseling Native American families, conducting parenting classes, and recruiting Native Americans as foster parents for tribal children.

Intensive Caring Unlimited
910 Bent Lane
Philadelphia, Pa. 19118
(215) 33-7510, Fax: (215) 233-5795

Support for parents experiencing problem pregnancies, children born prematurely or with special problems, or infant deaths. Offers support and information on the care of babies with special problems. Gives referrals and provides information nationwide.

Interracial Family Alliance
P.O. Box 16428
Houston, Tex. 77222
(713) 586-8949

Works for the community and social acceptance of interracial families and seeks solutions to the special problems of interracial families, such as the self-esteem of biracial children.

Interracial Family Circle
P.O. Box 53290
Washington, D.C. 20009
(301) 229-7326

For interracial couples and families and the adoptive and foster parents of mixed-race children. Provides support for such family groups as a viable family option.

Interracial Relationships Links
Internet: http://www.commonlink.com/~drc/race/inter.html

An Internet site with links to resources that support interracial and interethnic marriage and families.

Kevin Collins' Foundation for Missing Children
P.O. Box 590473
San Francisco, Calif. 94159
(800) 272-0012, (415) 771-8477

Offers support, experienced advice, and an immediate response to families of stranger-abducted children, while working to prevent abduction.

Kinship Alliance – International
17 Horton Plaza, Number 145
San Diego, Calif. 92101
(619) 989-1050

Conducts searches and assists persons in searching for missing children and adults, birth parents, adoptees, and adoptive parents.

Men/Fathers Hotline
807 Brazos, Suite 315
Austin, Tex. 78701
(512) 472-3237, Fax: (512) 499-8056
e-mail: Men@menhotline.org or
tfa@menhotline.org or DADS@Fathers.org

Crisis line and referral service for fathers and other men.

Men International
3980 Orchard Hill Circle
Palm Harbor, Fla. 34684
(813) 786-6911

Clearinghouse and resource center. Coalition of men's rights and divorce reform organizations. Works for equal rights for men, especially in domestic relations, and assists men who have been falsely accused of child abuse or rape.

Missing Children Help Center
410 Ware Boulevard, Suite 400
Tampa, Fla. 33619
(800) USA-KIDS, (813) 623-5437
Provides coordination among missing children, parents, and law enforcement. Assists parents in dealing with the legal system. Distributes information about and photographs of missing children nationwide.

Molesters Anonymous
c/o Batterers Anonymous
1850 N. Riverside Avenue, Number 220
Rialto, Calif. 92376
(909) 355-1100
Self-help group for child molesters.

Moms Online
Internet: http://www.momsonline.com
An Internet site for mothers, including a weekly magazine, tips, recipes, and other items of interest.

Mothers at Home
8310-A Old Courthouse Road
Vienna, Va. 22182
(800) 783-4666, (703) 827-5903
Fax: (703) 790-8587
Support and information for mothers who choose to stay at home to raise children.

Mothers Without Custody
P.O. Box 36
Woodstock, Ill. 60098
(800) 457-MWOC
Support for mothers living apart from their minor children, whether by choice or otherwise, and for mothers exploring custody options. Also provides member exchange.

National Association for Parents Rights
2033 Bancrat Road
Valdosta, Ga. 31602
(912) 241-0202, Fax: (912) 241-0402
Informs parents of rights regarding minor children. Organizes support groups for parents who have problems with children involved with government agencies.

National Association of Mothers' Centers
336 Fulton Avenue
Hempstead, N.Y. 11550
(800) 645-3828, (516) 486-6614

Fax: (516) 538-2548
Local support groups facilitate women's working to create personal and societal changes that will benefit mothers and families.

National Association to Advance Fat Acceptance
P.O. Box 188620
Sacramento, Calif. 95818
(800) 442-1214, (916) 558-6880
Fax: (916) 558-6881
e-mail: naafa@world.std.com
Works to improve the self-esteem and quality of life for fat people and to end discrimination against and negative messages about fat people. Sponsors pen pals and other programs.

National Center for Fathering
(800) 593-DADS
Internet: http://www.fathers.com
Works to develop practical resources that will help fathers in various parenting situations to be better fathers.

National Center for Men
P.O. Box 555
Old Bethpage, N.Y. 11804
(516) 942-2020
Works to eliminate sexism against men, specifically in the areas of sexual harassment, fathers' rights, divorce, reproductive rights, and paternity suits.

National Center for Missing and Exploited Children
2101 Wilson Boulevard, Suite 550
Arlington, Va. 22201
(800) 843-5678, (703) 235-3900
Referral and clearinghouse for information about missing children; also provides information on child pornography. Accepts calls from parents reporting missing children, people who think they have seen a missing child, and parents who want to report extrafamilial sexual abuse.

National Child Care Association
1029 Railroad Street
Conyers, Ga. 38207
(770) 922-8198, (800) 543-7161
Fax: (770) 388-7772
Provides education on and advocates quality, licensed, private child care and preschool services.

National Child Safety Council Watch Campaign

4065 Page Avenue
Jackson, Mich. 49204
(800) 222-1464, (517) 764-6070
Answers questions and distributes information on child safety, including drug abuse, household dangers, and reports of sightings of missing children.

National Coalition Against Domestic Violence

P.O. Box 18749
Denver, Colo. 80218
(303) 839-1852, Fax: (303) 831-9251
Coalition of service organizations and shelters for battered women. Phone referral service and programs for women in the United States, Canada, Puerto Rico, and the Virgin Islands.

National Coalition of Free Men

P.O. Box 129
Manhasset, N.Y. 11030
(516) 482-6378, (516) 794-5151
e-mail: ncfm@liii.com
Maintains a hotline and works for men's rights in the areas of abortion, divorce, child custody, the draft, abuse of men, sexual harassment, and false accusations of rape.

National Committee to Prevent Child Abuse Information Line

(800) 55-NCPCA, (312) 663-3520
TDD/TTY: (312) 665-3540
Recorded information on subjects including parenting, sexual abuse, child-abuse prevention, and substance abuse. Caller gives name, address, and the type of information needed.

National Congress of Neighborhood Women

249 Manhattan Avenue
Brooklyn, N.Y. 11211
(718) 388-6666, Fax: (718) 388-0289
Multiracial group of low- to moderate-income women working to improve their neighborhoods, play an advocacy role for low-income women, and empower women.

National Council on the Aging

409 3rd Street SW, Suite 200
Washington, D.C. 20024
(800) 424-9046
(202) 479-1200, Fax: (202) 479-0735
TDD/TTY: (202) 479-6674
Answers questions from seniors on services available to them. Sponsors groups dealing with employment for seniors, rural aging, adult day care, senior housing, and volunteer programs for seniors.

National Family Caregivers' Association

9621 E. Bexhill Drive
Kensington, Md. 20895
(301) 942-6430, Fax: (301) 942-2302
Association for individual caregivers and others working for the needs of family caregivers and improving the quality of caregivers' lives. Offers educational materials and resource information.

National Family Violence Hotline

1155 Connecticut Avenue NW, Suite 400
Washington, D.C. 20036
(800) 222-2000, (202) 429-6695
Provides referrals to hotlines and shelters, as well as assistance to persons seeking information or community services. Provides information on child abuse, spousal or partner violence, and elder abuse.

National Gay and Lesbian Domestic Violence Victims' Network

3506 S Ouray Circle
Aurora, Colo. 80013
(303) 754-7579
Support group for homosexuals abused by their partners.

National Genealogical Society

4527 17th Street N
Arlington, Va. 22207
(703) 525-0050, (800) 473-0060
Fax: (703) 525-0052
Promotes genealogical research; works for the preservation and publication of records from the national level down to churches, cemeteries, and families.

National Hospice Organization

1901 N. Moore Street, Suite 901
Arlington, Va. 22200
(800) 658-8898, (703) 243-5900
Provides information on caring for terminally ill patients and their families. Gives referrals to hospices throughout the United States.

National Institute on Aging

P.O. Box 8057

Gaithersburg, Md. 20898

(800) 222-2225

Government agency that offers materials on preventing disease, promoting health, nutrition, safety, the body, medical care and medications, diseases and disorders, and planning for later years.

National Multi-Ethnic Families Association

2073 N. Oxnard Blvd, Suite 172

Oxnard, Calif. 93030

Internet: http://www.latinoweb.com/nuestram

Produces a monthly newsletter, available on the Internet.

National Runaway Switchboard

3080 N. Lincoln Avenue

Chicago, Ill. 60657

(800) 621-4000, (800) 621-3230, (312) 880-9860, (312) 929-5150

Provides crisis intervention and referrals for youth. Offers conference calls to parents, shelters and other agencies, and delivers messages from runaways to parents or guardians. Operates twenty-four hours a day; affiliated with AT&T language line, which offers translation in 140 languages.

National Self-Help Clearinghouse

25 W. 43rd Street, Room 620

New York, N.Y. 10036

(212) 354-8525

Clearinghouse offering referrals on self-help groups throughout the United States.

Native American Community Board

P.O. Box 572

Lake Andes, S.Dak. 57356

(605) 487-7072, Fax: (605) 487-7964

Provides self-help programs and workshops on such topics as fetal alcohol syndrome, AIDS awareness, family planning, domestic abuse, and child development. Offers support services to Native Americans seeking employment and education.

North American Conference of Separated and Divorced Catholics

P.O. Box 1301

LaGrande, Oreg. 97850

(541) 963-8089, Fax: (541) 963-8089

Support for divorced and separated Catholics from others in the same situation. Also offers programs for children whose parents are divorced.

Older Women's League

666 11th Street NW, Suite 700

Washington, D.C. 20001

(202) 783-6686, Fax: (202) 638-2356

Information on and support for issues affecting middle-aged and older women, such as health care, jobs and pensions, and maintaining independence.

Overeaters Anonymous

6075 Zenith Court NE

Rio Rancho, N.Mex. 87124

(505) 891-2664, Fax: (505) 891-4320

Twelve-step support group for persons who want to stop compulsively overeating.

Parent Care

9041 Colgate Street

Indianapolis, Ind. 46268

(317) 872-9913, Fax: (317) 872-0795

Supports parents of premature and high-risk infants and provides information to parents, medical specialists, and related organizations. Supports formation of local groups.

Parents Anonymous

520 S. Lafayette Park Place, Suite 316

Los Angeles, Calif. 90057

(800) 421-0353, (213) 388-6685

Provides information and referrals to local self-help support groups at which parents work to prevent abusive behavior and improve their relationships with their children.

Parents Helping Parents

3041 Olcott Street

Santa Clara, Calif. 95054

(408) 727-5775, Fax: (408) 727-0182

Support for parents of children with special needs, including chronic or terminal illness. Provides assistance to new and ongoing parent support groups and resource centers.

Parents of Murdered Children

100 East 8th Street

Cincinnati, Ohio 45702

(513) 721-5683, Fax: (513) 345-4489

Self-help organization offering support for those who have had family members or friends murdered. Provides information about grief and the criminal justice system. Establishes self-help groups that meet regularly. Also works on violence prevention programs.

Parents Room
Internet: http://parentsroom.qwas.com
An Internet site and chat room for parents, including a special site for stay-at-home parents.

Parents United International
232 E. Gish Road
San Jose, Calif. 95112
(408) 453-7616, Fax: (408) 453-9064
Provides crisis and long-term support for families affected by the sexual abuse of a child. Offers self-help groups for children ages five through eighteen and for adults molested as children.

Parents Without Partners
401 N. Michigan Avenue
Chicago, Ill. 60611
(800) 637-7974, (312) 644-6610
Fax: (312) 321-6869
Provides support and activities for single parents with or without custody and information on child rearing. Promotes social awareness of the needs of single parents and their children.

Parentsoup
Internet: www.parentsoup.com
Internet site with links to a wide variety of resources. Includes a directory of organizations related to parenting, child care, fathers, mothers, etc., and toll-free phone numbers for groups dealing with elder care, family issues, health matters, and other items of interest to families.

Pearl S. Buck Foundation
P.O. Box 181
Green Hills Farm
Perkasie, Pa. 18944
(800) 220-BUCK, (215) 249-0100
Seeks sponsors to help impoverished Amerasian and other displaced children. Conducts searches to reunite American fathers with Amerasian children. Offers international and United States adoption services.

(Pen) Parents
P.O. Box 8738
Reno, Nev. 89507
(702) 826-7332, Fax: (702) 826-7332
Supports parents dealing with the death of a child (including during pregnancy) or a teenager. Provides support through correspondence for parents who do not have access to regular support groups, who are not comfortable in face-to-face groups, or who prefer corresponding.

Positive Steps
2605 Loftsmoor Lane
Plano, Tex. 75205
Internet: http://www.positivesteps.com
Provides information and resources to assist stepfamilies, works on legal issues affecting stepparents, and develops educational materials.

Pregnancy and Infant Loss Center
1421 East Wayzata Boulevard, Number 30
Wayzata, Minn. 555391
(612) 423-9372
Referral service to support groups, counseling, or other parents, for parents who have suffered miscarriage, stillbirth, or infant death. Provides information on funerals, high-risk pregnancy, and the problems of surviving siblings.

Project RACE
1425 Market Blvd., Suite 330-E6
Roswell, Ga. 30076
Fax: (770) 64-7101
e-mail: projrace@aol.com
National organization promoting the establishment of a multiracial classification for multiracial persons; web site provides links to other sites of interest to multiracial and interracial families.

Ray of Hope
P.O. Box 2323
Iowa City, Iowa 52244
(319) 337-9890
Self-help organization providing support to persons coping with suicide, loss, and grief. Organizes suicide survivor support groups. Gives training and consultation on suicide prevention.

Reunion Research
40609 Auberry Road
Auberry, Calif. 93602
(209) 855-2101
Internet: http://www.reuniontips.com
Promotes family and other group reunions with tips and information on resources and products for reunions.

RTS Bereavement Services – Lutheran Hospital, LaCrosse
1910 South Avenue
LaCrosse, Wis. 54601
(800) 362-9567, (608) 791-4747
Fax: (608) 791-5137
e-mail: Berservs@LHL.6undluth.org
Support, information, and referrals for parents who have suffered miscarriage, stillbirth, or infant death. Also offers information on fathers' and grandparents' grief.

Search Reports, Inc./Central Registry of the Missing
Hasbrouck Heights, N.J. 07604
(201) 288-4445, Fax: (201) 8055
Works to locate juvenile runaways, children snatched in custody disputes, and missing adults through a directory of missing-person flyers and data on unidentified deceased persons.

Services for the Missing
P.O. Box 26
Gibbsboro, N.J. 08026
(609) 783-3101, Fax: (609) 783-9442
Works to locate and recover missing adults, children abducted by parents, and juvenile runaways. Provides counseling and advice to families on safety.

Share – Pregnancy and Infant Loss Support
301 1st Capitol Drive
St. Charles, Mo. 63301
(800) 821-6819, (314) 947-6164
Fax: (314) 947-7486
Support, information, and referrals for parents who have suffered miscarriage, stillbirth, or infant death. Assists local groups in organizing.

Single Mothers by Choice
P.O. Box 1642, Gracie Square Station
New York, N.Y. 10028
(212) 988-0993
e-mail: matttes@pipeline.com
Support and information for women who have or are considering having or adopting a child out of wedlock. Sponsors play groups for members' children.

Stepfamily Association of America
650 J Street, Suite 205
Lincoln, Nebr. 68508
(402) 477-7837, (800) 735-8329
Fax: (402) 477-8317
Support and advocacy for stepparents and remarried parents and their children. Provides education, support groups, referrals, and children's services.

Stepfamily Foundation
333 West End Avenue
New York, N.Y. 10023
(212) 877-3244, (800) SKY-STEP
Fax: (212) 363-7030
Provides information on stepfamilies and counseling for persons in stepfamily relationships.

Supportive Older Women's Network
2805 N. 47th Street
Philadelphia, Pa. 19131
(215) 477-6000, Fax: (215) 477-6555
Establishes local support groups to help older women cope with loneliness, health and housing concerns, widowhood, families, and staying independent. Provides leadership training and community outreach.

Survivors of Incest Anonymous
P.O. Box 21817
Baltimore, Md. 21817
(410) 433-2365
Self-help support group for adults who were molested as children, based on the Twelve Steps and Twelve Traditions of AA.

THEOS
322 Boulevard of the Allies, Suite 105
Pittsburgh, Pa. 15222
(412) 471-7779, Fax: (412) 471-7782
Assists in planning and developing programs for widows and widowers in the United States and Canada.

TOPS Club (Take Off Pounds Sensibly)
4575 South 5th Street
P.O. Box 07360
Milwaukee, Wis. 53207
(800) 932-8677, Fax: (414) 482-4620
Self-help weight-loss support group using group dynamics, competition, and recognition. Participants are required to consult with a doctor about weight loss goals and diets.

Toughlove International
P.O. Box 1069

Doylestown, Pa. 18901
(800) 333-1069, (215) 348-7090, (215) 348-9874
Multinational network of weekly support groups for parents of troubled children. Provides workshops to help persons wanting to form new groups.

Unwed Parents Anonymous
P.O. Box 15466
Phoenix, Ariz. 85060
(602) 952-1463, Fax: (602) 952-1463
Adaptation of the Twelve Steps and Twelve Traditions of Alcoholics Anonymous to provide spiritual and emotional support for unwed parents and others affected by out-of-wedlock births. Provides support in working through the emotions that may result from a decision to give a child up for adoption. Advocates premarital abstinence.

Vanished Children's Alliance
1407 Parkmoor Avenue, Suite 200
San Jose, Calif. 95126
(800) 826-4743, (408) 971-4822
Provides counseling, assistance, case management, and multilingual translation services. Distributes photos and posters in North America and abroad and publishes an annual directory of missing children.

WAVE, Inc.
501 School Street SW, Suite 600
Washington, D.C. 20024
(800) 274-2005, (202) 484-0103
Works to provide educational opportunities, training services, and motivational activities for young people facing barriers to success.

Well Spouse Foundation
610 Lexington Avenue, Suite 814
New York, N.Y. 10022
(800) 838-0879, Fax: (212) 644-1338
e-mail: Wellspouse@aol.com
Emotional support network for spouses or partners of chronically ill patients. Establishes local groups; provides information and materials.

Widowed Persons Service
c/o AARP
61 E Street NW
Washington, D.C. 20049
(202) 434-2260, Fax: (202) 434-6474
e-mail: astudner@AARP.org

National outreach group of volunteers widowed for at least eighteen months who visit, support, and offer referrals to new widows and widowers.

Women on Their Own
P.O. Box 1026
Willingboro, N.J. 08046
(609) 871-1499
Puts women raising children on their own in touch with other women in the same situation for mutual support and help. Provides support, advocacy and referrals, and some small loans.

Women Work! The National Network for Women's Employment
1625 K Street NW, Suite 300
Washington, D.C. 20006
(800) 235-2732, (202) 467-6346
Fax: (202) 467-5366
Clearinghouse for technical assistance, public information, and information on funding and legislation for displaced homemakers, single parents, and others. Gives referrals and provides publications.

Youth Crisis Hotline
(800) HIT-HOME, (619) 292-5683
Fax: (619) 292-5460
Provides referrals and some counseling on runaways, gangs, child abuse, eating disorders, molestation, pregnancy, and suicide.

SUPPORT GROUPS FOR ADDICTIVE BEHAVIOR

Alcoholism and Drug Abuse

AA World Services
475 Riverside Drive
New York, N.Y. 10163
(212) 870-3400, Fax: (212) 870-3003
Free self-help program of recovery from alcoholism. Members work to recover from alcoholism and help others to achieve sobriety through a twelve-step program in which members share experiences, strength, and hope with each other. Gives referrals to local meetings.

Al-Anon Family Group
1600 Corporate Landing Parkway
Virginia Beach, Va. 23454
(800) 356-9996, (212) 302-7240
Fax: (212) 869-3757

A free self-help program of recovery from the family disease of alcoholism, based on the Twelve Steps and Twelve Traditions of Alcoholics Anonymous. Recovery is based on attending meetings and sharing experiences, strength, and hope. Gives referrals to local meetings.

Alateen
1600 Corporate Landing Parkway
Virginia Beach, Va. 23454
(800) 356-9996, (212) 302-7240
Fax: (212) 869-3757
A free self-help program based on the Twelve Steps and Twelve Traditions of Alcoholics Anonymous, for younger family members who have been affected by someone else's drinking. Gives referrals to local meetings and will send a free packet of information.

American Council on Alcoholism
2522 St. Paul Street
Baltimore, Md. 21218
(800) 527-5344, (410) 889-0100
Fax: (410) 889-0297
Provides referrals and information on available treatment and numbers to call for treatment services.

Children of Alcoholics Foundation
P.O. Box 4185, Great Center Station
New York, N.Y. 10163
(800) 359-COAF, (212) 754-0656
Fax: (212) 754-0664
Provides information on the effects on children of parental abuse of alcohol and other substances and looks for solutions to the problems of children of alcoholics.

Cocaine Anonymous
3740 Overland Avenue, Suite H
Los Angeles, Calif. 90034
(800) 347-8998, (310) 559-5833
Fax: (310) 559-2554
Internet: http://www.ca.org
Refers callers to local self-help groups for persons addicted to cocaine.

Cocaine Hotline
(800) COCAINE, Fax: (212) 496-6035
e-mail: cocaine@ix.netcom.com
Internet: http://www.riverhope.org/
A national drug abuse treatment referral service.

Families Anonymous
Box 3475
Culver City, Calif. 90231
(800) 736-9805, (310) 313-5800
Fax: (310) 313-6841
Twelve-step support group for persons dealing with drug abuse or related behavior problems of a family member or friend. Refers callers to the nearest FA meeting, which are held throughout the world. Also provides referrals to other twelve-step programs and other resources and organizations.

Families Worldwide
75 E. Fort Union Boulevard
Midvale, Vt. 84047
(800) 752-6100, (801) 532-6185
Fax: (801) 532-7769
e-mail: families@utw.com
A prevention and referral service for substance abuse. Offers counseling to alcoholics and drug abusers and their families. Families in Focus Program works with families through seminars and in-home visits. Vietnam Vetlink Program works with Vietnam Veterans and their families, especially those with a developmentally disabled child at home.

Marijuana Anonymous
P.O. Box 2912
Van Nuys, Calif. 91404
(800) 766-6779
Twelve-step support group for persons who want to recover from dependency on marijuana.

National Clearinghouse for Alcohol and Drug Information
P.O. Box 2345
Rockville, Md. 20847
(800) 729-6686
Provides information on alcohol and drug abuse from information specialists; will mail out materials. Gives referrals to local programs.

National Council on Alcoholism and Drug Dependence
(800) NCA-CALL, (212) 206-6990
Fax: (212) 645-1690
Provides information on drinking, alcoholism, and other forms of drug dependence among teenagers. Gives referrals to local counseling and treatment resources and has a list of publications.

National Drug and Alcohol Treatment Referral Hotline
(800) 662-HELP, (800) 662-9832 (Spanish)

Government agency that provides referrals for substance abuse treatment throughout the country and information on alcohol and drugs. Callers can speak with information specialists on adolescent use of alcohol and drugs or family problems caused by alcohol and drug abuse, or they can request that information be mailed.

Potsmokers Anonymous
208 W. 23rd Street, Apt. 1414
New York, N.Y. 10011
(212) 254-1777

Offers a nine-week program for persons in New York who want to stop smoking marijuana and intensive weekend sessions for persons from outside the New York area.

Rapha
5500 Interstate North Parkway, Suite 515
Atlanta, Ga. 30328
(800) 383-HOPE, (713) 944-1111

Assists callers in locating Christian psychiatric and substance abuse treatment centers.

Rational Recovery
P.O. Box 800
Lotus, Calif. 95651
(800) 303-CURE, (916) 621-4374
Fax: (916) 621-2667

Nonspiritual program of recovery from substance abuse and other addictive behaviors, including overeating. Self-help groups use Addictive Voice Recognition Technique to help people reject irrational thoughts and ideas that impede recovery.

Secular Organization for Sobriety
Box 5
Buffalo, N.Y. 14215
(310) 821-8430, Fax: (310) 821-2610

Nonspiritual, nonreligious recovery program for alcoholics and addicts. Encourages self-reliance and stresses personal responsibility.

Other Addictions

CODA (Co-Dependents Anonymous)
P.O. Box 33577
Phoenix, Ariz. 85067
(602) 277-7991, Fax: (602) 274-6111
Internet: http://www.ourcoda.org

A twelve-step self-help support group for codependent persons.

Co-Dependents of Sex Addicts (COSA)
9337-B Katy Freeway, Suite 142
Houston, Tex. 77024

A twelve-step self-help program for persons involved in relationships with persons who exhibit compulsive sexual behavior.

Love-N-Addiction
P.O. Box 759
Willimantic, Conn. 06226
(860) 423-2344

Self-help support group for women who are emotionally addictive and exhibit self-destructive behavior in relationships.

Sex Addicts Anonymous
P.O. Box 70949
Houston, Tex. 77270
(713) 869-4902

Twelve-step support group for persons who compulsively repeat sexual behavior that is detrimental to their lives.

Sex and Love Addicts Anonymous
The Augustine Fellowship
P.O. Box 650010
West Newton, Mass. 02165
(617) 332-1845

Twelve-step support group for persons recovering from sexually or emotionally compulsive behavior. Works toward long-term sexual and emotional sobriety.

Sexaholics Anonymous
P.O. Box 111910
Nashville, Tenn. 37222
(615) 331-6230, Fax: (615) 331-6901

Twelve-step self-help group for persons who want to stop self-destructive thinking and behavior, such as the use of pornography, adultery, incest, or criminal sexual activity.

ADOPTION, PREGNANCY, AND OTHER REPRODUCTIVE ISSUES

Abortion Alternatives Hotline
686 N. Broad Street
Woodbury, N.J. 08096
(800) 848-5683, (609) 848-1819
Fax: (609) 848-2380

Free, confidential pregnancy testing. Provides support to pregnant women, including help finding a place to stay; medical, legal, and psychological help; and baby formula, food, and toys. Gives referrals to U.S. pregnancy services.

Adoptee-Birthparent Support Network
3421 M Street NW, Number 328
Washington, D.C. 20007
(202) 686-4611, Fax: (301) 774-1741
Provides support, information, and education to members and works to help them come to terms with the effects of adoption. Provides search assistance to adoptees and birth parents who want to locate biological relatives.

Adoptees in Search
P.O. Box 4101
Bethesda, Md. 20824
(301) 656-8555, Fax: (301) 652-2106
Offers support groups, professional search assistance, and a voluntary match-up search registry.

Adoption and Family Reunion Center
Box 1860
Cape Coral, Fla. 33910
(813) 542-1342, Fax: (813) 549-9393
Provides emotional support for families, search assistance, direction to persons seeking missing relatives, and a network referral service. Promotes open adoption.

Adoptive Families of America, Inc.
3333 Hwy. 100 N
Minneapolis, Minn. 55422
(612) 525-4829, (800) 372-3300
Fax: (612) 535-7808
Umbrella organization for adoptive-parent support groups. Provides parenting resource materials for adoptive families, including those with children from other countries. Maintains a list of families willing to provide personal support.

ALMA – Adoptive Liberty Movement Association
P.O. Box 727, Radio City Station
New York, N.Y. 10101
(212) 581-1568, Fax: (212) 765-2861
Assists adults seeking birth parents or children. Conducts encounter groups, research, and classes in genealogical research. Sponsors program to help adoptive parents understand adoptees' search for their birth families.

Bradley Method Childbirth Hotline
(800) 4-A-BIRTH
Provides a free information packet on the Bradley Method of natural childbirth, including nutrition, exercise, and coaching. Refers callers to local teachers.

Childfree Network
7777 Sunrise Boulevard, Suite 1800
Citrus Heights, Calif. 95610
(916) 773-7178, Fax: (916) 786-0513
Support for persons who cannot or choose not to have children.

Committee for Single Adoptive Parents
P.O. Box 15084
Chevy Chase, Md. 20825
(301) 966-636, Fax: (301) 966-636
Provides information and assistance to single persons who have adopted or want to adopt children.

Concerned United Birthparents
200 Walker Street
Des Moines, Iowa 50317
(800) 822-2777, (515) 263-9541
National support and search organization. Works to open birth records for adoptees and their birth parents, develop alternatives to the current adoption system, and assist birth parents in coping with problems arising from adoption separation.

Couple-to-Couple League
P.O. Box 111184
Cincinnati, Ohio 45211
(513) 471-2000
e-mail: 73311.256@compuserve.com
Sponsors local groups that assist couples who wish to space pregnancies by timing intercourse in accordance with women's natural fertility cycle rather than by using contraceptives. Educational publications available in English, French, Hungarian, Polish, Russian, and Spanish.

Depression After Delivery
P.O. Box 1282
Morrisville, Pa. 19067
(800) 944-4773, (215) 295-3994
A clearinghouse for information on postpartum depression, providing referrals, educational materials, and support for affected women and their families.

Donors' Offspring
P.O. Box 37
Sarcoxie, Mo. 64862
(800) 291-1906, (417) 548-3679
Fax: (417) 673-1906
Self-help support group for donors, recipients, surrogate parents, offspring, and others affected by artificial fertilization. Provides referral service and helps in locating medical histories.

Gladney Center
230 Hemphill
Fort Worth, Tex. 76110
(800) GLADNEY
Provides services to birth parents, children, and adoptive parents, including residential facilities, medical care, educational programs, professional counseling, enrichment opportunities, licensed infant placement, and postplacement services. Provides similar services to women who want to remain in their home community during pregnancy.

La Leche League International
1400 Meacham
Schaumburg, Ill. 60173
(800) LA-LECHE, (708) 519-7730
Fax: (708) 519-0035
Internet: http://www.lalecheleague.org
Help, information, education, support, legal information, and encouragement for mothers who want to or are breast-feeding. Offers informal discussion groups and telephone support.

Lamaze: American Society for Psychoprophylaxis in Obstetrics
1200 19th Street NW, Suite 300
Washington, D.C. 20036
(800) 368-4404, (202) 857-1128
Provides information on the Lamaze method of prepared childbirth and on how to locate a local ASPO-certified childbirth educator.

National Adoption Center
1500 Walnut Street, Suite 701
Philadelphia, Pa. 19102
(800) TO-ADOPT, Fax: (215) 735-9410
Promotes adoption of minority children and children with special needs (older children, siblings who need homes together, and children with emotional, mental, or physical disabilities).

National Association of Surrogate Mothers
8383 Wilshire Boulevard, Suite 750
Beverly Hills, Calif. 90211
(800) 696-4664, (213) 655-2015
Supports surrogate mothers, enabling them to share experiences and information. Also lobbies for legislation and works for the legal rights of surrogate mothers.

National Foster Parent Association
226 Kilts Drive
Houston, Tex. 77024
(713) 467-1850, Fax: (713) 827-0919
Works to identify and promote the needs of foster children and foster parents. Informs foster parents of their legal rights. Provides information on foster care issues.

National Infertility Network Exchange
P.O. Box 204
East Meadow, N.Y. 11554
(516) 794-5772, Fax: (516) 794-0008
Peer support group, education, and referrals for persons who are infertile.

National Organization of Mothers of Twins Clubs
P.O. Box 23188
Albuquerque, N.Mex. 87192
(505) 275-0955
Umbrella group for groups that provide information on twins and twin care.

Organization of Parents Through Surrogacy
7054 Quito Court
Camarillo, Calif. 93012
(805) 482-1566, (805) 394-4116
Support for parents whose have had a child through surrogate parenting, including a phone network support service for members. Also provides information and referrals to infertile couples.

Orphan Foundation of America
1500 Massachusetts Avenue NW, Suite 448
Washington, D.C. 20005
(800) 950-4673, (202) 861-0762
Works to help older foster children through networking resources. Offers postsecondary education scholarships and workshops in independent living skills.

Planned Parenthood National Toll-Free Appointment Line
(800) 230-PLAN
Automatically connects callers to a local Planned Parenthood health center. Offers information on human sexuality and reproductive health.

Pregnancy Helpline Services
(800) 542-4453, (804) 384-3043
A twenty-four-hour helpline sponsored by a Christian maternity home that provides housing, education, medical care, and counseling for single, pregnant young women who wish to keep their children or place them for adoption.

Pregnancy Hotline
c/o National Life Center
686 N. Broad Street
Woodbury, N.J. 08096
(800) 848-LOVE, (609) 848-1819
Fax: (609) 848-2380
Provides guidance on pregnancy, free pregnancy tests, and medical, legal, and professional counseling referrals. Shelter, adoption, maternity, and baby clothing are available through local 1st Way affiliates. Directs callers to nearest pro-life pregnancy service.

Resolve, Inc.
1310 Broadway
Somerville, Md. 02144
(617) 623-1156
Works to increase public awareness about infertility and to educate people about their choices.

Triplet Connection
P.O. Box 99571
Stockton, Calif. 95209
(209) 474-0885, Fax: (209) 474-2233
e-mail: triplets@inreach.com
Helps parents prepare for and deal with triplets and larger multiple births. Provides support and facilitates networking. Offers information on such topics as breast-feeding, medical services, preventing premature births, and clothing and equipment exchanges. Also provides support for mothers who have lost one or more babies of a multiple birth.

Twinless Twins Support Group International
11220 St. Joe Road
Fort Wayne, Ind. 46835
(219) 627-5414, Fax: (219) 627-5414
e-mail: brandt@mail.fwi.com
Provides support to persons who have lost a multiple-birth sibling through death or disappearance and helps others dealing with multiple birth losses. Also works to reunite multiple-birth siblings who were separated through adoption or for other reasons.

DISEASES AND DISABILITIES, PHYSICAL AND MENTAL

Alliance of Genetic Support Groups
35 Wisconsin Circle, Suite 440
Chevy Chase, Md. 20815
(800) 336-GENE, (301) 652-5553
Provides information and support to persons and families affected by genetic disorders and referrals to appropriate genetic support groups and professionals.

Alzheimer's Association
919 N. Michigan Avenue, Suite 1000
Chicago, Ill. 60611
(800) 272-3900, (312) 335-8700
Fax: (312) 335-1110
Promotes family support systems for relatives of victims of Alzheimer's disease.

American Anorexia/Bulemia Association
293 Central Park West, Suite 1R
New York, N.Y. 10024
(212) 501-8351, Fax: (212) 501-0342
Organizes self-help groups for persons with eating disorders. Provides information, referral, and outreach services.

American Network for Community Options and Resources
4200 Evergreen Lane, Suite 315
Annandale, Va. 22003
(703) 642-6614
e-mail: ancor@clark.net
Umbrella group for more than six hundred agencies that provide services and support to persons with disabilities.

American Sudden Infant Death Syndrome Institute
6065 Roswell Road, Suite 876
Atlanta, Ga. 30328
(800) 232-SIDS, (800) 847-SIDS, (404) 843-1030

Provides support, information, and advice from physicians, counselors, and other parents for families affected by Sudden Infant Death Syndrome (SIDS).

Americans with Disabilities Act Information Line
(800) 514-0301, TDD: (800) 514-0383
Internet:
http://www.usdoj.gov/crt/adahom1.htm
Government service providing information on Titles II and III of the Americans with Disabilities Act. Information is available over the phone from specialists, or documents may be ordered by fax or mail.

The ARC
500 Border Street, Suite 300
Arlington, Tex. 76010
(817) 277-6003, Fax: (817) 277-3491
Promotes local, state, and national services, research, and legislation for the mentally disabled and their families.

Association for Children with Down Syndrome
2616 Martin Avenue
Bellmore, N.Y. 11710
(516) 221-4700, Fax: (516) 221-4311
Resource and information source for parents of children with Down syndrome. Provides referrals; offers programs in New York State for preschool-age children and their siblings and recreational programs and support groups for older children.

Association for the Help of Retarded Children
200 Park Avenue South, Suite 1201
New York, N.Y. 10003
(212) 254-8203, (212) 473-2225
Provides support, training, clinics, and residential facilities for the developmentally disabled and their families.

Association of Birth Defect Children
827 Irma Avenue
Orlando, Fla. 32803
(800) 313-ABCD, (407) 245-7035
Fax: (407) 245-7087
Provides support for persons with birth defects; puts parents of children with similar birth defects in touch with each other; offers help in dealing with problems that come with deformities.

Brass Ring Society
11117 Spring Hollow Road, Number 101
Oklahoma City, Okla. 73120
(800) 666-WISH
Seeks to fulfill the wishes of children with life-threatening illnesses.

Candlelighters Childhood Cancer Foundation
7910 Woodmont Avenue, Suite 460
Bethesda, Md. 20814
(800) 366-2223, (301) 657-8401
Fax: (301) 718-2686
e-mail: 75717.3513@compuserve.com
Provides information, support, and advocacy to families of children with cancer, survivors of cancer, and professionals who work with them.

Carry Hollander Center for SIDS
(800) 996-5002, (201) 996-5000
Provides support services, research, awareness, and education to families and others affected by the loss of a baby to Sudden Infant Death Syndrome (SIDS).

Center for Family Support
386 Park Avenue South
New York, N.Y. 10016
(212) 889-5464
Provides counseling and referrals to families with developmentally disabled children and sponsors parents' groups.

Children's Wish Foundation International
7840 Roswell Road, Suite 301
Atlanta, Ga. 30358
(800) 323-9474, (404) 393-9474
Seeks to fulfill the wishes of terminally ill children.

Dream Factory
315 Guthrie Green
Louisville, Ky. 40202
(800) 456-7556, (505) 584-3928
Seeks to fulfill the wishes of chronically or critically ill children and works to promote a more positive family atmosphere in the face of prolonged illness.

Federation for Children with Special Needs
96 Berkeley Street, Suite 104
Boston, Mass. 02116
(800) 331-0688, (617) 482-2915
Fax: (617) 695-2939
Coalition of groups concerned with children and

adults with disabilities. Provides information on resources, basic rights, and obtaining services. Works for parent involvement in the care of children with disabilities and chronic illnesses and supports parent training and information.

Friends of Karen
P.O. Box 217
Croton Falls, N.Y. 10519
(800) 637-2774, (914) 277-4547
Provides emotional help for parents of children with a life-threatening illness.

Health FaxLine
Centers for Disease Control and Prevention
AIDS and Diseases Fax Information Service
Fax: (888) 2332-3299
A number of documents related to diseases and other health issues are available from the Centers for Disease Control and Prevention (CDC) Fax Information Service as well as from its web site. Diseases covered include acquired immunodeficiency syndrome (AIDS), cholera, Epstein-Barr virus, hepatitis, influenza, Lyme disease, plague, rabies, and tuberculosis, among many others. Both nontechnical information for patients and technical information for health care providers can be obtained. These documents are updated as necessary.

HIV/AIDS Treatment Information Service
ACTIS/AIDS Treatment Mail Stop 9-S
2277 Research Boulevard
Rockville, Md. 20850
(800) HIV-0440, (301) 217-0023
Fax: (301) 738-6616, TDD/TTY: (800) 243-7012
An interagency federal project providing federally approved HIV/AIDS treatment information to people with human immunodeficiency virus (HIV) or acquired immunodeficiency virus (AIDS), their families and friends, health care providers, and others. Does not answer questions related to specific or individual medical management needs.

Lekotek Toy Resource Helpline
2100 Ridge Avenue
Evanston, Ill. 60201
(800) 366-PLAY, (708) 328-0001
Provides information on choosing appropriate toys and other play materials and developing creative play ideas for children with disabilities.

Make-a-Wish Foundation of America
100 W. Clarendon Street, Suite 2200
Phoenix, Ariz. 85013
(800) 722-WISH, (602) 279-9474
Seeks to fulfill the wishes of children who have terminal illnesses or other life-threatening conditions.

Mother's Voices
165 W 46th Street, Suite 1310
New York, N.Y. 10036
(212) 730-2777, Fax: (212) 730-4378
Group of mothers concerned about acquired immunodeficiency virus (AIDS) who work for legislation and funding for AIDS education, research, prevention, and treatment.

MUMS National Parent-to-Parent Network
150 Custer Court
Green Bay, Wis. 54301
(414) 336-5333, Fax: (414) 339-0995
e-mail: mums@netnet.net
For parents or caregivers of children with disabilities or serious health conditions. Matches parents whose children have similar conditions so that they can support each other.

National Alliance for the Mentally Ill
200 N. Gelbe Road, Suite 1015
Arlington, Va. 22203
(800) 950-6264
Provides emotional support and practical guidance to the mentally ill and their families. Offers referrals to local groups. Advocates legislation and funding for institutional and community-based settings for the seriously mentally ill.

National Association of Anorexia Nervosa and Associated Disorders
Box 7
Highland Park, Ill. 60035
(708) 831-3438, Fax: (708) 433-4632
Resource center and advocacy agency. Provides referral services and early detection programs; organizes self-help groups. Supports local and regional meetings.

National Center for Youth with Disabilities
University of Minnesota, Division of General Pediatrics & Adolescent Health
Box 721
420 Delaware Street SE
Minneapolis, Minn. 55455

(800) 333-6293, (612) 626-2825

Provides information and resources on adolescents with chronic illnesses and disabilities and on their transition to adult life.

National Coalition for Cancer Survivorship

1010 Wayne Avenue, 5th Floor

Silver Spring, Md. 20910

(301) 650-8868, Fax: (301) 565-9670

Internet: http://www.acess.digex.net/
~mKragen/carsearch.html

Provides support to cancer survivors and their families and friends. Facilitates peer support and maintains a list of organizations that are concerned with survivorship.

National Down Syndrome Congress

1605 Chantilly Drive, Suite 250

Atlanta, Ga. 30324

(800) 232-NDSC, (404) 633-1555

Fax: (404) 633-2817

Assists parents in finding solutions to children's needs, coordinates local parents' groups, and provides a clearinghouse for information on Down syndrome.

National Down Syndrome Society

666 Broadway

New York, N.Y. 10012

(800) 221-4602, (212) 460-9330

Fax: (212) 979-2873

Provides information and referral services to families, local support groups, and community programs.

National Eating Disorder Hotline and Referral Service

6655 S. Yale Avenue

Tulsa, Okla. 74136

(800) 248-3285, (918) 481-4044

Offers a referral service, an on-premise therapist, and general information on eating disorders.

National Information Center for Children & Youth with Disabilities

P.O. Box 1492

Washington, D.C. 20013

(800) 695-0285, (202) 884-8205

TDD/TYY: (800) 695-0285, (202) 884-8200

e-mail: nichcy@aed.org

Provides referrals to other organizations, performs searches of the center's database and library, and gives technical assistance to parents and groups.

National Information Clearinghouse for Infants with Disabilities and Life-Threatening Conditions

University of South Carolina, Center for Developmental Disabilities

Benson Building, 1st Floor

Columbia, S.C. 29208

(800) 922-9234, ext. 201, (803) 777-4435

Provides information about services available to families with infants and young children with disabilities and critical illnesses.

National Mental Health Association

(800) 969-NMHA, (703) 684-7722

Recorded message for callers to request mailed information on specific disorders or a directory of local mental health resources. Offers support groups, community outreach and education, information and referral programs, and other patient advocacy services.

National Organization for Rare Disorders

P.O. Box 8923

New Fairfield, Conn. 06812

(800) 999-6673, (203) 746-6518

Gathers and disseminates information on more than three thousand rare diseases. Facilitates networking between patients with the same disorder. Does not provide medical advice.

Parents of Children with Down Syndrome

c/o The ARC of Montgomery County

11600 Nebel Street

Rockville, Md. 20852

(301) 984-5777, Fax: (301) 816-2429

Sponsors meetings, provides support, and facilitates parent-to-parent counseling for parents of children with Down syndrome. Provides referrals to doctors and other professionals.

Pilot Parents

3610 Dodge Street, Suite 101

Omaha, Nebr. 68131

(402) 346-5220, Fax: (402) 346-5253

Provides peer support for parents of children with special needs through a parent-matching program. Provides information on developmental disabilities, medical services, and local support agencies.

Research! America

908 King Street, Suite 400 East

Alexandria, Va. 22314

(800) 366-CURE

Offers resource referrals, data, and contact names for organizations nationwide who offer support and information on a wide range of diseases and disorders.

Ryan White National Teen Education Program

381 Van Ness Avenue, Suite 1507

Torrance, Calif. 90501

1-800-933-KIDS, (310) 783-0575

Fax: (310) 783-0585

For children with acquired immunodeficiency syndrome (AIDS) and other catastrophic illness. Provides information, educational materials, and a referral service about AIDS and the teenage population. Offers counseling services and community outings for affected children and their families.

SIDS Alliance

1314 Bedford Avenue, Suite 210

Baltimore, Md. 21208

(800) 221-7437

Works to increase public awareness and funding for medical research and family awareness of Sudden Infant Death Syndrome (SIDS).

TEENS T.A.P. (Teens Teaching AIDS Prevention)

3030 Walnut

Kansas City, Mo. 64108

(800) 234-TEEN, (816) 561-8784

Fax: (816) 531-7199, TDD/TTY: (816) 561-9518

A program founded and run by teens for teens. Provides peer educators, peer support and counseling, and a teen buddy program that offers friendship and understanding to teens who have human immunodeficiency syndrome (HIV) or acquired immunodeficiency syndrome (AIDS) or who have family members or other loved ones with HIV or AIDS.

Women Organized to Respond to Life-Threatening Diseases (WORLD)

3948 Webster Street

Oakland, Calif. 94609

(510) 658-6930, Fax: (510) 601-9746

Support and information for women with human immunodeficiency syndrome (HIV) or acquired immunodeficiency syndrome (AIDS); sponsors retreats and classes.

—Irene Struthers

Glossary

ABC-X family crisis model: Theoretical model developed by sociologist Reuben Hill that seeks to explain why families differ in their abilities to deal with stressful events. In this model, "A" stands for the stressful event. "B" stands for the family's crisis-meeting resources. "C" stands for the definition the family gives to the event. "X" stands for the crisis, or the turning point (in a positive or negative direction) provoked by the crisis. For example, if a family finds that one of its children has been using drugs, this is a stressful event. This can provoke a crisis (X), leading to deteriorating or improving family relations. The nature of the crisis will depend on how other members of the family use their skills in dealing with the problem (B) and on how they define the problem (C).

Acquaintance rape: Rape committed by someone known to the victim, such as a friend, relative, or neighbor is referred to as "acquaintance rape." The most common image of the rapist is as a stranger breaking into a house or attacking a woman alone on a street. In reality, the majority of rapes are committed by men who are well known to their victims and often trusted by them. "Date rape," or forced sexual intercourse during a date, is one of the most common forms of acquaintance rape. In many cases, women are reluctant to report cases of date rape.

Afterbirth: The materials expelled from the uterus after the birth of a child. These materials include the placenta, amniotic sac, chorionic membrane, and umbilical cord.

Alternative families: Any families that depart from the traditional husband and wife family form. Single-parent, homosexual, unmarried, and multiple-partner families are all examples of alternative families. In the United States and many other developed countries since the 1970's, these varied family forms have increased in numbers and in acceptance although not necessarily in approval.

Amniocentesis: Diagnostic method often used by doctors before the birth of a baby. To perform an amniocentesis, the doctor inserts a long, hollow needle through the mother's abdomen into the amniotic sac, drawing a sample of the amniotic fluid. Cells discarded by the fetus are in this fluid. The doctor examines these cells microscopically for evidence of disease or birth defects. Amniocentesis can also determine the sex of the fetus.

Androgyny: Mixing of characteristics traditionally regarded as masculine and feminine. The word comes from the Greek words *andros*, which means "male," and *gynos*, which means "female." Sigmund Freud, the founder of psychoanalysis, argued that all human beings are androgynous; that men have female sides to their personalities and that women have male sides to their personalities. Some people maintain that androgyny is a desirable cultural goal, holding that men should develop their female qualities and that women should develop their male qualities. The term first came into wide usage in the early 1970's, when the women's movement became much more active than it had been earlier. Many activists, psychologists, and sociologists believed that rigid sex roles limited the rights and opportunities of women and even men, since men were expected to behave in accordance with sex-role stereotyping.

Aphrodisiacs: Food or chemicals believed to produce sexual arousal. Most medical authorities argue that there are no true aphrodisiacs in the sense of substances that produce sexual stimulation. However, some mood-altering drugs may influence the psychological inclination toward sexual activity. For example, alcoholic beverages may incline individuals toward sexual activity, but this is largely a consequence of the lowering of inhibitions and judgment by alcohol and of the social settings in which persons consume alcoholic beverages.

Artificial insemination: Medical technique used to help women have children. Doctors inject sperm near the cervix or into the uterus at the time of ovulation. The two types of artificial insemination are artificial insemination using a husband's sperm (referred to as AIH) and artificial insemination using the sperm of a donor other than the husband of the recipient (AID). All forms of artificial insemination are opposed by the Roman Catholic Church.

Attachment styles: In the psychodynamic perspective on human relationships, attachment styles are types of love relationships between adults. Psychodynamic researchers believe that people build their capacities for attachment to others from their earliest experiences with parents or with other primary adult caregivers. Infants, children, and adolescents develop three styles of bonding with others. These styles are identified as secure, anxious/ambivalent, and detached/avoidant. Secure attachment styles are characterized by self-confidence, self-esteem, and acceptance of the love partner. Anxious/ambivalent styles are believed to result when children have inconsistent and unreliable relationships with their parents. Those drawn to this type of attachment are prone to extreme emotions, sexual obsessions, and feelings of jealousy and mistrust. Detached/avoidant styles are believed to result when children experience criticism, emotional unavailability, or rejection from their caregivers. As adults, these persons often fear contact, commitment, and closeness in love relationships.

Authoritarian child rearing: Style of parenting that involves rigid rules and the expectation of unquestioning obedience to parents. The most common response of an authoritarian parent to any questioning of a rule by a child is: "Because I told you so." Punishment for breaking rules is emphasized in authoritarian child rearing, since authoritarian parents believe that children only behave well if they fear physical punishment. Many child psychologists argue that this type of upbringing tends to produce bullies and bigots. In this view, children develop anger toward parents who punish them. Since they are unable to express this anger toward their parents, they find weaker people to serve as scapegoats. Sociologist Melvin L. Kohn has argued that authoritarian styles of child rearing are linked to the economic activities of parents. Kohn found that parents in agricultural societies and working-class parents in industrial societies are more likely than middle-class parents to follow authoritarian child-rearing styles. He maintained that this is because parents who work at jobs in which they have little control over their own lives tend to emphasize the importance of obedience when dealing with their children.

Authoritative child rearing: Style of parenting that attempts to combine strict discipline of children with emotional support from parents. Authoritative child rearing places emphasis on rewards for good behavior, known as "positive reinforcement," rather than on punishment for bad behavior. Rules and discipline are consistent, whereby parents attempt to enable children to understand the necessity of rules and not simply to respond with unquestioning obedience.

Binuclear family: A nuclear family that has split into two families, usually through divorce and remarriage, is often referred to as "binuclear." The mother of the original family remarries and forms a new household and the father of the original family remarries and forms a second new household. Binuclear families have become common in the United States and other societies with high divorce rates. One of the biggest problems faced by members of a binuclear family is the problem of role confusion. Since binuclear families involve parents and children in two families, each of which has its own set of rules and expectations, family roles can become unclear. This can lead to conflict among family members.

Birth cohort: In demography, a birth cohort consists of all people who are born during the same period of time. This is usually all of those born during the same year, but it may also be used to refer to those born during the same decade or general period of time. Thus, those born during the Depression of the 1930's may be thought of as a single birth cohort.

Bisexuality: Sexual orientation of persons sexually attracted to members of both sexes. Bisexuals challenge the common identification of individuals as either heterosexual or homosexual. Many psychologists argue that all human beings are bisexual and can feel physical attraction to both sexes. From this point of view, people would be predominantly, rather than exclusively, heterosexual or homosexual.

Bond: Anything that connects people or ties people together. A bond between two people, such as a marriage or a romantic relationship, is referred to as a paired bond.

Boomerang kids: Adults who return to live in the homes of their parents after divorce, job loss, financial crisis, or other setback. Few parents of returned adult children require their children to pay room and board. Research generally indicates that parents are more willing to extend such services as cooking, laundry, and cleaning to returned sons than to returned daughters.

Celibacy: Abstention from all sexual activity. Many religions teach that celibacy is a virtue. In the Roman Catholic Church, priests are expected to be celibate. Despite changing attitudes toward premarital sexuality in the United States, a majority of parents still expect adolescent children to remain celibate until very late adolescence or adulthood.

Chromosomes: Each human being has forty-six chromosomes, in twenty-three pairs, that define human hereditary characteristics. These chromosomes are ribbon-like strands made up of genes which are, in turn, composed of DNA molecules. One pair of the chromosomes are sex chromosomes, which determine all sex-related characteristics. Sex chromosomes can be either an X chromosome or a Y chromosome. Each egg cell contains an X chromosome and each sperm cell contains a Y chromosome. When two X chromosomes are combined in a fertilized egg the result is a biological female and when an X chromosome and a Y chromosome are combined the result is a biological male.

Clitoris: Female organ located under the upper portion of the labia minora of the genitalia (sex organs). The clitoris is in some ways similar to the male's penis, since it has both a shaft and a glans and it becomes erect during sexual arousal. The nerve endings at the end of the clitoris are highly sensitive to stimulation, much more so than the nerve endings inside the vagina. Clitoral stimulation is therefore a particularly effective way for women to reach orgasm.

Companionate love: One of the types of love identified by Yale psychologist Robert L. Sternberg. Sternberg conceives of all love relationships as having three components: commitment, intimacy, and passion. Commitment consists of an emotional investment in a relationship and a sense of obligation. Intimacy involves sharing feelings and providing mutual emotional support. Passion is a matter of physical affection. Sternberg identifies companionate love as the type that involves a great deal of commitment and intimacy but little passion. This type of rela-

tionship tends to become common among people who have been married for many years.

Companionate marriage: Form of marriage based on ideals of mutual respect, friendship, and shared interests. The companionate marriage has become the predominant expectation in the United States and in other industrialized countries.

Comparable worth: Many feminists advocate a legal and political policy of comparable worth, under which jobs would be ranked according to their difficulty and skill requirements. Comparable occupations would then be paid equally, regardless of whether they are held primarily by men or women. Comparable worth policies gained support during the 1970's and 1980's, as women entered the full-time labor force in increasing numbers while continuing to be paid less than men. One of the difficulties with such an approach is that it is difficult to identify the worth of any particular job.

Complementary needs: Marriage therapists and theorists have argued that couples achieve maximum gratification from their relationship when they have complementary needs rather than similar needs. For example, the best mate for an ambitious person may not be another ambitious person, since their similar needs could cause them to clash. Instead, a mate who needs someone to admire will complement the ambitious mate's need for achievement.

Complex stepfamily: A family that includes children from previous marriages of both parents. Complex stepfamilies contrast with simple stepfamilies, which include children from the previous marriage of only one parent. In a 1991 study of complex and simple families published in the *Journal of Marriage and the Family*, researchers Noel Schultz, Cynthia Schultz, and David Olson found that simple stepfamilies generally have more strengths than the complex type. They found that complex stepfamilies tend to have more difficulties with personality conflicts, communication, conflict resolution, and parenting skills.

Consummate love: In the work of Yale psychologist Robert L. Sternberg, consummate love is a relationship that is endowed with all three dimensions of love: commitment, intimacy, and passion. In Sternberg's view, commitment consists of an emotional investment in a relationship and a sense of obligation. Intimacy involves sharing feelings and mutual emotional support. Passion is a matter of physical affection.

Cost of children: Most parents would agree that children can be extremely expensive. In early 1991 researcher Mark Lino used data from the U.S. Department of Agriculture to examine just how much children, on the average, cost their parents. He found that for families earning less than $29,900 per year, the cost of raising each child from birth to seventeen years of age was $86,100, or just under $4,800 per year. For families earning from $29,900 to $48,300 per year, the cost was $120,150, or about $6,675 per child per year. For families earning over $48,300 per year, the cost increased to $168,480, or $9,360 per child per year. This means that a middle-income family with three children could expect to spend over $20,000 each year raising them. Since these calculations did not include children over the age of seventeen, they did not include the costs of higher education.

"Crack babies": During the 1980's and 1990's the use of cocaine and in particular the highly refined form of cocaine known as "crack" increased sharply in North America. The use of cocaine by pregnant mothers became a noticeable problem. Fetuses can become addicted to this drug in the wombs of their mothers because the drug passes from pregnant mothers' bloodstream through the umbilical cord and into babies' bloodstream. One researcher found that as many as 25 percent of the babies born in inner-city hospitals in 1989 were born addicted to cocaine. Babies whose mothers were crack addicts were often born prematurely, were much smaller than other babies, and usually suffered severe brain damage.

Dating differential: Tendency of men to date women who are physically smaller, younger, of lower social status, or less well educated than themselves. The dating differential is a source of the marriage gradient, the tendency of women to "marry up" and the tendency of men to "marry down." Some social theorists and researchers have argued that the dating differential is a product of America's male-dominated culture. Others have maintained that similar tendencies are found in virtually all known cultures.

Demography: Study of the size, rate of growth, and composition of human populations. The study of the composition of populations includes factors such as proportions of people at various ages, ratios of males to females, ethnicity, living arrangements, and income distribution.

Developmental readiness: Most child psychologists adhere to some version of the concept of developmental readiness. From the perspective of many psychologists, children are best able to learn new skills at certain stages in their cognitive and neuromotor development. Before children have reached the proper stage of development, it may be difficult or impossible for them to acquire a given skill. Once they have passed the stage at which they are developmentally ready to acquire that skill, they may not be able to learn it as quickly or easily as they would have at a younger age.

DINS dilemma: Phrase used by therapists, marriage counselors, and others who work with married couples to describe a common problem in families in which both spouses work. "DINS" stands for "Double-Income, No Sex." Long working hours, the pressures of caring for children, and other stresses can limit dual-income couples' opportunities and desire for sexual activity and put strains on marriages.

Displaced homemaker: A woman who has been out of the labor market who returns to work after a divorce is a displaced homemaker. Displaced homemakers often have difficulty because they lack job skills and recent work experience. As divorce rates have risen, displaced homemakers have become increasingly common in the United States. One side effect of this phenomenon is that many women seeking retraining have become students at universities, local colleges, and vocational schools.

Dominant gene: Human gene that determines a hereditary trait. Each chromosome carries two genes for every hereditary trait. One comes from the father and the other from the mother. If a child has a gene for brown hair from the mother and a gene for blond hair from the father, the gene for brown hair will be dominant and the child will have brown hair. The gene for blond hair, in this case, is called a recessive gene. However, this child may grow up and marry a brown-haired person who also carries a recessive gene for blond hair. Their child may, in turn, may receive a gene for blond hair from each parent. Thus, hereditary traits that do not appear in either parent may show up in a child.

Egalitarian marriage: Marriage in which power and responsibilities are shared equally by the husband and the wife. Although marital relationships became more equal in the United States over the course of the twentieth century, full equality has not yet been achieved. Most household chores, for example, are still performed by women even in homes in which both husband and wife are employed full-time outside the home.

Empty love: In the psychology of love developed by Yale psychologist Robert L. Sternberg, empty love is a relationship based on commitment that nevertheless lacks two other important dimensions of love: intimacy and passion. Sternberg defines intimacy as shared feelings and emotional support and passion as physical affection. An example of empty love would be a couple married for many years who have developed a strong sense of obligation to each other but who enjoy little communication or sexual contact. Empty love usually produces a relationship that is long-lasting and stable but entails little satisfaction for those involved.

Equal Pay Act: In 1963 the U.S. Congress passed the Equal Pay Act, which forbids employers from paying women less than men for essentially the same jobs. This was a response to the increasing entry of women into the labor market and was one of the first federal legislative efforts against gender discrimination in the workplace.

Equal Rights Amendment (ERA): Proposed amendment to the U.S. Constitution that would have guaranteed equal rights for women. The ERA was first proposed in 1923. Proponents of the ERA maintained that a constitutional amendment was needed to ensure protection against sex discrimination. Opponents held that existing laws already prohibited discrimination on the basis of sex and that there was no need to alter the nation's basic law. In 1972 Congress approved the Equal Rights Amendment, an amendment to the Constitution that would forbid discrimination on account of sex. By the 1982 deadline, the ERA was ratified by slightly less than the three-quarters of the states required for adoption of a Constitutional amendment.

Extramarital sex: Sexual relations between a married person and someone other than that person's spouse. Extramarital involvements are considered to be a major reason for divorce. A Gallup Poll in 1990 established that less than 10 percent of respondents admitted to having engaged in extramarital sex, but there are questions about the truthfulness of these responses. Marriage therapists report that marriages often survive extramarital affairs and can sometimes be stronger after an affair.

Family circumplex model: This model is a representation of relationships within families used by family therapists and family researchers. In this representation, families are considered to have three primary dimensions: cohesion, or togetherness; flexibility, or the ability to change; and communication. The better the communication skills of families, the more they are able to move between extremes of cohesion and flexibility.

Family of origin: Persons' family of origin is the family in which they grow up before marrying and forming a distinct family. Families of origin affect families by marriage, because when persons marry, each joins the other's family of origin. In addition, people bring expectations, attitudes, and habits from families of origin to new families.

Family power: Researchers and therapists are often concerned with relative amounts of power held by family members and with the different kinds of power that exist in families. This is essential in order to understand how family members interact with one another. Researchers have identified a number of types of family power. Legitimate power exists as part of a person's formally defined power in a family. Thus, in some families fathers may exercise the most power over family spending because family members recognize this as part of fathers' role. Alternatively, mothers may exercise the most power over day-to-day decisions about children, because child care is primarily defined as part of mothers' sphere of influence. Reward power involves persons' ability to provide rewards, and coercive power involves persons' ability to provide punishments. Referent power involves emotional control. Thus, a husband or wife may use a spouse's emotional or physical attraction to guide behavior. Family members exercise informational power when they have some special knowledge. A wife who has carefully studied consumer guides on automobiles may have greater power than her husband when buying a car. Expert power is similar to informational power, but it involves respect for a family member as an expert in some area that affects family life. For example, if a wife is a lawyer and a husband a carpenter, the wife will tend to have the greatest power over legal decisions and the husband the greatest decision-making power over household repairs. In contemporary American families, husbands generally have more power than wives. However, since power comes in so many different varieties, it is very seldom the case that any family member holds no power.

Family systems approach: Researchers and therapists often describe families using a theoretical approach in which individual family members are seen as parts of an interdependent system. From a family systems perspective, the emotions and behaviors of individual family members can only be understood by examining the entire set of relations among all family members. These relations vary in degree of flexibility or rigidity along several dimensions. The boundaries of the family, for example, represent the extent to which the family is open to people and influences outside the family. The leadership and negotiation dimension describes the extent to which authority within the family is rigid or flexible. The organization dimension describes the level of stability or chaos within the family. The values dimension refers to whether the family puts individuals or the family as a whole first or whether the family is committed to traditional or nontraditional values. The family systems approach also sees families as varying in their degree of cohesion, or the amount of closeness or detachment in family relations, and in their degree of adaptability, or the ability to cope with change and stress. Many social workers and family therapists use a family systems approach to deal with family problems, arguing that problems are matters of how all family members are connected to one another.

Fatuous love: In the theoretical scheme of Yale psychologist Robert L. Sternberg, fatuous love is a relationship based on passion, which is de-fined as physical attraction, and commitment without the important third dimension of intimacy, defined as shared feelings and mutual emotional support. An example of this type of relationship would be a man and woman who fall in love over a weekend and make the decision to marry immediately without having developed any true understanding of one another's needs and backgrounds. Sternberg maintains that fatuous love is unstable because it lacks this depth of understanding.

Female-headed families: Single-parent families headed by women are referred to as female-headed families In most industrialized societies, the percentage of families headed by single women increased rapidly beginning in the 1960's. In the United States, for example, about 10 percent of families were headed by single women in 1960. By 1991, 21 percent of American families were headed by single women.

Field of eligibles: All persons who are eligible to marry someone are referred to as that person's field of eligibles. In theory, all unmarried persons of the opposite sex constitute the field of eligibles for unmarried persons in modern American society. In actuality, however, the field of eligibles is much more limited, since many Americans tend to regard as potential mates only those in their own racial group and in their own social class. Age can also limit the field of eligibles, since people rarely consider those much older or much younger than themselves as potential mates.

Fireplace: Also known as the hearth, long a symbol of the family. This is reflected in the term "hearth and home," in which the fireplace and the home are regarded as synonymous. Before other means of heating were invented, families gathered around the fireplace in the evening for warmth, so that the fireplace became the natural center of family life. Moreover, before Benjamin Franklin invented the Franklin stove in 1745, most cooking was done in the fireplace. The symbolic importance of the fireplace has continued, so that many modern homes contain fireplaces, even though central heating or space heaters provide effective warmth. Some people have argued that the television, as a modern center for family life, has become a contemporary version of the fireplace.

Frustration theory: Before the sexual revolution, it was often commonly thought that rape or other forms of sexual victimization of women were due to the absence of sexual outlets for men. Frustration theory held that men were frustrated by strict sexual standards and abstinence and that rates of rape would go down if a society developed greater sexual permissiveness. However, as American society became more sexually permissive during the sexual revolution, rates of rape actually went up. This increase in rape has sometimes been attributed to relative frustration: When a society becomes more permissive, expectations of sexual intercourse increase, but opportunities do not increase as much as expectations.

Gender: Social scientists often use the term "gender" to refer to the socially created psychological, social, and cultural features that distinguish males from females. This is contrasted with "sex," which refers to biological differences between men and women.

Gender gap in voting: When women first received the right to vote in national elections in the United States in 1920, many people thought that this would greatly change political life. Some thought that women would tend to be more emotional in their voting. Others thought that political life would be morally purer, since women would have higher moral standards. However, for most of the twentieth century, people voted as family units, with husbands and wives casting very similar votes. Moreover, women were much less likely than men to vote until 1976. By 1980, the gender gap in voting emerged, whereby men and women tended to vote for different candidates. Part of the explanation for this change is probably the change in family patterns. As the divorce rate rose, even women in stable marriages began to face the theoretical possibility of living on their own. At the same time, both married and single women entered the full-time labor force in greater numbers. Thus, a number of political issues emerged as distinctively women's issues.

Glass ceiling: Discrimination against women in hiring or promotion is forbidden by law. Nevertheless, it is widely agreed that women are often limited in their occupational ambitions by a "glass ceiling," an invisible barrier that makes it difficult for women to enter top positions. Most women who manage to reach the top in professional careers do so by sacrificing their family lives. By the mid-1980's about 52 percent of women executives were single and 61 percent had no children. Among men who were executives, 95 percent were married and 97 percent had children. The glass ceiling became an important issue for families as well as for individual women, as women's incomes became increasingly important parts of family incomes.

Head Start: Federally funded preschool program begun during the 1960's as a part of the War on Poverty. Head Start was designed to improve the educational preparation of poor children and to close the gap in school achievement between poor and middle-class children. Since parental involvement is an important influence on the education of children, one of the goals of Head Start has been to involve low income families as much as possible in the early childhood education of their children.

In vitro fertilization: Technique sometimes used to help couples who have difficulty conceiving children. Ova, or eggs, are taken from a woman and fertilized with the father's sperm in a laboratory petri dish. Several fertilized ova are then placed in the hopeful mother's uterus, leading to an increased chance of multiple births for couples who use this technique. About 20 percent of births from in vitro fertilization are twins and 5 percent are triplets. Since this is a sophisticated medical procedure, it tends to be quite expensive. Many opponents of abortion also oppose in vitro fertilization, since fertilized ova not placed in the uterus are often destroyed.

Infancy: Period of human life from birth to about age one during which children usually learn to crawl or walk. During infancy, persons' primary needs are to be fed when hungry and to be comforted when crying. Infants must learn two important skills: to sleep through the night and to control their hunger so that they eat only during the day. When infants learn to move about by themselves, they have entered the toddler stage of their development.

Infatuation: In the work of Yale psychologist Robert L. Sternberg, infatuation is a form of emotional involvement based mainly on physical attraction. Sternberg conceives of all love relationships as having three components: commitment, intimacy, and passion. Commitment consists of an emotional investment in a relationship and a sense of obligation. Intimacy involves sharing feelings and providing mutual emotional support. Passion is a matter of physical affection. Sternberg sees infatuation as a matter primarily of passion. It often comes in the form of "love at first sight," an intense desire for another person involving little emotional commitment or involvement. Infatuation frequently becomes obsessive, particularly when the object of infatuation does not return the feeling. People frequently idealize those with whom they are infatuated. Most infatuations end when those affected come to know the other person better or give up the attraction as hopeless. If an obsessive infatuation continues, however, it can be emotionally destructive and in some cases may even lead to stalking the object of attraction.

Intermarriage: Marriages between persons from different racial, ethnic, or religious groups are known as interracial, interethnic, and interfaith marriages, respectively. Interfaith marriages have become common in the United States, particularly among people in the various Christian denominations. Interracial marriage, on the other hand, remains relatively rare, especially between African Americans and whites.

Labor: The time at the end of pregnancy when a mother's body pushes out the fetus. Three stages of labor are generally recognized. During the first stage, the uterus contracts and the cervix dilates; during the second, the fetus is forced through the cervix and out of the vagina while the uterus continues to contract; and during the third, the mother's body expels the afterbirth.

Limerence: Technical term for a compulsive attraction to another person or an inability to stop thinking about another person. Limerence typically involves idealizing and daydreaming about another. This is usually regarded as a first step in forming a romantic bond.

Longevity: Length of a lifetime. Longevity is a family issue because women tend to outlive men. Part of the difference in longevity is due to the fact that men are more likely to smoke, drink, and engage in health-threatening and life-threatening behaviors than women. How-

ever, even when these activities are taken into consideration, women still tend to live longer than men. This suggests that sex differences in longevity may be due to genetic factors. Longer lifetimes are often a problem for women, because they are likely to outlive their husbands and frequently must live alone for part of their older years.

Marriage-enrichment programs: While marriage counseling is usually intended to help couples who are having difficulties in marriage, marriage-enrichment programs are designed for those who have satisfactory marriages that they want to improve or for those who want to prevent marital problems from developing. Courses and workshops to improve marriages began in the early 1960's, but the term "marital enrichment" was coined in 1971. In 1973 the Association for Couples in Marriage Enrichment (A.C.M.E.) was founded. Marriage enrichment programs are intended to improve husband-wife relationships, usually by improving communication.

Marriage gradient: The tendency for women to marry up and for men to marry down in terms of education, financial situation, and occupational prestige. Even though there has been a continuing trend over the course of the twentieth century toward greater equality between husbands and wives, the marriage gradient still often places greater power and resources in the hands of husbands.

Maternal impression: Commonly held superstition that prenatal experiences of mothers can affect unborn babies. While traumatic experiences may, in a few cases, cause such strong physiological reactions in mothers that babies in wombs may be affected, in most cases babies cannot share in their mothers experiences. There is no connection between the nervous system of the mother and that of the baby and no way that information can be passed from one to the other.

Matriarchy: Form of social organization in which power is chiefly held and exercised by women. Social organization in the United States tends to be either patriarchal, with power held by men, or egalitarian, with power held by both men and women. Some anthropologists and feminist theorists maintain that prehistoric human societies were matriarchal in character, but there are few truly matriarchal societies in the modern world.

Mixed-class family: A family is said to be mixed-class when the husband and wife are from different social classes, as measured by occupational prestige, income, and education. In the past, there were few distinctively mixed-class families, since women obtained their social class positions from their husbands. Nevertheless, husbands' and wives' families of origin sometimes belonged to different social classes. By the 1990's class distinctions between husbands and wives had become much more noticeable, because 60 percent of married women were employed full-time and one-third of those women were married to men who held less prestigious jobs. Since the members of different social classes have different tastes, interests, values, and goals, mixed-class families can sometimes produce family conflict.

Nature vs. nurture controversy: Debate over the extent to which human beings are determined by their biological characteristics or by upbringing. Gender characteristics are a central part of this controversy, because there is a great deal of disagreement over the extent to which male-female differences are inborn or the results of learning and training by families and the surrounding society.

Old age: The time at which old age begins is arbitrary. In some societies, people are considered old at age forty. In American society, age sixty-five has usually been used as the starting point for old age, because this was designated as retirement age. However, social scientists and social workers now recognize a number of stages of old age. The gerontologist Bernice Neugarten has divided old persons into three periods: the young-old, those aged roughly fifty-five to sixty-five who are still working and active; the mid-old, those aged sixty-five to seventy-five who are retired but usually in good physical and mental health; and the old-old, those aged seventy-five and over who often suffer from physical ailments and psychological difficulties, especially loneliness.

Ovulation: Regular monthly process in which an ovum (egg) is released into a woman's Fallopian tube. This occurs about once every twenty-eight days. The regularity of ovulation enables couples to practice the rhythm method of contraception, which involves abstaining from sex during the woman's fertile days.

Paraphilia: Any form of sexual behavior or interest that is outside the behaviors and interests usually regarded as normal or acceptable in society at large is technically referred to as paraphilia. Paraphiliac behaviors are often referred to in common speech as "kinky." Some kinds of paraphilia, such as being sexually aroused by women's shoes or underwear, are entirely harmless. Others, such as the desire for sex with young children, can involve inflicting psychological or physical damage on others. The distinction between normal sexual behavior and paraphilia is a social one and it may change over time. For example, oral sex was once regarded as paraphiliac, but in contemporary American society many persons consider oral sex between consenting partners normal and acceptable.

Patriarchy: Form of social organization in which power is chiefly held and exercised by men. Feminists sometimes use the word to describe the systematic domination and oppression of women by men. Researchers have found that a patriarchal relationship, in which a man is in complete control and a woman is economically dependent on the man, increases the likelihood of domestic violence and sexual exploitation.

Pedophilia: Sexual act between an adult and a child. People generally begin to engage in pedophilia while they are teenagers. It is estimated that there are about 4 million pedophiles in the United States and that about 95 percent of them are men. Most pedophiles are not suspected by their friends, spouses, or others around them.

Permanent availability: The notion that the frequency of divorce in American society makes Americans permanently available to others as potential marriage partners. This idea was introduced in the early 1960's by the social scientist Bernard Faber, who argued that marriage was ceasing to be a restriction on the possibility of an individual becoming a partner in future marriages.

Permissiveness: Style of child rearing in which relatively few restrictions are placed on children. Child rearing in the United States has tended to become more permissive over the course of the twentieth century, and this tendency has been especially marked in the years following World War II. The permissive approach to child rearing is often associated with the famous child-care manual *The Common Sense Book of Baby and Child Care* (1946) by Benjamin Spock. Spock emphasized considering the feelings and needs of children rather than obedience and discipline.

Pink-collar occupations: Label for occupations typically held by women. Secretary, typist, bookkeeper, and store clerk are all examples of pink-collar jobs. These kinds of occupations generally involve relatively little physical exertion, pay less than male-dominated jobs, and offer little opportunity for upward mobility.

PLISSIT model: Approach to sex therapy developed by therapist Jack Annon. This involves four types of treatments: permission giving (P), limited information (LI), specific suggestions (SS), and intensive therapy (IT). A permission-giving approach is appropriate when clients simply need reassurance that their sexual behavior or desires are harmless and morally acceptable. When clients' problem is the result of lack of knowledge, providing additional information is helpful. Specific suggestions involve exercises to help reduce anxiety over sexual concerns. Intensive therapy is appropriate when an individual or couple suffers from a serious sexual problem rooted in psychological difficulties requiring the help of a trained professional sex therapist.

Polygamy: Practice of having multiple mates. It includes both polygyny, whereby one man has more than one wife, and polyandry, whereby one woman has more than one husband. Although polygamy is an accepted social custom in many countries, it is a violation of the law everywhere in the United States.

Premarital sex: People engage in premarital sex when they have sexual relations before marriage. This may be between people who will later marry each other or between people who will not marry each other. Premarital sex has become more socially acceptable over time, but sex on the first date or during casual dating is still not the norm among most young adult Americans. The double standard in which premarital sex is more socially acceptable for men than for women has decreased, but it continues to influence how many Americans view sexual activity before marriage.

Primary and secondary relationships: A primary relationship is a relationship that is relatively long lasting, informal, and personal. Behavior in primary relationships tends to be spontaneous and intimate. Family relationships constitute the most important type of primary relationship. Secondary relationships, by contrast, are relationships between people who do not know each other very well. A relationship between a salesperson and a customer is a prime example of a secondary relationship.

Procreation: The producing of children through sexual intercourse. According to some religious beliefs, sexual intercourse is only acceptable for the purpose of procreation, even when it occurs between married partners.

Promiscuous sex: Compulsive pursuit of new sexual partners. When this pursuit reaches its most extreme form, it is said to be a sexual addiction. Promiscuous sex places people at risk of developing sexually transmitted diseases. With the appearance of AIDS in the mid-1980's, promiscuous sex became a major health risk.

Rape: Violent assault involving the penetration of the vagina, anus, or mouth by the penis of the attacker or by another object under force or threat of force or when the victim is unable to give consent. Most psychologists and sociologists argue that rape is basically a means by which men express power: either power over women or power over other men, depending on the sex of the victim. This does not mean that rapists do not often derive sexual pleasure from rape, since sexual feelings and the desire to feel powerful are often connected.

Recessive gene: Parents pass their physical traits to their children by means of genes in chromosomes. Each chromosome carries two genes for every hereditary trait. Sometimes a child inherits a different type of gene from each parent. For example, a child may inherit a gene for blue eyes from the father and a gene for brown eyes from the mother. The gene that determines the child's actual eye color is said to be the dominant gene. The other gene is recessive. Thus, a brown-eyed person may have a recessive gene for blue eyes. If that person produces a child with someone else who has brown eyes and a recessive gene for blue eyes, each parent may pass the recessive gene to the child. Thus, two parents with brown eyes can have a blue-eyed child.

Resource theory: Theory of who holds decision-making authority in a marriage. According to this theory, the spouse who holds greater resources will have more authority. Resources can include education, occupational prestige, or social status. Men usually hold more authority because they have higher levels of education and better jobs than women. However, as women obtain more education and move into more prestigious jobs, they should have greater familial authority.

Rhythm method: Contraception technique involving abstention from sexual relations during a woman's fertile days—that is, three or four days before and one day after ovulation. Those whose religious beliefs do not allow them to practice other contraceptive techniques often rely on the rhythm method, although the latter can be quite unreliable due to miscalculation.

Role models: The persons who provide patterns of behavior and attitudes for other individuals are the role models of those individuals. Immediate family members are usually the most important role models for children. Thus, one of the more important ways that parents and older siblings teach children is by providing models of behavior.

Roller coaster course of adjustment: In the work of family stress researcher Reuben Hill, families were found to adjust to crises by following a roller coaster course, involving a sudden plummet into hardship and disorganization, a gradual recovery, and a reestablishment of some level of family organization. For example, the birth of a stillborn child can plunge the family into intense grief that makes day-to-day life extremely difficult. Although the family may never "get over" this experience, its members gradually begin to work out ways of living together again. Eventually, the family returns to a steady state of everyday life, even though memory and grief may always remain with family members.

Romantic love: In the influential psychology of love of Robert L. Sternberg, romantic love is a relationship based on passion, or physical attraction, and intimacy, or shared feelings, but

entailing little or no commitment. Romantic love frequently begins with infatuation. It may develop into another type of love relationship, but if it does not, it tends to be emotionally intense but not long-lasting or stable.

Serial monogamy: The practice of having only one mate at a time but multiple mates over the course of a lifetime. Serial monogamy may be distinguished from strict monogamy, in which a person marries only once. Many people argue that serial monogamy has become a major family pattern in the United States, as divorce and remarriage have become more common. For example, it has been estimated that approximately half the marriages in 1990 will eventually end in divorce. Of those who divorce, about 75 percent will marry again. Slightly over half of these second marriages will also end in divorce, with 70 percent marrying a third time. Thus, it can be estimated that well over a third of Americans who marry will probably have at least two marital partners during the course of a lifetime and well over one out of every ten will have at least three.

Sex ratio: In demography, the sex ratio is the number of males per females in a population. The sex ratio varies from place to place. Alaska, where many men move to work on pipelines or in oil fields, has an extremely high sex ratio. Large urban centers, such as New York City and Washington, D.C. have sex ratios that are quite low. When there is an imbalance in the sex ratio, this can pose problems for those seeking mates.

Sex therapy: Sex therapy involves counseling and assistance to individuals or couples who have problems or concerns about their sexual behavior. This type of therapy generally entails learning about sexual anatomy, learning about one's own attitudes toward sexuality, overcoming irrational and undesired inhibitions in sexual behavior, and developing new sexual techniques. In the United States, certified sex therapists are trained professionals who have met requirements established by the American Association of Sex Educators, Counselors, and Therapists (AASECT).

Sexual revolution: Time of rapid change in values, attitudes, and behavior toward sex that occurred in the United States and in other industrialized countries in the 1960's and 1970's.

Sibling abuse: Physical or psychological abuse of children by brothers or sisters. It has been estimated that about half of all children in America are bitten, kicked, or punched by brothers or sisters each year. Children who abuse their siblings have most often learned abusive behaviors from their parents.

Simple stepfamily: Stepfamily that includes children from a previous marriage of only one of the parents. This is contrasted with a complex stepfamily, which includes children from previous marriages of both parents. Researchers generally find that simple stepfamilies have fewer stresses and conflicts than complex stepfamilies.

Social learning theory: Approach to the behavior of males and females that considers how the two sexes learn forms of behavior considered appropriate to their gender. Social learning theorists are particularly interested in looking at how young children learn to conform to gender roles they see acted out by their parents and by others in their society.

Socialization: The process of acquiring information and social roles needed for behaving in socially acceptable ways. The family is the chief agent of socialization in the United States, as in most societies. However, peers begin to become important sources of socialization during childhood and the importance of peers increases through the teenage years. Although childhood and adolescence are the most critical times for socialization, this process continues throughout life. Since different forms of behavior are acceptable in different groups, the socialization an individual receives from one group may be unacceptable to another. Adolescents, for example, may sometimes learn behaviors from other adolescents that are unacceptable to parents or teachers.

Spectatoring: Sexual dysfunction identified by sex researchers William H. Masters and Virginia Johnson. This problem occurs when men or women are self-consciously aware of their own performance during sex. Spectatoring can cause anxiety about sexual performance and interfere with pleasurable lovemaking.

Spouse abuse: Spouse abuse consists of physical or psychological violence against a marriage partner, usually the wife. It is difficult to say when a relationship is psychologically abusive, since this is a matter of definition. Spouse abuse is often related to the degree of involvement between partners. The more intimacy there is between a husband and wife, the greater the possibility of abusive incidents.

Stimulus-Value-Role Theory: The social scientist Bernard Murstein has argued that the process of mate selection goes through three stages. In the first, the "stimulus" stage, individuals are drawn to one another by physical or social attributes. Beauty, wealth, or prestige, for example, might make someone an appealing mate. In the second stage, the "value" stage, people who have been attracted to one another engage in comparing their values. This means that they learn about each other's interests, attitudes, ideals, beliefs, and religious orientations. If they find that they have enough in common, they may progress to a third stage. In the "role" stage, the two people learn to function in compatible roles. A man may learn to act out his idea of the role of a husband in a manner that is acceptable to his wife and the wife may learn to act out her idea of the role of a wife in a manner that is acceptable to her husband.

Styles of love: Researchers have identified six major styles of love relationships, which they have identified with Greek and Latin words. *Eros* is based on an attraction to someone as an ideal of physical beauty. *Ludus* refers to a playful relationship, in which love is based on the enjoyment of recreational activities. *Storge* refers to love that is based on friendship and mutual respect. *Mania* is anxious, obsessive love. *Pragma* is love that develops as a matter of practicality, such as the need to maintain a home or take care of children. *Agape* is a style of love that is chiefly concerned with the other person's well-being. All of these different styles may be present in varying combinations in any relationship, and varying styles may become dominant at different times during the course of a relationship.

Swinging: Form of extramarital sexual activity in which both husband and wife agree to engage in sex with other people. Most often, swinging involves two or more couples who agree to swap partners. Researchers know little about the effects of swinging on marital stability or on the emotional well-being of those who engage in it, but it is usually assumed that this type of activity can damage marriages and cause emotional problems.

Tender years doctrine: Legal presumption that after a divorce young children should be placed in the care of their mothers. This doctrine has generally been replaced by a "best interests of the child doctrine," in which both fathers and mothers are considered as potential custodians of children. In practice, however, mothers continue to receive custody of children following most divorces.

Thumb sucking: Most children derive comfort from sucking thumbs or other fingers during the toddler stage or early childhood. Early in the twentieth century, thumb sucking was regarded as a danger to the development of children and as an activity that was to be prevented. As recently as 1938, a book on child care published by the U.S. government, *Infant Care*, showed an illustration of a stiff cuff that could be used to keep an infant from bending its arm and sucking its thumb. Since World War II, however, attitudes toward thumb sucking have changed. Most medical experts now agree that this is a harmless activity and that preventing it or making children feel ashamed of indulging in it can cause psychological problems.

Title IX: A U.S. federal policy established in 1972 that prohibits sex discrimination in education.

Toddler stage: The period in child development between infancy and childhood is known as the "toddler" stage. The stage begins at about age one, when infants begin to crawl or walk, and ends at about age three. During the toddler stage, people change from infants to children. Since toddlers can move about but have not developed sufficient reason to know when they are in danger, they require a great deal of parental attention, particularly during the first year of toddlerhood. Baby-proofing a house, by removing dangerous and breakable items, is essential for coping with toddlers' energy and eagerness

to explore the world around them. Child-care experts generally agree that it is better to create a safe environment and allow toddlers to indulge their curiosity than to scold them for constantly getting into things. In the second year of toddlerhood, sometimes called the "terrible twos," children are able to exercise greater reason and become somewhat less of a threat to themselves. However, at this time they also begin to establish their identities by asserting independence from their parents. Therefore, the two-year-old child can often seem negative and rebellious. It is generally recommended that parents respond to this with firmness and consistency.

Tribes: The word "tribe" has a variety of meanings. Generally, it refers to a group of families who share a sense of belonging to the same community, reside in or identify with the same geographic area, and follow the same customs. In North America the word has political connotations. Tribes are American Indian (also called Native American) groups who have treaties with the United States or Canada. In the United States, tribes are usually recognized as domestic dependent nations with control over their own lands. Members of Indian groups are both citizens of the United States and members of their respective tribes. Since tribal membership is a matter of ancestry, belonging to an Indian tribe means belonging to an Indian family. A majority of American Indians marry non-Indians, which can create questions about tribal membership. For most tribes, any child with a parent who is a member of a tribe can also be a member. In 1990 the 1,937,391 individuals who belonged to recognized American Indian tribes were in 449,281 families. Slightly over 26 percent of these tribal families were single-parent, female-headed families. Thus, families among American Indian tribes were more likely to be single-parent families than were either white or African American families.

—*Carl L. Bankston III*

Select Bibliography

Families exist in every culture, everyone is a member of a family, and therefore all activities everywhere are by implication issues involving the family. As a result, ever new strains of research and writing which might qualify as "family studies" emerged in the late twentieth century. Whether dealing with formal academic disciplines such as sociology, psychology, law, medicine, religion or history, the study of contemporary affairs and public policy, feminist and gender studies, biography and autobiography, or the vast array of self-help literature one should be aware of the family component that is inherently present and therefore potentially useful to the student of the subject. As a result, this relatively brief bibliography must be selective.

A review of this bibliography's chief characteristics will be useful. First, recent studies figure more prominently than older works. This enables researchers to study the latest ideas on timely topics. This principle also enhances access to specialized bibliographies that will lead researchers to appropriate older works. Although many classic and pioneering works are included, they are often included for their historical value. Even the best works in this field tend to become quickly dated because of the rapid changes in public policy, law, and social values that shift the context in which the family develops and is evaluated.

General studies figure more prominently than specialist studies or works focusing on individuals. Synthetic works have been preferred when they are available, because they are of greater value to general researchers. More narrowly focused studies have been included where they fill important gaps, but seldom have accounts of personal and individual experiences been listed.

Some subjects, such as gender, abortion, education, and the workplace, inevitably touch on the condition and nature of family life. Those works that deal most directly with the family have been included here.

A wide range of reference materials has been included, enabling researchers to continue investigation at higher levels should they choose to do so. Most highly specialized contemporary academic studies or extensive lists of works published prior to 1980 are not included in this selective bibliography. However, they can be traced through such works as Joan Aldous and Reuben Hill, *International Bibliography of Research in Marriage and the Family, 1900-1972* (1967, 1974); the *Annual Review of Sociology* (1975-   ); the *Family Studies Database* (1995-   ); the *Inventory of Marriage and Family Literature* (1974-   ); and the *Sage Family Studies Abstracts* (1979-   ), which are included in the bibliography.

This bibliography is supplemented by more specialized bibliographies accompanying the longer articles in the *Encyclopedia of Family Life*. Article bibliographies are independent of this bibliography and should be consulted for the appropriate area of research.

This bibliography is divided into the following sections:

1. GENERAL WORKS AND BIBLIOGRAPHIES

Aby, Stephen H. *Sociology: A Guide to Reference and Information Sources*. Englewood, Colo.: Libraries Unlimited, 1987. The first comprehensive guide to sociological literature; easily used by nonspecialists. Selected by *Choice* magazine as an "Outstanding Academic Book" for 1987-1988.

Acock, Alan C., and Jeffrey N. Clair, eds. *The Influence of the Family: A Review and Annotated Bibliography of Socialization, Ethnicity, and Delinquency, 1975-1986*. New York: Garland, 1986. Nearly eight hundred annotated entries focus on intergenerational influences, divided into sections on family influence, ethnicity, and delinquency.

Aldous, Joan, and Reuben Hill. *International Bibliography of Research in Marriage and the Family, 1900-1972*. 2 vols. Minneapolis: Minnesota Family Study Center and the Institute of Life Insurance, 1967-1974. Contains more than twenty thousand computer-generated references. A supplementary series, *Inventory of Marriage and Family Literature* continues annually (see below).

Annual Review of Sociology. Palo Alto, Calif.: Annual Reviews, 1975- . Articles grouped according to broad classifications such as theory and methods, institutions and culture, and social processes. Essay topics, which change annually, have included the impact of divorce on children, stepfamilies, work and the family, and suburban communities.

Bahr, Stephen J., ed. *Family Research: A Sixty-Year Review, 1930-1990*. 2 vols. Lexington, Mass.: Lexington Books, 1991-1992. Covers various topics such as marital sexuality and gender roles that are organized by decade and subtopic. Contains extensive bibliographies and tables comparing research results.

Baker, Robert L. *The Social Work Dictionary*. 3d ed. Washington, D.C.: NASW Press, 1995. For nonspecialist researchers, this work is valuable for defining the wide range of terminology used in the various fields of social work, including family therapy, counseling, moral development, social theory, and criminal justice.

Baumgartner, James E., et al. *National Guide to Funding for Children, Youth, and Families*. 3d ed. New York: Foundation Center, 1995. Lists 3,272 grant-making foundations and 137 direct corporate programs dispensing more than $900 million in awards.

Becker, Lawrence C., and Charlotte B. Becker, eds. *Encyclopedia of Ethics*. 2 vols. New York: Garland, 1992. Covers a wide range of family-related topics from an ethical perspective, including abortion, moral absolutes, and the family.

Burguière, André, Christiane Klapisch-Zuber, Martine Segalen, and Françoise Zonabend, eds. *A History of the Family*. 2 vols. Cambridge, Mass.: Harvard University Press, 1996. Collection of essays in two volumes dealing with the history of the family from ancient through modern times in China, Japan, India, the Arab world, Africa, Europe, and the Americas.

Caplow, Theodore, et al. *Recent Social Trends in the United States, 1960-1990*. Montreal: McGill-Queen's University Press, 1991. In this first title in the Comparative Charting of Social Change series, some seventy-eight tables of data dealing with age groups, women, household resources, education, and values are organized so as to allow cross-national comparisons.

Chadwick, Bruce A., and Tim B. Heaton, eds. *Statistical Handbook on the American Family*. Phoenix, Ariz.: Oryx Press, 1992. More than four hundred tables, charts, and graphs provide a wide range of data on marriage, the quality of marriage and family life, divorce, children, sexual attitudes and behavior, living arrangements and kinship ties, working women, wives and mothers, family violence, and elderly families. Essential support for many kinds of research.

Cline, Ruth K. J. *Focus on Families: A Reference Handbook*. Santa Barbara, Calif.: ABC-Clio, 1990. Good starting point for undergraduates and high school students beginning research, providing statistics, background, definitions, and quotations for topics including single-parent families, stepfamilies, child abuse, and adoption. Half of each of the nine chapters is devoted to an annotated list of materials.

Contemporary Sociology: A Journal of Reviews. Washington, D.C.: American Sociological Association, 1972- . Each bimonthly issue critically reviews between fifty and sixty books, with important works being given more extensive treatment in review essays.

CQ Researcher. Washington, D.C.: Congressional Quarterly, ongoing. Formerly *Editorial Research Reports*, this valuable publication weekly focuses on a single topic of contemporary interest and debate, including such subjects as "Parental Rights," "Teaching Values," "Insurance Fraud," "Child Labor and Sweatshops," and "Teenage Violence." Each 12,000-word report contains an overview of the issues, background, an analysis of the current situation, and an assessment of outlook. It is also accompanied by a variety of sidebars and graphs and an annotated select bibliography of recent books, journal and newspaper articles, and reports. Always includes a list of organizations that can be contacted for further information.

The Family in America. San Diego, Calif.: Greenhaven Press, 1992. Compiled for young adults, the editors of the Opposing Viewpoints Series have drawn upon the writings of such respected authors and family researchers as David Popenoe, Lenore J. Weitzman, and Bryce J. Christensen to present the various sides to controversies such as "What Is the Status of the Family?", "How Does Divorce Affect the Family?", and "How Are Two-Career Parents Affecting the Family?" Current bibliography, lists of organizations, and critical thinking activities make this an excellent starting point for research into family issues.

Family Resources. Anoka, Minn.: National Council on Family Relations, 1970-1993. Database covering professional journals, government documents, dissertations, newsletters, audiovisual materials and instructional tools dealing with marriage, divorce, family trends, family relationships, marital and family therapy, and services to families. Though updating was ended in December, 1993, the database is now maintained as a closed file. See *Family Studies Database*, below.

Family Studies Database: 1970-December, 1995. Baltimore, Md.: National Information Services Corporation, 1995. A CD-ROM extension of *Family Resources* (see above), this English-language database currently includes 135,000 bibliographic records, with approximately 6,000 being added annually. Enables users to search at three different levels, in either English or Spanish.

Herron, Nancy L. *The Social Sciences: A Cross-Disciplinary Guide to Selected Sources.* 2d ed. Englewood, Colo.: Libraries Unlimited, 1996. An extensive and clear guide to 1,030 of the most important reference sources in the social sciences, including guides, reference books, hand-books, reviews of research, indexes and database, book reviews, bibliographies, directories, and biographical and statistical sources.

Herron, Nancy L., and Diane Zabel, eds. *Bridging the Gap: Examining Polarity in America.* Englewood, Colo.: Libraries Unlimited, 1995. A handbook containing twelve bibliographic essays devoted to issues that divide Americans, including child and elder care, children and learning, and the changing American family.

Inventory of Marriage and Family Literature. Anoka, Minn.: National Council on Family Relations, 1974-   . Annual publication, with online formats available. More than six hundred interdisciplinary journals are scanned for articles on marriage and the family. The inventory employs subject, author, and keyword indexes.

Kuper, Adam, and Jessica Kuper, eds. *The Social Science Encyclopedia.* New York: Routledge, 1996. Contains a wide range of authoritative, introductory articles related to the family and family history. More a broad, topical work than a ready reference, these articles will nevertheless be useful for a variety of research projects.

Kurian, George Thomas. *Datapedia of the United States, 1790-2000: America Year by Year.* Lanham, Md.: Bernan Press, 1994. Provides vital statistical information on a wide range of family topics, including households, marriage and divorce, distribution of money income of families, median income of families, and education. Pre-1970 statistics based entirely on *Historical Statistics of the United States from Colonial Times;* post-1970 statistics based on the annual *Statistical Abstract of the United States* and a variety of additional published statistics.

"Literature and Resource Review Essay," *Family Relations.* A valuable annual feature of this academic journal, reviews books, videos, and other resources. In 1996 it published an annotated bibliography of the winners, runners-up, and honorable mention awards granted in the 28th Annual National Council on Family Relations Media Awards Competition.

Marsiglio, William, and John H. Scanzoni. *Families and Friends.* New York: Addison-Wesley, Longman, 1995. Part of the "Hot Topics in Sociology" series, this minitext expands upon textbook coverage to provide direct background information, current data, and reference sources.

Masnick, George, et al. *The Nation's Families: 1960-1990.* Cambridge, Mass.: Joint Center for Urban Studies of MIT and Harvard University, 1980. Using the 1980 U.S. Census, the authors have compiled a variety of statistics useful in research on the American family.

National Directory of Children, Youth, and Family Services. 7th ed. Longmont, Colo.: Marion L. Peterson, 1991. This biennial publication lists social, health, juvenile justice, and special service agencies, including their addresses, phone numbers, fax numbers, and other information. Part two includes information on federal level programming. Lists health and welfare hotline numbers.

The Public Welfare Directory. Washington, D.C.: American Public Welfare Association, 1940- . This annual publication is the basic guide to human service programs in the United States and Canada. Identifies federal, state, regional, and county agencies for the United States and federal, provincial, and territorial agencies for Canada. Contains information on birth, death, marriage, and divorce records and eligibility for various assistance programs.

Ramachandran, V. S., ed. *Encyclopedia of Human Behavior.* 4 vols. San Diego, Calif.: Academic Press, 1994. Less technical than many psychological reference books, this interdisciplinary work contains 250 signed articles on subjects such as child abuse, marriage, and parenting. Each article in this outstanding set includes an outline, a glossary, a definition of the topic, cross-references, and a bibliography.

Sage Family Studies Abstracts. Thousand Oaks, Calif.: Sage Publications, 1979- . Each quarter, this publication provides approximately 250 abstracts of journal articles, books, government documents, and a variety of other materials related to courtship, marriage, divorce, sex roles, reproduction, life span development, family relationships, and family law.

Schmittroth, Linda, ed. *Statistical Record of Women Worldwide.* Detroit: Gale Research, 1991. Almost half of this volume's eight hundred tables are devoted to women of the United States and cover topics such as domestic life, education, and legal justice. Detailed subject index and table of contents allow easy identification of materials. Original sources of statistics include government agencies, polling organizations, private organizations, newspapers, journal articles, and books.

Smelser, Neil J., ed. *Handbook of Sociology.* Newbury Park, Calif.: Sage Publications, 1988. The first new general handbook in sociology in almost a quarter of a century, its chapters by experts cover the discipline's major fields and summarize trends in research. Extensive bibliography.

Sociological Abstracts. San Diego, Calif.: Sociological Abstracts, 1953- . The major periodical index to all fields of sociology, including the family. Many libraries provide this in CD-ROM formats.

The State of America's Children Yearbook. Washington, D.C.: Children's Defense Fund, 1997. Provides an excellent summary of the health status of American children; separate chapters on family income, health, child care, teen pregnancy, education, violence against children, and families in crisis. Evaluates selected programs designed to deal with these problems.

Touliatos, John, Barry F. Perlmutter, and Murray A. Straus, eds. *Handbook of Family Measurement Techniques.* Newbury Park, Calif.: Sage Publications, 1990. This tool for clinicians and researchers describes almost 1,000 measuring instruments divided into five categories: "Dimensions of Interaction," "Intimacy and Family Values," "Parenthood," "Roles and Power," and "Adjustment." Author and title indexes.

Wood, Elizabeth J., and Floris W. Wood, ed. *She Said, He Said: What Men and Women Really Think About Money, Sex, Politics, and Other Issues of Essence.* Detroit: Visible Ink Press, 1992. Using data from Floris Wood's *American Profile: Opinions and Behavior, 1972-1989* and the General Social Survey, the editors compare responses on vital issues.

2. AGING AND THE FAMILY

Bass, Scott A., Elizabeth A. Kutza, and Fernando M. Torres-Gil, eds. *Diversity in Aging: Challenges Facing the White House Conference on Aging.* Glenview, Ill.: Scott, Foresman, 1989. Pointing out that "the programmatic strategies of the past twenty years, in all likelihood, will be unresponsive to the dramatically changing needs of the population," the authors see the period 1990-2010, with baby boomers at their production peak, as a golden opportunity for restructuring American policy.

Bengtson, Vern L., ed. *Adulthood and Aging: Research on Continuities and Discontinuities.* New York: Springer, 1996. A collection of articles by senior scholars representing the wide range of approaches to research in the field, including surveys, personal interviews, personal reflections. A tribute to human development pioneer Bernice L. Neugarten.

Binstock, Robert H., and Linda K. George, eds. *Handbook of Aging and the Social Sciences.* 3d ed. San Diego, Calif: Academic Press, 1990. A review of research dealing with topics such as social structure, diversity, old age pensions, and leisure and time use. Includes an extensive section on "Families and Aging." Extensive bibliographies.

Chudacoff, Howard P. *How Old Are You? Age Consciousness in American Culture.* Princeton, N.J.: Princeton University Press, 1989. A good survey of age-consciousness in America, with discussions of integrating age groups in early American families and of intergenerational trends.

Coyle, Jean M. *Families and Aging: A Selected, Annotated Bibliography.* New York: Greenwood Press, 1991. Divides 778 entries into categories such as grandparents, adult children, widowhood, and ethnic minority groups. Covers books, articles, audiovisuals, and documents from 1980 to 1990.

Darnay, Arsen J., ed. *Statistical Record of Older Americans.* Detroit: Gale Research, 1994. Topics such as housing, homelessness, and loneliness are statistically illustrated with more than nine hundred charts, tables, and graphs taken from more than 140 public and private sources. More extensive than the second edition of *Statistical Handbook on Aging Americans,* edited by Frank L. Schick and Renee Schick (see below).

Fischer, David Hackett. *Growing Old in America.* New York: Oxford University Press, 1977. Beginning as the Bland-Lee Lectures at Clark University, the author produced one of the first historical treatments of aging, tracing evolving perceptions from "the exaltation of the aged" in the seventeenth and eighteenth centuries to "old age as a social problem" in the twentieth. Contains a number of statistical appendices.

Friedan, Betty. *The Fountain of Age.* New York: Simon & Schuster, 1993. A feminist pioneer argues that in trying to hold on to youth, many people deny the possibilities of age. The crucial challenge is "to continually make the occasions to deepen the touching and shared disclosure that is the true glue of intimacy," whether with friends, colleagues, children, grandchildren, or lovers.

Kastenbaum, Robert, ed. *Encyclopedia of Adult Development.* Phoenix, Ariz.: Oryx Press, 1993. Named "A Best Reference Source for 1993" by *Library Journal,* the 106 articles cover a wide range of topics, including divorce, religion in adult life, gender differences, and widowhood. The seventy contributors include specialists in education, family studies, communications, psychology, history, sociology, gerontology, physiology, psychiatry, nursing, and medicine. Unique in that it does not focus on aging or the aged.

Maddox, George L., ed. *The Encyclopedia of Aging: A Comprehensive Resource in Gerontology and Geriatrics.* 2d ed. New York: Springer, 1995. An authoritative one-volume work drawing upon the expertise of more than two hundred prominent gerontologists. Brief articles written with a limited amount of jargon makes this volume particularly accessible to nonspecialists. The bibliography alone covers more than one hundred pages. More than 80 percent of the book is new or has been revised since the original edition of 1986.

Manheimer, Ronald J., ed. *Older Americans Almanac.* Detroit: Gale Research, 1994. A comprehensive reference on the subject of aging in America, including treatment of the demography and diversity of aging; physical, mental, and social processes of aging; employment, finance, and retirement; health and wellness; social environments; and lifestyles. Contains lists of organizations, with addresses, phone numbers, and fax numbers.

Posner, Richard A. *Aging and Old Age.* Chicago: University of Chicago Press, 1995. An optimistic analysis of aging and the aged, which suggests that the 1990's, despite their problems, represents a golden age of influence for older Americans. Draws principally from economic and biological sources; contains extensive footnotes.

Riekse, R. J., and H. Holstege. *Growing Older in America.* New York: McGraw-Hill, 1996. A highly readable and exceptionally broad survey of gerontological research, which treats the aging of America as "a social revolution with far-reaching implications."

Roy, Frederick Hampton, and Charles Russell. *The Encyclopedia of Aging and the Elderly.* New York: Facts On File, 1992. A multidisciplinary collection of cross-referenced entries. Addresses for national and state organizations; bibliography.

Schick, Frank L., and Renee Schick, eds. *Statistical Handbook on Aging Americans.* 2d ed. Phoenix, Ariz.: Oryx Press, 1994. Including almost four hundred charts, tables, and graphs based on government sources and the census, this handbook recognizes the importance of aging in American social development. Contains sections on "Demographics," "Living Arrangements and Marital Status," "Households, Housing, and Informal Supports," and "Health Care Expenditures."

Schweitzer, Marjorie M. *Anthropology of Aging: A Partially Annotated Bibliography.* New York: Greenwood Press, 1991. Prepared under the auspices of the Association for Anthropology and Gerontology, this work includes references to books, book chapters, and articles, the most important of which are annotated.

Troll, Lillian E., ed. *Family Issues in Current Gerontology.* New York: Springer, 1986. Series of articles drawn from *The Journal of Gerontology* and the *Gerontologist,* focusing on family issues. Articles are divided into sections, including marriage, widowhood, parent-adult child relations, caregiving, kinship networks, childlessness, and divorce.

3. ART, MEDIA, AND THE FAMILY

Alali, A. Odasuo. *Mass Media, Sex, and Adolescent Values: An Annotated Bibliography and Directory of Organizations.* Jefferson, N.C.: McFarland, 1991. Contains 285 annotated entries organized into chapters dealing with sex-role portrayals, adolescents' attitudes and values, contraception, pregnancy, and health issues.

Cofer, Lynette Friedrich, and Robin Smith Jacobvitz. "The Loss of Moral Turf: Mass Media and Family Values." In *Rebuilding the Nest,* edited by David Blankenhorn et al. Milwaukee, Wis.: Family Service America, 1990. Argues that the combination of absent parents and terrifying television combines to undermine the moral value of the family.

Cowan, Geoffrey. *See No Evil: The Backstage Battle over Sex and Violence in Television.* New York: Simon & Schuster, 1979. An insider's account of the battle to create a "family hour" on network television.

Fisher, Kim N. *On the Screen: A Film, Television, and Video Research Guide.* Littleton, Colo.: Libraries Unlimited, 1986. An extensive annotated bibliography of sources.

Himmelstein, Hal. *Television Myth and the American Mind.* 2d ed. Westport, Conn.: Praeger, 1994. Building upon dramatic changes in the television industry since publication of the first edition in 1983, the author discusses the impact of the continual stream of commodities bombarding viewers and suggests ways that it might be countered.

Jowett, Garth S., Ian C. Jarvie, and Kathryn H. Fuller. *Children and the Movies: Media Influence and the Payne Fund Controversy.* New York: Cambridge University Press, 1996. Analyzes the first comprehensive investigation, in 1933, of the influence of movies on America's youth.

Lake, Sara. *Television's Impact on Children and Adolescents.* Phoenix, Ariz.: Oryx Press, 1981. This bibliographic source includes references to 515 books and journal articles covering the years 1976 to 1980. Specifically covers children's and adolescents' viewing habits, behavioral impact of television, and suggestions for improving the quality of viewing. Contains a subject index.

Lichter, S. Robert, Linda S. Lichter, and Stanley Rothman. *Prime Time: How TV Portrays American Culture.* Washington, D.C.: Regnery, 1993. A comprehensive study of "life" as it seems to exist on television. Extensive coverage of the family, including the advent of single-parent households, baby boomers, nontraditional families, parental controls, and family values. The authors argue that television's emphasis on sex and violence does not represent the values of most Americans.

Medved, Michael. *Hollywood vs. America: Popular Culture and the War on Traditional Values.* New York: HarperCollins, 1992. A noted film critic's attack on Hollywood's disregard for the values of most Americans, identifying the sixties as the decade when producers began to rely on the shock value of sex and violence rather than quality storytelling. Part III deals specifically with "The Assault on the Family." Became the center of a national controversy when Vice President

Dan Quayle attacked television programming at about the time of the book's publication.

Murray, John P. *Television and Youth: Twenty-five Years of Research and Controversy*. Stanford, Wash.: Boys Town Center for the Study of Youth Development, 1980. Murray's extensive bibliography includes 2,800 items covering the period 1955 to 1980, with some 60 percent drawn from 1975 to 1980. Most citations are from North American, Australian, British, and European sources.

Nussel, Frank H. *The Image of Older Adults in the Media: An Annotated Bibliography*. Westport, Conn.: Greenwood Press, 1992. Including scholarly, general, and activist literature, this work covers 558 annotated sources grouped in topical chapters such as ageism, children's literature, greeting cards, advice, film, and television.

Pearl, David, Lorraine Bouthilet, and Joyce Lazar, eds. *Television and Behavior: Ten Years of Scientific Progress and Implications for the Eighties*. Washington, D.C.: U.S. Government Printing Office, 1982. Includes a variety of articles on the impact of television, including "The Family as Portrayed on Television 1946-1978."

Postman, Neil. *Technopoly: The Surrender of Culture to Technology*. New York: Alfred A. Knopf, 1992. Argues that omnipresent technologies are replacing traditional freedom of choice.

Schramm, Wilbur, ed. *The Effects of Television on Children and Adolescents*. Paris: UNESCO, 1964. A classic annotated bibliography, noting the conclusions of 163 English- and foreign-language studies. Now dated, though important for historical analysis.

Signorielli, Nancy. *Role Portrayal and Stereotyping on Television: An Annotated Bibliography of Studies Relating to Women, Minorities, Aging, Sexual Behavior, Health, and Handicaps*. Westport, Conn.: Greenwood Press, 1985. An extensive annotated bibliography of books, reports, and articles, containing full bibliographic information and summaries of research results.

Stillman, Peter R. *Families Writing*. Cincinnati: Writer's Digest Books, 1989. Includes dozens of practical ideas for encouraging family bonding through writing, including sections on letters, poetry, and stories.

Trojan, Judith. *American Family Life Films*. Metuchen, N.J.: Scarecrow Press, 1981. This extensive 2,100-item compilation is designed to "provide a single, comprehensive resource" of films covering "the broad spectrum of family dynamics in America, past and present." Most entries cover educational or documentary films dealing with abortion, adolescence, and childhood development, although some 20 percent of the titles are dramatic features. Dated, as it covers only easily accessible 16-mm films.

Twitchell, James B. *Adcult USA: The Triumph of Advertising in American Culture*. New York: Columbia University Press, 1996. This survey of mostly twentieth century themes suggests that advertising has become the central institution in American culture. Drawing on both scholarly and popular culture sources, the author argues that advertising has become "the dominant meaning-making system of modern life" and rejects the notion that advertising "creates artificial desires." Well illustrated with a good bibliography.

Zimmermann, Patricia R. *Reel Families: A Social History of Amateur Film*. Bloomington: Indiana University Press, 1995. An idiosyncratic book beginning with the premise that amateur film ("home movies") has been overlooked by historians because of its association with the traditional family and its lack of association with the dominant power structures in the industry.

4. CHILDREN, CHILD DEVELOPMENT, AND EDUCATION

America's Children. San Diego, Calif.: Greenhaven Press, 1991. Designed for young adults as a part of Greenhaven's Opposing Viewpoints Series, this book excerpts published opinions from thirty-five experts, drawn from a wide range of sources, and arranges material in a pro/con format. Balanced treatment, reliance upon experts, and current book and periodical bibliographies make this an excellent starting point for research.

Apter, Terri. *The Confident Child: Raising a Child to Try, Learn, and Care*. New York: W. W. Norton, 1997. Valuing most of all the building of self-esteem, the author offers popular advice on parenting, including "How to Be an Imperfect Parent Without Ruining Your Child's Life," and "Raising Moral Children."

Bloom, Jill. *Parenting Our Schools: A Hands-On Guide to Education Reform*. Boston: Little, Brown, 1992. A children's author argues for the rights and responsibilities of parents regarding school reform.

Blustein, Jeffrey. *Parents and Children: The Ethics of the Family.* New York: Oxford University Press, 1982. Offers the first philosophically based theory of parenting; includes a section on family policy and a good bibliography of classical Western sources fundamental to North American families of European descent.

Carpenter, Kathryn Hammell. *Sourcebook on Parenting and Child Care.* Phoenix, Ariz.: Oryx Press, 1995. More than nine hundred entries contain information divided into twenty-six chapters, including the adoptive family, parental responsibilities, and the humorous side of parenting. Entries provide full bibliographic information, including price. Appendix includes parenting videotapes.

DeFrancis, Beth. *The Parents' Resource Almanac: Where to Write, Who to Call.* Holbrook, Mass.: Adams, 1994. Annotated references in twenty-seven chapters and nine appendices cover topics such as parenting techniques, grandparents, family travel, health, and children's literature. Each subject includes listings of books, periodicals, associations, videotapes, software, and various businesses and services. Comprehensive and practical.

Dewey, John. *School and Society.* Chicago: University of Chicago Press, 1900. The project for "psychologizing" American schools; called for experimentation and the use of new methods.

Dixon, Penelope. *Mothers and Mothering: An Annotated Feminist Bibliography.* New York: Garland, 1991. Contains 351 annotated entries for articles and books published between 1970 and 1990 that cover topics such as daughters, sons, family, psychoanalysis, and reproductive issues.

Erwin, Elizabeth, ed. *Putting Children First: Visions for a Brighter Future for Young Children and Their Families.* Baltimore: Paul H. Brookes, 1996. Emerging from the continued presence of social problems (such as poverty, violence, and health care issues) and recent legislative trends, this work integrates literature from early childhood education, special education, public policy, and medicine. Extensive discussion of family role includes a chapter on "The Impact of Family and Community Violence on Young Children and Their Families."

Franck, Irene M., and David Brownstone, eds. *The Parent's Desk Reference.* New York: Prentice-Hall, 1991. Includes 2,500 cross-referenced entries on such topics as cesarean section, early screening inventory, and Parent Locator Service, many of which include references. A Special Help section includes information on pregnancy, baby safety, books for children, and a variety of hotline phone numbers related to children's services.

Galinsky, Ellen, Carollee Howes, Susan Kontos, and Marybeth Shinn. *The Study of Children in Family Child Care and Relative Care: Highlights of Findings.* New York: Families and Work Institute, 1994. This extensive study found that two-earner families usually split shifts, roughly divided between the parents, in order to maximize parental care.

Gelles, Richard. *The Book of David: How Preserving Families Can Cost Children's Lives.* New York: Basic Books, 1996. By focusing on the case of one child as opposed to a system or a body of research literature, the author illustrates the many ways in which maltreated children are failed by the social systems and agencies "ostensibly designed for their protection."

Groze, Victor. *Successful Adoptive Families: A Longitudinal Study of Special-Needs Adoptions.* Westport, Conn.: Praeger, 1996. An academic study, based upon a systematic sample of 199 Iowa families involved in subsidized special-needs adoption.

Grubb, W. Norton, and Marvin Lazerson. *Broken Promises: How Americans Fail Their Children.* New York: Basic Books, 1982. The authors suggest that the crisis of the family can only be solved by recognizing the permanent role of the state in private lives and by articulating "a set of public responsibilities toward children."

Haas, Enid E. *Research Guide for Studies in Infancy and Childhood.* New York: Greenwood Press, 1988. Section one covers research strategies, describing twenty-five databases with a brief bibliography of online searching materials. Section two provides subject bibliographies organized in broad categories such as families and social/cultural development. Includes 1,400 annotated entries.

Harkness, Sara, and Charles M. Super, eds. *Parents' Cultural Belief Systems: Their Origins, Expressions, and Consequences.* New York: Guilford Press, 1996. A collection of essays that addresses the variety of beliefs which parents have about children. A sophisticated examination of the reality of child rearing.

Hawes, Joseph M., and N. Ray Hiner, eds. *American Childhood: A Research Guide and Historical Handbook.* Westport, Conn.: Greenwood Press, 1985. A necessary starting point for the study of American childhood, this book contains a series of detailed articles, each with an extensive bibliography, in which the family is routinely treated. Separate chapters on "Native American Children" and "Ethnicity and American Children."

Helfer, Mary Edna, Ruth S. Kempe, and Richard D. Krugman, eds. *The Battered Child.* 5th ed. Chicago: University of Chicago Press, 1997. First published in 1968, this is an updated version of one of the first works to raise American consciousness about the problem of child abuse. Includes parts dealing with the cultural, social, and economic background of the problem; assessment of specific cases; intervention, treatment, and legal issues; and prevention and policy issues.

Henderson, Ann T., and Nancy Berla, eds. *The Family Is Critical: A New Generation of Evidence.* Columbia, Md.: National Committee for Citizens in Education, 1994. Reviews research demonstrating the vital role of parents in their children's achievement.

Hewlett, Sylvia Ann. *When the Bough Breaks: The Cost of Neglecting Our Children.* New York: HarperCollins, 1991. Suggests the importance of government intervention in the raising of children.

Hurrelman, Klaus, ed. *International Handbook of Adolescence.* Westport, Conn.: Greenwood Press, 1994. Each chapter presents historical developments (1945 to 1990), education, family building, and other topics from various countries, enabling the researcher to deal with U.S. and Canadian issues comparatively.

Kilpatrick, William K. *Why Johnny Can't Tell Right from Wrong: Moral Illiteracy and the Case for Character Education.* New York: Simon & Schuster, 1992. Attacks the values-neutral education that has prevailed since the introduction of American moral relativism in the 1960's. Notable criticism of John Dewey's progressivism.

Lerner, Richard M., Anne C. Peterson, and Jeanne Brooks-Gunn, eds. *Encyclopedia of Adolescence.* New York: Garland, 1991. More than two hundred articles examine adolescence from a variety of perspectives, including physical, psychological, and social. Topics include cognitive development, pregnancy and childbearing, religion, and HIV infection. Contains an extensive subject index and effective illustrations.

O'Neill, Onora, and William Ruddick, eds. *Having Children: Philosophical and Legal Reflections on Parenthood.* New York: Oxford University Press, 1980. An anthology of writings dealing with moral issues involved in procreation and caring for children. In "Parents and Life Prospects," Ruddick proposes a "principle of parenthood" as a potential guide for judges determining cases of child abuse and neglect.

Pritchard, Michael S. *Reasonable Children: Moral Education and Moral Learning.* Lawrence: University Press of Kansas, 1996. Without rigidly defining "reasonable," the author establishes some commonly accepted characteristics of the term and contends that children should be taught this valuable social skill. Chapters include "Families, Schools, and Moral Education" and "Moral Diversity."

Rich, Dorothy. *Megaskills: How Families Can Help Children Succeed in School and Beyond.* New York: Houghton Mifflin, 1988. Emphasizes the need to impress upon children the need for self-discipline in attaining material and social success.

Rioux, J. William, and Nancy Berla. *Innovations in Parent and Family Involvement.* Princeton Junction, N.J.: Eye on Education, 1993. An argument for strengthening the ties between schools and families.

Scarre, Geoffrey, ed. *Children, Parents, and Politics.* New York: Cambridge University Press, 1989. Collection of essays by professors of philosophy, history, and bioethics dealing with the seldom examined moral status of children. Chapters cover the history of children, their place in a democratic polity, and the moral value of children in cases of severe disability and in relationship to pornography.

Scheffler, Hanna Nuba. *Resources for Early Childhood: An Annotated Bibliography and Guide for Educators, Librarians, Health Care Professionals, and Parents.* New York: Garland, 1983. Each of the sixteen chapters begins with an essay and includes an evaluative bibliography. Based on the collection at the New York Public Library's Early Childhood Resource and Information Center.

Scheffler, Hannah Nuba, Deborah Lovitky Sheiman, and Kathleen Pullan Watkins. *Infancy: A Guide to Research and Resources.* New York: Garland, 1986. Compiled for students, parents, and teachers, these annotated entries address development from the prenatal period to two years of age. Chapter ten lists books for babies.

Schmittroth, Linda, ed. *Statistical Record of Children.* Detroit: Gale Research, 1994. Nine hundred tables drawn from both governmental and private sources, many published here for the first time, cover health and medical care, nutrition, education, child care, adoption/foster care, welfare, poverty, child abuse, sports, and children as consumers. Contains a detailed table of contents and an extensive index for easy use.

Sheiman, Deborah Lovitky, and Maureen Slonim, eds. *Resources for Middle Childhood: A Source Book.* New York: Garland, 1988. Focusing on children between the ages of six and twelve, the annotated entries are divided into chapters such as family interactions and peer relationships.

Spock, Benjamin. *A Better World for Our Children: Rethinking American Family Values.* Bethesda, Md.: National Press Books, 1994. An impressionistic essay by the legendary author on child care, arguing that parents put too much pressure on their children to succeed athletically and academically and suggesting that parents should raise kids who want to be kind and helpful to others.

———. *Common Sense Book of Baby and Child Care.* New York: Duell, Sloan and Pearce, 1946. The child-care bible to the post–World War II generation of parents who routinely feared life-threatening and debilitating diseases such as meningitis and polio. Spock emphasized the understanding of child misbehavior and suggested less violence in punishing children. Sold twenty-eight million copies between 1946 and 1976.

Steinberg, Laurence, with B. Bradford Brown and Sanford M. Dornbusch. *Beyond the Classroom: Why School Reform Has Failed and What Parents Need to Do.* New York: Simon & Schuster, 1996. Argues that parents and educators must first change society in order to reform schools, reestablishing links between students and academic achievement.

Sutherland, Neil, Jean Barman, and Linda L. Hale, eds. *Contemporary Childhood and Youth: A Bibliography.* Westport, Conn.: Greenwood Press, 1992. Contains 7,328 unannotated entries grouped by region; covers books, government reports, articles, and theses published through 1990.

Wiggin, Kate Douglas. *Children's Rights.* Boston: Houghton Mifflin, 1892. The classic romantic view of children's rights, urging the development of child-centered kindergartens and milder forms of discipline.

Woodbury, Marda, ed. *Youth Information Resources: An Annotated Guide for Parents, Professionals, Students, Researchers, and Concerned Citizens.* New York: Greenwood Press, 1987. Examining both U.S. and Canadian English-language sources on adolescents, who are defined as ages thirteen to nineteen, this work provides more than one thousand annotated entries dealing with research and library use, research questions, and a wide variety of sources.

Zollar, Ann Creighton. *Adolescent Pregnancy and Parenthood: An Annotated Guide.* New York: Garland, 1990. References to seven hundred articles, books, and book chapters, plus additional references to the holdings of the Data Archive on Adolescent Pregnancy and Pregnancy Prevention (DAAPPP). Arranged by topical areas such as "Adolescent Fathers" and "Legal Issues." Somewhat difficult to use as it lacks a subject index and cross-references.

5. DATING, MARRIAGE, AND DIVORCE

Ahrons, Constance. *The Good Divorce: Keeping Your Family Together When Your Marriage Comes Apart.* New York: HarperCollins, 1994. A sociologist argues against identifying divorce as shameful and suggests that the children of divorce can lead happy lives.

Ahrons, Constance, and Roy H. Rodgers. *Divorced Families: Meeting the Challenge of Divorce and Remarriage.* New York: W. W. Norton, 1989. The authors believe that divorce is a natural response to a rapidly changing social structure. In the past people married for economic reasons, whereas in the late twentieth century they marry for love and companionship.

Applewhite, Ashton. *Cutting Loose: Why Women Who End Their Marriages Do so Well.* New York: HarperCollins, 1997. Attempts to dispel the myth of the lonely and financially deprived divorcee.

Bailey, Beth L. *From Front Porch to Back Seat: Courtship in Twentieth-Century America.* Baltimore: Johns Hopkins University Press, 1988. Argues that dating was a social "necessity" for people living in tenements, without access to piano and parlor.

Beal, Edward W., and Gloria Hochman. *Adult Children of Divorce: Breaking the Cycle and Finding Fulfillment in Love, Marriage, and Family.* New York: Delacorte Press, 1991. Offers practical advice, drawn from more than three hundred case studies, on breaking the cycle of divorce so often handed down in families.

Bernard, Jessie. *The Future of Marriage.* New York: World, 1972. Prophetic sociological study before the advent of the "domestic partnership" movement; attacks traditional marriage for forcing women into certain sex roles and for the creation of a system of "structured stress."

Broude, Gwen J. *Marriage, Family, and Relationships: A Cross-Cultural Encyclopedia.* Santa Barbara, Calif.: ABC-Clio, 1994. Starting from the premise that human beings everywhere marry and limit their choice of partners in relationship to basic needs, this work addresses a wide range of subjects including courtship, divorce, kinship, reproduction, prostitution, incest, and premarital pregnancy. Should be used with caution, as the customs of non-Western cultures are often represented from out-of-date sources.

Cherlin, Andrew. *Marriage, Divorce, Remarriage.* Rev. and enlarged ed. Cambridge, Mass.: Harvard University Press, 1992. Concise review of sociological research on the family. New research since the first edition of 1981 has suggested a more accurate titling: "Cohabitation, Marriage, Divorce, More Cohabitation, and Probably Remarriage." Contains an excellent discussion of demographic trends.

Christensen, H. T. *Handbook of Marriage and Family.* Chicago: Rand McNally, 1964. A dense, encyclopedic reference that held the field for three decades. Still useful.

Cutrona, Carolyn E. *Social Support in Couples: Marriage as a Resource in Times of Stress.* Thousand Oaks, Calif.: Sage Publications, 1996. A clearly written academic study that introduces and reviews the literature associated with social support processes between spouses.

DiCanio, Margaret. *The Encyclopedia of Marriage, Divorce, and the Family.* New York: Facts On File, 1989. Concise, readable, and thorough encyclopedia containing more than six hundred entries on topics as diverse as adoption, black families, breast-feeding, child support, cohabitation, parental leave, stepfamilies, and wife battering; extensive bibliography. Contains detailed author, title, and subject indexes and nine appendices containing practical aids such as sample nuptial agreements and directories of state child-care agencies.

Dym, Barry, and Michael Glenn. *Couples: Exploring and Understanding the Cycles of Intimate Relationships.* New York: HarperCollins, 1993. Two therapists outline the evolving stages of relationships to prepare couples for inevitable changes.

Fassel, Diane. *Growing Up Divorced: A Road to Healing for Adult Children of Divorce.* New York: Pocket Books, 1991. Suggests that traditional families are not well suited to modern society, where people live longer and have greater means for ending marriages; points to family violence and drug abuse as evidence of the vulnerability of traditional family forms.

Fineman, Martha. *The Illusion of Equality: The Rhetoric and Reality of Divorce Reform.* Chicago: University of Chicago Press, 1991. Argues that the language of divorce reform is deliberately used to mask genuine inequities.

Furstenberg, Frank F., Jr., and Andrew J. Cherlin. *Divided Families: What Happens to Children When Parents Part.* Cambridge, Mass.: Harvard University Press, 1991. The authors argue that the economic consequences of divorce are more important than the moral ones and that a "child support assurance" plan could help ease the transition.

Kalter, Neil. *Growing Up with Divorce: Helping Your Child Avoid Immediate and Later Emotional Problems.* New York: Free Press, 1990. The director of the Center for the Child and the Family at the University of Michigan argues for the central role of parents in helping children avoid both environmental and internal stresses; based on detailed clinical accounts.

Levinson, David, ed. *Encyclopedia of Marriage and the Family.* New York: Macmillan, 1995. Includes 169 articles by academics and professionals on a wide variety of family issues, including health-related problems, parenting, reproduction, gangs, cohabitation, and sociocultural influences on the family. Clear and concise writing make this easily accessible.

McManus, Michael J. *Marriage Savers: Helping Your Friends and Family Avoid Divorce*. Grand Rapids, Mich.: Zondervan, 1995. Prescriptions for overcoming marital problems, including reform of no-fault divorce laws and mandatory premarital counseling. Written from a Christian perspective.

Marston, Stephanie. *The Divorced Parent: Success Strategies for Raising Your Children After Separation*. New York: William Morrow, 1994. A marriage counselor's manual for navigating the uncharted waters of relationships following divorce.

May, Elaine Tyler. *Great Expectations: Marriage and Divorce in Post-Victorian America*. Chicago: University of Chicago Press, 1980. Good survey of the period, with an especially good treatment of marriage in the films of the 1920's.

Nofsinger, Mary M. *Children and Adjustment to Divorce: An Annotated Bibliography*. New York: Garland, 1989. Unique in providing separate bibliographies for professionals, parents, and children and young adults, each with its own introduction. Organization and audiovisual resource lists.

Popenoe, David, Jean Bethke Elshtain, and David Blankenhorn, eds. *Promises to Keep: Decline and Renewal of Marriage in America*. Lanham, Md.: Rowman & Littlefield, 1996. Emerging from a conference on the New Familism, the authors identify numerous trends regarding the family. Popenoe cautions, however, that lack of role models and high divorce rates might undermine recent moves toward greater family stability.

Rheinstein, Max. *Marriage Stability, Divorce, and the Law*. Chicago: University of Chicago Press, 1971. Argues that the conflict between America's high ideals for marriage and the relatively lax enforcement of divorce law created a healthy compromise.

Sussman, Marvin B., and Suzanne K. Steinmetz, eds. *Handbook of Marriage and the Family*. New York: Plenum, 1987. The standard interdisciplinary handbook in the field, replacing Christensen's classic *Handbook of Marriage and the Family* (1964). Contains more than thirty articles on subjects such as family theory, ethnicity, nontraditional family forms, family stress, and social policy. Many charts and tables; subject index.

Wallerstein, Judith, and Sandra Blakeslee. *The Good Marriage: How and Why Love Lasts*. Boston: Houghton Mifflin, 1995. Basing themselves on a study of fifty couples coping with marital problems, these psychologists reaffirm the need for love and intimacy in successful marriages.

_____. *Second Chances: Men, Women, and Children a Decade After Divorce*. New York: Ticknor & Fields, 1990. Based upon a fifteen-year study, the authors contend that divorce in a world where children feel unprotected continues to produce negative effects throughout adulthood.

Weitzman, Lenore J. *The Divorce Revolution: The Unexpected Social and Economic Consequences for Women and Children in America*. New York: Free Press, 1985. Deals with the development and usefulness of technical equality in divorce legislation, arguing that no-fault divorce works to the disadvantage of women. A ground-breaking early challenge to no-fault divorce.

Whitehead, Barbara Dafoe. *The Divorce Culture*. New York: Alfred A. Knopf, 1997. Argues that the "high-divorce society is creating a low-commitment culture." Identifies the mid-1960's as the turning point, when divorce became a form of personal expression and an opportunity rather than a devastating moral choice.

6. DEMOGRAPHICS AND FAMILY TYPES

At Issue: Single-Parent Families. San Diego, Calif: Greenhaven Press, 1997. This anthology of writings by liberal, centrist, and conservative experts provides a balanced introduction to the debate over why drug abuse, crime, and teenage pregnancy are so prevalent in single-parent families. Articles drawn from a variety of sources are printed in their entirety, along with source notes, extensive bibliographies, and annotated lists of organizations. A good starting point for young adults researching this topic.

Baca Zinn, Maxine, and D. Stanley Eitzen. *Diversity in Families*. 4th ed. New York: Addison-Wesley, Longman, 1996. A clear, sociological analysis of the family, beginning with the premise that much of what Americans believe about their families is mythical and symbolic. Unusual in treating diversity as the norm in modern family life. Views the family on both the "macro" and "micro" levels. Strongly based upon feminist scholarship.

Commonweal, November 22, 1991. Contains three articles debating the value of gay marriages.

Brent Hartinger argues in "A Case for Gay Marriage" that gay marriage would strengthen the American family.

Foster, Barbara, Michael Foster, and Letha Hadady. *Three in Love: Menages à trois from Ancient to Modern Times.* New York: HarperCollins, 1997. Carefully distinguishing the *menages à trois* from the violent and competitive love triangle, three practitioners of their passion argue for the *menages à trois* as a practical alternative to the two-partner family.

Gay Rights. San Diego, Calif.: Greenhaven Press, 1997. This anthology incorporates a wide spectrum of primary sources representing liberal, conservative, and centrist views. The writings of experts such as Jonathan Rauch, Richard Rorty, Anthony Kennedy, Antonin Scalia, and William H. Rehnquist are drawn together to answer such questions as "Should Society Legally Sanction Homosexual Families" and "What Rights Should Gays and Lesbians Have?" With extensive indexes and bibliographies, this is an excellent starting point for research involving homosexual families.

Gouke, Mary Noel, and Arline McClarty Rollins, ed. *One-Parent Children, the Growing Minority: A Research Guide.* New York: Garland, 1990. Contains 1,142 annotated abstracts divided into four sections, including one on types of families (fatherless, lesbian or gay, adoptive).

Gruber, Ellen J. *Stepfamilies: A Guide to the Sources and Resources.* New York: Garland, 1986. Thorough coverage of materials from 1980 to 1984, including some audiovisuals, organizations, and newsletters.

Johnson, W. R., and D. M. Warren, eds. *Inside the Mixed Marriage.* Lanham, Md.: University Press of America, 1994. Explains the "changing attitudes, patterns and perceptions of cross-cultural and interracial marriages."

Macklin, E., and R. Rubin, eds. *Contemporary Families and Alternative Lifestyles.* Beverly Hills, Calif.: Sage Publications, 1983. Includes an article on nonmarital heterosexual cohabitation.

Maggiore, Dolores J. *Lesbianism: An Annotated Bibliography and Guide to the Literature, 1976-1986.* Metuchen, N.J.: Scarecrow Press, 1988. Includes approximately 350 entries, including a section on lesbian families. Must be used with caution, as it excludes negative views of lesbianism.

Marciano, Teresa, and Marvin B. Sussman, eds. *Wider Families: New Traditional Family Forms.* Binghamton, N.Y.: Haworth Press, 1991. These sociologists suggest that traditional definitions of the family are not suited to modern society and that the traditional family actually coexists with a wider family.

May, Elaine Tyler. *Barren in the Promised Land: Childless Couples and the Pursuit of Happiness.* New York: Basic Books, 1995. The standard study on childlessness, including treatment of infertility, sterilization, and adoption.

The New American Family: Significant and Diversified Lifestyles. New York: Simmons Market Research Bureau, 1992. Drawn mainly from government sources, this work includes various tables and charts on shopping habits, income, and marital status for groups such as new mothers, baby boomers, empty nesters, and teens.

Rosenblatt, Paul C., Terri A. Karis, and Richard D. Powell. *Multiracial Couples: Black and White Voices.* Thousand Oaks, Calif.: Sage Publications, 1995. Based on extensive interviews with twenty-one interracial couples, this study analyzes the reasons behind a still uncommon practice in the United States, ultimately arguing against the racism that prevents understanding.

Seward, Rudy R. *The American Family: A Demographic History.* Beverly Hills, Calif.: Sage Publications, 1978. Incorporates the technique of family reconstruction through the collection of many fragments of information, such as births, marriages, and deaths.

Tessina, Tina. *Gay Relationships for Men and Women: How to Find Them, How to Improve Them, How to Make Them Last.* Los Angeles: Jeremy P. Tarcher, 1989. A therapist offers advice on alternative relationships and examines the dynamics of gay unions.

Wagner, V., ed. *The Family in America: Opposing Viewpoints.* San Diego, Calif.: Greenhaven Press, 1992. Includes articles on how homosexual partners are changing America and on the changing definition of "family."

Wells, Robert V. *Revolutions in Americans' Lives.* Westport, Conn.: Greenwood Press, 1982. The author provides a "demographic perspective on the history of Americans, their families, and their society."

_____. *Uncle Sam's Family: Issues in and Perspectives on American Demographic History.* Albany: State University of New York Press, 1985. Continues the examination of changing demographic trends begun in *Revolutions in Americans' Lives*.

Weston, K. *Families We Choose: Lesbians, Gays, Kinship*. New York: Columbia University Press, 1991. Reexamines the traditional definition of "family" in light of the growing acceptance of same-sex unions.

7. HEALTH, MEDICINE, AND THE FAMILY

Abortion. San Diego, Calif.: Greenhaven Press, 1997. An anthology of published writing by experts, presenting arguments for and against various policies and practices related to abortion. Topics include "Is Abortion Immoral?", "Should Abortion Rights Be Restricted?", and "Is Abortion Safe for Women?" Bibliography, illustrations, and list of organizations. A good starting point for research.

Ackerman, Nathan. *The Psychodynamics of Family Life*. New York: Basic Books, 1958. Revolutionized the treatment of mental disorders by encouraging psychiatrists to treat clients in the light of family process dynamics.

Alecson, Deborah Golden. *Lost Lullaby*. Berkeley: University of California Press, 1995. A moving study of a mother and father as they wrestle with the ethics of medical decision making following the birth of a daughter with severe brain damage.

Armstrong-Dailey, Ann, and Sarah Zarbock. *Hospice Care for Children*. New York: Oxford University Press, 1993. Emphasizes the various roles of family, volunteers, and health care providers in treating terminally ill children. Written by the founder of Children's Hospice International.

Aronheim, Judith, and Doron Weber. *Final Passages: Positive Choices for the Dying and Their Loved Ones*. New York: Simon & Schuster, 1992. Wonders at the effort of those around the dying to empathize with their plight. Considers the effort to legalize the right to die a "serious health threat."

Barnes, Grace M., and Diane K. Augustino, ed. *Alcohol and the Family: A Comprehensive Bibliography*. New York: Greenwood Press, 1987. Covers more than six thousand books, articles, and book chapters.

Brock, George W., ed. *American Association for Marriage and Family Therapy Ethics Casebook*. Washington, D.C.: American Association for Marriage and Family Therapy, 1994. Outlines the eight core principles, discussing the development of the code of ethics, results of a survey of therapists, list of procedures, decision tree, and questionnaires.

Callahan, Daniel. *Setting Limits: Medical Goals in an Aging Society*. New York: Simon & Schuster, 1987. Argues that in an age of declining resources, medical goals for treating the elderly should focus on preventive care and relief of suffering rather than on prolonging life without quality. Nominated for a Pulitzer Prize in 1987.

Caring for Kids with Special Needs: Residential Treatment Programs for Children and Adolescents. Princeton, N.J.: Peterson's Guides, 1993. Designed for parents and health care professionals, this work describes U.S. and Canadian facilities that deal with behavior disorders, substance abuse, depression, and other disorders. Provides a reference chart for 817 facilities. A section on program profiles includes descriptions of treatment programs, staff, facilities, and program costs.

Dallos, Rudi. *Family Belief Systems, Therapy, and Change: A Constructional Approach*. Milton Keynes, England: Open University Press, 1991. Explores "the intimate relationships in families from the standpoint of the people 'inside' them." Includes "Images of Families and the Family Life Cycle" and "Exploring Family Belief Systems."

Gaylin, Willard, and Ruth Macklin. *Who Speaks for the Child? The Problem of Proxy Consent*. New York: Plenum Press, 1982. Examines the difficult question of when a child should become part of the medical decision-making process.

Gladding, S. T. *Family Therapy: History, Theory, and Practice*. Englewood Cliffs, N.J.: Prentice Hall, 1995. An up-to-date text that comprehensively surveys the field in a surprisingly readable style. Particularly strong on recently published literature and on legal and professional issues. Includes sections on individual and family life cycles, healthy and dysfunctional families, the history of family therapy, and the variety of therapy techniques. Also includes the Codes of Ethics for the American Association for Marriage and Family Therapists and the International Association of Marriage and Family Counselors.

Goldstein, Eleanor, with Kevin Farmer. *Confabulations: Creating False Memories, Destroying Families*.

Boca Raton, Fla.: Sirs, 1994. Psychotherapists argue that a code of ethics is needed in the profession regarding unsubstantiated accusations based upon repressed memories. Argues that "books, tapes and seminars that are programmed for specific objectives are improper tools for psychotherapy."

Gormley, Myra Vanderpool. *Family Diseases: Are You at Risk?* Baltimore, Md.: Genealogical Publishing, 1989. This guide both describes hereditary illnesses and provides help in researching family disorders. Includes a number of charts, checklists, and addresses for helpful organizations.

Hobfoll, Stevan E., ed. *Stress, Social Support, and Women.* Cambridge, Mass.: Hemisphere Publishing, 1986. Fifteen articles by a wide range of experts, divided into five categories: "Developmental Issues in the Adjustment of Women," "Career, Marriage, and Family Stressors," "Violence Toward Women," "Women's Health," and "Bereavement and Old Age."

Hymovich, Debra P., and Gloria A. Hagopian. *Chronic Illness in Children and Adults: A Psychosocial Approach.* Philadelphia: W. B. Saunders, 1992. Analyzes chronic conditions and how they affect family life. Utilizes advanced academic techniques. Includes a chapter on "The Family System."

Jamison, Stephen. *The Final Acts of Love: Families and Assisted Dying.* New York: Putnam, 1996. Controversial book by a psychologist who has been close to a number of cases of assisted suicide. Suggests what those assisting in suicide should do in order to remain emotionally strong after the event.

Kabat-Zinn, Jon. *Full Catastrophe Living: Using the Wisdom of Your Body and Mind to Face Stress, Pain, and Illness.* New York: Delacorte Press, 1990. The founder of the Stress Reduction Clinic at the University of Massachusetts offers a program for reducing the ill effects of stress.

Kohl, Marvin, ed. *Infanticide and the Value of Life.* Buffalo, N.Y.: Prometheus Books, 1978. Examines the ethical problems involved in determining the potential quality of one's life and suggests protective measures for the most vulnerable human beings. Examines separately religious/ethical, medical/anthropological, psychological, legal, and ideological/philosophical subject areas.

Landau, Elaine. *The Right to Die.* Danbury, Conn.: Franklin Watts, 1993. Comprehensive survey of the issue for younger readers, including a discussion of the various forms of suicide and euthanasia and the denial of treatment for disabled infants.

Lauritzen, Paul. *Pursuing Parenthood: Ethical Issues in Assisted Reproduction.* Bloomington: Indiana University Press, 1993. Clear examination of the ethical issues evolving along with increasing levels of human reproductive technology.

Logue, Barbara J. *Last Rights: Death Control and the Elderly in America.* New York: Lexington Books, 1993. Extensive examination of the aging process and its impact on persons' wish to die or to assist others in dying. Includes suggestions for communicating end-of-life wishes to family members and friends. Based upon extensive research.

Lubin, Bernard. *Family Therapy: A Bibliography, 1937-1986.* New York: Greenwood Press, 1988. Comprehensive work including 6,167 cross-referenced entries. Author and subject indexes.

Marker, Rita L. *Deadly Compassion: The Death of Ann Humphry and the Truth About Euthanasia.* New York: William Morrow, 1993. Account of the dissolution of the marriage of Humphry and the co-founder of the Hemlock Society and Humphry's eventual suicide. Based on extensive interviews and written by an outspoken opponent of euthanasia.

Miermont, Jacques. *A Dictionary of Family Therapy.* Rev. ed. edited by Hugh Jenkins. Cambridge, Mass.: Blackwell, 1995. Designed for more advanced research, this work focuses on psychiatry within family and social circumstances. Originally published in French in 1987, the extensive bibliography is weighted with European and British studies.

Minuchin, Salvador, and Michael P. Nichols. *Family Healing.* New York: Simon & Schuster, 1993. Drawing upon a lifetime of work, this book explains the hidden rules that stifle development within families.

Moreno, Jonathan D., ed. *Arguing Euthanasia: The Controversy over Mercy Killing, Assisted Suicide, and the "Right to Die."* New York: Simon & Schuster, 1995. Book that discusses the hotly-contested issues surrounding euthanasia.

Muldoon, Maureen. *The Abortion Debate in the United States and Canada: A Source Book.* New

York: Garland, 1991. Chapters concerning demographics, sociological research, opinions, philosophical perspectives, law, politics, religious positions, and advocacy groups each contain bibliographies and notes. General index.

Mullens, Anne. *When Timely Death? A Consideration of Our Last Rights.* Toronto: Knopf Canada, 1996. An important book by a prize-winning Canadian medical reporter, integrating numerous in-depth interviews. Funded by an Atkinson Foundation Award for Public Policy, the author did extensive research in Canada, the United States, the Netherlands, and in other countries.

Page, Penny Booth. *Children of Alcoholics: A Sourcebook.* New York: Garland, 1991. Chapters include annotated entries of books, articles, and pamphlets from 1969 to 1990, covering family issues, treatment, recovery, and general reference.

Rae, Scott B. *The Ethics of Commercial Surrogate Motherhood: Brave New Families?* Westport, Conn.: Praeger, 1994. Discusses the legal status of surrogate motherhood and changes in parent and child law.

Rothman, Barbara Katz, ed. *Encyclopedia of Childbearing: Critical Perspectives.* Phoenix, Ariz.: Oryx Press, 1993. About 250 articles treat the subject from a multidisciplinary approach, including topics on amniocentesis, the antiabortion movement, cesarean birth, midwife-attended birth, and imaging techniques. General index.

Satir, Virginia. *Conjoint Family Therapy.* Palo Alto, Calif.: Science and Behavior Books, 1964. The first major work to suggest the importance of seeing both members of a couple together at the same time during therapy. Highly readable, thus contributing to its influence.

Sauber, S. Richard, Luciano L'Abate, Gerald R. Weeks, and William L. Buchanan, eds. *The Dictionary of Family Psychology and Family Therapy.* 2d ed. Newbury Park, Calif.: Sage Publications, 1993. Defines often confusing terminology in the context of its original use.

Sherman, Barbara Smiley. *Directory of Residential Treatment Facilities for Emotionally Handicapped Children and Youth.* Phoenix, Ariz.: Oryx Press, 1988. Arranged by state, this work provides addresses, types of placement, children served, tuition, setting, and referral requirements.

Stimmel, Barry. *The Facts About Drug Use: Coping with Drugs and Alcohol in Your Family, at Work, in Your Community.* New York: Haworth Press, 1993.

Written in lay language, part one classifies drugs and discusses symptoms, effects, and dependency; part two covers use patterns, preparations, withdrawal, and treatment; part three covers a variety of contemporary issues such as multiple drug use, AIDS, pregnancy, and the "war against drugs." First published in 1991 by *Consumer Reports.*

Stuart, Richard B., and Barbara Jacobson. *Weight, Sex, and Marriage.* New York: W. W. Norton, 1987. Analyzes weight loss in the context of family relationships, with particular attention to the subtle ways in which spouses undermine one another's efforts.

Substance Abuse and Kids: A Directory of Education, Information, Prevention, and Early Intervention Programs. Phoenix, Ariz.: Oryx Press, 1989. Descriptive program profiles of services for children to age eighteen, including information on addresses and phone numbers, personnel, age/grade level served, and staffing.

Substance Abuse Residential Treatment Centers for Teens. Phoenix, Ariz.: Oryx Press, 1990. Covers more than one thousand residential and inpatient programs for treating alcohol, drug, and behavioral disorders. Includes contact information, date established, parent organization, affiliations, licensure, addictions treated, fees, and follow-up.

Trager, Oliver, ed. *Abortion: Choice and Conflict.* New York: Facts On File, 1993. Provides full text of editorials and cartoons from leading U.S. newspapers. Divided into sections: "Abortion and the Courts," "Politics and Abortion," "Pro-Life v. Pro-Choice," and "Health, Youth, and Abortion." Well indexed.

Tribe, Laurence H. *Abortion: The Clash of Absolutes.* New York: W. W. Norton, 1990. This Harvard law professor reviews the social and legal aspects of abortion, pointing to the Supreme Court's 1992 decision in *Planned Parenthood v. Casey* as a turning point in the debate, affirming the legality of abortion but allowing new state freedoms to restrict it.

8. HISTORY, KINSHIP, AND GENEALOGY

Abin, Mel, and Dominick Cavello, eds. *Family Life in America, 1620-2000.* New York: Revisionary Press, 1981. Contains a wide range of articles by experts on various aspects of the history of the family, including an article by Eugene Genovese on the roles of slaves as husbands, wives, and parents.

Achenbaum, W. Andrew. *Shades of Gray: Old Age, American Values, and Federal Policies Since 1920.* Boston: Little, Brown, 1983. Traces the development of government policy on aging, including the impact of the Depression and President Ronald Reagan's policies. Outlines a "modernization model" for developing future policy.

Adler, Mortimer, ed. *The Great Ideas: A Syntopicon of Great Books of the Western World.* Chicago: Encyclopedia Britannica, 1952. Provides a good bibliography of classical Western ideas of the family, which form the basis of family life among North Americans of European descent.

American Family History: A Historical Bibliography. Santa Barbara, Calif.: ABC-Clio, 1984. More than 1,100 references divided into four categories: "The Family in Historical Perspective," "The Family and Other Social Institutions," "Familial Roles and Relationships," and "Individual Family Histories."

Beauvoir, Simone de. *The Second Sex.* 2 vols. New York: Alfred A. Knopf, 1953. First published in France in 1949, this pathbreaking book contains the noted existentialist's plea that women not yield to the "eternal feminine" of motherhood, but rather choose their manner of living.

Benson-von der Ohe, Elizabeth, and Valmari M. Mason. *An Annotated Bibliography of U.S. Scholarship on the History of the Family.* New York: AMS Press, 1986. Detailed descriptive annotations of journal articles, books, book chapters, and dissertations from 1975 to 1983.

Bremner, Robert, et al. *Children and Youth in America: A Documentary History.* 3 vols. Cambridge, Mass.: Harvard University Press, 1970-1974. The best overview of the history of children in the United States.

Calhoun, Arthur W. *A Social History of the American Family from Colonial Times to the Present.* 3 vols. Cleveland: Arthur H. Clark, 1917-1919. Long considered the definitive history of the American family, this work perpetuated a number of stereotypes that have since been disproved or modified by more extensive research. Characterized the century-long shift in American family policy as a "movement of political democracy" in which the individual was the principal social unit. The "new view," he suggested, was "that the higher and more obligatory relation is to society rather than to the family."

Cayton, Mary Kupiec, Elliott J. Gorn, and Peter W. Williams. *Encyclopedia of American Social History.* 3 vols. New York: Charles Scribner's Sons, 1993. One section devoted specifically to "Family History," with extensive essays on "Family Structures," "Gender Roles and Relations," "Sexual Behavior and Morality," "Courtship, Marriage, Separation, and Divorce," "Reproduction and Parenthood," "Life Stages," "Childhood and Children," "Adolescence," "Old Age," and "Death."

Clark, Clifford Edward, Jr. *The American Family Home, 1800-1960.* Chapel Hill: University of North Carolina Press, 1986. Looks at family values embodied in the house itself. The fifties house, for instance, with its low-pitched roofs, attached carports, and fences gave "a sheltered look," which exuded isolation, privacy, and containment.

Degler, Carl N. *At Odds: Women and the Family in America from the Revolution to the Present.* New York: Oxford University Press, 1980. The first comprehensive treatment grouping these two distinct but related topics. The author draws together a wide array of contemporary evidence including handbooks, manuals, personal letters, and diaries to demonstrate how modern conceptions of women and family are often at odds with their historical ideals.

D'Emilio, John, and Estelle B. Freedman. *Intimate Matters: A History of Sexuality in America.* 2d ed. Chicago: University of Chicago Press, 1997. This standard history of American sexuality sheds much light on the formation and maintenance of families as well as on the shaping of social and cultural patterns.

Demos, John. *A Little Commonwealth: Family Life in Plymouth.* New York: Oxford University Press, 1970. A pioneering monographic study that dispelled many myths about the family in early America through a penetrating study of the complete range of evidence. Provides a detailed description of the range of family activities and functions that have been taken over by specialized institutions.

_____. *Past, Present, and Personal: The Family and the Life Course in American History.* New York: Oxford University Press, 1986. A collection of studies, most of which were previously published in journals during the 1970's and 1980's. Stresses the gradual and evolutionary change in the American family that make it difficult to precisely identify the emergence of the "modern" family.

Doane, Gilbert H., and James B. Bell. *Searching for Your Ancestors: The How and Why of Genealogy.* 5th ed. Minneapolis: University of Minnesota Press, 1980. A standard reference since the first edition of 1937, this revision includes information on more than thirty-five ethnic groups. A particularly accessible book, because it is written with a common-sense approach and is divided into two sections: "How to Search for Your Ancestors" and "Special Searches." Chapter thirteen covers the search for ethnic roots among Native Americans, Canadians, Mexicans, Puerto Ricans, and Cubans. Chapter fourteen focuses on genealogical searches in twenty-eight countries outside the Western Hemisphere.

Eakle, Arlene, and Johni Cerny, eds. *The Source: A Guidebook of American Genealogy.* Salt Lake City, Utah: Ancestry, 1984. A thorough resource compiled by experienced genealogists, this work provides an introduction for beginning researchers. The core is divided into three sections: major record sources (including family sources such as cemetery records and marriage and divorce records); a seventy-page list of genealogical sources; and special resources relating to the research of Native American, Spanish and Mexican American, Jewish American, African American, and Asian American families.

Eichholz, Alice, ed. *Ancestry's Red Book: American State, County, and Town Records.* Salt Lake City, Utah: Ancestry, 1989. Includes ten regional overviews, with a historical summary for each state and discussions, lists, and addresses for obtaining records. Brief descriptions of census records, archives, maps, and church records.

Engels, Frederick. *The Origin of the Family, Private Property, and the State.* Chicago: C. H. Kerr, 1902. Originally published in 1884, this work contains the classic Marxist interpretation of the family as a component of economic society.

Filby, P. William, comp. *American and British Genealogy and Heraldry: A Selected List of Books.* 3d ed. Boston: New England Historic Genealogical Society, 1983. Including references to almost ten thousand genealogical sources, this classic bibliography includes a substantial number of entries on Canadian, American, and British sources.

Filby, P. William, and Mary K. Meyer, eds. *Passenger and Immigration Lists Index.* Detroit: Gale Research, 1981. Originally published in three volumes, now annually supplemented. Includes more than two million names of immigrants arriving in the United States and Canada, mainly from the seventeenth through the nineteenth centuries, arranged alphabetically and drawn from more than three hundred sources.

Fildes, Valerie A. *Breasts, Bottles, and Babies: A History of Infant Feeding.* Edinburgh, Scotland: Edinburgh University Press, 1986. The first thorough history of infant feeding, paying particular attention to changing perceptions and attitudes.

Fisher, Helen. *Anatomy of Love: A Natural History of Mating, Marriage, and Why We Stray.* New York: W. W. Norton, 1992. An anthropological view linking sexual behavior with evolution; determines that serial monogamy has been the norm. As an ethnologist, the author assumes that "human beings have a common nature, a set of shared *unconscious* tendencies . . . encoded in our DNA."

Gordon, Linda. *Heroes of Their Own Lives: The Politics and History of Family Violence, Boston 1880-1960.* New York: Viking, 1988. A model historical examination of one locality; for similar coverage on a broader scope see Elizabeth Pleck's *Domestic Violence,* below.

_____. *Pitied but Not Entitled: Single Mothers and the History of Welfare.* New York: Free Press, 1994. A noted historian examines government attitudes and policies toward single mothers.

_____. *Woman's Body, Woman's Right: A Social History of Birth Control in America.* Rev. ed. New York: Penguin, 1990. First published in 1976, this was the first detailed examination of the birth control movement. A thorough book, the family is treated throughout, unlike many more modern works on the same subject.

Gordon, Michael, ed. *The American Family in Social-Historical Perspective.* 3d ed. New York: St. Martin's Press, 1983. Includes a series of articles by specialists dealing with such topics as affection between parents and children in the Chesapeake region, parental power and marriage patterns in early Massachusetts, and the nineteenth century cult of true womanhood.

Griswold, Robert L. *Fatherhood in America: A History.* New York: Basic Books, 1993. Examines changing paternal roles and stereotypes throughout history.

Grossberg, Michael. *Governing the Hearth: Law and Family in Nineteenth-Century America.* Chapel Hill: University of North Carolina Press, 1985. In attempting to explain the creation of domestic-relations law, the author takes a broad approach, examining the "major instruments of policy making": appellate court opinions, legislative acts, commission reports, political commentaries, and public and professional journals, treatises, and polemics.

Guide to Genealogical Research in the National Archives, rev. ed. U.S. National Archives and Records Service. Washington, D.C.: National Archives Trust Fund Board, 1985. A well-organized introduction to the records of the National Archives. This is the premier guide to federal records, including guides to passenger arrival lists, naturalization records, military records, land and court records, and records of the Bureau of Indian Affairs.

Handlin, Oscar. *The Uprooted.* 2d ed. Boston: Little, Brown, 1973. A widely influential book that caricatured the immigrant family as a collection of socially uprooted newcomers, overwhelmed by the forces of industrialization and urbanization.

Hawes, Joseph M. *The Children's Rights Movement: A History of Advocacy and Protection.* Boston: Twayne, 1991. A highly readable introduction that traces the historical development of the children's rights movement from the foundation of child protection laws in the seventeenth century to the role of big government in the twentieth. Contains a chronology and an extensive bibliographic essay.

Hawes, Joseph M., and N. Ray Hinter, eds. *Children in Historical and Comparative Perspective: An International Handbook and Research Guide.* New York: Greenwood Press, 1991. Includes specific chapters on Canada and the United States, which serve as updates and extensions of the authors' *American Childhood: A Research Guide and Historical Handbook* (1985).

Hawes, Joseph M., and Elizabeth I. Nybakken. *American Families: A Research Guide and Historical Handbook.* Westport, Conn.: Greenwood Press, 1991. In eleven chapters, the authors synthesize the literature of the discipline, the range of methodologies, the family during specific historical periods, and a wide range of special topics such as "women and families," "African American families," "Native American families," and "immigrant working class families."

Hewitt, Nancy A., ed. *Women, Families, and Communities: Readings in American History.* Glenview, Ill.: Scott, Foresman, 1990. With a selection of readings, the author examines major themes in American history by looking at "the ways that ordinary mothers, wives, and daughters contributed to the development of their families and communities." Contains a number of articles on immigrant and minority families.

Hey, David. *The Oxford Guide to Family History.* Oxford, England: Oxford University Press, 1993. Simple but authoritative guide to research in family history in encyclopedic form. Filled with suggestions for unorthodox sources of information; focus on British family history.

Howard, George Elliott. *A History of Matrimonial Institutions.* 3 vols. Chicago: University of Chicago Press, 1904. Represented the advent of the social scientist as a new authority in making legal judgments about marriage.

Kaminkow, Marion J., ed. *Genealogies in the Library of Congress: A Bibliography.* Baltimore, Md.: Magna Carta, 1972. A comprehensive bibliography of family histories from the United States and Great Britain, including more than twenty thousand items.

Kemp, Thomas J. *International Vital Records Handbook.* Genealogical Publishing, 1990. A practical guide to obtaining vital records from the United States, Canada, and sixty-six other countries. Includes many forms that can be photocopied when applying for materials.

Lamphere, Louise. *From Working Daughters to Working Mothers: Immigrant Women in a New England Industrial Community.* Ithaca, N.Y.: Cornell University Press, 1987. A detailed study of both family and work spheres of women in the industrial community of Central Falls, Rhode Island, from 1915 to the late 1970's. Pays particular attention to the French-Canadian and Polish communities in the earlier period and to the Portuguese and Colombian communities in the more recent period.

McLaren, Angus. *A History of Contraception: From Antiquity to the Present Day.* Oxford, England: Basil Blackwell, 1990. Unlike many such histories, this work posits that there have always been societies that at some point have taken steps to limit their offspring and that each age "gave its own meaning to effective family planning."

Mason, Mary Ann. *From Father's Property to Children's Rights: The History of Child Custody in the United States.* New York: Columbia University Press, 1994. Beginning with the assumption that social attitudes and legal norms relating to the triangular relationships between parents, children, and the state provide "the basis of social continuity within a nation," the author traces the evolution of legal rules on custody and control of children.

May, Elaine Tyler. *Homeward Bound: American Families in the Cold War Era.* New York: Basic Books, 1988. A thorough historical account of the American family adjusting to peace, prosperity, and the baby boom; suggests that Cold War tensions "prompted Americans to create a family-centered culture."

Meltzer, Milton. *Cheap Raw Material: How Our Youngest Workers Are Exploited and Abused.* New York: Viking, 1994. Links contemporary attempts to end labor exploitation of children to the historical practice of industrial America and the ancient world.

Mintz, Steven, and Susan Kellogg. *Domestic Revolutions: A Social History of American Family Life.* New York: Free Press, 1988. Superb and highly readable overview of the American family from the seventeenth to the late twentieth century. The authors argue that the changes in the American family that became prominent during the 1970's and 1980's have in fact been developing for three hundred years.

Moch, Leslie Page, and Gary D. Stark, eds. *Essays on the Family and Historical Change.* Arlington: Texas A&M University Press, 1983. A collection of articles by specialists, including John Modell's "Dating Becomes the Way of American Youth."

Moore, Gloria, and Ronald Moore, eds. *Margaret Sanger and the Birth Control Movement: A Bibliography, 1911-1984.* Metuchen, N.J.: Scarecrow Press, 1986. Includes 1,300 entries written by and about Margaret Sanger. For the period until her death, entries are grouped by year, with Sanger's writings first.

Mount, Ferdinand. *The Subversive Family: An Alternative History of Love and Marriage.* New York: Free Press, 1992. A British journalist argues against much of the revisionist history of the family.

Nasaw, David. *Children of the City at Work and at Play.* Garden City, N.Y.: Anchor/Doubleday, 1985. Strong on early twentieth century urban life, the author examines the significance of adults' and children's shared street and tenement space.

Neagles, James C., and Mark C. Neagles. *The Library of Congress: A Guide to Genealogical and Historical Research.* Salt Lake City, Utah: Ancestry, 1990. This work "describes significant materials in the Local History and Genealogy Reading Room," as well as other parts of the Library of Congress. Part three describes "key source materials by region and state."

Palmer, Phyllis. *Domesticity and Dirt: Housewives and Domestic Servants in the United States, 1920-1945.* Philadelphia: Temple University Press, 1989. Demonstrates how women of color historically have been thought of differently from other American women in the conception of work and family and are expected to put work before family.

Phillips, Roderick. *Putting Asunder: A History of Divorce in Western Society.* New York: Cambridge University Press, 1988. Authoritative account linking the rise of divorce to other historical movements such as secularization, industrialization, and feminism.

Pleck, Elizabeth. *Domestic Violence: The Making of American Social Policy Against Family Violence from Colonial Times to the Present.* New York: Oxford University Press, 1987. Surveys principally the urban response to child abuse, including such groups as the Society for the Prevention of Cruelty to Children.

Pollock, Frederick, and Frederic W. Maitland. *The History of English Law Before the Time of Edward I.* 2 vols. Cambridge, England: Cambridge University Press, 1898. Traces the earliest developments in Western family law as it was passed down to the United States.

Riley, Glenda. *Divorce: An American Tradition.* New York: Oxford University Press, 1991. Traces the history of divorce in America from the early seventeenth century to the present; urges people to avoid moral judgments on divorce.

Rothman, Ellen. *Hands and Hearts: A History of Courtship in America.* New York: Basic Books, 1984. Demonstrates how the elaborate rules of "courtship" were transformed into a new category—"dating"—during the 1950's.

Schneider, D. M. *American Kinship: A Cultural Account.* 2d ed. Chicago: University of Chicago Press, 1980. Overview of American kinship as a cultural system. A brief introduction to the study of symbols associated with the family.

Scott, Donald M., and Bernard Wishy. *America's Families: A Documentary History.* New York: Harper & Row, 1981. Emphasizes the extent of family diversity from the earliest days of European settlement.

Smith, Jessie Carney, ed. *Ethnic Genealogy: A Research Guide.* Westport, Conn.: Greenwood Press, 1983. Deals specifically with problems confronting those searching for African American, American Indian, Asian American, or Hispanic ancestors, with separate extended chapters for each group.

Soliday, Gerald L., ed. *History of the Family and Kinship: A Select International Bibliography.* Millwood, N.Y.: Kraus International Publications, 1980. Begun as a special project of the *Journal of Family History*, this bibliography of some 6,200 entries represents the first generation of work in the field of family history. Includes sections specifically devoted to "Theoretical and Comparative Works," "Canada," and the "United States."

Stead, William T. *If Christ Came to Chicago.* Chicago: Laird and Lee, 1894. Muckraking by a respected British journalist, who demonstrated how "very little reverence" there was for children in Chicago and, by implication, in other American cities.

Stearns, Peter N. *Encyclopedia of Social History.* New York: Garland, 1994. Extensive guide by a noted social historian. A wide range of family-related topics is covered, including ancestor worship, divorce, extended family, generations, godparenting, kinship, naming practices, and inheritance systems. Each entry includes a brief bibliography.

Steinfels, Margaret O'Brien. *Who's Minding the Children: The History and Politics of Day Care in America.* New York: Simon & Schuster, 1973. The principal history of day care in America.

Stone, Lawrence. *The Family, Sex, and Marriage in England, 1500-1800.* New York: Harper & Row, 1977. The classic account of the English family at the time of the settlement of North America.

Sutton, John R. *Stubborn Children: Controlling Delinquency in the United States, 1640-1981.* Berkeley: University of California Press, 1988. Demonstrates the historical roots of many American attitudes, originating with the Massachusetts stubborn child law.

Trattner, Walter I. *Crusade for the Children: A History of the National Child Labor Committee and Child Labor Reform in America.* Chicago: Quadrangle Books, 1970. Standard history which provides much testimony and analysis of the relationship between family and labor.

Weiner, Lynn Y. *From Working Girl to Working Mother: The Female Labor Force in the United States, 1820-1980.* Chapel Hill: University of North Carolina Press, 1985. Traces the merging of the rhetoric of patriarchal middle-class society with the reality of women in the American workplace.

Welfeld, Irving. *Where We Live: A Social History of American Housing.* New York: Simon & Schuster, 1988. The author, a policy analyst for the U.S. government's Department of Housing and Urban Development, suggests the power of housing in shaping the social landscape.

Westermarck, Edward. *The History of Human Marriage.* 5th ed. 3 vols. London: Macmillan, 1921. A useful, extensive survey of the history of marriage to 1900.

Wishy, Bernard. *The Child and the Republic: The Dawn of Modern American Child Nurture.* Philadelphia: University of Pennsylvania Press, 1968. Traces the dawning of a new era in American family life, when children were viewed as innocents and not simply as little adults.

9. Law and the Family

Avery, Rosemary J., ed. *Adoption Policy and Special Needs Children.* Westport, Conn.: Auburn House, 1997. Written by a former worker in a New York state agency, this work seeks to widen the knowledge of adoption policies that have focused traditionally on infant adoptions.

Blackstone, William. *Commentaries on the Laws of England.* 4 vols. Chicago: University of Chicago Press, 1979. The authoritative commentary on English law, first published in 1769, which formed the foundation of much of family law in the United States; rejected entirely the notion that marriage was sacramental and sacrosanct, instead believing that it should be defined by civil contract.

Buzawa, Eve S., and Carl G. Buzawa, eds. *Domestic Violence: The Changing Criminal Justice Response.*

Westport, Conn.: Auburn House, 1992. Includes an article on "The Court's Response to Interpersonal Violence."

Clark, Homer H., Jr. *Law of Domestic Relations.* 2d ed. 2 vols. St. Paul, Minn.: West, 1987. Demonstrates how American law incorporated British family law, despite the lack of ecclesiastical courts. See also the abridged student edition (1988).

Curry, Hayden, Denis Clifford, and Robin Leonard. *A Legal Guide for Lesbian and Gay Couples.* 9th ed. Berkeley, Calif.: Nolo Press, 1996. Intended for general readers, this how-to manual was prepared to help lesbian and gay couples in "taking charge of the legal aspects of their lives." Includes chapters on creating families, gay parenting, estate planning, buying a home, heterosexual marriages, and going separate ways. Also contains sample documents for preparing durable powers of attorney, proxies for health care, wills, codicils, and cohabitation agreements.

Dolgin, J. L. "The Family in Transition from *Griswold* to *Eisenstadt* and Beyond." *The Georgetown Law Journal* 82 (1994).

Family Diversity Project. *Official Registration of Families with the Secretary of State, May 1991.* Describes how nontraditional families can register as nonprofit associations with the California secretary of state.

Fischer, Louis, and Gail Paulus Sorenson. *School Law for Counselors, Psychologists, and Social Workers.* 3d ed. New York: Longman, 1996. Contains an extended examination of the Family Educational Rights and Privacy Act of 1974.

Garrow, David J. *Liberty and Sexuality: The Right to Privacy and the Making of Roe v. Wade.* New York: Macmillan, 1994. The definitive legal history of the decision on abortion, beginning with the legal debates of the 1920's and 1930's and concluding with a chapter on "Liberality and Sexuality Since *Roe v. Wade.*" Includes an extensive bibliography and more than two hundred pages of notes. Essential.

Glanzer, Perry L. *Parental Rights and Public Education.* Colorado Springs, Colo.: Focus on the Family, 1996. A twenty-nine-page summary of the parent's rights movement from the perspective of a conservative Christian organization.

Glendon, Mary A. *The Transformation of Family Law: State, Law, and Family in the United States and Western Europe.* Chicago: University of Chicago Press, 1989. Emphasizes the importance of ethnic diversity in the transformation of family law and views the 1960's as a watershed in the transformation of ideas that had remained relatively static for centuries. The author focuses on England, France, Germany, and the United States but examines other policies as in the Scandinavian system, in which there is "genuine judicial supervision of the spouses' financial arrangements for children."

Hilton, N. Zoe, ed. *Legal Responses to Wife Assault: Current Trends and Evaluation.* Newbury Park, Calif.: Sage Publications, 1993. This work is designed to "promote appropriate and effective legal responses to wife assault." Each chapter begins with a review of trends and literature before dealing with the various questions from the position of contributors' own expertise. Separate sections deal with the police, the courts, and victims.

Houlgate, Laurence D. *Family and State: The Philosophy of Family Law.* Totowa, N.J.: Rowman & Littlefield, 1988. Out of the 1980's debate over whether domestic relations law should be individualistically or family based, the author seeks to create a new point of examination in the philosophy of family law. Authoritative but clearly written, each chapter is introduced with a representative court case.

Jacob, Herbert. *Silent Revolution: The Transformation of Divorce Law in the United States.* Chicago: University of Chicago Press, 1988. Examines the nature of policy making in the United States to demonstrate why divorce law changed so dramatically after 1965. Based upon government documents, legal and scholarly literature, and extensive interviews with individuals involved in bringing about change.

Leonard, Robin D., and Stephen R. Elias. *Family Law Dictionary: Marriage, Divorce, Children, and Living Together.* Berkeley, Calif.: Nolo Press, 1988. Two lawyers define more than five hundred legal terms and phrases relating to family law. Clearer than *Black's Law Dictionary*, which is designed for law students and professionals.

Lerman, Lisa. *Prosecution of Spouse Abuse: Innovations in Criminal Justice Response.* Washington, D.C.: Center for Women Policy Studies, 1981. Demonstrates that although there have been reforms in policy to protect abused spouses, much of the public and many police officers still believe that spousal disagreements are best handled privately.

Millman, Linda Josephson. *Legal Issues and Older Adults*. Santa Barbara, Calif.: ABC-Clio, 1992. Part one addresses such issues as health care, housing, family law, and legal services; part two lists related private and government organizations. Bibliography.

O'Donnell, William J., and David A. Jones. *The Law of Marriage and Marital Alternatives*. Lexington, Mass.: D. C. Heath, 1982. This work dealing with the rising tide of alternatives to marriage is valuable for clearly defining a number of variables such as legalistic, ceremonialized, common-law, proxy, putative, companionate, liberalized, and technical models of marriage.

Robinson, Lelia. *The Law of Husband and Wife, Compiled for Popular Use*. Boston, 1899. Emphasized judicial bias toward paternal authority, "because it is so generally the case that the money, property, income, means of support, and education are in the father's possession rather than the mother's."

Samuelson, Elliot D. *Unmarried Couples: A Guide to Your Legal Rights and Obligations*. New York: Insight Books, 1992. Addresses special issues related to unmarried domestic partners, including prenuptial agreements, adoption, custody, inheritance, and pensions. Appendices include a list of common law marriage states, state provisions to enact living wills, and sample forms.

Schouler, James. *A Treatise on the Law of Domestic Relations*. 5th ed. Boston: Little, Brown, 1895. Offering a summary of family law at the end of the nineteenth century, the author argues that "the law of the family is universal. . . . The ties of wife and child are for all classes and conditions; neither rank, wealth, nor social influence weighs heavily in the scales."

Sloan, Irving J. *Living Together: Unmarrieds and the Law*. Dobbs Ferry, N.Y.: Oceana, 1980. Emanating out of the *Marvin v. Marvin* cohabitation case, this brief work seeks to indicate what rights unmarried cohabitants possess. Useful in research regarding this famous case and its impact. Appendices include copies of the judicial decision, the trial court judgment and opinions, and copies of decisions in *Hewitt v. Hewitt* and *McCall v. Frampton*.

Sugarman, Stephen D., and Herma Hill Kay, eds. *Divorce Reform at the Crossroads*. New Haven, Conn.: Yale University Press, 1990. A collection of essays by professors of law, which examine the larger implications of no-fault divorce. Following an overview, the authors cover topics dealing with custodial arrangements, the economics of divorce, the law's perception of "family" after divorce, and child support.

Taylor, Bonnie B. *Education and the Law: A Dictionary*. Santa Barbara, Calif.: ABC-Clio, 1996. Beginning with an overview of the history and sources of education law, the author provides starting points for research into related issues. Includes an extensive alphabetical listing of important cases in education law.

Ten Broek, Jacobus. *Family Law and the Poor*, edited by Joel F. Handler. Westport, Conn: Greenwood Press, 1971. Pathbreaking series of articles first published in 1964 and 1965 in the *Stanford Law Review* demonstrating that the law discriminated against the poor on the basis of their poverty, in violation of the Fourteenth Amendment to the United States Constitution. Lays the foundation with a discussion of Poor Law and Common Law in Elizabethan England.

Wallerstein, Judith S., and Sandra Blakeslee. *Second Chances: Men, Women, and Children a Decade After Divorce—Who Wins, Who Loses—And Why*. New York: Ticknor & Fields, 1989. Defining contribution to the debate over long-term psychological effects of divorce on children; controversial.

Wardle, Lynn D., Christopher L. Blakesley, and Jacqueline Y. Parker. *Contemporary Family Law: Principles, Policy, and Practice*. 4 vols. Deerfield, Ill.: Callaghan, 1988. Good survey of family law, which demonstrates the historical importance of common law.

10. PARENTING AND FAMILY RELATIONSHIPS

Akner, Lois F. *How to Survive the Loss of a Parent: A Guide for Adults*. New York: Quill, 1993. A manual for working through the natural grief associated with parental loss.

Alexander-Roberts, Colleen. *The Essential Adoption Handbook*. Dallas: Taylor, 1993. Written for prospective adoptive parents, this work draws upon the experiences of more than one hundred adoptive parents to provide suggestions, forms, and tips for smoothing the adoptive process. Includes information on single-parent adoptions.

At Issue: Domestic Violence. San Diego, Calif.: Greenhaven Press, 1996. In a relatively brief book, the editors bring together a wide variety of viewpoints on the incidence of spousal abuse. Articles are printed in their entirety with notes; extensive bibliography and annotated list of relevant organizations.

August, Eugene R. *Men's Studies: A Selected and Annotated Interdisciplinary Bibliography.* Littleton, Colo.: Libraries Unlimited, 1985. Almost six hundred entries, including materials on men's rights, divorce and custody, and men in families.

Bart, P. B., and E. G. Moran, eds. *Violence Against Women: The Bloody Footprints.* Newbury Park, Calif.: Sage Publications, 1993. Contains articles on father-daughter incest.

Bartholet, Elizabeth. *Family Bonds: Adoption and the Politics of Parenting.* Boston: Houghton Mifflin, 1993. Argues that adoption should be seen "as a uniquely positive form of family" that is not necessarily inferior to the biological family.

Berry, Mary Frances. *The Politics of Parenthood.* New York: Viking, 1993. Demonstrates the way in which mythical perceptions of motherhood and the family affect policy.

Blankenhorn, David. *Fatherless America: Confronting Our Most Urgent Social Problem.* New York: Basic Books, 1995. Argues that America's most urgent challenge at the close of the twentieth century is the "re-creation of fatherhood as a vital social role for men," otherwise there will be "continued societal recession."

Bly, Robert. *The Sibling Society.* Reading, Mass.: Addison-Wesley, 1996. This noted explorer of human mythic sensibilities speaks out against U.S. culture, in which adults do not grow up, thus placing themselves in a tenuous moral position in relationship to their children.

Books to Help Children Cope with Separation and Loss: An Annotated Bibliography. 4th ed. New Providence, N.J.: R. R. Bowker, 1993. Refers to classic and modern works, many of which are readily available in public and school libraries.

Bradshaw, John. *Family Secrets: What You Don't Know Can Hurt You.* New York: Bantam Books, 1995. Argues that even small secrets can be destructive of relationships within a family. This counselor and theologian provides a step-by-step plan for constructively bringing secrets to light.

Bryan, Mark. *The Prodigal Father: Reuniting Fathers and Their Children.* New York: Clarkson Potter, 1997. Discusses the great burden absent fathers place on mothers; outlines an "emotional boot camp" for rebuilding relationships.

Buscaglia, Leo. *The Disabled and Their Parents: A Counseling Challenge.* 3d rev. ed. Thorofare, N.J.: C. B. Slack, 1994. This nationally famous counselor and lecturer urges parents to develop the innate potential of each child, rather than trying to fit them into particular molds. Inadequate counseling, he believes, leads to loss of human potential.

Canter, Lee, with Marlene Canter. *Assertive Discipline for Parents.* New York: Harper & Row, 1988. Suggests that by establishing family "law" and expecting children to live up to it, parents could avoid anger and punitive measures in child rearing.

Cardarelli, Albert P., ed. *Violence Between Intimate Partners: Patterns, Causes, and Effects.* Boston: Allyn & Bacon, 1997. Views family violence as a part of a "wider spectrum" that includes terrorist bombings, drive-by shootings, and other social acts of violence. The author argues that all intimate relationships carry the risk of violence as partners move through life in varied stages of intimacy. Contains an extensive bibliography.

Chadwick, Bruce A., and Tim B. Heaton, eds. *Statistical Handbook on Adolescents in America.* Phoenix, Ariz.: Oryx Press, 1996. Based on detailed statistics drawn from the 1990 U.S. Census and several public domain databases, this work examines a wide range of topics associated with adolescence. Sections include "Demographics," "Family Types," "Living Arrangements of Children and Adolescents," "Adolescents' Perceptions of Parents and Adults," "Parent-Child Conflict," "Adolescents' Household Chores and Allowance," "Adolescents' Involvement with Extended Family," and "Adoption."

De Young, Mary. *Incest: An Annotated Bibliography.* Jefferson, N.C.: McFarland, 1985. Covers mainly the period 1975-1985 and includes statistical studies, book reviews, and definitions.

Dobson, James. *Dare to Discipline.* New York: Bantam Books, 1977. First published in 1970, this is a practical, Christian-oriented book by a clinical professor of pediatrics against the permissive society. Explains why children crave firm control.

Dreikurs, Rudolf. *The Challenge of Parenthood.* New York: Plume/Penguin, 1992. Written in Austria during the 1930's, this work was a protest against the growth of fascism. This book was influential in the United States, especially during the 1950's, because the author believed that American democracy was a fruitful proving ground for new theories of child rearing, based on the notion of family councils and parliamentary order.

Engeldinger, Eugene A. *Spouse Abuse: An Annotated Bibliography of Violence Between Mates.* Metuchen, N.J.: Scarecrow Press, 1986. Extensive index of 1,783 entries including scholarly and popular English language books, theses, dissertations, government publications, articles, handbooks, and pamphlets through 1983. Name and subject indexes.

Finkbeiner, Ann K. *After the Death of a Child.* New York: Free Press, 1996. Based on extensive interviews and the latest in grief research, this study examines the short- and long-term changes that occur in relationships between parents after the death of a child.

Finkelhor, David, Richard J. Gelles, Gerald T. Hotaling, and Murray A. Straus, eds. *The Dark Side of Families: Current Family Violence Research.* Beverly Hills, Calif.: Sage Publications, 1983. Includes a chapter on "Violent Men or Violent Husbands."

Forward, Susan, with Craig Buck. *Toxic Parents.* New York: Bantam Books, 1989. Extreme account of how parents abuse their children, somewhat indiscriminately linking incest and beating with occasional moralizing and other forms of "psychological pressure."

Gelles, Richard J. *Family Violence.* 2d ed. Newbury Park, Calif.: Sage Publications, 1987. Shows that when women are isolated from social networks, they are more likely to be victims of violence.

_____. *The Violent Home: A Study of Physical Aggression Between Husbands and Wives.* Beverly Hills, Calif.: Sage Publications, 1974. Pioneering study in which the extent of acceptance of spousal abuse was brought to light.

Gelles, Richard J., and C. Cornell. *Intimate Violence in Families.* 3d ed. Newbury Park, Calif.: Sage Publications, 1997. Particularly valuable for its twenty-page bibliography.

Gelles, Richard J., and Donileen R. Loseke, eds. *Current Controversies on Family Violence.* Newbury Park, Calif.: Sage Publications, 1993. Includes an article suggesting that alcohol and other drugs are associated with violence but do not cause it.

Gelles, Richard J., and M. A. Straus. *Intimate Violence: The Causes and Consequences of Abuse in the American Family.* New York: Simon & Schuster, 1988. Based upon fifteen years of research and more than 6,000 interviews.

Ginott, Haim. *Between Parent and Child: New Solutions to Old Problems.* New York: Avon Books, 1972. Focuses on the need for mutual respect in the parent/child relationship. Designed to "help parents identify their goals in relations to children."

Gordon, Thomas. *P.E.T.: Parent Effectiveness Training.* New York: Penguin, 1970. Suggests that parents should try to bridge the generation gap with counseling techniques, such as emotionally neutral "behavioral messages."

Helfer, Ray E., and C. Henry Kempe, eds. *The Battered Child.* 4th ed. Chicago: University of Chicago Press, 1987.

Hotaling, Gerald T., David Finkelhor, J. T. Kirkpatrick, and Murray A. Straus, eds. *Family Abuse and Its Consequences.* Beverly Hills, Calif.: Sage Publications, 1988. Includes an article on courtship violence and possible precautions.

Kemmer, Elizabeth Jane. *Violence in the Family: An Annotated Bibliography.* New York: Garland, 1984. Covers 1,055 English-language periodicals and books from 1960 to 1982. Author and subject indexes.

Koss, Mary P., et al. *No Safe Haven: Male Violence Against Women at Home, at Work, and in the Community.* Washington, D.C.: American Psychological Association, 1994. Emerging from the American Psychological Association's Task Force on Male Violence Against Women, the authors present an overview of the problem, which is followed by separate sections on violence at home, at work, and in the community and a detailed set of recommendations for therapists, institutions, and government agencies.

Levinson, David. *Family Violence in Cross-Cultural Perspective.* Newbury Park, Calif.: Sage Publications, 1989. Shows that child abuse and spouse abuse are higher when nonfamily violence is prevalent.

McCue, Margi Laird. *Domestic Violence: A Reference Handbook.* Santa Barbara, Calif.: ABC-Clio, 1995. Good introduction for students and researchers, this work carefully defines the various behaviors known as "domestic violence," provides historical background, biographical sketches, a chronology, and a good bibliography of print and nonprint sources.

Mack, Dana. *The Assault on Parenthood: How Our Culture Undermines the Family.* New York: Simon & Schuster, 1997. Argues that the current notion of "family values" is in fact an institutional assault on the family in which parental autonomy has been replaced by "experts" such as lawyers, psychologists and social workers. A well-argued defense of the Republican Project for American Renewal.

Melina, Lois Ruskai. *Adoption: An Annotated Bibliography and Guide.* New York: Garland, 1987. Intended for a wide audience, this annotated bibliography contains 845 works arranged in thirteen topical chapters covering infants, special needs, intercountry and minority adoption, sealed records, proadoption issues, and termination of parent rights. Author and subjects indexes.

Miller, Alice. *For Your Own Good: Hidden Cruelty in Child-Rearing and the Roots of Violence.* Translated by Hildegarde Hannum and Hunter Hannum. New York: Noonday Press, 1983. A psychotherapist argues that trauma is an inevitable part of childhood, as parenting is an unconscious pattern of behaviors in which the parent always triumphs over the child. Controversial.

Nelson, Barbara J. *Making an Issue of Child Abuse: Political Agenda Setting for Social Problems.* Chicago: University of Chicago Press, 1984. Shows that the historical background of parent-child relations, in which child abuse was not regarded as a widespread problem until the 1960's, still bears on policy issues.

Nordquist, Joan. *Domestic Violence: Spouse Abuse, Marital Rape.* Santa Cruz, Calif.: Reference and Research Services, 1986. A slim volume covering both scholarly and general interest literature.

Paul, Ellen, ed. *The Adoption Directory: The Most Comprehensive Guide to Family-Building Options, Including State Statutes on Adoption, Public and Private Adoption Agencies, Adoption Exchanges, Foreign Requirements and Adoption Agencies, Independent Adoption Services, Foster Parenting, Biological Alternatives, and Support Groups.* 2d ed. Detroit: Gale Research, 1995. Comprehensive. Provides an inside look at the adoption process as prospective adoptive or foster parents would see it. Section one includes state and province statutes and adoption agencies in the United States and Canada. Based on questionnaires sent out to almost 7,000 agencies. Includes a glossary and bibliography.

Reiss, A. J., Jr., and J. A. Roth, eds. *Understanding and Controlling Violence.* Washington, D.C.: National Academy Press, 1994. Includes a chapter on "Violence Between Spouses and Intimates: Physical Aggression Between Men and Women in Relationships."

Rowe, David C. *The Limits of Family Influence.* New York: Guilford Press, 1994. Emphasizes the importance of genetic factors that are often overlooked in the study of child development.

Scarf, Maggie. *Intimate Worlds: Life Inside the Family.* New York: Random House, 1995. Deals with the mental health and perceptions of family members.

Society 34 (November/December, 1996): 29-69. Includes a symposium on "Licensing Parents," featuring eight articles by David J. Lykken, Byron M. Roth, Jack C. Westman, Howard G. Schneiderman, Eli Ginzberg, William M. Epstein, William A. Donohue, and Robert A. Gordon.

Straus, Murray A., and Richard J. Gelles, eds. *Physical Violence in American Families: Risk Factors and Adaptations to Violence in 8,145 Families.* New Brunswick, N.J.: Transaction Books, 1990. Based on extensive studies of family violence conducted between 1975 and 1985. Finds that wives assault husbands as often as husbands assault wives but that the rate of injury is only one-seventh as great. Centuries-long trends continue, with substantial reduction in the rates of child and wife abuse.

Straus, Murray A., Richard J. Gelles, and Suzanne K. Steinmetz. *Behind Closed Doors: Violence in the American Family.* New York: Doubleday/Anchor, 1980. Demonstrates the relationship between the physical punishment of children and these children's later physical violence against spouses. Argues that although family violence occurs in all socioeconomic categories, it is most prevalent among disadvantaged minorities and the poor.

Straus, Murray A., and Gerald T. Hotaling, eds. *The Social Causes of Husband-Wife Violence.* Minneapolis: University of Minnesota Press, 1980. Shows that societal forms of violence, such as war, are linked to increases in interpersonal violence.

Includes a chapter on family violence in Mexican American and Jewish ethnic groups.

Swerdlow, Amy, Renate Bridenthal, Joan Kelly, and Phyllis Vine. *Household and Kin: Families in Flux.* Old Westbury, N.Y.: Feminist Press/McGraw-Hill, 1981. Examines changing family structure from a feminist perspective.

Van Hasselt, V. B., R. L. Morrison, A. S. Bellack, and M. Hersen, eds. *Handbook of Family Violence.* New York: Plenum, 1988. Includes an article on physical aggression between spouses.

Viano, E. C., ed. *Intimate Violence: Interdisciplinary Perspectives.* Washington, D.C.: Hemisphere, 1992. Includes an article on "Woman Abuse Among Separated and Divorced Women."

Westman, J. C. *Licensing Parents: Can We Prevent Child Abuse and Neglect?* New York: Plenum Press, 1994. The influential book which proposes that parents should be required to meet the same minimum requirements which the government now requires for adoption, to ensure that children are well cared for.

Windell, James. *Discipline: A Sourcebook of Fifty Fail-safe Techniques for Parents.* New York: Collier/Macmillan, 1991. Following earlier patterns of "assertive discipline," the author argues for withholding special privileges for misbehavior and using rewards as a powerful tool in the "personnel" management of children.

11. RACE, ETHNICITY, AND THE FAMILY

Allen, Walter R., Richard A. English, and Jo Anne Hall, eds. *Black American Families, 1965-1984: A Classified, Selectively Annotated Bibliography.* New York: Greenwood Press, 1986. Contains 1,153 references, providing subject descriptors for each reference. Some annotations.

Auerbach, Susan, ed. *Encyclopedia of Multiculturalism.* 8 vols. New York: Marshall Cavendish, 1994, 1998. Broadly inclusive reference work containing many articles touching on family issues among North America's diverse peoples.

Baron, Augustine, Jr., ed. *Explorations in Chicano Psychology.* New York: Praeger, 1981. Includes a significant article by Oscar Ramirez and Carlos Arce on "The Contemporary Chicano Family."

Bibliography of Native North Americans. Santa Barbara, Calif.: ABC-Clio, 1992-   . This database consists of some sixty thousand records drawn substantially from *Ethnographic Bibliography of North America,* edited by George Peter Murdock and Timothy J. O'Leary. Covers sources on the history and culture of 290 Canadian, American, and Northern Mexican groups, incorporating many titles relevant to research on family issues.

Billingsley, Andrew. *Climbing Jacob's Ladder: The Enduring Legacy of African-American Families.* New York: Simon & Schuster, 1992. An important account of a stabilizing influence in the history of African Americans.

Blackwell, James E. *The Black Community: Diversity and Unity.* 3d ed. New York: Addison-Wesley, Longman, 1991. In this panoramic sociological view of African Americans the author discusses the black family, economic life, education, and religion.

Blasinghame, John. *Slave Testimony: Two Centuries of Letters, Speeches, Interviews and Autobiographies.* Baton Rouge: Louisiana State University Press, 1977. Contains poignant testimony to the nature and value of the family among slaves; useful for a wide range of research projects.

Bradburn, Norman H., Seymour Sudman, and Galen L. Gockel. *Side by Side: Integrated Neighborhoods in America.* Chicago: Quadrangle Books, 1971. Using extensive data from the National Opinion Research Center, the authors examine the variety of social perceptions among different racial groups in the United States.

Camarillo, Albert. *Chicanos in a Changing Society: From Mexican Pueblos to American Barrios in Santa Barbara and Southern California, 1848-1930.* Cambridge, Mass.: Harvard University Press, 1979. Demonstrates how changing work patterns, particularly associated with migrant labor, affected Hispanic families.

_____. *Mexican Americans in Urban Society: A Selected Bibliography.* Oakland, Calif.: Floricanto Press, 1986. Includes 2,133 annotated entries which guide researchers to books, articles, dissertations, and government publications on Chicano studies, family, history, employment, religion, and education.

Carrasquillo, Angela. *Hispanic Children and Youth in the United States: A Resource Guide.* New York: Garland, 1991. Chapters cover family, diversity, history, education, language issues, health, the criminal justice system, and labor force. There are also profiles of Hispanic children's advocacy groups and a directory of social welfare and immigration organizations.

Chavez, Linda. *Out of the Barrio: Toward a New Politics of Hispanic Assimilation.* New York: Basic Books, 1991. A former staff director of the U.S. Commission on Civil Rights argues that Hispanics are for the most part assimilating well into American culture; argues against bilingual education programs.

Chicano Database. Berkeley, Calif.: Chicano Studies Library Publications, University of California, 1990-   . Entries in this database are drawn from *Arte Chicano* (compiled by Ahifra M. Goldman and Tomas Ybarra-Frausto), the *Chicano Anthology Index, Chicano Periodical Index,* and *Chicano Index,* among other sources. Updated semiannually on CD-ROM, this work includes references to books, academic and popular magazines, journals, anthologies, poetry, songs, literature, and plays.

Davis, Lenwood G. *The Black Family in the United States: A Revised, Updated, Selectively Annotated Bibliography.* New York: Greenwood Press, 1986. Includes 772 entries, several of which treat new topics such as abortion, genocide, polygamy, military families, racism, and sterilization. Major books are listed in a separate section.

Dickson, L. "The Future of Marriage and Family in Black America." *Journal of Black Studies* 23 (1993). Discusses prospects for the development of marriage and family life among African Americans.

Frazier, E. Franklin. *The Negro Family in the United States.* Chicago: University of Chicago Press, 1939. A classic study by an African American that attributed family disorganization to the legacy of slavery and assumed that by adopting "modern" patterns this disorganization would disappear.

Gall, Susan B., and Timothy L. Gall, eds. *Statistical Record of Asian Americans.* Detroit: Gale Research, 1993. Contains approximately nine hundred tables, graphs, and charts covering the lives of American and Canadian citizens of Chinese, Japanese, Korean, Vietnamese, Cambodian, Filipino, and Hawaiian descent. Topics include the family, domestic life, education, housing, religion, and demographics.

Griswold del Castillo, Richard. *La Familia.* Notre Dame, Ind.: University of Notre Dame Press, 1984. Extensive research enabled the author to determine that the Hispanic family changed dramatically as economic circumstances changed—more so than European immigrant families under comparable circumstances.

Gutman, Herbert. *The Black Family in Slavery and Freedom, 1750-1925.* New York: Pantheon Books, 1976. Through extensive use of plantation records, census data, and other materials, the author showed that the family as a cultural institution remained intact despite slavery.

Horton, Carrell Peterson, and Jessie Carney Smith, eds. *Statistical Record of Black America.* Detroit: Gale Research, 1990. Recognized by *Library Journal* as one of the most important reference books of 1990, the tables and statistics in this work are drawn from government publications, journals, books, newspapers and associations. Includes treatment of education, the family, health and medical care, religion, and interracial dating.

Hoxie, Frederick E., and Harvey Markowitz. *Native Americans: An Annotated Bibliography.* Metuchen, N.J.: Scarecrow Press, 1991. An annotated listing of books and articles dealing with Native American reference, history, culture, and modern life. Topics include family and tribal life, law and government, and self-identity.

Jewell, K. Sue. *Survival of the Black Family: The Institutional Impact of United States Social Policy.* New York: Praeger, 1988. Argues that the "policies, procedures, and assumptions underlying the social and economic policy of the 1960's and 1970's contributed to the disintegration of the black two-parent and extended families."

Jones, Jacqueline. *Labor of Love, Labor of Sorrow: Black Women, Work, and the Family from Slavery to the Present.* New York: Basic Books, 1985. A good survey of the impact of the African American cultural experience on the development of the family; argues that the "status of black women after the war cannot be separated from their roles as wives and mothers within a wider setting of kinship obligations."

Kanellos, Nicolas, ed. *The Hispanic-American Almanac: A Reference Work on Hispanics in the United States.* Detroit: Gale Research, 1993. Twenty-five topical chapters deal with history, family, demographics, language, law, labor, women, religion and the arts. Covers the descendants of people who emigrated from Spain, Mexico, Puerto Rico, Cuba, and the Spanish-speaking countries of the Caribbean and Central America.

McFadden, Margaret, consulting ed. *Women's Issues.* 3 vols. Pasadena, Calif.: Salem Press, 1997. Wide-ranging reference work containing nearly 700 essays on subjects relating to North American women. A large proportion of these articles deal with family issues.

"Model Strategies in Bilingual Education: Family Literacy and Parent Involvement." Washington, D.C.: U.S. Education Department, March 1993. Practical advice on a variety of school programs for parents of bilingual children.

Mokuau, Noreen, ed. *Handbook of Social Services for Asian and Pacific Islanders.* New York: Greenwood Press, 1991. Includes separate topical chapters on the aged, youth, family violence, and history and chapters on ethnic groups such as Japanese Americans, Chinese Americans, Filipino Americans, Vietnamese Americans, Indigenous Hawaiians, Samoans, and Chamorros. Index.

Murry, Velma McBride, and the Consortium for Research on Black Adolescence. *Black Adolescence: Current Issues and Annotated Bibliography.* Boston: G. K. Hall, 1990. Each topical chapter, such as "family relationships," includes a literature review, a list of annotated references, and a list of additional references.

Myers, Hector F., Phyllis G. Rana, and Marcia Harris, eds. *Black Child Development in America, 1927-1977: An Annotated Bibliography.* Westport, Conn.: Greenwood Press, 1979. Includes more than 1,200 annotated references to books and periodical literature, grouped in five categories: personality development, social development, language development, physical development, and cognitive development.

Ploski, Harry A., and James Williams, eds. *The Negro Almanac: A Reference Work on the African American.* 5th ed. Detroit: Gale Research, 1989. Includes an extensive section on "The Black Family."

Reddy, Marlita A., ed. *Statistical Record of Hispanic Americans.* Detroit: Gale Research, 1993. In 922 tables and graphs, the demography, family, education, health, culture, justice, and economics of Americans and Canadians of Hispanic, Mexican, Cuban, and Puerto Rican descent are portrayed. Provides useful comparative data for Asians, blacks, whites, and Latinos.

Roschelle, Anne R. *No More Kin: Exploring Race, Class and Gender in Family Networks.* Newbury Park, Calif.: Sage Publications, 1997. Reviewed in *Choice* (October, 1997), this book is a general work dealing with the issues of race and gender as they affect family life in the United States.

_____. *Statistical Record of Native North Americans.* Detroit: Gale Research, 1993. Includes more than one thousand tables, charts, and graphs covering the family, demographics, education, culture and tradition, health, social and economic conditions, business and industry, land and water management, government relations, and law enforcement for the United States and Canada. Mainly drawn from U.S. and Canadian government statistics, although some records from state and tribal agencies are included.

Siems, Larry, ed. and trans. *Between the Lines: Letters Between Undocumented Mexican and Central American Immigrants and Their Families and Friends.* Tucson: University of Arizona Press, 1992. Provides the personal side to research on immigrant families.

Slonim, Maureen. *Children, Culture, and Ethnicity: Evaluating and Understanding the Impact.* New York: Garland, 1991. Provides a multidisciplinary overview of how children are affected by ethnicity. One chapter deals specifically with family systems and four others with Asian, Hispanic American, African American, and European cultures.

Staples, R., and L. B. Johnson. *Black Families at the Crossroads: Challenges and Prospects.* San Francisco: Jossey-Bass, 1993. At a critical moment in the self-identity of African Americans, these authors explore the various issues related to the core institution of the people.

"Strong Families, Strong Schools: Building Community Partnerships for Learning." Washington, D.C.: U.S. Education Department, September, 1994. Utilizing the "Goals 2000" legislation, this work makes the case for increasing family involvement in public schools.

Taylor, Ronald, ed. *Minority Families in the United States: A Multicultural Perspective.* Englewood Cliffs, N.J.: Prentice Hall, 1994. Examines the variety of family cultural patterns in the United States, focusing on Mexican, Puerto Rican, Chinese, Japanese, and American Indian families.

Torres-Gil, Fernando. *Hispanics in an Aging Society.* New York: Carnegie Corporation, 1986. Recognizing that immigrant groups such as Hispanics will outnumber descendants of earlier European immigrants in many parts of the United States, the author argues for a close examination of the peculiar circumstances of the Hispanic aged.

Vecoli, Rudolph J., ed. *Gale Encyclopedia of Multicultural America.* 2 vols. Detroit: Gale Research, 1995. Contains more than one hundred original articles addressing distinct ethnic and ethno-religious groups in the United States, each containing a section on "Family and Community Dynamics." Native American groups are not comprehensively treated, although a dozen representative tribes are included.

Washington, Valora, and Velma La Point, eds. *Black Children and American Institutions: An Ecological Review and Resource Guide.* New York: Garland, 1988. Beginning with an essay that examines African American children and schools, family, the criminal justice system, and health, this work provides an annotated bibliography and a list of related organizations such as the Children's Defense fund and the National Urban League.

Zambrana, Ruth, ed. *Understanding Latino Families: Scholarship, Policy, and Practice.* Thousand Oaks, Calif.: Sage Publications, 1995. An excellent introduction to a variety of issues surrounding the Latino family structure. Includes a twenty-page bibliography.

12. Social Issues or Sociology of the Family

American Values. San Diego, Calif.: Greenhaven Press, 1995. Drawing from a wide range of respected sources, this work examines questions such as "How Important are Family Values?" and "How Do Religious Values Influence America?" The writings of activists and social critics such as Malcolm S. Forbes, Jr., Pat Buchanan, and Cornel West are arranged in a pro/con format. Providing many sides to the debate and containing bibliographies, illustrations, and organization contacts, this is a superb starting point for research.

Anderson, Michael. *The Social and Political Economy of the Household.* New York: Oxford University Press, 1994. A noted authority on the sociology of the family explores the interrelationships found in the household.

———. *The Sociology of the Family.* London: Harmondsworth, 1980. First issued in 1971, This work provide a good introduction to the varie-

ties of perspectives which are and which have been used in the study of the family. Articles focus on urban families in Britain and the United States and are grouped in various sections involving change and diversity in family systems, relationships of adults with parents and wider kin, the choice of a spouse, patterns of interaction between spouses, marital dissolution, and parents and their small children.

Bellah, Robert N., Richard Madsen, William M. Sullivan, Ann Swidler, and Steven M. Tipton. *Habits of the Heart: Individualism and Commitment in American Life.* Berkeley: University of California Press, 1985. Decries increasingly individualistic values, which lead Americans to place individual goals over the well-being of the family and community.

Berger, Brigitte, and Peter L. Berger. *The War over the Family: Capturing the Middle Ground.* Garden City, N.Y.: Anchor Press, 1983. In an attempt to build bridges between extreme positions taken regarding the "bourgeois family," the two authors review the ideological battleground and tensions of modernization, before providing "a reasonable defense" of the traditional family.

Berns, Roberta M. *Child, Family, School, Community: Socialization and Support.* 4th ed. New York: Harcourt Brace, 1997. Analyzes the variety of contexts in which children are socialized, including the family, the school, child/family/school interaction, the community, the peer group, and the mass media.

Blake, Judith. *Family Size and Achievement.* Berkeley: University of California Press, 1990. Addresses the role of family size in educational expectations and the importance of family size relative to other measures of family background.

Blankenhorn, David, Steven Bayme, and Jean Bethke Elshtain, eds. *Rebuilding the Nest: A New Commitment to the American Family.* Milwaukee: Family Service America, 1990. A collection of essays by experts who propose varying viewpoints as to the nature of family decline. David Popenoe argues that Americans should recommit themselves to strong families; while Dennis Orthner suggests that the family is in transition, rather than decline.

Borgatta, Edgar F., and Marie L. Borgatta, eds. *Encyclopedia of Sociology.* New York: Macmillan, 1992. The first extensive guide to the field of sociology since the revolutionary changes of the 1960's and 1970's. Contains a wide range of authoritative articles on family and related issues, including family and household structure, family law, family planning, family policy in Western societies, family roles, family size, and family violence. This idea of a comprehensive encyclopedia grew out of the editor's work with a series of handbooks commissioned during the 1960's, including Harold T. Christensen's *Handbook of Marriage and the Family* (1964).

Burr, Wesley R., R. Hill, F. I. Nye, and I. Reiss, eds. *Contemporary Theories About the Family.* New York: Free Press, 1979. A variety of articles by well respected theorists; argues that gender roles are socially constructed.

Carlson, Allan C. *Family Questions: Reflections on the American Social Crisis.* New Brunswick, N.J.: Transaction Books, 1988. Argues that the "matriarchal welfare state" has been more disruptive to the family than poverty itself.

Christensen, Bryce J. *Utopia Against the Family.* San Francisco: Ignatius Press, 1990. The director of the Rockford Institute Center on the Family in America argues that the concept of "family" should not be redefined to include nontraditional groups, for by such redefinition a variety of special interests can use the word to promote their causes.

Christian Coalition. *Contract with the American Family.* Nashville, Tenn.: Moorings, 1995. Clarifies the political position of a powerful conservative organization, including their opposition to the U.N. Convention on the Rights of the Child.

Coontz, Stephanie. *The Way We Never Were: American Families and the Nostalgia Trap.* New York: Basic Books, 1992. Carefully examining the gender and family myths promoted in American popular culture, the author opposes the idea that a return to "traditional values" will solve current problems.

Daly, Kerry. *Families and Time.* Thousand Oaks, Calif.: Sage Publications, 1996. Outlines a theory designed to generate new research, in which the time available to families is seen as a highly diverse, socially constructed concept rather than a simple reality.

Elkind, David. *Ties That Stress: The New Family Imbalance.* Cambridge, Mass.: Harvard University Press, 1994. Argues that the old rigid boundaries defining the family were beneficial to children, but often stifling to parents. Introduces a model of the new "vital family."

Garbino, James. *Raising Children in a Socially Toxic Environment.* San Francisco: Jossey-Bass, 1995. Designed to encourage the middle class to action, the author delineates many factors that heighten the vulnerability of children, including television, unsupervised exposure to "adult things," large schools, single-parent families, and rigid economic policies.

Gallagher, Maggie. *Enemies of Eros: How the Sexual Revolution Is Killing Family, Marriage and Sex, and What We Can Do About It.* Chicago: Bonus Books, 1989. A clever social critique of feminism and its effect upon the family.

Gubrium, J. F., and J. A. Holstein. *What Is Family?* Mountain View, Calif.: Mayfield, 1990. Explores the question from the perspective of psychoanalysis and discourse analysis.

Hite, Shere. *The Hite Report on the Family: Growing Up Under Patriarchy.* New York: Grove Press, 1995. A controversial account by a pioneer in the study of sexuality, arguing against the notion of family decline and examining the changing family in terms of natural evolutionary development.

Jones, Landon. *Great Expectations: America and the Baby Boom Generation.* New York: Ballantine Books, 1986. Examines the complex mix of economic, social, and cultural factors that affected the composition of the family following World War II.

Keniston, Kenneth, and the Carnegie Council on Children. *All Our Children: The American Family Under Pressure.* New York: Harcourt Brace Jovanovich, 1977. Makes the case for public advocacy on behalf of children.

Klein, David M., and James M. White. *Family Theories: An Introduction.* Thousand Oaks, Calif.: Sage Publications, 1996. Good introduction to the social methodologies involved in the study of the family.

Lakoff, George. *Moral Politics: What Conservatives Know That Liberals Don't.* Chicago: University of Chicago Press, 1996. The author examines how politicians link morality to politics through the concept of the family and argues that conservatives have exploited the connections more effectively than liberals.

Lamanna, Mary Ann, and Agnes Riedman. *Marriages and Families: Making Choices Throughout the*

Life Cycle. Belmont, Calif.: Wadsworth, 1994. A readable, introductory survey dealing with contemporary family experience.

Lasch, Christopher. *Haven in a Heartless World: The Family Besieged.* New York: Basic Books, 1977. Shows how early in the twentieth century "doctors, psychiatrists, teachers, child guidance experts, officers of the juvenile courts, and other specialists began to supervise child-rearing, formerly the business of the family."

McDonald, Gerald W., and F. Ivan Nye, eds. *Family Policy.* Minneapolis: National Council on Family Relations, 1979. A series of articles by experts examining the development of family policies in the United States and Europe.

Mann, Michael, ed. *International Encyclopedia of Sociology.* New York: Continuum, 1984. Some 750 short articles, mostly written by authors affiliated with the London School of Economics. Also published as *The Macmillan Student Encyclopedia of Sociology.*

Ostheimer, A. L. *The Family: A Thomistic Study in Social Philosophy.* Washington, D.C.: Catholic University of America, 1939. Deals with the theory of natural law as it applies to the relationship between family and state.

Russell, Bertrand. *Marriage and Morals.* Garden City, N.Y.: Garden City Publications, 1929. Work that recommended complete sexual equality in marriage and trial marriages that would not be binding until wives' first pregnancy.

Sadler, Judith DeBoard. *Families in Transition: An Annotated Bibliography.* Hamden, Conn.: Archon Books, 1988. The bibliography includes 970 works grouped in topical chapters that treat single parents, adoptive and foster families, parental kidnapping, working parents and latchkey children, and homosexual relationships. Separate indexes for subjects, authors, book titles, and article titles.

Salter, David F. *Crashing the Old Boys' Network: The Tragedies and Triumphs of Girls and Women in Sports.* Westport, Conn.: Praeger, 1996. Written from the perspective of a father who sees "antiquated beliefs" about sports as a bar to equitable treatment for his daughter. Includes resources for obtaining assistance.

Schroeder, Pat. *Champion of the Great American Family: A Personal and Political Book.* New York: Random House, 1989. A critique of the handling of family issues by the political and business communities, notable chiefly because it was written by the chair of the House of Representatives' Select Committee on Children, Youth and Families.

Skolnick, Arlene. *Embattled Paradise: The American Family in an Age of Uncertainty.* New York: Basic Books, 1991. Combating scholars who see a decline in the institution of the traditional family in America, the author reevaluates in light of the emotional quality of life.

Skolnick, Jerome, and Arlene Skolnick, eds. *Family in Transition.* 9th ed. New York: Addison-Wesley, Longman, 1997. Authoritative collection of both classic and modern essays on issues affecting the family, including parenting, divorce, gender roles, and demographic trends. The ninth edition introduces a chapter on family diversity, with readings on African American, Hispanic, and lesbian and gay families.

Sweet, James A., and L. L. Bumpass. *American Families and Households.* New York: Russell Sage Foundation, 1987. Deals with the effect of declining growth on the nature of the family, demonstrating that the increased capability of women in competing for jobs made it more economically and psychologically "expensive" to raise children.

13. Work, Economics, and the Family

Ambry, Margaret. *The Official Guide to Household Spending.* 2d ed. Ithaca, N.Y.: New Strategist, 1993. Designed principally for business use, this work provides a wealth of information about family economics and values. Organized by product and service categories, each chapter is divided into sections on highlights, spending trends, spending by age, spending by income, spending by household type, and spending by household size.

Barnett, Rosalind C., and Caryl Rivers. *He Works/She Works: How Two-Income Families are Happier, Healthier, and Better Off.* New York: HarperCollins, 1996. Suggests that women should be more relaxed about work and parenting, should trust the child-care system, and should develop their own individual identities.

Baum, Alice S., and Donald W. Burnes. *A Nation in Denial: The Truth About Homelessness.* Westview Press, 1993. Dismissing the traditional claims that homelessness is caused by poverty and economic disarray, the authors argue that it is instead a condition of disengagement from "family, friends, neighborhood, church, and community," as well as a loss of self.

Beeghley, Leonard. *What Does Your Wife Do? Gender and the Transformation of Family Life.* Boulder, Colo.: Westview Press, 1996. Seeks to demystify the rapid social changes of the twentieth century by explaining how premarital sex, abortion, divorce, and women's employment affect family life.

Berrick, Jill Duerr. *Faces of Poverty: Portraits of Women and Children on Welfare.* New York: Oxford University Press, 1995. By examining the actual lives of poor persons, the author provides a human face to a frequently debated social issue.

Blau, Peter M., and Otis D. Duncan. *The American Occupational Structure.* New York: Free Press, 1967. Demonstrates that family size, as well as parental resources, affects sibling achievement.

Brazelton, T. Berry, M.D. *Working and Caring.* Addison-Wesley Publishing, 1985. A top pediatrician offers advice to parents on balancing work with the raising of children.

Conrad, Pamela J. *Balancing Home and Career: Skills for Successful Life Management.* Los Altos, Calif.: Crisp Publications, 1990. A practical primer with tips on negotiating each day between the demands of home and work.

Craig, Betty L. *Careers in Home Economics.* St. Paul, Minn.: EMC, 1992. Represents the possibilities of applied studies in the management of the home.

Ellwood, David T. *Poor Support: Poverty in the American Family.* New York: Basic Books, 1988. Suggests the need for greater government support for health care and a higher minimum wage for the working poor of America.

Free to Be Family: Helping Mothers and Fathers Meet the Needs of the Next Generation of American Children. Washington, D.C.: Family Research Council, 1992. A blueprint for reversing trends toward divorce, premarital sex, and crime, all of which threaten the family.

Garfinkel, Irwin. *Assuring Child Support: An Extension of Social Security.* New York: Russell Sage Foundation, 1992. Based on a fifteen-year study, the author argues for guaranteed child-support payments for single parents.

Gerson, Kathleen. *Hard Choices: How Women Decide About Work, Career, and Motherhood.* Berkeley: University of California Press, 1985. Shows that the prototypical family—a legally married husband and wife living together for a lifetime, with the wife raising the children and the father supporting the family—is anachronistic.

Goldscheider, Frances K., and Linda J. Waite. *New Families, No Families? The Transformation of the American Home.* Berkeley: University of California Press, 1991. Two sociologists analyze recent data to suggest changes in child care and housework.

Hareven, Tamara K. *Family and Kin in Urban Communities, 1700-1930.* New York: New Viewpoints, 1977. Suggests that family change has been uneven across the country and that families themselves have been active agents in change rather than simply passive recipients; shows that families could provide stability in an economically debilitating environment.

Henslin, James M. *Homelessness: An Annotated Bibliography.* 2 vols. New York: Garland, 1993. Volume one contains annotated entries on books, book chapters, journal articles, and newspapers. Volume two groups the same entries, less annotations, under forty-one subtopics.

Hewlett, Sylvia Ann. *When the Bough Breaks: The Cost of Neglecting Our Children.* New York: Basic Books, 1991. Locating the declining state of the family in a "parenting deficit" caused by two wage-earner families, this economist argues for a major response from business and government.

Hochschild, Arlie, and Anne Machung. *The Second Shift: Working Parents and the Revolution at Home.* New York: Viking, 1989. Based on a long-term study of working couples, the author analyzes the division of domestic work and child care. Discusses strategies for success, including flexible role assignments.

Jencks, Christopher. *The Homeless.* Cambridge, Mass.: Harvard University Press, 1994. Examining the discrepancies in homeless figures issued by the government and various advocacy groups, the author recommends ways in which housing could be made available at a reasonable cost.

Johnson, Clifford M., Andrew M. Sum, and James D. Weill. *Vanishing Dreams: The Growing Economic Plight of America's Young Families.* Washington, D.C.: Children's Defense Fund, 1988. Argues that Americans born after the late fifties are "suffering a frightening cycle of plummeting earnings and family incomes, declining marriage rates, rising out-of-wedlock birth rates, increasing numbers of single-parent families, and skyrocketing poverty rates." Identifies "ten key findings" that explain the phenomena.

Kahn, Alfred J., and Sheila B. Kamerman. *Income Transfers for Families with Children.* Philadelphia: Temple University Press, 1983. Demonstrates that American governmental policies tend to help better-off families rather than lower-income families.

Kamerman, Sheila B., Alfred Dahn, and Paul Kingston. *Maternity Policies and Working Women.* 2d ed. New York: Columbia University Press, 1993. A useful summary of current practices emphasizing the inadequacy of maternity policy in the United States.

Kamerman, Sheila B., and Alfred J. Kahn. *Child Care, Family Benefits, and Working Parents: A Comparative Study.* New York: Columbia University Press, 1981. Emphasizes the role of women in the labor force in providing more choice in developing their own lifestyles.

Kenen, Regina. *Reproductive Hazards in the Workplace: Mending Jobs, Managing Pregnancies.* New York: Haworth Press, 1993. A good introduction to the reproductive toxicology that has become so prevalent with the entry of more women into the workplace.

Kozol, Jonathan. *Rachel and Her Children: Homeless Families in America.* New York: Fawcett Columbine, 1988. Utilizing a representative case, the author shows how easy it is to fall into homelessness in an uncertain economy. Winner of the Robert F. Kennedy Book award.

Lindsey, Linda L. *Gender Roles: A Sociological Perspective.* Englewood Cliffs, N.J.: Prentice-Hall, 1990. Clarifies a number of gender issues, showing, for example, that the median age of marriage for women was higher in the 1980's than at any time since 1890.

Popenoe, David. *Disturbing the Nest: Family Change and Decline in Modern Societies.* New York: Aldine De Gruyter, 1988. Reviews the argument that greater opportunities for women benefit society as a whole.

Radigan, Anne L. *Concept and Compromise: The Evolution of Family Leave Legislation in the U.S. Congress.* Washington, D.C.: Women's Research and Education Institute, 1988. A summary of congressional action on a controversial issue; important in the intersection of traditional values toward economy and the family.

Robinson, John P., and Geoffrey Godbey. *Time for Life: The Surprising Ways Americans Use Their Time.* University Park: Pennsylvania State University Press, 1997. Counters Juliet B. Schor's contention that Americans are overworked (see below), suggesting instead that workers have gained as much as an hour in leisure time since 1965. Analyzing how Americans feel about "time," they argue that most of the gains have gone into watching television. Includes chapters on trends in housework, family care, and gender differences.

Sanders, Darcie, and Martha M. Bullen. *Staying Home: From Full-Time Professional to Full-Time Parent.* New York: Little, Brown, 1992. Based on interviews with 350 stay-home mothers, this study argues that most women find that the benefits of educational control and increased family cohesiveness outweigh social isolation and loss of income.

Schor, Juliet B. *The Overworked American: The Unexpected Decline of Leisure.* New York: Basic Books, 1991. Proposes longer holidays, shorter work weeks, and more balanced domestic gender roles in providing a better quality of life.

Skolnick, Arlene S. *The Intimate Environment: Exploring Marriage and the Family.* 6th ed. New York: Addison-Wesley, Longman, 1996. Integrates sociological findings with historical, psychological, and anthropological insights. Incorporates data from the 1990 U.S. Census and the 1994 University of Chicago study of Americans' sexual behavior.

Tilly, Louise, and Joan W. Scott. *Women, Work and Family.* New York: Henry Holt, 1978. Two historians explain the traditional historical model as a family-based economy, in which each person performs jobs according to age and sex.

Vogel, Lise. *Mothers on the Job: Maternity Policy in the U.S. Workplace.* New Brunswick, N.J.: Rutgers University Press, 1993. Traces the evolution of pregnancy policy in the workplace, demonstrating how the United States government's reluctance to develop family and maternity policy has led to a number of poorly coordinated government programs.

Wolf, Robin. *Marriages and Families in a Diverse Society*. New York: Addison-Wesley, Longman, 1996. An accessible textbook that balances social and interpersonal perspectives. Includes male and female perspectives on various family issues.

Zigler, Edward F., and Meryl Frank, eds. *Parental Leave Crisis: Toward a National Policy*. New Haven, Conn.: Yale University Press, 1988. Articles by a variety of specialists, including Congresswoman Patrician Schroeder, explain America's lack of maternity policy and make the case for rectification.

Zill, Nicholas, and Christian Winquist Nord. *Running in Place: How American Families Are Faring in a Changing Economy and an Individualistic Society*. Washington, D.C.: Child Trends, 1994. Based on government surveys, this book examines the efforts of families to cope with economic pressures.

Zucker, Elana. *Being a Homemaker/Home Health Aide*. 4th ed. Englewood Cliffs, N.J.: Brady/Prentice-Hall, 1996. Good text in the study of practical home management.

—John Powell

Encyclopedia of Family Life

List of Entries by Category

For additional assistance in locating articles, consult the lists of cross-references at the end of each essay and the reference set's comprehensive index.

SUBJECT HEADINGS

AGING AND ELDERLY CARE

Age of consent
Ageism
Aging and elderly care
Alzheimer's disease
Baby boomers
Death
Displaced homemakers
Elder abuse
Employee Retirement Income Security Act (ERISA)
Empty nest syndrome
Euthanasia
Family demographics
Family life cycle
Filial responsibility
Friend networks
Funerals
Gender longevity
Generational relationships
Grandparents
Grief counseling
In loco parentis
Inheritance and estate law
Intergenerational income transfer

Life expectancy
Living wills
Menopause
Midlife crises
Nursing and convalescent homes
Older Americans Act (OAA)
Retirement
Retirement communities
Sandwich generation
Senior citizen centers
Sheehy, Gail
Social Security
Townsend movement
Widowhood
Wills and bequests

ARTS, MEDIA, AND ENTERTAINMENT

Advertising
Ageism
Art and iconography
Cassatt, Mary
Children's literature
Children's magazines
Comer, James P.

Computer recreation
Cooney, Joan Ganz
Cultural influences
Enculturation
Entertainment
Family advice columns
Film depictions of families
Film ratings
Gray, John
Haley, Alex
Holidays
Literature and families
Myths and storytelling
News media and families
Pornography
Recreation
Rockwell, Norman
Senior citizen centers
Sexual revolution
Television depictions of families
Television rating systems
Youth sports

CHILDHOOD AUTHORITIES

Brazelton, T. Berry
Bruner, Jerome

Clark, Kenneth and Mamie
Coles, Robert
Comer, James P.
Cooney, Joan Ganz
Edelman, Marian Wright
Erikson, Erik H.
Gessell, Arnold L.
Kagan, Jerome
Lathrop, Julia C.
Mendenhall, Dorothy Reed
Murphy, Gardner and Lois
Spock, Benjamin

CHILDREN
Abandonment of the family
Adoption issues
Age of consent
Aid to Families with Dependent
    Children (AFDC)
Alateen
Allowances
Alsager v. District Court
Amerasian children
Attachment theory
Attention-deficit hyperactivity
    disorder (ADHD)
Baby-sitters
Baby talk
Battered child syndrome
Bedtime reading
Behavior disorders
Big Brothers and Big Sisters of
    America (BBBSA)
Birth defects
Birth order
Bonding and attachment
Breast-feeding
Child abandonment
Child abduction
Child abuse
Child Abuse Prevention and
    Treatment Act (CAPTA)
Child and dependent care tax
    credit
Child care
Child Care and Development
    Block Grant Act
Child custody
Child molestation
Child prodigies

Child Protection and Toy
    Safety Act
Child rearing
Child safety
Child support
Child Support Enforcement
    Amendments
Child Welfare League of
    America (CWLA)
Childhood fears and anxieties
Childhood history
Children born out of wedlock
Children's Bureau
Children's Defense Fund (CDF)
Children's literature
Children's magazines
Children's rights
Community programs for
    children
Competition during childhood
Computer recreation
Corporal punishment
Curfews
Day care
Disciplining children
Educating children
Education for All Handicapped
    Children Act (EHA)
Equality of children
Family therapy
Favoritism
Foster homes
Gangs
Gomez v. Perez
Guardianship
Head Start
Health of children
Imaginary friends
In loco parentis
In re Gault
Infanticide
Juvenile courts
Juvenile delinquency
Latchkey children
McKinney Homeless
    Assistance Act
Megan's Law
Missing Children's
    Assistance Act
Nannies

National Center for Missing
    and Exploited Children
    (NCMEC)
Only children
Orphans
Parental divorce
Parental Kidnapping Prevention
    Act (PKPA)
Pediatric AIDS
Puberty and adolescence
Separation anxiety
Stranger anxiety
Substitute caregivers
Sudden infant death syndrome
    (SIDS)
Supplemental Nutrition
    Program for Women, Infants,
    and Children
Time-out
Toilet training
Tough love
Uniform Child Custody
    Jurisdiction Act (UCCJA)
United Nations Convention
    on the Rights of the
    Child
Youth sports

COURT CASES
Alsager v. District Court
Gomez v. Perez
In re Baby M
In re Gault
Loving v. Virginia
Reed v. Reed
Roe v. Wade
Wisconsin v. Yoder
Zablocki v. Redhail

DEMOGRAPHICS
Abortion
Acquired immunodeficiency
    syndrome (AIDS)
African Americans
Alternative family types
Amerasian children
Baby-boom generation
Birth control
Blended families
Childless/truncated families

Intergenerational income transfer
Living wills
Love
Marriage squeeze
Mother-daughter relationships
Mother-son relationships
Names
Nursing and convalescent homes
Parental divorce
Patriarchs
Primogeniture
Retirement
Retirement communities
Sandwich generation
Social Security
Substitute caregivers
Suicide
Wealth
Wills and bequests

HEALTH AND MEDICAL ISSUES

Abortion
Acquired immunodeficiency syndrome (AIDS)
Aging and elderly care
Al-Anon
Alateen
Alcoholism and drug abuse
Alzheimer's disease
Americans with Disabilities Act (ADA)
Apgar, Virginia
Attention-deficit hyperactivity disorder (ADHD)
Battered child syndrome
Behavior disorders
Birth control
Birth defects
Brazelton, T. Berry
Breast-feeding
Child molestation
Child Protection and Toy Safety Act
Child safety
Childbirth
Childhood fears and anxieties
Childlessness
Circumcision

Codependency
Death
Disabilities
Eating disorders
Eating habits of children
Education for All Handicapped Children Act (EHA)
Elder abuse
Electra and Oedipus complexes
Ellis, Albert
Emotional abuse
Emotional expression
Eugenics
Euthanasia
Family and Medical Leave Act (FMLA)
Family caregiving
Family counseling
Family crises
Family therapy
Fertility and infertility
Freudian psychology
Gender longevity
Genetic counseling
Genetic disorders
Gray, John
Grief counseling
Health of children
Health problems
Heredity
Human Genome Project
Imaginary friends
Kübler-Ross, Elisabeth
Learning disorders
Life expectancy
Maslow, Abraham
Masters, William H., and Virginia E. Johnson
Mendenhall, Dorothy Reed
Menopause
Mental health
Midlife crises
Mothers Against Drunk Driving (MADD)
Multiple births
Nursing and convalescent homes
Pediatric AIDS
Planned Parenthood Federation of America (PPFA)

Postpartum depression
Pregnancy
Puberty and adolescence
Recovery programs
Reproductive technologies
Roe v. Wade
Salk, Jonas
Sanger, Margaret
Separation anxiety
Sexuality and sexual taboos
Skinner, B. F.
Spock, Benjamin
Sterilization
Stranger anxiety
Sudden infant death syndrome (SIDS)
Suicide
Supplemental Nutrition Program for Women, Infants, and Children
Support groups
Surrogate mothers
Teen mothers
Test-tube babies
Toilet training
Watson, John B.
Wattleton, Faye
Wilson, William G.

HOMES AND HOUSING ISSUES

Addams, Jane
Child abandonment
Cohabitation
Communal living
Elder abuse
Empty nest syndrome
Foster homes
Full nest
Group marriage
Habitat for Humanity International (HFHI)
Home ownership
Home sharing
Homeless families
Household
Hull House
McKinney Homeless Assistance Act
Nursing and convalescent homes

Mommy track
Mother-daughter relationships
Mother-son relationships
Motherhood
Postpartum depression
Pregnancy
Pregnancy Discrimination Act
Reproductive technologies
Roe v. Wade
Single-parent families
Sterilization
Surrogate mothers
Teen mothers
Test-tube babies
Violence Against Women Act
Widowhood
Women's roles

ORGANIZATIONS AND GOVERNMENT PROGRAMS
Al-Anon
Alateen
American Association for
    Marriage and Family
    Therapists (AAMFT)
Big Brothers and Big Sisters of
    America (BBBSA)
Child Welfare League of
    America (CWLA)
Children's Bureau
Children's Defense Fund (CDF)
Family History Library
Focus on the Family
Habitat for Humanity
    International (HFHI)
Head Start
Human Genome Project
Mothers Against Drunk Driving
    (MADD)
National Center for Missing
    and Exploited Children
    (NCMEC)
National Council on Family
    Relations (NCFR)
Parents Without Partners (PWP)
Planned Parenthood Federation
    of America (PPFA)
Systematic Training for Effective
    Parenting (STEP)
Townsend movement

Vanier Institute of the Family
    (VIF)
Zero Population Growth
    movement

PARENTING
Adoption issues
Bedtime reading
Child abandonment
Child care
Child custody
Child rearing
Child support
Childlessness
Children born out of wedlock
Corporal punishment
Curfews
Day care
Disciplining children
Electra and Oedipus complexes
Empty nest syndrome
Familism
Family advice columns
Family counseling
Family Support Act
Family unity
Father-daughter relationships
Father figures
Father-son relationships
Fatherhood
Fatherlessness
Favoritism
Filial responsibility
Foster homes
Friend networks
Full nest
Gay and lesbian families
Generational relationships
Guardianship
Incest
In-laws
Juvenile courts
Least interest principle
Love
Mother-daughter relationships
Mother-son relationships
Motherhood
Nannies
National Council on Family
    Relations (NCFR)

Only children
Parental divorce
Parenting
Parents Anonymous (PA)
Parents Without Partners (PWP)
Paternity suits
Planned Parenthood Federation
    of America (PPFA)
Sandwich generation
Second shift
Siblings
Son preference
Stepfamilies
Substitute caregivers
Systematic Training for Effective
    Parenting (STEP)
Time-out
Tough love
Uniform Child Custody
    Jurisdiction Act (UCCJA)
Unwed fathers
Vanier Institute of the Family
    (VIF)
Visitation rights

PEOPLE
Addams, Jane
Allport, Gordon
Apgar, Virginia
Bernard, Jessie Shirley
Bethune, Mary McLeod
Bradshaw, John
Brazelton, T. Berry
Bruner, Jerome
Cassatt, Mary
Clark, Kenneth and Mamie
Coles, Robert
Comer, James P.
Cooney, Joan Ganz
Edelman, Marian Wright
Ellis, Albert
Erikson, Erik H.
Gessell, Arnold L.
Gray, John
Haley, Alex
Hall, G. Stanley
Hochschild, Arlie Russell
Kagan, Jerome
Kohlberg, Lawrence
Kübler-Ross, Elisabeth

Index

A page number or range in **boldface** type indicates a full article devoted to that topic.

ENCYCLOPEDIA OF FAMILY LIFE

Genetic disorders, 128-129, **676-680**

Genetics, 55, 68, 115, 216, 462-463, 466, 594, 722, 1203

Genghis Khan, 1320

Georgia, Republic of, 608

Gerber, Frank, 491

Gerbner, George, 457

German, 365

German measles, 128, 706

German Society of New York, 1244

Germanic tribes, 1075

Germans, 727, 729

Germany, 46, 129, 465, 467, 630, 790, 1141, 1312; war brides from, 1351

Gerry, Elbridge, 260

Gershom ben Juddah, 788

Gessell, Arnold L., **680**

Getty, J. Paul, 316

Getty family, 316, 491

Giannini, A. P., 491, 493

GIFT. *See* Gamete intrafallopian transfer

Giles, Jesse, 5

Gill, Charles, 262

Gilman, Caroline, 846

Gilmer, Elizabeth M., 480-481

Gimbutas, Marija, 896

Girl Scouts, 302, 1152, 1345

Glendenning, Frank, 441

Godchildren, 299

Godfathers, 299

Godparents, 299, 475, 611, **680-683**, 1111

Goes, Hugo van der, 88

Goldstein, Sidney, 988

Golem, 246

Golombok, Susan, 650

Goltz, J. Walter, 320

Gomez, Zoraida, 684

Gomez v. Perez, **684**

Gonorrhea, 234, 603, 1200. *See also* Venereal disease

Gonzaga family, 88

Goode, William, 400

Goodwin, George, 254

Gordon, Thomas, 1284

Gordy, Berry, 319

Gore, Albert, Sr., 1049

Gottfredson, Michael R., 591

Grandfathers, 54, 473, 576, 688, 912, 1037, 1236

Grandmothers, 101, 473, 688, 690, 896, 1037, 1080, 1141

Grandparents, 6-7, 11, 20, 43, 66, 77, 86, 89-90, 99, 134, 170, 188, 190, 192, 223, 256, 289, 292, 312-313, 329-332, 413, 470-471, 473-474, 485, 545, 592, 594, 608, 622, 673, **684-691**, 765, 770, 790, 795, 808, 816, 820, 824, 837-838, 840, 976, 984, 997, 1040, 1080, 1162, 1184, 1244, 1258, 1265, 1377

Gray, John, **691-692**

Great Britain, 111, 154, 621, 666, 670, 683, 704, 892; war brides from, 1350. *See also* England

Great Depression, 47, 96-97, 474, 737, 744, 836, 864, 997, 1015, 1141, 1154, 1319, 1363

Great Society, 262, 700

Greece, 40, 370, 762, 960

Greeks, 129, 562, 658, 718; art of, 86

Greenaway, Kate, 244

Gregory K., 1022-1024

Gregory VII, Pope, 1199

Grief counseling, **692-693**

Griffith, D. W., 612

Grimm, Jacob, 244

Grimm, Wilhelm, 244

Griswold v. Connecticut, 1085, 1154-1155

Group marriage, **693-694**, 807

Group Marriage Alliance, 694

Guardianship, **694-696**

Guatemala, 15

H. L. v. Matheson, 7

Habitat for Humanity International (HFHI), **697-698**, 1348

Hague Convention on the Civil Aspects of International Child Abduction, 159

Haiku, 247

Haiti, 655

Haitians, 319

Haley, Alex, 35, 485, 535, 562, 658, **698**, 699, 847, 976

Haley, Jay, 559

Hall, G. Stanley, 670, 680, **698-700**, 898, 962

Hammer v. Dagenhart, 259

Handsome Lake, 991-992

Hannah, 960

Hansberry, Lorraine, 849

Hareven, Tamara, 809, 835

Harlow, Harry, 855, 862

Harlow, Margaret, 855

Harper, James M., 134

Harrington, Michael, 340

Harris, C. J., 1024

Harroff, Peggy, 26

Haven House, 392

Hawaiians, 976, 1018

Hawke, Ethan, 668

Hawkins, Paul, 932

Hawthorne, Nathaniel, 845

Hays, Will H., 618

Hays Production Code, 618, 620

Head Start, 244, 262-263, 340-341, 355, 420-421, **700-703**, 970, 1173, 1291

Head Start Expansion and Improvement Act, 700

Health of children, **704-711**

Health problems, **711-717**

Healthy Meals for Healthy Americans Act, 1275

Healthy People 2000, 145

Heart and Lung Association, 1345

Heart disease, 1269

Hebrews, 23, 450, 562, 879, 960, 1198, 1206, 1294. *See also* Jews; Judaism

Heidegger, Martin, 670

Heimlich maneuver, 203

Heinecken, Christian, 183

Hell's Angels, 616

Hemophilia, 128, 485, 721, 1039

Hennig, Margaret, 572

Henry Street Settlement, 1189

Henry VIII (of England), 1249

Henson, Jim, 312

Hentz, Caroline, 846

Hercules, 183

Heredity, 115, **717-722**

Heritability, 719, 721

Herrnstein, Richard J., 466

Heterosexuals, 8, 277, 320, 324, 326, 384, 504, 597, 647, 649-650, 891

Hetfield, James, 668

HFHI. *See* Habitat for Humanity International

XXII